A REVOLUTION IN EATING

Arts and Traditions of the Table

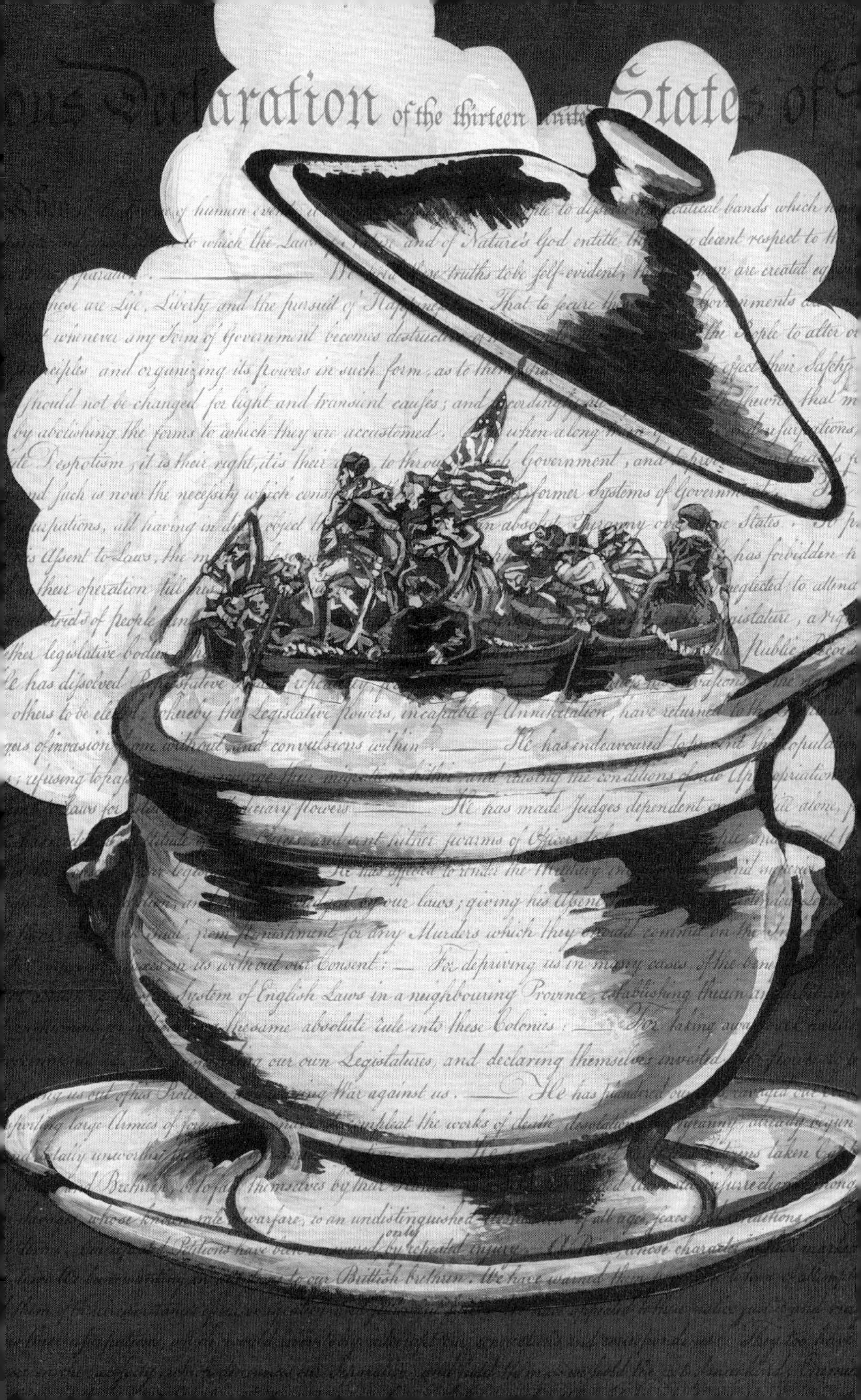
Declaration of the thirteen
States

A REVOLUTION IN EATING

How the Quest for Food Shaped America

James E. McWilliams

COLUMBIA UNIVERSITY PRESS : NEW YORK

Columbia University Press : *Publishers Since 1893* : New York Chichester, West Sussex

Copyright ©2005 Columbia University Press

Library of Congress Cataloging-in-Publication Data

McWilliams, James E.

  A revolution in eating : how the quest for food shaped America / James E. McWilliams.

    p.   cm.—(Arts and traditions of the table)

  Includes bibliographical references and index.

  ISBN 0-231-12992-0 (cloth : alk. paper)

    1. Gastronomy—History.   2. Food habits—United States.—History.   I. Title.   II. Series.

  TX633.M3 2005

  394.1'2'0973—dc22   2004061867

Acknowledgment is gratefully made for permission to reproduce the following: **ii.** Illustration by Martha Lewis; **viii [detail].** From R. B., *The English Empire in America* (London: Crouch, 1685). Lawrence H. Slaughter Collection, Map Division, The New York Public Library, Astor, Lenox and Tilden Foundations; **18 and 25.** From Charles de Rochefort, *Histoire naturelle et morale des îles Antilles de l'Amérique* (Rotterdam: Leers, 1681). Courtesy of the American Philosophical Society Library, Philadelphia; **28.** Courtesy of the Annenberg Rare Book and Manuscript Library, University of Pennsylvania, Philadelphia; **61.** From Johan von Staden, *Americae Pars Tertia* (Frankfurt, 1592). Courtesy of the Library Company of Philadelphia; **54 and 64.** Courtesy of the Rare Books Division, The New York Public Library, Astor, Lenox and Tilden Foundations; **94.** From Theodor de Bry, *America*, pt. 1, *Admiranda narratio, fida tamen, de commodis et incolarum ritibus Virginiae . . . Anglico scripta sermone a Thoma Hariot* (Frankfurt: Bry, 1590). Courtesy of the Rare Books Division, The New York Public Library, Astor, Lenox and Tilden Foundations; **97, 130, 142, and 147.** From Theodor de Bry, *America*, pt. 2, *Brevis narratio eorum quae in Florida Americae provicia Gallis acciderunt* (Frankfurt: Bry, 1591). Courtesy of the Map Division, The New York Public Library, Astor, Lenox and Tilden Foundations; **88, 106, and 112.** Courtesy of the Arents Collections, The New York Public Library, Astor, Lenox and Tilden Foundations; **139.** From Thomas Hariot, *Americae pars, nunc Virginia dicta* (Frankfurt: Wechel, 1590); **166 and 171.** Courtesy of the Library Company of Philadelphia; **200, 210, and 214.** From *Maryland Gazette*; **240 [detail], 248, and 249.** Spencer Museum of Art, University of Kansas, Gift of Mr. & Mrs. Dolph Simons Jr.; **261.** Courtesy of the Library of Congress, Washington, D.C.; **278 and 287.** Courtesy of the Massachusetts Historical Society, Boston; **310.** From Amelia Simmons, *American Cookery* (1796; facsimile, New York: Oxford University Press, 1958; reprint, New York: Dover, 1984).

CONTENTS

A REVOLUTION IN EATING

Getting to the Guts of American Food

Underlying the rich symbolic universe that food and eating always represent . . . there is the animal reality of our living existence.
Sidney Mintz, *Tasting Food, Tasting Freedom*

A Meal: How It Might Have Looked

On a warm spring afternoon in 1650, Rebecca Cole stepped out of her garden, entered her kitchen, and began to cook. Maryland, where the Cole family had migrated from Middlesex, England, was becoming well known not
only for its profitable tobacco crops but also for its ample corn, abundant
garden vegetables, and healthy supply of meat. And that combination, as it
did on most days, would make up the evening meal. Rebecca had started
soaking corn kernels at the crack of dawn to soften them for pounding, an
exhausting task made necessary by the lack of a local gristmill. She knew
that she needed about six cups of cornmeal to feed her husband, five children, and herself. So for the next couple of hours, Rebecca and her two
daughters dutifully hunched over a large mortar, took wooden pestles in
hand, and reduced a tub of white corn kernels into a gritty heap of meal.

Meanwhile, out in the barn, Robert Cole and his son, Robert Jr., contemplated a decision: pork or beef? The fact that they even had a choice
reflected Robert's preparation as a husbandman. Two months earlier, when
the weather was still cool, he had slaughtered two piglets and a calf. The
pigs were about seven months old, the age when their muscle density was
low, fat content high, and stringy connective tissue still pleasantly soft to
the palate. The calf was around two years old and similarly primed for consumption and preservation. Slaughtering a piglet was a turbulent task. It
began with a rapid cut to the beast's throat, followed by a prolonged period
of squealing and bloodletting. The beast was then scalded in a vat of boiling
water to loosen its sharp and wiry bristles so they could be easily brushed
off. Robert gathered the offal (the word literally denotes the "off fall" after
the slaughter) from the barn floor to make sausage. He then hacked the

corpse into two large chunks, called flitches, and placed them aside. The cow met a similarly brutal fate, but its slaughter took longer, resulted in a louder and deeper death rattle, and required greater precision: Robert had to not only kill it but also find its joints and dissect it into clean cuts of chucks, ribs, loins, and rounds. For all the commotion and mess that ensued, however, the slaughter was the easy part.

Robert Jr. and his brother managed the more physically taxing jobs of smoking the pork and pickling the beef. Smoking pork was a procedure dating back to the Middle Ages that sealed in fat and protected freshly cut meat from spoilage. The boys tossed the pork flitches in a large tub of salt, turning them over repeatedly, and then hung the coated slabs on metal hooks in order to air them out. After a day or two, the boys hauled the salted pork to the chimney, which served as a substitute for a smokehouse. With the pork hanging in the shaft, the wood smoke clogged the chimney and slowly coated the meat's surface, enhancing its flavor while extending its shelf life. Pickling beef involved submerging the cuts in a brine and vinegar solution that the boys prepared with salt, spices, and saltpeter. The process took place in large wooden barrels and didn't so much impart flavor as give the acid in the vinegar time to kill the enzymes that decomposed meat. The boys secured the barrels and rolled them to the corner of the barn. With the girls and Rebecca still pounding the corn in the kitchen, the boys stood in the barn, considered their inventory, and made their decision. They chose beef.

After placing three pounds of meat in a warming pan over the kitchen fire, Rebecca demanded that her servant, a trained dairymaid, quickly fetch some milk and butter. The dairymaid had spent the entire morning in the kitchen, where the dairy was housed, scalding milk pans, trays, pots, and churns in an eighteen-gallon copper pot. Whatever did not fit into the cauldron had to be cleaned individually. A colonial dairy had to be pristine. Any residual milk that dried on the surface of a container or shelf might carry bacteria that would result not only in a soured product but very possibly in widespread and potentially fatal illness. The maid, who had learned her skill back in England, could milk a single cow in about ten minutes. Out in the barn, after cleaning the equipment, she did just that to seven of the Coles' milk cows. She allowed the warm milk to cool in a tub and then strained it through a sieve concocted from a hollowed-out wooden bowl covered in a linen towel. The strained milk rested in earthenware milk trays for several hours, giving the cream a chance to coagulate at the top. The dairymaid then skimmed the thick cream with a slotted wooden paddle, leaving behind the thinner milk that Rebecca had requested. The weather that day was dry and warm, so the churning of the cream into butter took only a couple of hours rather than several. Once the butter had formed, the dairymaid squeezed out the buttermilk and fed it to the hogs, a practice that improved the taste of the meat. As late afternoon set in, she covered the bottom of a butter dish with salt, spooned in the thick butter, patted it down, and sprinkled the top with another layer of salt. She then carried a chunk of it over to Rebecca, whose cornmeal awaited.

As Rebecca warmed the meat and folded the butter and milk into the boiling cornmeal, Robert sent his boys out to the cider house, a small structure adjacent to the barn. The boys had spent several long afternoons mashing hundreds of apples gathered from the Coles' modest orchard into a gloppy pulp of apple meal. They placed the sweet mass of fruit in cider bags that the daughters had woven out of human and animal hair. The boys then picked up the bags and proceeded to twist and squeeze them as quickly and as tightly as they could, pressing the apple juice into a vat called a Mobby tubb. The Coles were a family of modest means—capable, at least, of affording a servant—but they did not own a cider press, which traded for about two thousand pounds of tobacco. Nevertheless, the boys improvised well enough. After inserting a four-inch tap into the tub, they decanted the liquid into a second tub to separate the juice from the lees. After bottling the apple juice in earthenware jugs and corking them, they placed the containers in a cool dugout beneath the barn. The boys now grabbed three of these bottles and rushed back to their two-room, six-hundred-square-foot house, where they plunked the earthenware containers on the table alongside the root vegetables that Rebecca had picked from her garden and roasted in the wide hearth.

Placing jugs of cider on a table was a fairly remarkable thing for the boys to do, as the vast majority of seventeenth-century families in colonial America lacked such amenities as a dining table and chairs. The Coles were unusual in having both. But the luxuries ended there. The girls threw a worn tablecloth over the pine table, and, after Rebecca pulled a loaf of cornbread from the hearth, the family carried either rickety chairs or tree stumps to the table. They shared a few wooden and pewter utensils to serve their food into pewter bowls. Then everyone began to eat. It was an event that would have made Miss Manners's head spin. The Coles ripped the meat off the bone with their dirty hands and shoved it in their mouths. Food scraps were soon scattered across the table. There were no forks, spoons, or individual cups or tankards. The cider pots were passed upon request to the person who wanted a drink. No napkins civilized the scene, as the coarse wool that made the boys' britches and the dark serge of the girls' dresses served that purpose just fine, as did the tablecloth. And so, rapidly and with gusto, the Coles consumed beef, cornmeal with butter and milk, corn bread, carrots, beans, and cider. As the sun descended, as the shadows outside stretched across the farm, and as the embers glowing in the hearth turned ashen, Rebecca and the girls began to clean.

The Coles lacked candles after all, and sleep beckoned.

Food Then, Food Now

The dinner table might seem like a strange place to begin exploring life in colonial America, but the Coles' meal has much to teach us—and not only about America's past but also about the way we eat and think about food today. What strikes me the most about the Coles' meal is how intimately the family knew its food. In this respect, they were hardly alone. The settlers who migrated to the English colonies in America, much like the Native Americans who had been living off the land for tens of thousands of years, produced the food they consumed. Simple as this act might sound, it's actually a hard reality for us to digest. Today our meat comes to us cut, cleaned, approved, and tightly bound in plastic wrap and Styrofoam. Vegetables are picked, washed, waxed, inspected, stickered, and displayed alongside one another in a shiny spectrum of commercial abundance. Our job is to choose, and the options are perpetual and endless. In Austin, Texas, where I buy my food, I can find tomatoes from Holland, fish from Massachusetts, and melons from Mexico on any given day of the week and on any given day of the year. A shopper in Portland, Oregon, or Nashville, Tennessee, can do the same thing on the same day, no matter the season. None of this food is especially fresh. The fish is frozen, the tomatoes hothouse grown, and the vegetables, for all their sprucing up, a bit tired and pale. But it's all there, all the time, and the toil and blood and dirt and sweat that brought that food to my plate remains conveniently beyond the sanitized frame of my shopping experience. Nothing, in fact, about the modern task of obtaining food reminds us that, before the American Revolution, the vast majority of Americans produced their own food. Which is to say that they killed their own game, caught their own fish, brewed their own beer, slaughtered their own livestock, sowed their own wheat, tilled their own fields, chopped down and burned their own fuel, grew their own vegetables, and reaped their own harvests. Men, women, and children—

free and slave, indentured and independent, European and Native—tied themselves to the land in ways that Americans today would find gruesome, excruciating, and impossibly time consuming. If food, as one writer suggests, "is one of the means by which a society creates itself," then I'd like to think that this difference between them and us matters.

Most of us, of course, would understandably be loath to give up the convenience of our local supermarket. Even so, many would still like to see this difference—that is, the gap between producing and consuming food—diminished. Without in any way romanticizing the colonial era, one might suggest that there is something about the Coles' effort to provide their own food that contemporary societies are finally beginning to regain. We increasingly hear the buzzwords "sustainability," "organic farming," and "slow food." We're constantly reminded about the importance of paying closer attention to the land and the particular foods that it's most naturally suited to support. High-profile chefs spend mornings visiting local farms, buying whatever happens to be available, and building menus around those ingredients. In France, an unlikely hero named Jose Bové became a national icon by ransacking the McDonalds that sprouted up in his tiny village, deeming the fast-food chain an affront to localism, fresh food, and general good taste. Home cooks routinely seek out farmers' markets rather than relying exclusively on conventional retailers for their produce, cheese, and meat. College students are spending summers interning on organic farms, where they not only pick pesticide-free vegetables but learn to slaughter animals with nothing more sophisticated than a sharp knife. (One student of mine recently returned from a Vermont farm where, he bragged, everything he ate over the entire summer was either harvested or killed that same day—often by him. He was having a hard time readjusting to cafeteria food.) Mainstream consumers are starting to become wary of genetically modified foods and pesticide use. It bothers many of us that the flavor of, say, a rack of lamb can be replicated in a lab and reduced to a capsule. In short, a quiet revolution in food is taking place in the Western, industrialized world, and it's a revolution toward sustainability, slow food, and greater intimacy with what we eat. For these reasons, too, the Coles have much to teach us.

Food Frontiers

For all its contemporary relevance, though, this book concerns the past. As we study the history of colonial British America through food, as we consider the Coles' experience, and as we recognize that food, as one historian writes, "shapes us and expresses us," we must constantly remind ourselves that the colonists were first and foremost *frontiersmen*. Their geographical distance from home directly shaped the relationship that they nurtured with the land, and it was a relationship that relatively urbanized Europeans at the time would also have found gruesome, excruciating, and impossibly time consuming. The hands-on, workmanlike intimacy so evident in my reconstruction of the Coles' meal proved especially true for poor and common colonists. Nevertheless, with rare exceptions, even wealthy Americans could not avoid getting their hands dirty in the production of their own food. Back home in Europe, food bustled through thriving markets, sophisticated commercial outlets, and well-established merchant warehouses. Back home, Robert most likely would have bought meat from a market vendor, Rebecca would have obtained cheese and milk from a commercial dairy, and the boys would have hauled cider home from the local press. In such a specialized and diverse economy as Europe's—and with England's economy being perhaps the most advanced in the world at the time—these options would have been cheaper, easier, and more efficient. As a whole, the free migrants to colonial America came from a relatively modern economic system.

But America in the seventeenth century was primitive. It generally lacked shops and other commercial outlets for food and drink. It did not have an economic infrastructure comparable to England's intricate networks of exchange. It was for a good reason that, as late as 1808, a popular American cookbook had to provide instructions on how to buy food in a market setting. "The large stall-fed ox beef is the best," the writer explained. "Dent it with your finger and it will easily rise again; if old it will be rough and spongy and the dent remain." For veal, she advised, "veal bro't to market in panniers, or in carriages, is to be preferred to that bro't in bags, and flouncing on a sweaty horse." And for salmon, "strictly examine the gills—if a bright redness if exchanged for a dull brown, they are stale." The point cannot be overstated: America throughout most of its colonial era was rough and, from the European perspective, woefully undeveloped. At the most basic level, the origins of American cooking are deeply rooted in this roughness, in this dire necessity imposed by frontier conditions, in the fact that Americans had *no choice* but to produce their own food. The intimacy and familiarity with food that the frontier demanded of all Americans shaped their lives in fundamental and lasting ways, and its impact was furthered by the fact that the frontier never closed throughout the colonial era. Such a literal and nearly universal hand-to-mouth relationship with the food they ate, a connection much tighter than it was in Europe at the time, became emblematic of life for all colonial Americans.

Luckily, the roughness of colonial life was tempered by the profusion of natural resources in British America. For all the challenges that the colonists faced, they rarely starved. English visitors were astonished at the region's material abundance. Officials of the Virginia Company, the English joint-stock company that underwrote Virginia's settlement, chose an apt metaphor when it asked, "Why should not the rich harvest of our hopes be seasonably expected?" It was a fair question. Richard Haklyut, an active promoter of English colonization of North America, looked at the colonial landscape and predicted, not unreasonably, that the colonies, once established, would "yelde unto us all the commodities of Europe, Affrica, and Asia . . . and supply the wantes of all our decayed trades." His father, Hakluyt the Elder, never visited America but still had praise for its "excellent soile," waxing effusive about "many other sundry kinds of hides there now presently to be had, the trade of Whale and Seale fishing, and of divers other fishings in the great rivers, great bayes, and seas there." He gushed over "the knowen plentie and varietie of Flesh, of divers kind of beasts at land there," touting the "sufficient victuall" that the land would surely provide with minimal effort. Immediately after reaching the Massachusetts Bay in 1630, John Winthrop ventured out in a small boat and, much to his surprise, "tooke in less than 2 howers, with a few hooks, 67 coddfishe most of them very great fishe some 1 yard and 1/2 longe." Later in the century, in the same region, an English set-tler praised the area as "an apt place for the keeping of cattle and swine, in which respect this people are the best stored." Land promoters and settlers alike agreed that the American landscape yielded a cornucopia of material wealth. A family like the Coles didn't have to travel far to grub up the ingredients for their meal. This abundance on the frontier was a perpetual aspect of the colonial condition and thus a solid foundation of American cooking.

The "Melting Pot"

It was not, however, the only foundation of American food. A search for the origins of American cooking brings us into a melting pot roiling with racial and ethnic interaction. The term "melting pot" can be misleading in the context of colonial America. Normally, the expression optimistically refers to the assimilation of nineteenth- and twentieth-century immigrants into the dominant American culture. In the seventeenth and eighteenth centuries, however, the idea of a melting pot implies something more complicated and unfinished. At this time, people were not so much assimilating into a dominant culture as they were trying to figure out precisely what the dominant culture would be. Sometimes they blended, at other times they clashed, but more often than not the colonists managed a compromised negotiation of traditional habits. There is perhaps no clearer lens through which to view this process than that of food.

And, as the Coles suggest, there is perhaps no food more symbolic of this cultural interaction than Indian corn. The first white settlers to North America arrived with customary dietary habits in place, and they explicitly excluded what herbalist John Gerard called "a heathan graine." Through the explorations of sixteenth-century adventurers and Spanish traders, the English had come to know Indian corn before settling colonial North America in the early seventeenth century. Their knowledge of it, however, was as a food more fit for swine than for people. Literally, the English fed Indian corn to pigs. But for the Native Americans who called North America home, corn was life. It grew easily and abundantly, required little labor, and could be planted alongside beans and squash throughout the forest, among the trees, in space unbound by fences or tilled fields. Indian corn yielded a crop several times greater than English wheat. It freed time up for other work, not to mention leisure activities. It was versatile. In every respect, Indian corn made sense. It was, for all of these reasons, fully commensurate with and integrated into the Native Americans' economic and social systems of production. The English, however, just didn't understand.

The cultural contrast was unavoidable and stark. And what especially bewildered the English settlers even more than the actual consumption of corn was that Indian women worked it while the men hunted. Women, first off, were not supposed to work in the field. And hunting, as the English saw it, may have served a purpose in rare times of need, but ultimately it was a sport, a diversion, a luxurious distraction from real work, an activity that, as John Winthrop explained, "toyles a man's bodye overmuch." No image could have cut more sharply against the grain of English civilization than that of women farming the land while men hunted the woods.

Voices of disapproval thus echoed through the colonies. Upon arriving in Virginia in 1615 and observing the local inhabitants, John Smith remarked how "the women be verie painefull [hard working] and the men often idle," an assessment based on the cultural norm that working essentially meant cultivating crops and tending livestock. Francis Higginson observed of the Indians in 1630 that "men for the most part live idly, they doe nothing but hunt and fish. Their wives set their corn and doe all their other worke." Edward Johnson, another New Englander, agreed. He noted that "women were generally very laborious at their planting time, and the Men extraordinarily idle." This popular condemnation evidently stuck, for even in the next century, a young Yale graduate wrote of Native Americans that "the superior strength of the man is used, not in protecting & lightening the burdens of the weaker sex, but in depressing them." This apparent perversion of what the English believed to be the crux of civilized behavior—husbandry—further discouraged their acceptance of a food popularly deemed the epitome of barbarity.

Nevertheless, here were the Coles in 1650, sitting at their pine table and eating Indian cornmeal. Indeed, it would be difficult to find a colonial American who did not eventually incorporate Indian corn into his diet. Every English family in the Chesapeake Bay region and the Lower South, and most families in New England, overcame their prejudices, grew the crop, and consumed it regularly. Even the American gentry came around to Indian corn. A hundred years after the Coles' meal, a recipe published in Williamsburg, Virginia, geared toward upper-class women, featured "Indian Meal Pudding." It instructed: "Take eight ounces of mush [cornmeal], six Ounces butter, six Ounces sugar, the Yolks of six Eggs, and White of one. Mix the Butter in the Mush while still warm, beat the Eggs light, mix the Sugar with them, and add to the Mush when cool. Put Mace, Nutmeg, and Wine to your Taste." The presence of such a recipe raises critical questions: How did a food fit for swine evolve into haute cuisine? How did the English finally come to accept Indian corn? Did this acceptance convey cultural cooperation or dominance? The ways in which colonists answered these questions tell us a lot about early American food.

The cultural negotiation of food wasn't, of course, limited to the English and the Native Americans. The sharing of food traditions has been endemic to every human society's culinary development. At no time in modern history, however, have so many cultures with so many culinary possibilities at their disposal found themselves vying for space in the same geographical region as they were in colonial British America. Not only had thousands of Native American cultures already established and developed societies in North America, but the same area would also become home—willingly or not—to English, French, Dutch, German, Swedish, Scottish, Scotch-Irish, Irish, and African settlers, among others. As tens of thousands of Europeans moved to this New World, as colonial Americans moved up and down the coast of North America (and then from the coast to the interior), as Africans endured the Middle Passage, and as Native Americans interacted with these new peoples, cooking techniques and habits intermingled and influenced one another in exciting ways. The origins of American cooking and culture can thus be further explored in this second foundation of American cooking—the often tense, often peaceful, blending of customary habits, beliefs, and cooking traditions in a new and very strange world. The diversification of America was endless and dynamic. Food was always at the vital center of this process.

Distinctions

On these foundations, colonial British Americans built a culinary tradition. Initially, however, it was a patchwork of regional cuisines characterized by discrete qualities. Throughout the seventeenth and early eighteenth centuries, each region of colonial British America developed precise ways of working the land. Each region also developed precise labor arrangements to carry out that work. A detailed investigation into American food, therefore, demands a careful look at the way that colonial and early Americans chose to do something that too often we take for granted: use the land. What people grew, how they grew it, and who grew it all contributed to the unique cooking and eating habits of each colonial region. Each factor helps us answer the even more important question of why they ate what they ate. Every region, it turns out, had its own answer.

More than any other region of colonial British America, New England mastered the art of feeding itself. Residents prized their mixed economy as a judicious system of food production that protected them from dangerous fluctuations in the temperamental transatlantic market. Their work spread the gamut. They grew Indian corn; grazed livestock; cultivated squash; produced cider, beer, and rum; and maintained extensive vegetable gardens both for their own subsistence and for sale in other markets. New Englanders exploited the region's ample supply of cod, mackerel, and shellfish that thrived in the coast's especially rich waters. New England settlers hunted game when the beef and pork supplies ran low. They kept a few chickens, churned their own butter, pressed their own cheese. And they did it all with family labor. Rather than rely on slaves or indentured servants, sons helped fathers out at sea and in the field while daughters assisted mothers in the garden and around the hearth. These arrangements and pursuits did not generate tremendous wealth, but rarely (if ever) did New Englanders have to look beyond their own borders for food. New England never turned its land over to a single, dominant crop for sale in international markets, and, because of this decision, it was able to pour its resources into a healthy, diversified range of agricultural pursuits. Rather than purchasing the expensive labor to grow a staple crop, New England achieved the remarkable accomplishment of feeding itself by itself. Driven by the love of God and England, it developed a cuisine of abundance that stayed more loyal to traditional cooking habits than did that of any other region of British America.

To even better appreciate New England's success, one need only look at the West Indies. Not unlike New England, the British West Indies began as small, mixed economies, but it wasn't long before sugar became king. By the 1650s, Barbados, St. Kitts, Antigua, and a dozen or so other islands had turned over virtually all of their land to sugar. And, as the Spanish precedent had shown throughout the sixteenth century, sugar not only meant great wealth. It also meant slavery. Indeed, hundreds of thousands of West Africans were transported to the West Indies against their will to toil in sugar fields that proved to be killing fields. Sugar, coinciding as it did with the rise of Europe's café culture, sold so well that English planters often became wealthy enough on the backs of their slaves to leave the disease-plagued islands altogether, entrusting their estate to an overseer. Blacks came to comprise more than 75 percent of an island's population and often as high as 90 percent. The British West Indies could not have stood in sharper contrast to the English society that was simultaneously developing in New England. Profits were immense compared with New England's modest earnings, and they all went back into sugar and slavery. Diversification was unheard of; exploitation, the norm.

Food in this environment was a virtual afterthought—but it couldn't be ignored. In a twist that ensured the prevalence of African cooking habits in early America, masters determined that it was cheaper to allot scrubby patches of land to their chattel than to import ample supplies of food. Slaves were rarely able to feed themselves well enough to stay healthy, especially in such a physically taxing environment. Malnourishment was common. Nevertheless, their cooking traditions came to dominate the West Indian foodways and, in so doing, imparted a strong African flavor to the region's food while establishing alongside New England another model of food production for other colonial regions to consider as they evolved into their own societies. New England's was a cuisine of abundance, but the West Indies' was a cuisine of survival, and while most individual African slaves did not survive into maturity, their foodways certainly did.

In foodways as well as geography, the rest of colonial British America fell somewhere between. The Middle Colonies—New York, Pennsylvania, New Jersey, and Delaware—generally gravitated toward the New England model, but with important differences. The Middle Colonies devoted a great deal of time to growing wheat for export. Although it never approached the status of a cash crop such as sugar, wheat did occupy enough of the region's resources to shape its labor force into a mixture of servant, family, and slave labor. This ethnically and religiously diverse stretch of colonial America also raised livestock to sell overseas, eat at home, and trade with families and merchants in New York City and Philadelphia. Pennsylvania maintained thousands of milk cows that became the basis of a thriving dairy industry; cheese and butter became readily available products from this region. Distilleries and breweries fueled tavern life in Philadelphia and New York, as farmers could easily grow barley alongside wheat, purchase molasses from visiting merchants, and build distilleries, breweries, and hop houses on their relatively large plantations. Rockfish and perch pulled from the Delaware, Hudson, and Susquehanna Rivers became dietary staples. Venison was a very popular source of meat, due to the Middle Colonies' extensive woodlands. Some areas within the Middle Colonies managed to build larger versions of the mixed farms that marked the New England landscape. And like their northern counterparts, they rarely had to import food. Others specialized, using slaves and servants to operate commercial wheat plantations, sophisticated dairy farms, or even ironworks and distilleries. As a result, settlers depended on other areas of the Middle Colonies or other regions of British America— mainly New England—for corn, beef, beer, and whatever else they could not provide on their own. If New England's was a cuisine of abundance, the Middle Colonies' cooking habits was a cuisine of diverse moderation.

The southern colonies—Maryland, Virginia, the Carolinas, and Georgia—hewed closer to the West Indian example. But here, too, there are important qualifications. By growing a staple crop primarily with slave labor, the South most obviously approximated West Indian ways. Slaves working tobacco in the Upper South and rice in the Lower South cultivated crops that allowed them to play critical roles in shaping the foodways of these two regions. As in the West Indies, planters typically minimized costs by allowing slaves to produce their own food, sometimes with ingredients that the masters provided, other times with whatever slaves could obtain and cultivate through their own efforts. This arrangement profoundly influenced the way that all Southerners ate, whites and blacks included. Unlike in the West Indies, however, the Upper South never reached levels of slavery exceeding more than 40 percent while parts of the Lower South often approached 60 percent. The slave system in the South was obviously brutal, but not nearly as indifferent to life as it was in the West Indies. Malnourishment and disease didn't cripple slave life in the South, as it did on the islands. The effort to preserve African cooking traditions in the South may not have been as extensive as it was in the West Indies, but neither was it as stunted. Rice and tobacco planters rarely generated enough cash to leave their plantations and live as absentee landlords. And because planters did form a strong culture of their own, they, too, developed a cuisine that did its best to approximate their traditional habits. It wasn't easy. For with a significant portion of the Upper South's labor being indentured servants, with poor whites intermingling with African slaves, and with Native Americans never far from the English periphery of settlement, the South pioneered a cooking style that wavered somewhere between a cuisine of adaptation and one of preservation. In so doing, the South constituted yet another distinct culinary model in British America, further enhancing the patchwork of cuisines that developed well into the 1740s.

The British Invasion

Unique as these traditions became, however, these regional cooking habits began to converge by the middle of the eighteenth century. The first factor blending regional cooking habits into a discrete American culinary style ironically involved the pervasive embrace of all things British in the three decades before the Revolution. Americans have a (bad) habit of looking at their early history as an inevitable movement toward independence and democracy. We understandably tend to favor a kind of "American exceptionalism" approach to our past whereby the founders' appeal for an antimonarchical government came to fruition inexorably and according to some natural law of justice. It might come as a surprise, therefore, to learn that as the Revolution approached, colonial Americans were actually becoming increasingly English in the way that they thought, dressed, spoke, entertained, and, of course, cooked and ate. As the political system that they had identified with since the Glorious Revolution fell into irreparable disrepair, American colonists were consuming more English goods, following more English styles, and trying to behave in a more English fashion than ever before. Insofar as there was a dominant cultural influence on American cooking prior to the Revolution, it was—despite all the ethnic and racial diversification—undoubtedly English.

Central to what one historian has labeled a thorough "Anglicization" of American cultural life in the mid-eighteenth century was a "commercial revolution" that captivated the colonies in the 1740s. The American economy had become so strong through the cultivation and exportation of cod, tobacco, wheat, and rice that, for the first time in its history, common people could finally afford to purchase common English imports. Nowhere was this transformation more obvious than in the kitchen. Within a decade, primitive colonial kitchens had become well stocked not only with conveniences, including forks, spoons, knives, cups, and bowls, but also with finery, including colanders, funnels, flour dredges, teakettles, fish kettles, stewpots, posnets, saucepans, drinking pots, salvers, and, perhaps most notable, cookbooks. The widespread acquisition of these cooking-related goods imposed a unity of sorts on the polyglot regional differences that otherwise prevailed throughout colonial British America. To be sure, colonists continued to follow regional habits, but they now cooked with similar utensils in similarly designed kitchens. The popularity of these goods up and down the coast, as well as in the hinterlands, became an important precondition for the emergence of an identifiable American style of food.

The Alcoholic Republic

Americans drank, and they drank a lot. It's in that pervasive habit, moreover, that a second factor driving the convergence of regional foodways emerged. Early in the colonial era, settlers consumed mainly homemade beverages such as beer and cider because these drinks were relatively easy to make and were cooked during production, an essential requirement when water was often tainted. Colonists young and old, male and female, black and white, and from all regions drank throughout the day, moderately, as a form of nourishment and, at times, entertainment. Initially, the vast majority of the beer and cider consumed was produced by women and children who worked the task of beverage production into their regular rounds of food preparation. By the end of the seventeenth century, however, farms had started to specialize production to the point that taverns arose to produce drinks in much larger quantities than individual homes were able to do. Eventually, taverns responded to the demand for more diverse menus by importing a variety of drinks that were not produced locally. The most notable of these drinks—at least in terms of colonial American food—was rum. Rum became so popular that it soon outpaced beer and cider as the colonywide beverage of choice. In so doing, rum helped pioneer a systematic intercoastal trade that brought the various regions of British America into routine contact. By the 1740s, American merchants were trading regularly within the colonies as well as the empire. Colonists eager to sample the foods of other regions were soon placing orders for bread and beer from Philadelphia, beef from New England, okra and rice from Carolina, and ham from Virginia. The more systematic this trade became, the more the colonies' culinary habits became less and less foreign to one another. And, in an especially tragic twist, rum helped weaken the cultures of Native Americans as it brought those of white settlers together, thus furthering the convergence of an American cuisine.

This Land Is My Land

A third and final precondition behind the convergence of regional cooking styles involved the rise of a republican political ideology throughout the American colonies. By the 1770s, as the Revolution approached, the cultural transition from a fragmented to a more unified approach to cooking culminated not so much in a particular dish or group of foods—as regions continued to rely on local ingredients—but, rather, in the way Americans thought about food. And, strange as it might seem, the way they thought about food was integral to the way they thought about politics. It's a fairly complicated connection, but it goes something like this: The emerging political notion that "the people" should elect virtuous leaders, and that those virtuous leaders should make decisions that benefit the common good as well as the individual pursuit of happiness, had its deepest roots in America's widespread ownership of land. Proportionally, more white men owned land in colonial British America than in any other colony or country in early modern Europe. America's vast availability of land, in addition to the relatively egalitarian way in which Americans distributed it, predisposed them to embrace republican principles in a way that the mother country never could.

Why? As historians regularly point out, land tied colonists into transatlantic markets and ultimately made British America an impressively stable and wealthy place. But that's not all. We must never overlook the fact that Americans' deep ties to the land also did something far more basic and sustaining: it fed them. British America was remarkable in never having to import food. Thomas Jefferson perhaps best understood the connection among land, food, and political ideology. In his *Notes on the State of Virginia*, he famously explained that "dependence . . . prepares fit tools for the designs of ambition." But the larger context of this quotation is often overlooked: "We have an immensity of land courting the industry of the husbandman. Is it best then that all our citizens should be employed in its improvement, or that one half should be called off from that to exercise manufactures and handicraft arts for the other?" His answer: "Those who labour in the earth are the chosen people of God, if ever he had a chosen people, whose breasts he has made his peculiar deposit for substantial and genuine virtue." Food, in short, became one obvious manifestation of this virtue, a virtue critical to the political philosophy that carried America toward revolution. It would be a truism to say that an ample and independent food source was a basic requirement for political independence. But the process whereby regular Americans such as the Coles sustained themselves did much more than just enable colonists to pursue radical political notions. It directly shaped what those political notions were.

Getting to the Guts

In the process of cooking a basic meal, the Coles vividly remind us that the British American origins of American cooking are many. These origins can be glimpsed in the intimacy that colonial Americans had with their food, in their cultural exchange with Native Americans, in colonial British America's growing ethnic diversity, in the emergence of regional foodways, in colonial Americans' adoption of English consumer goods, and, finally, in the melding of political ideology and food production. I will be elaborating on all these topics in the pages ahead. In so doing, though, I hope to move the field of American culinary history to another level. We currently know a lot about what colonial Americans ate, and I reliably go over that common ground. More important, however, I will also attempt to explain not only *what* colonial Americans ate but also *why* they ate it. Therein, I believe, lies the true story of America's culinary origins. Therein one grabs its guts.

There's a saying that only a historian could make a topic like sex seem boring. I hope, as I search America's cooking origins, that I don't do the same for food. After all, it's so common as to seem mundane, and, like sleep and sex, it's also ubiquitous to the point of blending into the historical scenery. Perhaps that's why we've overlooked it as long as we have in our ongoing effort to understand our complex and constantly changing heritage. But by no longer allowing food to remain "hidden in plain sight," by remembering that history is also about "the animal reality of our living existence," and by shining the spotlight on it during an especially transitional time in American history, I want not only to tell a story about how we once were but to provide some insight into who we are today. And—however immodest the goal might be—why.

CHAPTER I

ADAPTABILITY

The Bittersweet Culinary History of the English West Indies

Sweetness is a desire that starts on the tongue with the sense of taste,
but it doesn't end there.
Michael Pollan, *The Botany of Desire*

THE ORIGINS OF AMERICAN COOKING might have started with sweetness,
but sweetness got off to a sour start. When Christopher Columbus made
his second voyage to America in 1493, he stopped in the Canary Islands to
pick up a barrel of sugarcane stems. Although Native Americans had never
grown the crop, sugar was a plant that Columbus, whose mother-in-law
owned a small sugar plantation in Madeira, thought might thrive in the
rich soil of the West Indies. When he planted the samples in Hispaniola,
however, he confronted an unexpected problem. The rapid proliferation
of brown rats suggested that Columbus had loaded more than just cane
stems and provisions onto the *Santa María* during his brief sojourn. Rats
also sought familiar comforts in a strange land, and, much like the Spanish—who were gulping down imported wheat bread, olives, olive oil, garlic,
and gluttonous quantities of red wine—the rodents gorged themselves on
flavors to which they were also well accustomed. They did what rats had
done for thousands of years: they infested fields of freshly planted cane
shoots, becoming pervasive pests before the Spanish planters had even
harvested their first modest sugar crop. For the Spaniards, these rats multiplied into nagging and persistent reminders of home.

Most Spaniards reluctantly tolerated the nuisance of living with a rat
population that soon outnumbered them. One individual, however, was
bothered enough by the gnawed canes scattering his small garden to take
action. How this particular man (whose name escapes the legend) obtained
his misinformation remains unknown, but someone, somehow, convinced
him that the solution to the island's rat problem could be found in, of
all things, the mongoose. An Indian mongoose at that. This enterprising
planter, under the impression that the mongoose would hunt West Indian

rats with the same fervor that it attacked cobras back home, arranged to have several mongooses imported to the Spanish West Indies. When the creatures arrived, the planter set them free to extinguish the rodents.

The planter, it turns out, had made a terrible mistake. The mongooses promptly disappeared, whereas the rats, by contrast, continued to thrive on sugarcane. And, to make matters worse, the island's supply of fowl diminished. The reason was simple enough. The Indian mongoose is diurnal—it feeds during the day. The rat forages at night. On the West Indian islands, the rat and the mongoose passed each other at dusk and dawn, leaving the rats to proliferate as they had always done while the mongooses adjusted to life in the New World by competing quite voraciously with Spanish hunters for a scarce supply of wild birds.

How the Spanish Adapted Sugar to the Caribbean and Destroyed the Native American Population

The legend of the rat and the mongoose is exceptional because, if indeed true, the planter's act would have been just about the only sugar-related decision made by the Europeans to backfire. These animals might have passed in the night, but the sugarcane taking root in the West Indies burrowed into the soil and climbed toward the heavens. For the better part of four centuries, sugar did nothing less than dominate life in the West Indies. Because the ways in which colonial Americans ate responded directly to the ways in which they worked the land, we must take a close look at the history of that dominance.

Nature engineered sugar to adapt and thrive. Sucrose is an organic chemical belonging to the carbohydrate family. The cane from which it grows is in fact a type of grass whose scientific name is *Saccharum officinarum*. Civilizations with tropical or subtropical climates have grown sugar for more than ten thousand years, beginning in New Guinea and moving on to the Philippines, India, Egypt, the Azores, and, finally, the New World with Columbus. Sugar's history of seamless adaptation to foreign climes owes its success to asexual propagation. With decent soil, ample moisture, and frequent sunshine, a single stem graced with a single bud can cover a cleared field with tender green shoots in a matter of weeks. No cross-fertilization required. On the islands of Hispaniola, Puerto Rico, and Cuba, Spanish planters embraced the welcome discovery that their neatly planted rows of cane shoots reproduced abundantly. Growing almost an inch a day for six weeks, the stalks reached an impressive plateau of about fifteen feet, ripening sixteen months after planting. Sugar, if the first few decades of Spanish experimentation were any measure, seemed tailor-made for Spain's West Indian venture. It comes as no surprise that, as early as the 1520s, planters were exporting small amounts of the "white gold" back to Europe, tempting the taste buds of many of a café dweller, urging them to demand more while watching the price of their new commodity tick upward.

But sugar asked for a lot in return. For one, it sucked the life out of the soil, requiring twice the nutrition of the native maize. If the Spanish really wanted to capitalize on sugar exportation, they would have to spread the crop over vast stretches of land. Therefore, the most obvious obstacle, at least from the Spanish perspective, was the Taino Indians, who had been living on Hispaniola for almost fifteen hundred years. They had no intention of stepping aside to make room for a foreign crop that sweetened tea and rotted teeth, much less a foreign people hoping to become rich off such a frivolity. The Tainos had moved to Hispaniola (and Cuba) from South America around the time of Christ's birth. They developed a peaceful and cohesive civilization that, despite attacks by Caribs, eschewed war and integrated its ways into the natural rhythms of the islands on which they lived. The canoe (*canoa*), hammock (*hamaca*), and relatively spacious, circular homes constructed of river cane and palm leaves marked the Tainos' landscape and culture with an aura of sensible adaptation to a unique environment. In terms of industry, the Tainos manufactured jewelry from coral, shell, bone, and stone. They wove baskets, embroidered cotton belts, carved wooden chairs, and decorated pottery. As far as we can tell, they lived a generally quiet, healthy, and harmonious life.

The Tainos' dietary habits especially reflected their responsiveness to the island's natural environment. They obtained their protein from fish and wild animals (mainly snakes and birds) and cultivated manioc (*yuca*), sweet potatoes (*batata*), peanuts, and various squash, peppers, and beans. The Tainos grew these crops haphazardly, mixing them on small mounds, or *conucos*, carefully molded to prevent erosion and maintain well-irrigated soil. These foods successfully intermingled with a variety of wild root vegetables that served to further resist erosion, produce minerals, and provide raw material for potash. Cassava became the most popular of these roots. The Tainos would grub up cassava, squeeze out its poisonous juice (prussic acid), and bake the doughy root into flat bread. The Spanish might have eyed this land with a covetous glare, but, as the Tainos saw it, the land was their land, their sacred space, their ancestral home, their source of food and happiness. And they had no intention of going gently.

Never one to be deterred by such circumstances, Columbus—who admitted to his journal that the Tainos were "the best people in the world and above all the gentlest"—entertained a solution consistent with Spanish goals: relocate them. In 1495, after it had become clear that the Native Americans were unwilling to cooperate as servants, Columbus sent four hundred Taino Indians from Santo Domingo to Seville with the explicit intention of selling them into slavery. The plan never fully materialized, and each year until 1499 his shipments of Taino refugees diminished before fizzling out completely in 1500. It wasn't that Spain didn't want slaves. The Spanish had, after all, been using African slaves in the Canary Islands for decades. It was rather that the queen didn't approve of Columbus's presumptuous aggrandizement of what she now considered her barbarian (but potentially Christianized) subjects. "What power from me has the admiral to give anyone my vassals?" she asked. There was also the issue of the Tainos' failing health. One Genoese trader remarked on their poor suitability as slaves, saying, "They are not a people suited to hard work, they suffer from the cold and do not have a long life." The cause of the Tainos' unpopularity in the Spanish slave market, another merchant surmised, was due to "unaccustomed cold."

The weather had nothing to do with the Tainos' enervation. Instead, it was biological disaster that altered and ultimately settled the incipient land dispute between the Spanish and the Tainos. The most deadly stowaway that the Spaniards smuggled to the New World was smallpox. More than any other single factor, smallpox cleared the land of its local inhabitants. However one tries to spin the story of America's agricultural origins, planting cane shoots came at nothing less than the cost of an unfathomable human tragedy carried out by invisible but highly contagious microbes. It was a disease for which the Spanish had evolved immunity but the Native Americans, having lived in isolation from the world's most deadly pathogens for thousands of years, had no defense. And so, with ruthless logic and precision, smallpox decimated them in perhaps the most devastating "virgin soil epidemic" in world history. The numbers are disputed but, according to one authoritative estimate, Native Americans on Hispaniola declined from 3 to 4 million strong before European contact to near extinction sixty years after Columbus's arrival.

This turn of events hardly caused the Spanish to pause. In fact, with the land now cleared of so many Native Americans, it may have actually intensified their quest to plant and process the product that gave rats more reason to live. After all, God obviously was telling the Spanish that they were a superior people divinely ordained to exploit the landscape as they saw fit. Or so they thought. Whatever the rationale, the Spaniards forged ahead. They planted sugar, battled rats, and slowly but surely built small but viable plantations on Spain's arc of Caribbean possessions. The process began incrementally, almost unthinkingly, but it proceeded nonetheless. Relying on technology that had not changed since the tenth century, and using presses originally designed to process olive oil, Caribbean planters tried and repeatedly failed to manufacture serious amounts of sugar between 1505 and 1520. Experimentation was rampant, but exportation was minimal. The diminished presence of the Tainos, however, sparked a period of rapid sugar expansion supported primarily by the importation of the animal-powered sugar mills. The transition to more ambitious sugar endeavors also hinged on the importation of sugar masters from the Canary Islands to teach otherwise ignorant planters how to process cane. The infrastructure of economic success was, in short, slowly coming together.

Armed with these assets, a handful of renegade planters began to consolidate the sugar industry while the rest of the colony continued to search for real gold. With plans for a vertical three-roller mill on hand and a competent sugar maker at the ready, Cristobal de Tapia of Santo Domingo built a fully equipped sugar plantation in 1522, powering his mill with a team of eight oxen. Tomás de Castellon of Puerto Rico received a grant to establish a similar sugar mill in 1523. Francisco de Garay followed suit from Jamaica in 1527. Scores of mills eventually dotted the landscape as the quest for gold proved increasingly elusive and the demand for sugar potentially explosive. The mills arose to accommodate the productive sugar farms that the Spanish settlers had been developing for about a decade. Royal support in the form of loans and land grants from Charles I came through to provide financial support for these ventures. By the 1530s, the infrastructure was starting to pay off. The Spanish were coming to enjoy a nascent but quite sound system of West Indian sugar production that operated under the constant groan of rolling mills.

As well as the groan of involuntary labor. With the surviving Tainos proving to be chronically unreliable workers, in both the hollow gold mines and the lush sugar fields, Spanish planters began to import African slaves to plant their cane, power their mills, and fabricate their sugar. At first, the enslaved Africans trickled into the islands. De Tapia, for example, imported fifteen slaves obtained from Portuguese traders to operate his new Santo Domingo mill. But as the mills proved moderately successful, as a few more modest royal grants came through, and as the Dutch and Portuguese tightened their greedy grasp on the slave trade with lucrative state-sponsored contracts, the slave supply increased. By the 1530s, it wasn't unusual to find plantations brimming with 150 to 200 slaves. De Castellon, who established the first Puerto Rican mill, reported nearly 3,000 slaves on the island by 1530 (compared with only 327 whites). By the 1540s, slave importers were counting by the thousands. And by the 1560s, plantations with 500 or more slaves were hardly anomalous. Few could have predicted what the future held in store, but from the comfortable perspective of hindsight we know that these sugar pioneers were about to give birth to a slave society.

None of it was really planned. The Spanish had originally settled to find gold and support themselves by planting wheat, growing grape vines, and cultivating barley. Throughout the early sixteenth century, however, they realized that the original rationalization of "God, glory, and gold" might reasonably take a back seat to the pursuit of growing and selling sugar. Settlement and plantation development, the planters began to think, could replace the initial plans for extraction and expansion. These men might not just conquer a world in the name of king and country but, with sugar, shape that world to better sustain their own personal fantasies of grandeur. Through the potentially enormous profits generated by "white gold," sugar might not just sweeten European coffee, but become something much, much bigger: the basis of a new society—a society where planters ruled.

These dreamy notions became the sweet stuff of settlers' ambitions, sustaining the bountiful hope of a rich and possibly even independent society on Spain's colonial fringe. Much to the amusement of the Spanish elite back home, sugar planters even mustered the gumption to apply for titles of nobility. None were granted, but the hubris behind their requests speaks volumes about sugar's role in shaping the early culture of the Spanish West Indies. For Spanish planters building plantations between 1530 and 1580, in stark contrast to their young black workforce, the future looked bright.

Sugar Production, Slavery, and the English Takeover of the Industry

Grand dreams thus proliferated throughout the Spanish West Indies—but dreams are all that they remained. In order to understand how the Spanish ultimately lost the international bid for West Indian sugar, and to see how the English consequently came to dominate it, we must first take a closer look at sugar itself—the way it was grown and the many tasks it required. For it's only in the intricate details of production that the importance of this crop to American foodways begins to emerge.

Growing sugar was, for the most part, a relatively basic affair. Sun, soil, and water fueled the photosynthetic reactions that fattened soaring stalks of cane without constant planter intervention. Once ripened, though, sugarcane became an impatient and impetuous crop, demanding ongoing human labor. If its juice, with 13 percent sucrose content, wasn't extracted within two weeks after ripening, the canes dried, rotted, and fermented. The window of opportunity for harvesting this crop was therefore brief. There was no way around it: capitalizing on sugar required laborious efforts by planters hoping to reap nature's bounty in the quest for economic profit and, perhaps, a little personal fame.

With the harvest's onset, workers dove into their tasks. They hacked canes at their tough bases with long, curved machetes, loaded the reedy stalks into wooden oxcarts, and hauled them to the plantation's three-roller

Slaves processing sugar in the West Indies

The canes had to be crushed in a three-roller mill soon after cutting, or they would dry out.

mill, which was powered by oxen, horses, wind, or water. The machines and techniques used by the Spaniards were the same as those that had been used by the Portuguese since the late fourteenth century; the work was skilled, but there wasn't much of a learning curve to master. For hours on end, men unloaded piles of cane, passed them down a human chain, and delivered them to mill workers who pushed and pulled the canes through wooden rollers until they flattened into dry husks. The extracted juice seeped into a funnel, from where it flowed to the next stage of production. Workers saved the mashed canes to burn as fuel.

They next gathered the liquid in large pots and boiled it. The moment when impurities separated from the sugar called for immediate action. If the mixture boiled too long, the impurities might redissolve and taint the entire process. Strikers, as they were called, removed the liquid from heat at exactly the right moment and allowed the cleaned solution to thicken into a syrup called massacuite. After letting the mixture rest for a few hours, boilers reheated it and added egg whites, animal blood, or a substance called milk of lime. This material was made in a lime kiln by dissolving burned lime into water. When mixed with cane juice, milk of lime removed even finer impurities from the cane—stuff like dirt, pigment, tannins, and other complex carbohydrates. Like a moth to a flame, these impurities coagulated around the milk of lime, forming small brown clumps that were easy to remove with a skimmer. After heating the solution to yet another boil, slowly lowering the heat, adding another round of milk of lime, skimming off more scum, and delivering a final blast of heat, the boilers and strikers finally sent a thick, dark distillation of massacuite to the next team of workers.

Collecting the purified sugar in large, shallow pans, workers once again boiled off excess water. This process resulted in a gooey substance consisting of about 60 percent sugar. A second, much slower evaporation yielded a super-saturated mixture that workers poured into cone-shaped clay molds capable of holding anywhere from five to thirty pounds of liquid. As the highly viscous solution cooled inside the molds, workers stirred it rapidly to help precipitate the crystallization of raw brown sugar. After a few days of rest, the clay molds were turned upside down so that any accumulated molasses could drip into copper collecting bins. Finally, workers repacked the sweet wet clay into new molds and set it to rest for another week, allowing residual moisture to evaporate. The end result, if all went well, was a yellowish sugar loaf that workers wrapped in vibrant blue paper (to make it appear whiter than it was) and shipped to agents in London and Antwerp.

The molasses, of course, hardly went to waste. Ever resourceful, colonists distilled it into the rum that lubricated social life once the day's grueling work reached an end.

As elaborate as sugar production was, there wasn't a single stage in the process that the Spanish didn't master. Ultimately, however, they failed to establish a permanently profitable sugar plantation in the West Indies. Their failure had nothing to do with a lack of expertise or motivation. The Spanish enjoyed ample land, capital, know-how, drive, sun, rain, oxen, mills, and lime. They drew on ready access to transatlantic resources, the Crown's active support, a growing European sweet tooth, and an ample supply of ships. Every precondition for a booming sugar business was in place. Every precondition, that is, except the most critical one: manpower. Despite the early importation of African slaves throughout the 1520s and 1530s, the Spanish ultimately failed to import a constant, disposable, efficient, and relatively cheap supply of workers to clear the fields, stir the cane juice, strike the liquid, haul the massacuite, tend the fires, turn the mills, and pack the sugar. Bluntly put, they lacked—in spite of all of their efforts—a reliable quantity of what would soon become sugar's historical counterpart: slaves.

Why the oversight? It actually wasn't so much an oversight as it was a matter of poor timing. After the Spanish had decimated the indigenous population thoroughly enough to rule them out as a reliable source of labor, they turned, as we've seen, to the African slave trade to meet their labor needs. They did so, however, without a full appreciation for the growing international competition for the new transatlantic trade in human flesh. In fact, they turned to the slave trade under the assumption that the Atlantic Ocean continued to be their own "private lake," a place where they could continue to navigate without interference, proceed at their own pace, dominate without challenge. The Dutch, French, and English, however, had entered the colonization game. As they watched the Spanish start to exploit sugar and slavery, these competing European powers quickly made it be known that the slave market was up for grabs. A fierce quest for market control ensued, with the private lake becoming a turbulent ocean. Following the Spanish lead, European countries jumped into the Atlantic world later in the sixteenth century, caught the sugar bug, and began to allot their resources accordingly. An intensely competitive game of transatlantic domination ensued.

As far as the West Indies are concerned, the Spanish lost that game. The details of this transition make for a story beyond the scope of this book,

Barbados, 1650

This map of Barbados dates from the time when the English were beginning to adopt sugar as the staple crop of the West Indies and slavery as the labor system to work it.

but the upshot is simple enough. When, in 1588, the English navy finally routed the Spanish Armada off the coast of England, the tide of international power shifted, with decisive consequences. This change in geopolitical power allowed the English to dispatch their newly impressive naval force to control West African slave markets as well as acres upon acres of fertile sugar land in the West Indies. The Spanish, turning as they did to mine a new niche in South America, hardly went vanquished. They moved on to new ventures while the English (and the French) proceeded to attain thorough control of the West Indies. It took a while, and it required learning a few hard lessons in places such as Roanoke, Plymouth, Massachusetts Bay, and the Chesapeake Bay, but between 1624 and 1641 the English moved on to colonize Barbados, St. Kitts, Nevis, Antigua, Montserrat, and twelve other West Indian islands. In 1651, England—on the verge of stealing the slave trade from the Dutch—essentially sealed its West Indian dominance by taking Jamaica from Spain. By the mid-seventeenth century, the transition of power from the Spanish to the English in the West Indies was complete. The brutal world that they went on to create in these beautiful islands became the bittersweet, fertile foundation of America's culinary origins.

The Ultimate Reason Behind the Preservation of West African Foodways in America

The English were a people accustomed to knowing where their food came from. Sugar, however, was an exception to the rule. When artisans, farmers, serfs, and aristocrats plunked imported rocks of sugar into their cups of steaming coffee and tea, they hardly imagined the widespread cruelty wreaked to provide such a powerful flavor. Sugar played the most significant role in forcing nearly 11 million Africans to the New World between 1500 and 1800. No description can capture the cruelty of this historical reality. Nevertheless, by the early seventeenth century, at a time when the English were settling the North American colonies that would eventually become the United States, sugar and slavery had done nothing less than define life in the British West Indies. White gold and black slaves, once the stuff of Spanish dreams, quickly turned the British West Indies into England's most profitable colonial region.

The means to this "success" hinged on a straightforward accomplishment. The English developed a more reliable and affordable access to West African slaves at the very time that they were building their plantations. Whereas the Spanish turned to sugar production well before the slave system had matured, the English embraced sugar well after the slave trade had become established. This difference in timing proved critical. Moreover, by the late seventeenth century, the English wouldn't just tap this system of labor, but would nearly own it. Their growing monopoly on the slave trade, which reached its pinnacle in 1700, further ensured the dominance of sugar as the staple crop of the West Indies. The ruthless drive to mass-produce sugar continually demanded the equally ruthless exploitation of the laborers purchased to grow it. Sugar and slavery coexisted as two sides of the same coin. Together they shaped the culture, social system, and economic development of the English West Indies.

For the slaves who underwrote these developments, sugar left nothing but bitterness. The slave trade destroyed families, killed spiritual expression, and undermined the material world of transplanted Africans.

This cultural holocaust was comprehensive, ruinous, and unrelenting. Remarkably, however, slaves refused to acquiesce to the brutality completely. They refused to sacrifice their basic sense of humanity. In fact, faced with such adversity, West Indian slaves discovered unique ways to forge a culture that blended their African heritage with New World conditions, however desperate those conditions may have been. Cast adrift in a sea of violence and greed, they sought, against all odds, to cling to at least a semblance of their inherited traditions.

The most notable of these traditions was culinary. Slaves, whom plantation owners viewed as essentially equivalent to other investments such as cows and farming implements, came to dominate the foodways of the West Indies. Due in large part to the planters' frugal decision to import as little food as possible, plantation owners forced slaves to provide a substantial portion of their own sustenance. This demand became, in turn, the source of culinary empowerment and innovation that would help define American food to this day. Rarely do we look to the historically dispossessed for insight into a pervasive cultural tradition. Nevertheless, forced into a wrenching labor system that would send millions of Africans to the Americas, slaves became the unlikely founders of a distinctive way of American cooking. Sugar, in short, led to slavery; slavery influenced a distinctive West Indian way of eating; and that West Indian way of eating eventually moved to the mainland colonies that would become the United States.

West African Foodways

But it all started in West Africa. Culinary history is a story about adaptation. But the adaptation that characterized the involuntary migration of Africans to the West Indies was especially intense, creative, and widespread—in essence, unprecedented in scope. The origins of West African cereal cultivation and livestock domestication began ten thousand years ago with farming techniques that spread to the region through the Nile Valley by way of the savanna corridor. From this migration, two distinct agricultural systems eventually emerged. First, around 1500 B.C., in the more northern and drier savanna zone, residents who had once spent their lives foraging for wild millet and sorghum while fishing for their protein adapted agricultural practices from their Nile Valley neighbors. Central to this adaptation was the decision to replace wild crops with cultivated wheat and barley. Later, they further stabilized their increasingly sedentary culture by grazing livestock. To diversify their yields and expand their culinary options, these savanna farmers came to rely on a number of other cultivated crops, including rice, cowpeas, sesame, okra, fluted pumpkins, gourds, calabashes, and watermelons. These farmers practiced a combination of agricultural pursuits that lasted until African colonization. Second, in contrast to savanna agriculture, forest agriculture started around A.D. 800 when sedentary communities of hunters and fishermen were delighted to learn that several Southeast Asian crops could be grown using the same agricultural techniques that their savanna neighbors employed up north. Bananas, plantains, Asiatic yams, Asiatic rice, cocoyams (taro), and sugarcane came to the region via Madagascar, and, with the help of the native guinea yam and oil-palm tree, these goods fueled development throughout the more tropical areas of West Africa. Only in rare cases did farmers from both regions trade these crops. Instead, they grew them primarily for subsistence purposes. This more southern system also became stable enough to last until the colonization era.

These relatively insular agricultural habits shaped the West African landscape and foodways until the early sixteenth century. By then, however, Europeans (and some freed slaves returning from Brazil) began to introduce American crops to the continent. A sampling of these new crops—including maize, cassava, peanuts, avocado pears, tomatoes, potatoes, pineapples, and cacao—transformed and broadened the West African diet while leading to much greater yields than the indigenous crops produced. This growth, in addition to altering the diet of millions of Africans, encouraged Africa to develop internal and international trade networks. Two crops in particular, cassava and maize, played a powerful role in weaving Africa into foreign markets. Cassava arrived in West Africa during the sixteenth century, but the dogged root crop got off to a slow start. It wasn't until the eighteenth century, in fact, that returning Brazilian slaves popularized cassava by teaching cooks how to remove the prussic acid from the root and bake it into flat bread. In time, cassava—native to South America—became critical to West African agriculture not only because of its taste but also because its durability and easy storage made it an ideal insurance crop against the failure of other crops. Maize became even more central to the African diet than did cassava. An equally durable, more nutritious, and even more prolific crop than cassava, maize contributed to the expansion and health of the entire West African population. Two types of maize dominated. The flint, or "hard," variety first came to Spain with Columbus and then worked its way to Africa via Italy, the Levant, and Egypt; from there it went up the Nile, across the Sudan, and into the savanna regions of Africa. The "soft" varieties, or flour maize, arrived on the African coast with the

Portuguese. Cassava and maize were thus revolutionizing African cuisine while African foods were doing the same in the West Indies.

Contrary to older characterizations of Africa as being technologically "backward," we now know that West African farmers were hardly averse to innovation. They actively and strategically invented and assumed technologies supportive of their particular needs, geography, and cultural values. The effort to obtain food played an important role in dictating the conservative pace of technological change throughout Africa. Iron making, which was especially popular in West Africa because of the region's lack of bronze or copper, followed close on the heels of settled agricultural systems. Through its production of hand-held hoes in particular, West Africa came to rival contemporary iron-making efforts in Europe and the Middle East. But iron making was just one example among many. To accommodate the rising demand for fish and local trade, West Africans built a diversity of seaworthy craft. Dugout canoes made by African artisans reached up to eighty feet in length, could carry up to one hundred people, and were reliable several miles off shore. Reed boats, plank boats, and dhows further allowed traders and fishermen to navigate Africa's circuitous rivers, lakes, and coastal inlets. Concerning inland transportation, Africans domesticated animals and relied to some extent on teams of pack animals to move goods. They readily incorporated tools for manufacturing cotton into their technological capabilities (with the notable exception of the spinning wheel).

The region's modest rate of technological advance helped ensure that West Africans continued to practice their traditional agricultural systems while Europe was colonizing the West Indies and incorporating new, American crops. Forest dwellers living in the southern regions persisted as "long forest fallow cultivators." They grew root crops, legumes, fruits, and oil palms in patches of rough-hewn clearings, working over extensive areas of land. They complemented these crops with free-ranging pigs, goats, and fowl, but avoided cattle and horses because of the havoc constantly wreaked by the tsetse fly. Farmers in the south generally slashed and burned small plots, planted crops, held exclusive rights to the land while it was under cultivation, and relinquished those rights when the land fell fallow. Men and women labored both individually and cooperatively with sturdy, wrought-iron tools, especially hoes. The farming that these southern West African residents practiced was mostly subsistence in nature, but the addition of American crops and more sophisticated boats into their system pulled them, however slowly, toward more market-oriented production.

African farmers who settled and developed the northern region of West Africa also continued traditional methods after colonization. They practiced a mixed system of grain production and pastoral farming over much smaller plots of land. Relying on shorter fallow periods, deeper hoeing techniques, and elaborate irrigation mechanisms, these farmers cultivated crops such as pearl millet, wheat, barley, sorghum, okra, watermelon, and sesame. Free from the ravages of the tsetse fly, livestock thrived in this region without yokes and chains. Farmers grew enough not only to subsist but also to sell, and the region's craft specialization and intricate governmental infrastructure attested to the vibrancy of that trade. Olaudah Equiano, an Ibo slave who worked in the West Indies, offered a rare African perspective on this regional farming habit. "Our tillage," he wrote in 1791, "is exercised in a large plain or common, some hours' walk from our dwellings, and all the neighbours resort thither in a body. They use no beasts of husbandry, and their only instruments are hoes, axes, shovels, and beaks, or pointed iron to dig with." African farmers also used these tools throughout West Africa to cultivate crops to make *fufu*, which was a boiled starch, as well as onions, a collard green called *palava*, and chickpeas. Because they consumed most of what they produced, rather than exporting it, Africans in both the savanna and forest regions were able to carefully gear agricultural decisions to culinary demands even after American goods flooded their shores.

Cooking methods and recipes varied throughout West Africa, but a couple of techniques and dishes characterized the region's cooking habits as a whole. Perhaps most notably, African chefs relied on liberally spiced, one-pot meals—the most popular of which was pepper soup, a dish that was essentially a stew. The logic behind this meal was exquisitely simple: scrape off as much meat as possible from the bones of slaughtered animals, allow nothing to waste, toss it in a pot, and start cooking it. Organs, feet, beaks, tripe, oxtail—whatever could be salvaged—found their way into the slowly simmering stew. Many cooks fortified this haphazard mixture with fish and flavored it with spices such as Guinea pepper, African bird pepper, and—the defining ingredient—dried hot peppers. This stew was leavened with a fair amount of *fufu*, which lent it a creamy, thickened texture. In addition to pepper soup, fish stews became a staple of the West African diet. Cooks (once again, in a single pot) sautéed sea bass with onions, chili pepper, and spices. They complemented the meal with okra, a vegetable whose gooey consistency lent the ubiquitous dish a welcome thickness. One plant that was particularly central to African culture was the baobab tree, which grew well in the savanna. Africans used its bark to make rope, its sap to make medicine, and its trunks to build coffins. But it was for food that the baobab was most prized and exploited. African cooks used its leaves to thicken stew, made a grainy meal from its pulp to incorporate into bread, and squeezed cooking oil from its seeds. Seeds from a wide variety of plants, in fact, made it into African cooking practices. Cooks would grind watermelon, pumpkin, and squash seeds into a pulp and season meat and vegetable dishes with it. They would also toast the seeds, work them into a powder, and make a drink with them by bringing the ground seeds to a boil along with raisins, rice, honey, and fruit juice, and then straining the results.

African cooks shared their ingredients, recipes, and techniques on market days. A market day in a West African village was a social and culinary extravaganza. An especially popular dish was *kilishi*, which consisted of roasted meat basted in oil, herbs, and spices. It was not uncommon for women to dry the meat in the sun for a week and then marinate it for several more days before serving it up. Stalls typically accommodated two enormous pots and one chef. In one pot, cooks sautéed beef, goat, and lamb. In the other, they made a rich sauce with a yam base and leavened it with ground baobab leaves. After ladling the sauce over some meat and adding some *enjibotchi*, which is a rice-based sauce, the cook had a hearty meal to offer clients. Breads made from the baobab tree and gingerbread cakes were commonly sold at market, as was *kulli-kulli*—a fried patty made of oil, peanuts, spices, and pepper—and *karra*, which were meal dumplings or bean cakes deep fried in palm oil. In so many ways, the market was the most obvious manifestation of this region's vast and complex culinary offerings—offerings that reflected thousands of years of crop production, diversification, and adaptation. Offerings, moreover, that slaves would not soon forget when they were forcibly relocated to the other side of the Atlantic Ocean.

West Indian Foodways

At the same time that West Africans were pioneering local cooking procedures, Caribbean Natives were practicing their own timeworn agricultural and culinary habits. While every Native Caribbean culture (there were hundreds) developed distinctive food habits, they shared several commonalities. Fishing, most notably, dominated the culinary life of Caribbean Natives. Almost all their protein came from fish and shellfish. Native Americans fished extensively and enthusiastically, developing a thorough knowledge of the region's waterways, the feeding habits of different species of fish, and various methods for catching a variety of prey. The shallow, sandy flats throughout the West Indies proved to be fertile breeding grounds for needlefish, bonefish, porgy, parrotfish, angelfish, and wrasses—all of which swim in schools visible from a considerable distance in a canoe. Native Americans learned that these species frequently fed in shallow waters when the tide approached and, accordingly, relied on nets and weirs weighted with clay sinkers to harvest their prey at the right time. Farther out to sea, in and around coral reefs, fishermen sought other fish through other means. Fish that live around reefs tend to be sedentary loners reluctant to stray too far from their food source. Native American fishermen visited these reefs with wooden or tortoiseshell hooks to snag triggerfish, grouper, hogfish, and hinds. Another option was to set a basket trap at dusk and check it in the morning. The advantage to this technique was that the morning's catch was a discrete amount and thus could help determine how much foraging a tribe had to do that day. Another benefit was that fish caught in a basket trap had a tendency to attract other fish of the same species, thereby increasing yields. The major drawback to using a trap, however, was that a fisherman might pull up a basket with a bunch of fish bones and a well-fed nurse shark, as sharks also found the traps rather attractive places once a critical mass of prey had congregated. It will come as no surprise that Caribbean communities invariably settled within a mile of the coast, and that 70 percent of these settlements were on east coasts of the islands, where reefs predominated and waters remained less turbulent.

The land was as valuable to the Caribbean Natives as the sea. As mentioned, they relied heavily on cassava, a pinkish cigar-shaped tuber indigenous to South America. Not unlike northern West Africans, the Caribbean Natives cleared small patches of land in the inland forests to grow crops in these rough clearings. The cassava plant is a shrubby perennial that reaches about six feet tall. Native Americans grew cassava by planting ten-inch sections of the stem a couple of inches deep and about four feet apart. The plants grew well and matured after about nine months. The root's chief advantage is its durability. The cassava root matures when it reaches eight to twelve inches long and two to four inches in diameter, and it can rest in the ground for up to three months before being harvested, a quality that significantly diminished labor demands. (Europeans, not incidentally, would later discover the same advantage in the potato.)

After soaking the root in water or heating it gently and then removing the brown fibrous bark in order to eliminate the poisonous prussic acid,

Native American cooks prepared the white root in a variety of ways. More often than not, they ground it into a meal or grated it to make dry, flat cassava cakes over a griddle. On other occasions, they simply boiled or fried it and ate it whole or extracted the starchy interior to make a kind of sweet bread (later called *pan de bono* by the Spaniards). However manipulated, the poison lost its potency for humans after extraction and served as an effective preservative for meat and, in some cases, a poison to stun fish. Sometimes Natives made something called *cassareep* from a cassava root by squeezing out the juice; mixing it with a little sugar, cloves, and cinnamon; and reducing the solution to a syrup. *Cassareep* became a widely applicable and flavorful sauce for many meat dishes. As a final testament to cassava's versatility, the Caribbean Natives were even known to brew it into beer.

Cassava was only one of many crops cultivated in cleared patches of thick oceanic forest. Groups of sedentary agricultural people grew potatoes, tobacco, maize, beans, pumpkins, cocoyams, squash, peppers, and pineapple. When they first arrived, the Spaniards seemed particularly impressed by the common agricultural arrangement of maize, beans, squash, and peppers. Peter Martyr, the royal historian at the time of contact, wrote, "The sweet pepper is called *boniatai* and the hot pepper is called *canibal*, meaning sharp and strong." They were similarly impressed with the many cayenne peppers and the way that they provided more heat with less grinding. Columbus found the indigenous crops so plentiful and well suited to his taste that he remarked, "Thanks to God, that he has given us a sample of all the things of that land without danger or fatigue to our people." Native Americans grew the cabbage palm tree to harvest its blooms for their tender hearts. On many islands, Native Americans enjoyed coconuts, papaya, arrowroot, guayaba, and the mamey apple. Some archaeological evidence indicates that they even harvested seagrass, turtlegrass, sponges, and algae to eat. In 1595, Robert Davies visited Dominica and reported how the locals came out to his ship in canoes "and brought in them plantans, pinos and potatoes." Ten years later, George Percy had a similar experience. "Many Savage Indians," he wrote, "came to our ships with their canoas, bringing us many kinds of sundry fruites as Pines, Potatoes, Plantons, Tobacco, and other fruits." Additional accounts involve frequent attempts to trade cassava bread and roasted maize for iron tools and weapons.

Meat was much less common than fish among the West Indian Natives, but it did include turkeys, guinea fowl, and musk duck. Native Americans never domesticated animals for food (with the possible exception of the duck), but they hunted game on a regular basis. Residents ate manatee, moray eel, land crabs, mangrove oysters, porpoises, and monk seals. They consumed a variety of small reptiles and birds, as well as worms, sea urchins, rats, land snails, whelks, and littoral crabs. All these animals were cooked and eaten whole, and, with the rat at least, the brain was removed to eat separately, as a delicacy of sorts. Native Americans boiled whelks and snails with the shell still on and then removed it once the meat was cooked. With the birds, reptiles, and turtles, Native Americans consumed their eggs as well. A sixteenth-century engraving by Theodore de Bry depicts eleven dugout canoes, each holding two Native Americans, rowing out to two Spanish galleons and greeting them with proffered dead birds.

As with Africans, the job of cooking generally fell to women. Native Americans built a male and female space within their houses, and the female space always included the cooking space. Shards excavated by archaeologists indicate that inhabitants cooked in large utilitarian ceramic pots, much like West Africans were doing on the other side of the Atlantic. Pottery designed for cooking was about one-eighth of an inch thick, formed into a boat shape, and ceremoniously decorated with reddish human and animal heads. Archaeologists have found whole bowls and pots as well as intact water bottles and griddles. On some islands, the Native Americans incorporated sponge spicules into the clay to give the pottery added durability. They used conch shells to make plates, scrapers, and knives. Archaeologists have also discovered ample evidence of technological ingenuity. Caribbean Natives, for example, embraced rotary technology. A typical kitchen thus might have had grinding stones for maize and more refined milling stones and presses for cassava. Cooking spaces included straining bags for squeezing the poison from cassava, carrying poles to transport cooking water, and fire tongs made from mussel shell to keep embers aglow. The generally stoneless character of the land led to the use of wooden, shell, or bone knives, as well as manufactured clay stones to hold pots above the fire. Spits may have been used to roast meat, as charcoal has commonly been found in excavation sites. As with the Africans, cooking implements remained modest but eminently pragmatic. With them, Native Americans prepared the food that defined their culture: roots and tubers, maize, terrestrial animals, marine fish, and marine mollusks. As far as the archaeological evidence goes, their culinary decisions, as with the West Africans, seem to have served them well.

Slaves' Control of Their Own Diet

West African and Native Caribbean agricultural and culinary traditions developed in total isolation from each other for thousands of years. The Middle Passage, however, brought them together and, in so doing, reminds us with particular poignancy that America's culinary history is inextricably linked with suffering. The Africans were the first to endure the pain. The brutal journey that brought slaves from West Africa to the West Indies forced these historically disparate traditions together, but not before imposing abrupt dietary changes on the Africans. Food options and health conditions aboard slave ships worsened dramatically. Gone, after all, were the generously sauced and spiced meat dishes, rich grains, and access to a plethora of tropical fruits and vegetables. Gone were the delicious stews sold and bartered at market stalls. Enslaved Africans, cramped and chained below deck, now choked down a cold mush of yams, cassava, and rice served to them in a long trough more appropriate for farm animals than human beings. Slave traders who expressed more concern with the health of their cargo might complement the pallid mush with old cod and shrimp. Sometimes, but very rarely, slaves even ate food prepared with flour, palm oil, and red peppers. Whatever the availability of these goods, and whatever the captains chose to serve, slaves at this stage of dispossession had absolutely no voice about how their meals were prepared, and their "thin and weake" appearance upon landing, according to one observer, reflected rapidly deteriorating dietary conditions on board slave ships. Many slaves refused to abide their new fate and threw themselves to the sharks. Others slipped into fatal illness, "chiefly owing," as another witness put it, "to the evil practice of mixing sea water with fresh . . . to make it go further." If one single event best signaled the onset of impending dietary doom for West Africans, it was this brutal trip across the Atlantic Ocean.

Upon landing in the West Indies, however, the food situation unexpectedly improved. As the slave population burgeoned throughout the Caribbean (through increased importation, not natural increase), circumstances conspired to give slaves a genuine opportunity to maintain some control over their own diet. The underlying reason behind this development was anything but a newfound English respect for the Africans' cultural heritage. Instead, it was something much more predictable and mundane: frugality. As we've seen, sugar dominated the West Indies. And sugar was nothing if not a capital-intensive pursuit. Planters continually sought ways to reduce capital costs. Slaves and their provisions initially comprised a whopping 30 to 40 percent of a plantation's expenditures. After comparing the price of importing food for slaves with the cost of having slaves cultivate their own crops, masters generally favored the latter as a more economical option. Accordingly, planters set aside garden plots and a few of the least desirable planting fields for their slaves to eke out something of a subsistence living.

One points to a "positive" aspect of slavery with caution, but this situation mutually benefited masters and slaves. Planters avoided the cost of heavy food imports, limiting their purchases to a little grain, meat, and "refuse fish" (stale cod no longer fit for the market, often bought off Middle Passage ships that had obtained the cod from New Englanders delivering rum to Africa). Slaves, for their part, enjoyed the chance to apply familiar farming habits to New World soil. Contemporaries were quick to praise the arrangement. Alexander Campbell, a St. Vincent planter, remarked on the "custom" of granting slaves their own provisioning ground, saying that it was "universally considered the greatest benefit to a planter that his Negroes should have a sufficient quantity of provisions, and the more money the Negroes got for themselves, the more attached they were to the property." Improbable as it seems, economic calculation yielded to slaves the smallest degree of freedom. It was an opportunity they didn't squander.

A caveat is in order, however. Historical and archaeological evidence currently suggests that West Indian slaves often suffered considerable malnourishment. The combination of master-allotted provisions and slave food production on master-allotted land never fully met the slaves' nutritional needs. It's true that most slaves died of disease and accidents, not starvation. Nevertheless, food supply *was* a regular problem in the West Indies, and it surely contributed to these related ailments. Slave remains reveal dental evidence of hypoplasia, a deterioration indicating extreme dietary deficiency. A London agent visiting Barbados in 1776 reported slaves "robbing cornfields and slaughtering cattle for food" because their own supplies had run dry. The future founding father Alexander Hamilton, who was born in Nevis ("the bastard son of a Scotch peddler," according to John Adams, who spoke the truth), said of the West Indian slaves that "their proprietors appropriate only small portions, to the purpose of raising food; they are very populous, and therefore, the food raised among themselves goes but little way." The manager of an Antigua plantation reported in 1781 that slaves were notably thin "for want of a sufficiency of Food, and I am obliged to ease them as much as possible in their Labour. Never were provisions of all sorts so dear." The fact that slaves played any role at all in supplying their own provisions was itself a remarkable opportunity within the oppressive confines of the slave system. We mustn't lose sight, however, of the fact that it was a compromised accomplishment haphazardly achieved. In the end, we're left with the assessment that even partial self-sufficiency had the long-term affect of incorporating West African cooking practices into the American experience. Like most of the history of early American food, it's a bittersweet conclusion at best.

African–Native American Efforts to Forage and Catch Fish

That said, slaves did draw on their long history of adaptation to become highly flexible farmers, hunters, and fishermen after landing in the West Indies. Readily willing to adjust West African habits to New World soil, they sensibly followed the lead of the Native Americans who relied on cassava, beans, sweet potatoes, roots, berries, fish, and shellfish for their sustenance. Slaves, who hardly found these foods strange, quickly integrated them into their diet while combing the landscape alongside the Native Americans for nuts, berries, and wild plants. Some of these goods—most notably the sweet potato, maize, and cassava—not only had become central to an emerging Afro-Caribbean diet but also had worked their way back to Africa, where they became critical to evolving West African foodways. Slaves joined the Native Americans in making the most of the South Pacific–introduced mango, *dasheem*, cocoyam, *cocoes*, and breadfruit. Bananas, yams, plantains, and coconuts—items common to both regions before the Columbian exchange—became especially critical to the Africans as they worked, cultivated, and cooked in their new environment.

Nowhere was the slaves' reliance on local examples more evident than in the effort to obtain fish. As we've seen, the Native Americans were exceptional fishermen, and fish provided their main source of protein. Fishing was so ingrained in the Native Americans' daily routine that they actually had a term of reproach for "a man who does not know how to fish." Their techniques astounded visitors. In 1665, a French traveler expressed a popular opinion about these fishermen when he remarked how "they are marvelously ingenious in fishing with a hook." Local fishermen often fished with hand lines from dugout canoes, a technique made possible by their crafting of hooks from dense wood, strong fish bones, or shards of turtle shell. Baiting hooks with chunks of fish or meat, they trolled the expansive flats for larger species. Some hooks were even durable enough for Native Americans to catch sharks, which they would immobilize with a spear thrust to the brain before hauling into the canoe. Through the use of retrievable wooden spears, Native American fishermen not only stunned sharks, but captured sea turtles, manatees, rays, and large fish. One European inhabitant described the practice this way: "One goes at night in a canoe to places where many torn weeds have been noticed on the water's surface. . . . He who holds the harpoon is at the prow of the canoe. . . . As soon as the turtle feels his wound, it flees with all its strength, violently dragging the canoe behind." Once the turtle drowned, the fishermen hauled it into the boat.

A particularly wily method of catching large turtles involved sneaking up on them as they were in the throes of copulation, securing a slipknot around an otherwise distracted flipper, and hauling the male (he was the one invariably on top) into the canoe. An account from 1667 described the procedure in restrained terms:

The turtle mounts. . . . I shall not go into all the details of this action; suffice it to say that it is done on the surface in such a way that they can be easily discovered: two or three people quickly jump in a canoe, race towards them, and easily coming alongside, pass a slip knot over the neck and flipper . . . or grab them with a hand on the neck. Sometimes they take both, but ordinarily the female escapes.

It hardly seemed fair, of course, but then again those fish stunned with root poison didn't have much of a chance either. Nor did those nabbed by birds that the Native Americans trained to hunt them.

Masters took note. Intent on keeping their tables well stocked with fish and shellfish, they recognized these methods as highly effective and, in turn, offered slaves incentives to follow suit. In order to feed themselves and get a temporary pass from field work, many Africans actively embraced the opportunity to become fishing slaves. They had, of course, fished at home in Africa, but neither as often, for the same fish, nor with similar methods. With their long tradition of embracing human-driven technologies, however, they thrived in their adaptation of local habits. Slaves especially excelled at trolling for fish. Using sardines as bait, they developed a thorough knowledge of fish feeding habits. They also relied on native fish pots, but eventually improved them by designing an elaborate weir to attach to them. Fish drugging worked just as well for slaves as it did for Native Americans. "They built dams in inlets," a resident wrote in 1665. "There they throw their intoxicant, composed of quicklime, water, sludge, and the sugar of certain plants . . . the fish suddenly jump, dive, leap, and gambol." Slaves also used turtle-shell hooks attached to homemade vegetable-fiber lines and set up a row of poles along a fishing bank. Fishing at night with torches, they relied on nothing but their hands to grab fish swimming in shallow pools. Wielding harpoons to pull larger animals such as manatee and stingrays from the ocean, slaves kept their consumption of fish ample and diversified. Masters obviously benefited from these efforts. One anonymous observer remarked of the planters, "I have known people for whom a seine, a canoe, and a few negroes sufficed to amass a brilliant fortune." Slaves might have been working in the service of their master, but they made the most of these skills for themselves, too. An eighteenth-century traveler condemned the poor rations that masters gave to their slaves and then remarked that "slaves are obliged to seek out [their food] elsewhere, either in their particular skills, or in the work which they do for themselves in the free time allotted them. In this regard shellfish offer them great resources, because of the quantity which is found in the sea or the streams." Through all these adaptations, fish became central to the diet of slaves in the West Indies while reflecting the most conspicuous way that the slaves adhered to Native American practices.

Transplanted African Traditions

In addition to depending on the Native Americans for advice about obtaining and growing food, slaves shaped their diet with practices brought directly from Africa. When they cured pork and bacon, raised livestock and poultry, fried fish in palm oil, and cultivated guinea corn, yellow yams, guinea peas, okra, and kola nuts, slaves consciously evoked the unique flavors and cooking techniques of their ancestors. As they had done in West Africa, slaves cultivated the land with hoes, kept tilled gardens, and generally grew plants from cuttings rather than seed. Animal husbandry significantly enriched their West Indian diet with African traditions. Slaves raised a wide variety of fowl, a practice that led one Virginia traveler to refer to them as "chicken merchants." Guinea fowl, ducks, geese, turkey, and pigeons frequently made their way onto the fire, thus furthering the range of culinary choices available to slave families. A visitor to the Leeward Islands noted that a slave's "poultry and his [live]stock are his wealth." He continued, "A Negro without stock is miserable." Although less common, it wasn't unheard of for slaves to raise a few cattle and pigs. An active internal trade in cowhides and goatskins attests to the modest presence of these animals on slave grounds. In Antigua, slaves not only fed themselves with small livestock, goats, and hogs but occasionally provisioned departing ships with these goods as well. In such ways did slaves balance the old and the new in the ongoing effort to stay alive, eat as well as possible, and maintain a compromised African identity under the most adverse circumstances.

The yam, which has its origins in the Pacific islands but was grown in Africa for centuries, was a West African crop that became especially critical to the slaves' diet and cultural identity. Slaves mainly cultivated the yellow guinea yam and the *cush-cush* (also called *yampee*), mixing these yams with as many as six other varieties imported directly from West Africa. Aside from being a good source of starch, yams rotted slowly and could be cooked in many ways. If slaves didn't fry them in palm oil, they mashed them with wooden mallets, shaped them into patties, and then grilled them over coals. Or they might dredge the mashed yams in cornmeal or cassava flour and eggs and fry them into croquettes. Slaves produced and consumed enough yams for European observers to make mention of their "yam grounds"—relatively large areas within their allotted land dedicated to this crop. On some plantations, masters even allowed slaves to grow yams on fallow sugar fields. This decision proved doubly beneficial to the master because it kept slaves fed while replenishing the tired ground with lost nutrients. Back in Africa, the yam was so central to dietary subsistence that it was linguistically linked to the verb "to eat." Slaves made sure that the association remained intact in the New World.

Caribbean Natives and West Africans thus negotiated a wide range of influences, equipment, practices, and ingredients within the confines of an otherwise brutally oppressive existence officially dominated by white sugar planters. But how influential, in the grand scheme of things, were their eating habits? The course of change in the West Indies always followed the dictates of sugar. And thus it was through importation rather than natural increase that the slave population grew immensely throughout the seventeenth and eighteenth centuries while the white and Native American populations proportionally diminished. As the demography of the British West Indies changed to meet the growing labor demands of a growing industry intent on meeting Europe's sweet tooth, the culinary practices just sketched began to become the exclusive domain of slaves. And as slaves came to comprise up to 90 percent of the population on some British American islands, they made agricultural and cooking decisions that automatically shaped the region's overall culinary habits. Drawing on a wide variety of crop possibilities and cooking techniques, slaves pioneered food habits that a stubborn historical record has ignored, leaving too much to the imagination. Nevertheless, enough crumbs of evidence survive to convince us that within the slaves' worn bowls the ingredients of a genuine American cuisine emerged. Those ingredients combined to have a substantial culinary influence not just in the West Indies but throughout British America.

The Evolution of African-Caribbean Culinary Habits

Finding these ingredients, much less trying to make sense of them, is an exercise in scholarly humility. Slaves condemned to life on a sugar plantation left no written records. Historians don't enjoy the luxury of mining account books, treatises, sermons, or bills of exchange for information on how slaves used their provisioning grounds. To a very large extent, the food they cooked over their kitchen fires and the feelings they experienced while adapting to New World conditions are simply lost. Other historical decisions and opinions remain frustratingly vague at best, and the clues that we do have trickle down through snippets of European observation. Nevertheless, however biased these surviving accounts may be, they still go a long way toward uncovering a rudimentary picture of the culinary culture of West Indian slaves. These European men had a lot to say about the way that slaves in the West Indies prepared food. With a dose of skepticism, we should listen to what they have to say.

The allotted provision ground that slaves worked fell into three general categories. Most notably, slaves worked their ubiquitous yam grounds. Not exceeding forty square feet, these plots reflected a distinct West African practice. Slaves labored on the yam grounds in small gangs, much as they had done back home. One difference, however, involved timing. Slaves now had to grow the yams rapidly and couldn't leave them sitting in the ground after they ripened because the land they worked reverted back to the master once the yams matured. With a "clean and ameliorated surface to plant," masters turned the yam ground over to a new crop of canes. This impending demand for the plot forced slaves to alter their cultivation techniques in subtle ways. Ultimately, they had to speed it up. Small kitchen gardens were a second type of allotment. Gardens abutted slave homes, often providing the only buffer between individual cottages. Gardens became common and effective enough to justify a law, passed in Grenada in 1788, requiring planters to allot each adult slave at least one-fortieth of an acre "contiguous to the Negro Houses for the purpose of cultivating gardens for their sole use and benefit." Gardens provided slaves with the necessary space to raise small stock and poultry while cultivating tree crops, vines, and vegetables. Mountain ground was a third space for slaves to grow cassava, maize, and a range of other staple vegetables. These hard-scrabble plots stood on deeply sloped grounds that were difficult to clear and more difficult to cultivate. Unfit for sugar cultivation, the mountain ground suffered frequent erosion and even the occasional avalanche. Although slaves often received from one-half of an acre to two acres of this land, the density of the soil and its exposure to harsh winds helps explain the slaves' periodic malnourishment.

Despite the many drawbacks to their allotments, slaves made the most of them. Traveling throughout Jamaica in the eighteenth century, William Beckford admired the slave grounds for their organization and inventive methods of operation. Noting the "very husbandlike and beautiful appearance" of slave plots, Beckford described how "all kind of ground provision and corn, as well as the plantain, are successfully cultivated in the mountains." Both crops were favorites of the slaves because they demanded little attention. Confirming the master's tendency to allow slaves time to work their own fields, he remarked that "this is done by negroes in their own grounds and on those days which are given to them for this particular purpose." As a result, "it does not enter into the mass of plantation labor." Beckford often tinged his remarks with an air of cultural superiority, but he nonetheless demonstrated an honest interest in the connections between the slaves' crop decisions and geographical circumstances. "They generally make choice of such sorts of land for their ground as are encompassed by lofty mountains," he explained, "and I think that they commonly prefer the sides of hills, which are covered with loose stones, to the bottoms upon which they are not so abundant." He noted that some slaves "will have a mixture of both, and will cultivate the plantain tree upon the flat, and their provision on the rising ground." Beckford's account abounds with references to the slaves' abundant produce, including "fruit and garden stuff" cacao, corn, ginger, and "other minor productions of the country."

Beckford wasn't alone in finding the slaves' provisioning system worth a lengthy description. Although nineteenth-century observers might seem like inappropriate sources for understanding slave provisioning in the seventeenth and eighteenth centuries, their perspectives are in fact quite helpful because they allow glimpses into slave agricultural habits at their maturity. John Stewart visited several West Indian islands in the early nineteenth century, primarily as a merchant. He seemed especially interested in the ways that slaves worked the land to obtain their own food.

Identifying the slaves' gardens as their principal means of support, Stewart remarked how the industrious slave would keep himself fed, even in times of scarcity. In a book published in 1806, George Pinckard, another traveler, noted that "those who are industrious have little additions of their own, from vegetables grown on the spot of ground allotted to them." Referring to the garden plot, he mentioned "the pig, goat, or other stock raised about their huts in the negro yard." Pinckard seemed genuinely surprised to find on one estate "a pig, a goat, a young kid, some pigeons, and some chickens, all the property of an individual slave." Another Englishman observed how "slaves always have time to cultivate their yams, tannias, plantains, bananas, sweet potatoes, okras, pineapples, and Indian corn." The gardens caught his attention as well. In "every garden" he found "a hen coop" for "a half dozen fowls," a "pigsty," and "goats tied under the shade of some tree." On one occasion, he saw that "an old negro woman was stationed near" the animals to ensure that "they were not kidnapped."

Visitors frequently remarked on the trees that slaves cultivated in their gardens. F. W. N. Bayley described how slaves shaded their homes from "the scorching heat of the tropic sun" by planting "luxuriant foliage," including trees such as "the mango, the Java plum, the breadfruit, the soursop, the sabadilla and the pomegranate." An anonymous Englishman in eighteenth-century Jamaica marveled at what he called "Guinea trees" or "Guinea palms." These trees, of which this visitor said he saw hundreds, yielded "wine and oil" through the production of a fruit that "makes its appearance at the top of a cone resembling a high bush black-berry." The cone, as this observer likely embellished it, "is a size of a gallon keg, and the purple protuberances of this magnificent berry as big as a two ounce ball." Bunches of fruit could indeed weigh up to twenty pounds. Whatever the dimensions of the berries, slaves harvested them, crushed them in a wooden mortar, and boiled the juice in water. The liquid gathered from skimming this mixture "was palm oil, which constitutes an important item in African commerce and food." Slaves, he wrote, "prefer it to butter." Although he may not have known it, this traveler was observing one of the slaves' most important West African traditions. Guinea trees, which grew to more than one hundred feet, produced kernels that West Africans called *dende*, and *dende* were routinely squeezed for palm oil back in Africa. Slaves brought *dende* seeds to the New World and successfully grew the trees, whose nuts provided one of the most basic smells and tastes of their lost homeland. The nuts' pulp yielded deep yellow oil that had to be consumed soon after pressing because its high level of fatty acids made it prone to rapid spoilage. Oil squeezed from the kernel, by contrast, had a reddish tint and lasted longer in storage. When slaves depleted their supply of palm oil, they often found ways to dye other oils yellow and red for no other reason than to approximate the appearance of their customary cooking oil.

The slaves' reliance on fish, turtles, and pigs also made a significant impression on European travelers. Domesticated pigs originally imported from Spain, France, and England roamed the craggy hillsides at will, eventually becoming feral and thus fair game for capture. Eating everything from wild grass to garbage, pigs generally cared for themselves (unlike cattle, which usually needed enclosures). Pork, for this very reason, became much more central to the Afro-Caribbean diet than beef. Slaves came to rely heavily on pigs for pork fat, ham, bacon, sausage, and salt pork—foods that they enthusiastically incorporated into their New World diets whenever they could. Shellfish was also a popular item for slaves. They would regularly catch conch, marinate it in lime juice, and stir it into a stew of beans. Flying-fish pie, which slaves made with boiled flying fish, avocado, and mashed plantains, became a common slave meal, as did a variety of meals made with crabmeat. Sea turtles, the hapless victims of so many hunting tricks, provided an especially easy and versatile food source. Richard Bradley, an Englishman traveling in eighteenth-century Barbados, said of the turtle that "its flesh [is] between that of veal and lobster, and is extremely pleasant either roasted or baked." He claimed to have learned about preparing turtle from "a Barbadian lady."

The primary advantages of undomesticated food sources such as turtle, fish, feral pigs, crabs, and mollusks was the ease with which slaves could obtain them, the minimal labor required for their maintenance, and the variety of uses to which these ingredients could be put. Indeed, the cooking methods that slaves pioneered and adapted further reflected a practicality borne of necessity. With cooking utensils few and far between, and with free time always at a premium, most slave cooking occurred in a single large pot. It was in this capacity that their market-day traditions served them well. Slaves relied most heavily on an especially open-to-interpretation dish called *callaloo*. This one-pot soup incorporated ingredients as diverse as pokeweed, wild herbs, garlic, salt cod, crab, okra, and, in some cases, salt pork. Pepperpot, not unlike their pepper soup, remained another common meal for island slaves. Consisting of pigs' tails, tripe, a wide variety of vegetables, sea-turtle meat, *casereep*, brown sugar, and an array of seasoning, pepperpot would eventually make its way to the mainland colonies, and even into the quarters of George Washington's slaves. *Akee* stew was another very popular slave dish. *Akee* was a fruit grown in West Africa that traveled to the New World with slaves, who mashed the fruit into patties and fried them in palm oil. Slaves sometimes referred to *akee* as "vegetable brains," and Englishmen often noted its similarity to scrambled eggs. After mashing and frying the fruit, slaves added salt cod, onions, and tomatoes and allowed the stew to simmer for many hours. Sometimes beef was thrown into the mix. *Akee,* like cassava, had the further advantage of containing a poison that could be easily extracted and used to kill fish. A final dish that dominated the West Indian diet was fish-head stew. Obviously a way to extend leftovers, this meal consisted of a stock made from fish carcasses, pork fat, onions, tomatoes, beans, nutmeg, cilantro, and ginger.

Slave Markets in the West Indies

Even if these culinary habits had never left the plantation, they would still remain historically significant as remarkable examples of cultural adaptation. As it turns out, however, the foodways practiced by West Indian slaves had an impact that extended well beyond the individual slave garden, fishing ground, and kitchen. Slave cooking practices became very public matters as slaves actively drew on their cooking knowledge not only to feed themselves but, as they had done back home, to trade in local markets. Historians have identified "huckster slaves" as those men and women who dominated the local food trade throughout the West Indies. Given that the West Indies included Spanish, French, Dutch, and English colonies, one might expect the region's larger culinary developments to reflect these European influences. However, the slaves' vigorous participation in the internal market of the islands moved their culinary activity to the center of the region's cuisine. When, in the late eighteenth century, William Dickson snootily reported seeing slaves walking "several miles to market with a few roots, or fruits, or canes, sometimes a fowl or a kid, or a pig from their little spots of ground which have been dignified with the elusive name of 'gardens,'" he was identifying a critical cultural trend. And when two other travelers watched "busy marketeers" selling "an infinite variety of products," including "sweet potatoes, yams, eddoes, Guinea and Indian corn, various fruits and berries, vegetables, nuts, cakes," they, too, confirmed the popularity of this important social and economic development in the evolution of an Afro-Carribean society.

The cultivation of garden plots, the hunting of game, the raising of a little livestock, and frequent fishing ventures enabled slaves to occasionally produce a modest surplus that they would sell locally. "In this Island," an English clergyman said of Barbados in 1725, "the Negroes work all week for their masters, and on the Lord's Day they work and merchandize for themselves." Slave managers often tried to diminish Sunday trading activity, but, according to the clergyman, "the force of custom" undermined the "managerial resolve" to stop it. Financial benefits go a long way to explaining this "force of custom." F. W. N. Bayley estimated that a "tray of vegetables, fruits, calabashes, etc. brought in six or seven shillings"—more than a day's wage for a free laborer in New England. Poultry and livestock sales could bring in another ten shillings. Not that this income placed the slaves in a new social or legal category. Most of them, of course, used this extra cash merely to survive, complementing allotments from their masters and the foods they prepared on their own with items bought and bartered at the Sunday market. Market transactions hardly met the dietary or other material needs of the slaves. Nevertheless, an exceptional few approached some semblance of independence. "I have known several negroes," said Bayley, who had "accumulated large sums of money, more than enough to purchase their emancipation." Others, he noted, possessed tremendous "power of earning" but "frequently neglected it," a tendency that he blamed on a labor system that "leaves too many contented with what they deem sufficient for nature." Somewhat improbably, Bayley then lightly chastised the slaves for too often being content with "only cultivat[ing] sufficient ground to yield them as much fruit, as many vegetables as they require for their own consumption." They therefore had, according to Bayley, "none to sell."

Bayley wouldn't have been the only white person upset with what he perceived as the slaves' lack of productivity. Poor whites also hawked their wares at the Sunday markets, selling their surplus farm produce to other poor whites, blacks, and the occasional plantation owner. We're familiar with the historical image of slaves routinely pilfering from their masters' inventories. In the West Indies, however, theft regularly occurred in the other direction, with poor whites helping themselves to slave supplies before market day, something that they could do with impunity. Many whites, according to William Dickson, "depend for a subsistence on robbing the slaves . . . and illegally converting to their own use articles of greater value." The "injured party," he added, "has no redress." Poor white hucksters also made it a habit, as Dickson remarked, "of buying stolen goods from the negroes, whom they encourage to plunder their owners of everything that is portable." Whites depended on slaves in other ways, too. They often owned stores in town and needed slaves to provide raw materials and prepared foods from their gardens and kitchens to keep their stores stocked. Market transactions tied poor whites and slaves into complicated knots of interdependence, and food was often the binding force.

For all its novelty, though, the relationship between slave hucksters and whites was always somewhat schizophrenic. On the one hand, legislators continually worked to diminish the influence of slave traders. A law passed in Barbados in 1668 required justices of the peace to punish whites who purchased produce from slaves. Another bill approved six years later outlawed the sale of goods to blacks. A law ratified in 1708 forbade any white person to send a slave on his behalf to dispose "of any goods, wares, merchandize, stocks, poultry, corn, fruit, roots, or other effects." On the other hand, while legislators hoped to ban slaves from the internal market through these stipulations, they ultimately failed to contain a trade that they obviously, to some extent at least, depended on. Slaves and whites routinely and openly violated these laws. By 1733, Barbados revised the 1708 act to enumerate goods that slaves could legally sell, and by 1749 the legislators indirectly confirmed the popularity of slave hucksters by passing a law forbidding people to loiter at "huckster shops" (while saying nothing about the shops themselves). By the end of the century, legislative attempts to prevent slave participation in Barbados's internal market ceased almost completely. The only restriction left on the books limited slave huckstering to the "public market place called the Shambles adjoining the Old Church Yard."

We tend to think about markets in impersonal terms, a tendency perhaps best evoked by the overplayed "invisible hand" metaphor. But for whites living in the West Indies, the market became the most vivid reminder that the slaves' status as chattel was nothing if not an absurd legal fiction. Inventories suggest that as the huckster market became a more entrenched economic reality throughout the West Indies, whites' reliance on imports for their own diet diminished while their reliance on slave foods increased. This arrangement was cheaper, the ingredients were fresher, and the spices were more abundant. The humanity of chattel must have been quietly confirmed when wheat, beef, and beer imports declined and slaves found themselves standing face-to-face with a new and unexpected customer: their owner. Indeed, with interruptions to Atlantic trade increasing throughout the eighteenth century, it was by no means unheard of for masters to barter with their own slaves for excess corn, chickens, yams, and shellfish in exchange for manufactured goods, more land to cultivate, or even hard cash to spend at the market. The circumstances dictating these unlikely transactions could hardly be deemed free or fair, but they nonetheless emphasize the powerful role of slave cooking in the larger West Indian culture. As the Sunday market became a significant weekly event for both whites and blacks, it increasingly assumed a carnivalesque atmosphere as slaves directly shaped the terms of exchange as well as the goods exchanged. Such scenes were, of course, fleeting and rare, but they nonetheless powerfully reiterate the irony that an enslaved people could wield tremendous culinary influence in a foreign land.

Connections with the Mainland

This influence didn't end in the West Indies. It turns out that during the decades when the island slaves were pioneering culinary transformations and disseminating those changes through local markets, the British mainland colonies were forming critical ties to their West Indian counterparts. No bond would be tighter than that which formed between Barbados and Carolina. Throughout the late seventeenth and early eighteenth centuries, when slaves were developing their culinary habits in the West Indies, young planters seeking to establish larger plantations encountered something of a land crisis, and they looked to Carolina as a place to expand. Opportunities there seemed ripe. In 1681, eight English proprietors had convinced Charles II that they could turn a handsome profit in Carolina should he be generous enough to grant them the wide swath of land running from Virginia to Florida. They weren't sure how they would make the land produce revenue, but they knew from the West Indian experience that it would involve slaves. In a perversion of the normal order of colonial expansion, Barbadian emigrants purchased slaves in the West Indies, packed their bags, and went to Carolina. They figured that, once settled, they'd quickly find a way to put their bound labor to profitable use. For several years, aspiring Carolina planters, after learning that sugar would not adapt to the swampy low-country environment, practiced a remarkably diversified range of activities. Trading deerskins, potash, corn, and timber, Carolina was soon supplying the West Indies with ample provisions, prompting Barbadians to call it "a colony of a colony" and a place where "slaves were in search of a staple."

The search was short, and the staple turned out to be rice. It was an ironic twist, but slaves familiar with rice from West Africa helped planters figure out how to grow this often stubborn and always fastidious crop in the swampy stretches of the Carolina Lowcountry. Even more so than sugar, rice demanded exquisite timing, intricate knowledge of tidal patterns and irrigation, and a well-trained and tightly coordinated labor force. The coast of West Africa provided ample opportunity to hone these requirements. By the late seventeenth century, English planters adopted these methods on a scale approaching that of Barbadian sugar plantations. Within a few years, the planters' efforts paid off. Not only did the humid coastal waterways of the Lowcountry prove to be an ideal incubator for rice seeds but population growth in Europe steadily intensified the region's demand for rice. Carolina gradually weaned itself from its role as a "colony of a colony," established Charles Town as a bustling center of finance and shipping, and by 1721 had divided into North and South Carolina. As in the sugar industry, slaves underwrote these developments.

The Carolina rice boom lured hundreds of white Barbadians who packed thousands of slaves. A young Englishman named John Yeamans was part of this migration. After a few years in the Lowcountry, he responded to a questionnaire sent by King James II, explaining that "least we presume too farr wee shall only say that these settlements have been made and upheld by Negroes and without constant supplies of them cannot subsist." When a Carolinian needed more slaves, he could take out an ad like the following in a Barbadian paper:

To the owner of every Negro-Man or Slave, brought tither to settle within the first year, twenty acres [will be granted]; and for every woman Negro or slave, ten acres of land; and all Men-Negros, or slaves after that time, and within the first five years, ten acres, and for every woman-Negro or slave, five acres.

Because of this brutal system—a system sustained by racial superiority, a denial of humanity, and a desperate need for labor—British America's most distant and paradoxical culinary origin would continue to thrive in the thirteen mainland colonies, especially in the southern ones. The most oppressed and dispossessed group in colonial British America thus planted a kernel of American cuisine in a place that would eventually become the United States. It's in the Carolina Lowcountry where these roots would be watered with the blood of slaves coming from Africa who—much like their West Indian counterparts— took advantage of frontier conditions to control their own foodways.

The Big Picture

Hobbesian to the core, life in the British West Indies was indeed nasty, brutish, and short. It's hard to imagine anything surviving the brutality of a sugar plantation besides the white granules themselves. Nevertheless, the extension of West Indian cooking practices to Carolina ensured not only that certain foods would become central to North America's culinary origins, but also that a cultural mentality about food would migrate and evolve with them. The story of food in the West Indies set precedents that would directly shape the broader cooking habits of the mainland colonies. Two stand out.

First, Europeans had for centuries defined their culinary habits according to what the upper classes ate. Court traditions and royal fiat influenced the culinary standards of nations and popular conceptions of what constituted a "proper diet." As seems only natural, throughout most of Western history, the least oppressed enjoyed the most influence when it came to establishing food expectations. This situation would change dramatically in the West Indies. Unique New World conditions conspired to reverse the trajectory of cooking habits. The demands of a sugar economy endowed slaves with the modified power to shape their own cooking decisions. Demographically, they soon became a vast majority of the population. The planters' obsessive quest for sugar profits stunted the development of an upper-class cuisine, and, eventually, the West Indian diet was an Afro-Caribbean diet. This sharp reversal from the European tradition would powerfully shape cooking throughout America. America's cooking origins, as the West Indies suggest, were decidedly humble. Literally and figuratively, they evolved from the ground up.

Second, the West Indies epitomized the need for culinary adaptation on the fringe of an empire. Adaptation was, as I have already mentioned, integral to every culinary migration. Never, though, had it been so dramatic, so radical, and demanded so much *flexibility*. With Native Americans, English, and Africans confronting one another with starkly different cooking traditions, the cuisine that evolved in the West Indies required residents to suspend traditional judgments, apply whatever inherited culinary knowledge was applicable, and be ready and willing to taste something new. It was a broad habit that every migrant to the colonial American frontier had no choice but to accept. Unless they settled in that other British American colony that might be called the alter ego of the West Indies: New England.

CHAPTER 2

TRADITIONALISM

The Greatest Accomplishment of Colonial New England

Tradition is a guide and not a jailer.
W. Somerset Maugham

IT MUST HAVE BEEN A HARD SELL. Nevertheless, John Winthrop Jr., son
of the Massachusetts Bay Colony's first governor, traveled to England in
1662 to make his case. And not just to England but to the Royal Society
of London, the elite institution into which he'd been recently inducted.
Winthrop, who was then the governor of Connecticut, stood in front of the
world's prominent intellectuals and scientists, including Samuel Hartlib,
a Royal Society leader and author of *Legacy of Husbandry* (1655), to argue,
of all things, the virtues of Indian corn. On the surface, corn's benefits
were hardly newsworthy to his audience. Englishmen had been feeding
corn to their livestock for over a century after maize had come to Europe
from the New World, and the practice was, by the time of Winthrop's visit,
completely accepted by the average husbandman. Winthrop, however, had
a different case to make.

The earnest colonist rose before this august body and argued that Indian corn was not only, in the words of a leading English herbalist, food fit
"for swine," but food perfectly fit for human beings as well. So fit, in fact,
that it could be a viable replacement for wheat. One can only imagine the
thoughts that raced through the minds of Hartlib and his colleagues as
their newest member delivered the following oration:

The English [in New England] make very good Bread of the Meale, or flour of it
being ground in Mills . . . but to make good bread of it there is a different way of
ordering it, from what is used about the Bread of other Graine, for if it be mixed
into stiff past[e], it will not be good as when it is made into a thinner mixture a
little stiffer than the batter for Pancakes, or puddings, and then baked in a very
hot oven, standing all day or all night therein.

It would have been like someone today saying that we should eat dog food. Perhaps most alarming to the traditionalists, however, was the cultural baggage that Indian corn carried for English colonists living in New England. Winthrop continued:

This Corne the Indians dress it in severall manner for their food sometimes they boyle it whole, till it swell, and breake, and become tender, and then eate it with their Fish, or Venison in stead of bread . . . sometimes they bruise it in a mortar and boyle it and make very good food of it, baking it under the embers.

Winthrop's novel plea amused many and convinced none. That he felt compelled to make the speech at all, however, reminds us how emblematic Indian corn was in the larger culinary adjustment that colonial settlers had to make in their new world. Their acceptance and incorporation of Indian corn into the English diet—indeed, their unabashed celebration of it—was but a small brushstroke on the larger canvas of New England cooking.

New England and the West Indies: A Study in Contrasts

New England's first permanent settlement might have been composed of men and women of English descent, but it couldn't have been more different from its West Indian counterpart. Settlers had little interest, for one, in promoting a staple crop for export. Instead, New England consisted of restless Puritans hell-bent on utopia. These pious and relatively well-off malcontents aimed to reform the Anglican Church by building a "a city on a hill" on the Massachusetts coast. In theory, their society would become one that England would admire and emulate—certainly not a goal shared by those voracious sugar planters down the coast. New England would create a culture that would thrive on the search for grace, the establishment of small communities bound by love, and the prevalence of a communal rather than the individualistic mentality that defined life down in the tropics. Dominated as Puritan life was by men such as John Winthrop and Cotton Mather, New England's conspicuous piety has understandably become the bread and butter of its history.

These pious people, however, weren't interested in achieving only religious reform. They also wanted to replicate the English culture from which they had come. Mother England was a beloved and shared heritage for the migrating Puritans. Unlike the Pilgrims who preceded them, and unlike their West Indian brethren to the south, the Puritans had no interest whatsoever in abandoning inherited ways of life. Further strengthening their mission was the fact that they were unified in their goals and background. Settlers who shaped New England life during the seventeenth century came from a similar class background (middle), geographic location (East Anglia), ethnicity (English), and sense of religious toleration (absolutely none). The first settlers' original hopes of spiritual perfection might have devolved into the ranting jeremiads and hysterical witch persecutions. Even so, no region of colonial America succeeded so quickly and so thoroughly in adopting English habits to the New World. Indian corn, and what New Englanders did with it, reflected that accomplishment, an accomplishment that ironically helped to make New England cooking a fair approximation of the homeland's and, as a result, the polar opposite of the cuisine developing in the West Indies.

The Natural Environment and the Challenges Therein

For all their shared qualities, New England settlers immediately disagreed over whether they could achieve their goals. In *History of the Colony and Province of the Massachusetts Bay*, Thomas Hutchinson was an earnest naysayer. He wrote, "The air of the country [of New England] is sharp, the rocks many, the trees innumerable, the grass little, the winter cold, the summer hot, the gnats in summer biting, the wolves at midnight howling." Thomas Graves begged to differ, claiming, "This much I can affirm in generall: I never came in a more goodly Country in all my life, all things considered." For some, it was paradise. For others, a hell on earth.

No matter how settlers viewed the New World, however, the desire to eat familiar food was critical to the self-appointed task of bringing England to New England. The founders of the Massachusetts Bay Colony were, like Graves, legitimately optimistic that they could transplant Old World agriculture and foodways to New World soil. "The country is yet raw," wrote Robert Cushman, "the land untilled; the cities not builded; the cattle not settled." All true enough. But the *potential* to till, build, and settle was boundless. Upon landing in the Bay Colony, Winthrop (the elder) stepped ashore and gushed over its natural resources, exclaiming that "heere is foule and fish in great plenty," adding, "our grounds are apt for all sorts of roots, pumpkins, and other fruits, which for taste and wholesomeness far exceed those in England." Francis Higginson bragged to friends back home how "the fertility of the soil is to be admired at, as appeareth in the abundance of grass that groweth everywhere." Another summed up the founders' prevailing mood when, commenting on the region's natural resources, he explained, "It is scarce to be believed." With their hearts and minds not only on God but on the material reality of their daily lives, these were a people ready and eager, if nothing else, to believe.

But not without a dash of skepticism. Another round of opinions suggests the early difficulty in fulfilling the land's potential. Despite the vocal optimism of the colony's investors, and despite the land's obvious potential to feed this spiritual army of souls, what most of the first settlers listened to was their growling stomachs. Thomas Dudley arrived in the Massachusetts Bay in 1630 to find "the colony in a sad and unexpected condition, above eighty of them being dead in the winter before, and many of those alive weak and sick, all the corn and bread among them hardly sufficient to feed them a fortnight." Dudley was witnessing the dreaded "starving time"— that gruesome, if unavoidable, period of adjustment when immigrants arrived faster than settlers could feed them. Between the much anticipated shipments of English provisions, William Hubbard explained, "the people of the country in general were, like the poor widow, brought to the last handful of meal in the barrell, before the said ship arrived." A distraught servant wrote home to his father that "if theis ship had not come when it ded we had bine put to a wonderful straight but thanks be to god for sending it." He added, "Here we may live if we have suppleyes every yere from olde eingland other weyse we can not subeseste."

But subsist they would have to do, and settlers immediately hacked away at the ground, only to discover that the land wasn't quite as fertile as advertised. "This soil is like your woodland in England," sneered one settler, "best at first yet afterward grows more barren." Winter staples trickled through ice-clogged harbors, and the summer yielded a modest store of fresh food that often stretched into mid-fall. Nevertheless, even as a rudimentary seasonal agricultural system came together, and even as settlers got their farms and gardens up and running, families continued to face scarcity during those cruel weeks when one season's supply diminished before the next season's matured. In the best of all worlds, settlers would have immediately grown rye, oats, wheat, and buckwheat—as any self-respecting Englishman would have instinctively done. They quickly found, however, that their wheat "came to no good," and instead had to resort to the dreaded Indian corn. The cultivation of familiar domestic animals met a fate similar to that of wheat, foundering as it did on the lack of English grass. "Hay," said Dudley, "is inferior in goodness to our reed and sedge in England, for it is . . . devoid of nutritive vertue." Lacking time, seeds, equipment, and labor, gardeners encountered their own set of problems. Winter vegetables in the mid-seventeenth century consisted almost completely of dried peas. Pease porridge stew became a monotonous staple that taunted the taste buds of many a New Englander. Should a family have been fortunate enough to own them, the butter churn and cheese press would have collected dust throughout the winter because, due to the poor hay, farmers avoided "overwintering" their cattle, saving their cows instead for the spring's modest offering of fresh grasses. Like so many other luxuries, the absence of these basic goods required divine patience from the men, women, and children trying with decidedly mixed results to replicate English life on the colonial frontier while satiating their considerable hunger. How long that patience would hold out was another question.

Native American Foodways and the English Reaction to Them

The most logical short-term solution was to do as the West Africans and whites would soon do in the West Indies—follow the lead of the Native Americans. The northeastern cultures—the Narragansetts, Micmacs, Pequots, and Mohegans in particular—enjoyed a sound diet based on a combination of hunting, gathering, and a rough form of agriculture specializing in beans, squash, and maize. Like Native Americans throughout colonial British America, the New England cultures closely adhered to the ecosystem's natural rhythms. In the West Indies, this intimacy with the environment pushed Caribbean Natives to live sedentary lives on the coast, spending their days fishing, foraging, and practicing small-scale agriculture. In New England, however, with its greater diversity of flora and fauna, not to mention abrupt weather shifts, following the cycles of nature meant leading a more migratory lifestyle. Native American settlements were temporary and—as the English saw it—crude affairs. When fish were spawning, Native Americans would build a small village on the Merrimack River and fish. When wild game was flourishing, they would pack up their villages (usually consisting of small wigwams), store their food in a pit, and chase game. Everywhere they traveled, they would clear a few acres of forest by burning the underbrush and planting maize, squash, and beans in a single patch of land. Native American women would periodically check back to weed, "earth-up," and harvest their crops. These three activities structured the Native Americans' seasonal cycle of work, making their world go round.

The English—burdened with a stubborn sense of "civilization"—would have disagreed, but there was nothing haphazard about the Native Americans' methods for obtaining food. Instead, the seasons predictably dictated the course of change, and they followed with sensible strategies. In March, just after the ice broke, Native Americans took to the rivers and seas to catch fish that thrived so plentifully that one could hardly place his "hand into the water, without encountering them." The sea offered cod, which the Native Americans caught by line and hook; the tidewaters teemed with brook trout, smelt, striped bass, and flounder, which they speared with harpoons; and the rivers supplied alewives, sturgeon, and salmon, which they usually caught with nets. A duly impressed Frenchman remarked, "From the month of May to the middle of September, they are free from all anxiety about their food; for the cod are upon the coast, and all kinds of fish and shellfish." The Native Americans broiled the fish fresh or roasted them on a spit made of twigs. Many Native American groups made a fish chowder as well as a fish soup not unlike the French *soup de poisson*, a dish that involved boiling fish in water, removing the fish, and incorporating vegetables to thicken the broth. The arrival of the alewives told the Native Americans that it was time to start hunting migratory birds. Women and children took to the fields to gather duck eggs while men interrupted their fishing duties to pursue geese, brants, and mourning doves. When bird season waned, Native American men took to the seas and hunted whales, porpoises, and seals while women foraged for nuts and wild plants. These activities kept mobile villages satisfied until October, when villagers arranged themselves into much smaller teams and scattered into the forest to pursue caribou, deer, moose, and beaver. Hunting these animals proved relatively easy until February, when the snow began to melt, thereby making it much harder to track wild game. It was—and this was the rub as far as the English were concerned—not at all uncommon for Native Americans to feel intense hunger for several weeks, until the cycle resumed and the fish arrived to spawn.

The first English settlers had little choice but to adjust to these methods. Initially at least, the idea didn't strike them as so horrific. Their enthusiasm showed in their effusive observations of the region's fish supply, observations that indirectly supported the Native Americans' food-gathering strategies. William Wood, for one, commented on the arrival of alewives "in such multitudes as is almost incredible, pressing up such shallow waters as will scarce permit them to swim." The English also seemed willing to follow the Native American lead when it came to hunting game. "For beasts," wrote Francis Higgenson with enthusiasm, "there are some beares. . . . Also there are several sorts of Deere. . . . Also Wolves, Foxes, Beavers, Otters, Martins, great wild cats, and a great beast called a Molke [moose] as bigge as an Oxe." But it was the wild birds that really caught their attention. "If I should tell you," Wood wrote to a friend back home, "how some have killed a hundred geese in a week, fifty ducks at a shot, forty teals at another, it may be

Native Americans preparing the emetic "black drink"

In every way imaginable, the Eastern Woodland Indians practiced foodways that differed from those of the New England settlers. The division of labor between men and women, as well as assumed periods of scarcity, were aspects of Native American culture that the English found to be especially troublesome.

counted impossible though nothing more certain." Native Americans taught the English to grow maize and squash, and the English rapidly accepted these foods into their diet. Like the Native Americans, they placed these goods directly in the ashes of a smoldering fire, roasted them, and moistened them with animal fat (usually bear grease). In all these ways, the English who had yet to start building traditional farms in earnest adjusted to life in a strange, new world. In all these ways, that is, but one: they refused to experience the periodic hunger that the Native Americans so readily tolerated.

One environmental historian has called this phenomenon "the paradox of want in a land of plenty," and it was a paradox that the English couldn't abide. When a Native American explained, "It is all the same to us, we shall stand it well enough; we spend seven and eight days, even ten sometimes, without eating anything, yet we do not die," the proper Englishman cringed. Following the natural cycles of nature in New England inevitably entailed some period of scarcity, but the mere thought of denial amid such abundance grated against English sensibilities and ultimately pushed the settlers even harder to build their farms and become self-sufficient in English ways. "They are convinced," a French visitor wrote of the Native Americans, "that fifteen to twenty lumps of meat or of fish dried or cured in the smoke, are more than enough to support them for the space of five to six months. Since, however, they are a people of good appetite, they consume their provisions very much sooner than they expect." This perpetual miscalculation, as the English saw it, suggested nothing less than a willful lack of civilization. Any English predisposition to adjust to Native ways—however fleeting—was quickly defused by the prospect of temporarily going hungry.

Adding to the English sense of cultural superiority was the perceived sloppiness of the Native Americans' agricultural methods. Laboring with nothing more sophisticated than clamshell hoes, Native Americans cultivated disparate crops in a single, uncleared field by literally tossing the mixed seeds on top of one another. Corn stalks served as beanpoles for the kidney beans they routinely cultivated. Gourds found shade under corn stalks. As sensible as these methods were (they kept erosion to a minimum and naturally replenished the soil's nutrients), this agricultural system struck the ordinary Englishman as disorderly and wasteful. Where were the neat rows of grain? the fences? the plowed furrows? They also found the Native practice of clearing land through brush fires to be a curious habit at best. Thomas Morton explained that "the Salvages are accustomed to set fire of the Country in all places were they come," while William Wood noted that fire "consumes all the underwood and rubbish." Why, they wondered, would Native Americans so casually destroy their fuel supply? "Having burnt up the wood in one place," wrote Roger Williams, "they are faine to follow the wood; and so to remove to a fresh new place for the wood's sake." Nothing could have been more foreign to the settled nature of English agriculture. Completing the English disdain for Native American agricultural practices was the fact that women labored in the fields. This job, every right-thinking Englishman agreed, was decidedly men's work.

Observing "crops" strewn with debris, charred patches of land, and Native American women laboring to harvest a village's food, the original English settlers worked even harder to replicate their English agricultural habits as thoroughly and rapidly as possible. Native Americans could help them in times of dire need. Otherwise, they were only in the way.

The Successful Replication of English Agriculture

So, for a people intent on replicating the foodways of home, the early years were rough. However, in one of American history's most momentous culinary transitions, times would soon change. Without an agricultural revolution or a significant technological innovation, times would change to the extent that New England would become self-sufficient in its food supply. Not only would it become self-sufficient, but it would—Indian corn notwithstanding—do so in a thoroughly English manner. It was a feat that no other colonial region (with the possible exception of the Middle Colonies)—mired as its settlers were in the exploitation of a staple crop—would accomplish. This unprecedented transition matured in the eighteenth century, and it did so gradually—so gradually, in fact, that few historians have paid the accomplishment much heed.

By the end of the seventeenth century, New England's food supply had become, by any standard, abundant, varied, and annually available. Colonists had successfully worked several English grains alongside their fields of Indian corn by the 1660s. While wheat did poorly in the winter, settlers now knew that "our lands are aptest for Rye and Oats." Rye joined Indian corn as the most popular grain in the early-eighteenth-century diet, and the supply of traditional wheat—while still low compared with that at

Settlers traveling past a field still dotted with stumps

This engraving from the mid-eighteenth century shows a recently cleared forest in the process of becoming an English-style family farm. By building fences, planting gardens and crops, and grazing livestock, New Englanders replicated the local economy of their homeland more effectively than did settlers in any other region of British America.

home—improved considerably throughout the century. The importation of English clover and other meadow grasses, their subsequent proliferation over the New England landscape, and the increased availability of rye and wheat hay soon allowed farmers to milk their cows throughout the year. Provisions now lasted well into the winter and early spring, and even families of modest means could afford the land, cattle, and equipment necessary to provide a yearly supply of butter and cheese. Supplies of beef and pork increased dramatically as well. Fat oxen dominated estate inventories between October and January, and New Englanders became avid practitioners of brining and pickling their meat supply in order to extend it into leaner times. Vegetables, finally, became a prominent part of the New England diet. Kitchen gardens were the rule rather than the exception, so much so that by the 1730s, New Englanders were bequeathing cellar vegetables and kitchen gardens to their children. A modest stash of carrots and onions might have seemed like small potatoes, but, on the New England frontier, it beat dried peas.

While the spiritual goals of the founders fizzled, Puritans found themselves living in a culinary paradise. Understanding how they created it is central to our understanding of this second, radically different, origin of American food.

Work

Unburdened by the consuming demands of a staple crop, and unwilling to follow the Native American example, New Englanders worked hard to achieve the foodways of home. There is always considerable toil behind the production and consumption of food. Nowhere was that toil carried out as comprehensively or as consistently as it was in New England, where citizens strove to make New England approximate old England. Again, because it was the only region of colonial British America that lacked a staple crop, the vast majority of its inhabitants spent the vast majority of their time building and maintaining farms that collectively provided the region with a familiar self-sufficiency. To overlook the toil behind this effort is to miss one of the essential origins of American cooking. To understand colonial New England in its most commonplace manifestations, to see the past in all its hard-nosed grittiness, we have to be curious about more than just what the settlers ate. It's tempting to call American food anything that was native to America. That criterion, however, would obscure an important source of American cooking and downplay the critical processes that had to occur before food hit the plate (assuming, of course, that plates were even available).

Thus we must first consider precisely *how* these settlers on the colonial frontier produced their food. We must explore in some depth the specific decisions behind New England's culinary transition to relative abundance and culinary familiarity. We must not only ask what colonists ate, how they manipulated their food in the kitchen, and what that food looked like on the table—but also wonder how the food got there to begin with. To do that, we must pay a lengthy visit to the family farm.

Kitchen Gardens

New England cooking has its most basic origins in an almost entirely overlooked aspect of daily life, an aspect that amply confirms the grinding drudgery behind the seemingly simple act of providing food for the family: the kitchen garden. The term itself has a diminutive connotation. It shouldn't. For colonial Americans—and especially New Englanders—the establishment and cultivation of a year-round kitchen garden was an elaborate undertaking essential to any household's economic and dietary well-being. It was with considerable understatement that Charles Marshall, an English gardener and author of a popular eighteenth-century horticultural manual published in Boston, deemed the kitchen garden "an object of some consequence to the comfort of human life." Such may have been the case back home in England, where established markets structured daily economic life and rendered gardens a mere "comfort." But for New England families, most of whom did not enjoy immediate access to retail outlets or organized centers of exchange, the kitchen garden became nothing less than a key to survival. New England kitchens maintained an open door to the garden for a very good reason. They fully depended on the offerings that this critical plot of land eked from the region's notoriously stubborn, unforgiving, and rock-strewn soil.

The kitchen garden had its roots in the timeworn expectation that one of a housewife's proper duties was to lavish her meals with herbs, roots, fruits, and vegetables. In *Five Hundred Points of Good Husbandry* (1557), Thomas Tusser broke into verse over this widespread cultural assumption:

Wife, in to thy garden, and set me a plot
With strawberry roots, of the best to be got
Such growing abroad, among thorns in the wood
Well chosen and picked, prove excellent good

One wishes that he had stuck to prose (although that was pretty bad, too), but the point is clear enough: this was women's work. We would be mistaken to assume, however, that the colonial housewife could have replicated the English garden in all its sophistication and adornment. While the colonial garden has its direct origin in the more elaborate English garden, the gardens that New England women cobbled together were necessarily simplified frontier versions of traditional English designs. Granted, many of the crops sown were exactly the ones sown in English gardens, but "it is . . . extremely unlikely," a student of American gardens writes, "that [colonists] would take pains to reproduce any small, unrelated feature of the Old World garden." Indeed, the challenges of frontier life allowed little room for frivolities. The New Englander's garden was a rough reflection of an English ideal that had been honed for centuries.

The task of establishing a kitchen garden was as important as building the roof over a family's head. A garden had to be properly situated, adorned, and arranged in order to maximize its productivity. The ideal shape was an oblong plot, although a rough square sufficed. The plot had to be level, but, if setting it on a slope was unavoidable, it should "be southward, a point either to the east or west . . . but not to the north because crops come in late and plants do not stand the winter so well in such a situation." The calculating planter also understood that "to have a little [northern exposure] under cultivation, so situated, is desirable." The plot had to be kept as dry and warm as possible—no easy task in wet and cold New England. Placing the garden far from areas of heavy run-off while sheltering it from north and east winds with fences, walls, and trees helped achieve these conditions. Trees were often closely shorn hedges or dense evergreens, both of which had the advantage of keeping the garden free of foliage come fall. Alternatively, and more popularly, families combined the orchard with the garden, planting pear, apple, plum, and cherry trees around what they hoped would become a blooming cornucopia of garden produce.

Home gardeners obsessed about the soil's composition. "A free moderate loam, or some fresh maiden soil not too light," Marshall wrote, " is necessary." If this type of soil did not naturally exist, families spared no effort in enriching the soil with manure, rotted vegetables, wood ashes, and salt until they achieved the desired quality. Dung application was more science than art. Trees needed soil rich in horse dung. Most vegetables, however, thrived best in dirt liberally mixed with cow dung. Any section of the garden benefited from hog and sheep dung as long as it was "well-mixed" and evenly distributed. Too much dung of any sort had counterproductive results. "Let not the ground be glutted with dung," one horticulturist warned, "for a little at a time, well-rotted, is sufficient." A garden rich in onions, leeks, and other similar superficial rooting plants demanded more frequent infusions of dung. Vegetables with deeper roots, however, such as beets, carrots, and cauliflower, always came up less bitter when dung was applied lightly. Dung that clotted the soil or remained too damp always ran the risk of attracting worms, grubs, and unwanted insects. Too much dung could also make plants grow so fast that they lost their flavor. Knowledge of dung, in short, was power.

The gardener had to churn, turn, and aerate the soil. The ground, Marshall warned, "should never be long without stirring," and the garden should always enjoy "a free, sweet, and rich soil, by proper digging to forward well-flavored productions." A friable and "free" ground encouraged plant roots to expand, ensuring that they would not be "impeded in the quest for food." A "sweet" soil allowed for "food that may be wholesome." A "rich" soil made it so "that there may be no defect of nutrient." If the soil contained too much clay, gardeners trenched and retrenched until the garden maintained its fertility throughout the autumn and winter months. Once the ground reached "proper heat," every inch of it was "contrived to be constantly and successfully cropped."

Maintaining this condition, of course, was easier said than done. Work was backbreaking and time consuming. Granted, many New England colonists owned or had access to a plow and oxen. Humphry Gilbert of Ipswich, Massachusetts, for example, left to his wife, among other goods, "one paire of oxen" and "plou & tacklin." Salem's William Bacon owned "2 oxen" and "one cart, and plow, and plowgeere." William Stevens of Newberry had "one oxe" and "a yoake chayne and plow and plow irons." These men weren't unusual. But there were also plenty of men like John Goffe, whose agricultural implements consisted of "one pitchfork, one spade," and "1 shoovell and 1 pickaxe," or Wenham's John Fairfield, whose inventory confirmed ownership of "a pitchfork and a dung fork" but little else in the way of agricultural equipment. Reality, of course, often fell short of theory, leaving gardeners literally to scrape by with whatever they could get their hands on. Which often left them with their hands around a clamshell.

With the soil effectively dunged and aerated, fences built, and young trees firmly set, gardeners turned to planting, sowing, and maintaining the vegetable garden. However numerous and burdensome, these tasks closely adhered to a fairly predictable monthly cycle. The winter months, contrary to expectations, were anything but idle times for the New England gardener. "Let everything be done now that the weather and circumstances will permit," a guide advised. Gardeners recognized that the month of January, "when it was an open season (that is, clear) is a very important one in the way of gardening." This was a time of year "in which the loss of a single day is of consequence." Gardeners spent frigid midwinter mornings and afternoons hauling dung to elevated hotbeds in order to keep the soil rich. Despite the cold weather, many gardeners planted cucumbers of the "short prickly" variety, as well as several kinds of melons. They put lettuce directly into the ground, usually by the garden wall. Ideally, gardeners equipped all these plants with "frames," devices that were basically large aerated boxes—sort of minigreenhouses made of either glass or (more likely) oil paper—that protected the tender vegetable shoots from frost and snow. Hotbeds nurtured asparagus seeds, which could sprout as early as late February. Gardeners would dig up the ground "a full spade deep" and plant a spread of carrots. Some manuals suggested planting "mint on heat," deciduous trees, grapevines, "cabbages at distances," raspberries, and currants. Depending on available space, gardeners sowed spinach, beans, "cabbages at distances," and peas—all in raised beds. The miscellaneous maintenance during January was, especially for smaller families, seemingly endless. It included turning manure and compost heaps (making sure to remove "any very dry long strawy and exhausted parts"), repairing and sharpening tools, trenching and preparing the ground, pruning trees, destroying webs and nests, weeding, procuring tree sections for grafting, and tying saplings to stakes. Working in the bitter cold must have tested the mettle of many gardeners, but they toiled nonetheless under the knowledge that "many things might be prepared in the winter, in readiness for the spring, which are too often neglected."

Early spring was "very valuable to the good gardener," but it offered little room for pause, intensifying the daily routines of weeding, churning manure and compost, sticking peas, and maintaining hotbeds. Gardeners treated the soil for immediate planting and sowing. They applied manure, dug borders for run-off (as snow melted), dressed herb and strawberry beds, weeded asparagus beds, grafted trees, sifted compost, and planted vines along the walls. March was the month to do any rearranging of the garden, draw a blueprint, and decide what was going to go where. The seedlings of several plants and herbs that planters had set in warm beds back in the winter now had to be removed to the warmer ground. Gardeners shifted mint, thyme, strawberries, asparagus, artichokes, cauliflower, and lettuce out of the beds in order to clear room for the next line-up of crops that had to be sowed in the warmer and wetter months. During the first week, planters sowed radishes, asparagus, beets, parsley, red cabbage, and turnip radishes. During the second, they moved on to "turnips on a gentle heat." And throughout the last week of the month, housewives placed in the beds "broccoli of the purple autumn sort," "herbs of all sorts," and "grass seeds for plants." The work was endless, but at least the weather was improving.

The latter half of spring brooked little relaxation. Gardeners earthed up sweet potatoes, collected more dung for hotbeds, tied up cabbages, and insulated the blossoms budding on trees. Additionally, they sowed pumpkins, gourds, brussels sprouts, kidney beans, more herbs ("culinary and medicinal"), "basil on heat," cucumbers and melons, celery, and radishes. Gardeners moved chives and garlic from beds to open ground. May ratcheted up the gardener's schedule even further. Old routines persisted: more weeding, earthing up, thinning, stirring the ground. But now gardeners had to make sure that cucumber plants enjoyed shade in addition to fulfilling the new tasks of claying the grafts of trees into place and topping off the blossoms of beans. They also planted the kidney beans, lettuce, and celery that they had sowed in April, while also sowing new endive, purslaine, savoy, peas, and spinach. "The products of spring," Charles Marshall wrote, "are the rewards that sweeten labour: All the senses are gratified."

The summer offered a rare chance to savor that gratification. "It is in this month," Marshall explained, speaking of June, "that the gardener begins to find some pause in his labor." Basically, the housewife's main gardening task from June through early September was to keep close tabs on the garden's progress. She had to make sure that nothing "stand[s] in need of the necessary assistance of culture, or good management." Keeping the crops well watered kept gardeners busy, as did the standard demands of weeding, thinning, grafting, and pruning. Planting was one job that intensified during the summer, as "most weather at this season is very advantageous for pricking out, or planting, and it must not be neglected." Gardeners moved more cucumbers, melons, pumpkins, gourds, cabbages, leeks, celery, and herbs out of their beds and into the ground. Miscellaneous tasks included gathering herbs for drying, culling ripening seeds for fall sowings, picking and storing garlic and shallots, and preparing "vacant ground for cropping." Housewives scattered seeds into beds for cauliflower, cabbages, radishes, carrots, and "onions for winter and spring." So while the summer allowed some respite from the toil, gardeners were nonetheless wise to "let nothing be omitted that may tend to crown the garden's credit with a continued production of fine vegetables and fruits."

Gardening routines slowly resumed their customary intensity in the early fall. First and foremost, planters worked to revive what was by now an exhausted ground. "An attention of this sort, stirring the ground and raking it," Abercrombie explained, "will give it a freshness and culture highly pleasing and creditable." Incessantly, throughout September and October, they aerated, applied dung, composted, raked, and stirred. The ground near the walls had to be enriched for new fruit trees. Dragging frames out of the barn, housewives placed them over the cucumbers, cauliflower, and melons as the night air dipped toward freezing. Fathers and sons culled apples from taller trees while mothers and daughters thinned the shorter ones. Boys hauled fruit to the barn or cellar for cider production. Onions, shallots, and garlic were taken up, dried, and hung in the barn or kitchen. Gardeners sowed spinach, turnips, onions, endive, beans, chervil, and sorrel in raised beds (under frames) while moving lettuce, broccoli, celery, and brussels sprouts to the ground. If the garden boasted an especially warm plot, housewives could plant lettuces and strawberries. Come late September and early October, the entire family would converge on the garden to plant trees and shrubs, the most onerous aspect of which involved digging huge holes in the hard ground. Leaf clearance proved to be yet another constant challenge. Miscellaneous jobs during this time of the year included trimming the buds off cauliflower plants, hoeing between rows of cabbages, killing caterpillars ("for they do mischief rapidly"), gathering seeds to dry, and thinning spinach crops. Through such work, gardeners bestowed on their plot "that proof of good culture."

The end of fall brought a new cycle, but not before gardeners completed several perfunctory jobs. They drained any stagnant water from the garden, as hard freezes would soon ensue. A number of crops had to be picked and stored during November, including beets, leeks, turnips, radishes, sweet potatoes, Jerusalem artichokes, and celery. Families often packed these crops in dry sand and kept them in the cellar for the winter. After frost settled over the ground for several nights in a row, gardeners harvested the young cauliflower and broccoli plants, packed them in "balls of earth," and placed them in the cellar with the other vegetables. Come December, the garden, according to Marshall, was "no longer decorated with flowers or verdure." Nevertheless, Marshall reminded his readers, "it contains many things of promise which demand attention." Weather was no excuse to keep the garden from running at full tilt. "If this month be called dreary," he wrote, "yet still the face of nature has its charms . . . even when covered with snow." Frost demanded that gardeners move and protect many plants, but settlers came to regard freezing as generally a good thing because— even if it killed some crops—it dried out the soil and prepared it "for future produce." Gardeners spent the month making sure that seeds stayed dry, weeding out any rotten fruit, taking up musty straw from storage rooms, dunging hotbeds, tying up endives, grinding sharp edges on their tools, sowing some beans and peas, planting mint, and, somehow, resting up for the familiar demands of a new year.

The Ideal and Reality of the Kitchen Garden

The scenario just sketched is a horticultural fantasy. One imagines that few colonial New England gardeners ever came close to achieving it. Indeed, our skepticism would be legitimate should we question the extent to which the impressive range of crops catalogued in gardening manuals reflected the messy reality of life on the ground. Fortunately, several surviving documents imply that the gap between the ideal and the reality of the New England garden remained a modest one.

Two insights into New England's successful approximation of the English garden come from John Josselyn, a settler who wrote a book called *New-Englands Rarities Discovered*, and John Higginson, author of *New England's Plantation*. As for radishes, Josselyn noted, "I have seen them as big as a man's arm." He explained that fennel "must be taken up, and kept in a warm cellar all winter," that the peas in New England "are the best in the world," that "asparagus thrives exceedingly," and that "our fruit trees prosper abundantly." He mentioned cucumbers, all kinds of herbs, turnips, lettuce, strawberries, blackberries, mushrooms, and red beets—all described in the manuals. The region's orchards especially impressed Josselyn. "Our fruit trees prosper abundantly," he explained. "Apple trees, quince trees, cherry trees, plum trees I have observed with admiration." One farmer found a prominent place in Josselyn's account because he "made five hundred hogsheads of syder out of his own orchard in one year." Higginson, for his part, remarked that "our turnips, parsnips, and carrots are here both bigger and sweeter than is ordinarily to be found in England." He continued, "Also divers excellent pot-herbs, grow abundantly among the grasse, as Strawberrie leaves in all places of the Country, and plenty of Strawberries in their time, and Winter Savoy, Sorrell, liverwort, Carwell, and Watercresse." In their comprehensiveness, Josselyn's and Higginson's comments on garden produce reflect their neighbor Edward Johnson's observation that "you have heard in what extreme penury these people were at first . . . [now] this poor wilderness hath not only equalized England in food, but goes beyond it in some places." Even allowing for exaggeration, the claim speaks volumes about how far the region had come in providing the garden herbs and vegetables that confirmed their English heritage.

Wills further indicate the prominent place of English-style kitchen gardens in the regional economy. Salem's Thomas Payne stipulated that "first unto my wife I give my house I now live in, gardens & housefuitting with my two acre lotte with the pffits (profits) accrewing therefrom." The inventory attached to William Ager's will referred to "one house and garden plot," valued at an expensive £16. Newbury's Henry Fay owned a "house and about seven acres and a halfe of land lyeing adjoyning a barne, orchard, and garden." References—as in John Trumble's Rowley inventory—to "hous and barne, gardings orchard" are common enough to suggest that the kitchen garden was anything but a novelty. Perhaps the most convincing proof of the garden's popularity, however, lies in the fact that New England settlers did not have to import vegetables, fruit, or herbs. A relatively healthy population whose members not uncommonly lived past seventy years, we know they ate them.

Livestock in Colonial New England

New Englanders couldn't live on vegetables alone. Dairy and beef were equally essential. Pilgrims imported the region's first livestock in 1624—"three heifers and a bull"—but by the late seventeenth century, farmers typically owned from one to four milk cows, plus two or three "dry" cows. It was the rare homestead, no matter how poor, that lacked at least one of each.

New Englanders came by their love of cattle naturally. Settlers had migrated from a culture where livestock ownership was a basic part of material life. Having enjoyed a continuous surplus of beef and dairy products since the Middle Ages, England never had to import these consumer goods. In fact, by the seventeenth century, English farmers were systematically exporting dairy and beef products throughout the rest of Europe, sending them to Portugal, France, and Spain. The process of enclosing and consolidating farms throughout the sixteenth century enhanced the English dairy and beef industry by encouraging production for profit rather than local subsistence. Grasses remained abundant; barns, ubiquitous; and butchering, brining, smoking, and dairying skills, taken for granted. Cow cheese, butter, and milk became items that every Englishman, rich or poor, consumed as a matter of course. They were, therefore, staples of an English diet that migrants had every intention of replicating in the New World. To lose cattle was, in a sense, to lose the English identity.

Demand for beef and dairy products in early New England was intensified by the fact that settlers were starting from scratch. To ameliorate the initial dearth, they imported what they considered to be a reliable supply of cows. In the spring of 1631, English farmers sent to New England a few dozen red cows and heifers. More cattle arrived in 1632, when the *Whale* delivered seventy cows; the *Charles*, eighty; and the *James*, sixty-one heifers. During the following year, the *Griffen* unloaded one hundred cows and the *Regard*, fifty. The reality of the region's early material conditions, however, undermined these efforts. Despite the frequent importation of livestock and the vast availability of land to graze it on, settlers soon found themselves struggling to protect their animals from a danger they hadn't anticipated: wolves. Even with a £20 bounty for a wolf's head on the law books, residents routinely awoke to find their hastily built stables the scene of late-night carnage. Grass (or the lack thereof) was another problem. Beasts initially languished on "such wild Fother as was never cut before" and—poorly sustained by the less nutritious native grasses—celebrated their first New England spring by either promptly dying of malnutrition or "drying up" (becoming unable to produce milk). Complaining of the native grasses, one livestock owner said, "Our beasts grow lousy feeding upon it, and are much out of heart and liking." Compared with England, New England's early organizational efforts, shelters, and natural grasses paled. As a result, so did its early cow supply.

A number of well-planned policies, however, supported conditions for a thriving livestock supply. Winthrop recognized the settlers' right to acquire as much ground as they deemed necessary under the presumption that "as men and cattle increased, they appropriated some parcells of ground by enclosing and manurance." John Smith praised "the abundance of [English] grass that groweth everywhere," a condition that explained just "how our kine and goats, horses, and hogs do prosper here and like well of this country." Daniel Gookin soon called the region "an apt place for the keeping of cattle and swine." New Englanders started to transplant English grasses by mid-century. In fact, their cattle did. The manure of imported cows contained the seeds for the very same pasture grasses that blanketed southern England. By the 1660s, Josselyn observed how "our English-clover grass thrives very well." Another gentleman from Rhode Island wrote that "in this province is also the best English grass." By the 1720s, white clover grass blanketed the pastures of Connecticut and Massachusetts so thickly that, as Thomas Hutchinson wrote to King George III, "To grazing, sir; your majesty has not a finer colony for grass in all your dominions."

Household inventories further suggest just how well the average New England farmer did in approximating England's substantial livestock holdings. Newbury's minister, the Reverend James Noyes, left an estate with "eight cowes, a two year old steere and two calves," and "one churne and a cheesepress with tubs and buckets and keelers." Joseph Morse of Ipswich bequeathed to his wife a cow and recorded an inventory containing "one chirne, one barrell and keeler, one powdering tub, 6 small cheeses, butter." Andover's John Osgood passed to his kin "fowre oxen, two steers . . . six cows . . . seven young cattle," as well as "barrells, tubbs, trayes, cheese-moates and payles . . . a firkin of butter . . . cheese." Thomas Barker died in Rowley in 1651, giving his wife "all my goods, household stuffe, cattell," a parcel that also included "butter . . . eight cows and heifers . . . three calves . . . 24 sheep." Margery Knowlton of Ipswich left an inventory that made reference to "the shop Kitching and buttery," as well as a space that included "butter and tub," "firkin, form, and half tub" for cheese, and "3 cows and one heifer." These examples merely scratch the surface of a population of hardscrabble English farmers who had acquired the ability to provide their own dairy and beef by the end of the seventeenth century.

Dairy Production

Producing quality dairy began in places well beyond the dairymaid's domain—out in the pasture, in the garden, and behind stable doors. A milk cow's diet was a delicate phenomenon. As such, it demanded constant attention from vigilant husbandmen intent on a steady supply of dairy goods. A healthy milk cow required a diet based on a changing balance of hay, grains, garden produce, and grass in order to produce decent milk throughout the year. Farmers who couldn't afford to feed their cows anything except hay or straw during the frigid winter months were left owning a cow that took up precious space and couldn't pay its rent. Farmers could wait until the seasonal spring clover carpeted the meadows in early March, but, even then, as a result of the fallow winter, the cow would produce milk erratically at best. And it would be thin, tasteless milk at that.

Getting a cow to yield winter milk required a winter diet rich in moistened hay, oats, corn stalks, rye grass, cabbage leaves, and softened roots, especially turnips and carrots. In a pinch, brewers' refuse—the waste left over from making beer—could serve as adequate winter grub for cows, although it tended to produce milk that was too thin to make hard cheese. Beans and potatoes composed a diet that fostered thicker milk and tastier cheese and butter, but, cows being cows, an enormous quantity of the stuff was needed. Keeping cows warm further enhanced milk production, as did

ensuring that any dietary changes happened gradually. A calm environment, moreover, was also helpful. Although the advice came from a nineteenth-century manual, the author echoed a timeless sentiment of responsible husbandry when he wrote, "Cows . . . should be treated with constant
gentleness, never struck, or spoken harshly to, but coaxed and caressed."

A cow's shelter further influenced milk production. Barns had become
standard features of the New England landscape by the mid-seventeenth
century, and many of them contained discrete cow houses inside. John
Oliver's Newbury will, for example, refers to a "barn and cow house purchased by Mr. Gerish." In Ipswich, John Satchwell owned a "home stall,
with barne, [and] cowhouse," all of which he bequeathed to his wife. John
Fairfield's Wenham estate included "a dwelling house and a cow house."
The combination of "dwelling house, barn, and cowhouse" was a common
inventory entry. A barn or specialized cow house enabled farmers to gather
manure, keep hay and fodder dry and sweet, and provide their livestock with
a reasonable amount of warmth. The ideal cow house sat aside a hill, thereby
creating room below for a cellar to which dairymaids could haul milk to cool.
It had windows for frequent ventilation, an entrance for carts, bays for hay
storage, feeding troughs, and, sometimes, a cistern. Again, though, that was
the ideal.

The reality was that most women didn't work in a dairy but, rather, in
a specifically designated area of the kitchen. This small space usually sat
on the north end of the house in order to reduce exposure to the sun. It
was also a place where no other products were produced besides dairy.
"Milk and cream are exceedingly sensitive to the slightest taint in the air,
in everything with which they come in contact," a manual warned. This
room normally contained a shelf at window height, thereby allowing fresh
air to circulate freely around pots of milk set out to foster cream production. By the eighteenth century, many households enjoyed the resources
to build discrete dairy houses. Farmers located these structures near the
place of milking and, if possible, close to a source of fresh water. Cleanliness mattered above all else, and the designation of a distinct area for milk
production helped keep the process cleaner, if for no other reason than that
housewives knew to scrub these areas with added elbow grease. Spilled
milk was literally something to fret over. "No matter if it is but a single
drop," a manual explained, "if allowed to soak into the floor and sour . . . it
is sufficient to taint the air in the room."

Once a tub of milk was set in the cellar, barn, or dairy, several transformations followed. Cows make butter in their udders, and it exists as little

round globules suspended in the milk's cheesy matter. Nature not only forms the butter, but even takes care of the subsequent separation as the globules rise to form the uppermost layer of cream. Winter milk, being thicker, required more time for the butter and curds to separate, and the dairymaid often added a little water or heat in order to precipitate the process. The dairymaid strained the milk into earthenware milk trays, allowed the cream to form, skimmed it with a wooden skimmer, put cream into cream pots, and eventually churned it into a solidified state. Dairymaids always tried to churn on the same day that they milked, but a grace period of three or four days could be tolerated. Sooner churning, however, meant firmer and richer butter.

Churning was a dreaded chore that typically occurred in the coolness of the morning. It took upward of fifty minutes but rarely more than ninety, unless it was exceptionally cold outside. Churning resulted in a thickened mixture of butter and buttermilk, and most of the latter was extracted through a vent hole in the churn. Farmers usually served the buttermilk to the pigs, and some of the whey from the buttermilk was reserved and worked back into the butter. The dairymaid spooned the butter into a dish, spread it into a thin layer, and covered it with salt—about an ounce of salt to a pound of butter. After salting several layers of butter, the maid finally covered the tub with a linen cloth and set the mass to rest for a few hours. She then rinsed the butter with water in an attempt to remove any lingering buttermilk. The maid poured cold water over the mixture and worked it in with her hands, allowing the water to bind with the buttermilk and leech the buttermilk out of the butter. After several rounds of rinsing (up to twelve), the dairymaid kneaded the mixture to eliminate residual liquid. She had to work quickly so as not to soften the butter too much with warmth from her hands. The last step was to pack the butter into firkins that had been thoroughly scoured and dusted with wood ash. Any leftover fat particles from the previous batch would reliably ruin fresh butter.

Studies suggest that this entire process—as laborious and precarious as it was—remained a common New England household activity through the entire colonial period. For wealthier New England families in particular, about 30 percent of whom had butter on hand during the recording of an inventory, churning butter was a daily activity performed by servants. Even the poorest families, though, made butter, with 20 percent of them showing evidence of ownership in surviving inventories. Churns, for all classes of people, were one of the most commonly owned kitchen utensils.

Dairymaids toiled under Gervase Markham's assessment that "there be many mischiefs and inconvenience which may happen to butter in the churning, because it is a body of much tenderness," but they did so knowing that the end product wasn't going to come from anywhere else. Thus they churned to eat well and remain loyal to their heritage.

As the dairymaid churned butter, the sugar in the extracted milk converted itself into lactic acid. Lactic acid, in turn, precipitated curdling. Curds meant cheese, and the New England dairymaid, in her ongoing quest to live as a proper English farm family member, made it regularly. Cheese production, however, couldn't be undertaken half-heartedly. Unlike butter, it demanded not so much a strong forearm but a finely calibrated sense of timing and balance. Too much cream in the milk might have enhanced a cheese's taste, but it also led to a gooey consistency that kept poorly, resisted packaging, and had to be consumed immediately. Overly skimmed milk, by contrast, ensured a hard, brittle block of cheese that lacked flavor and texture. It took years of experience to attain the proper viscosity through the steady addition of cream to curdling milk. Once the milk curdled, the dairymaid removed the whey by passing the mixture through a filter, leaving behind only dry curds. From there, she cut the curds into rough cubes, salted them down, and placed them in a cheese press, a device that gently mashed the crumbly curds into a consistent whole over the course of two or three days. Once the cheese was pressed, the dairymaid sliced the blocks into neat squares, salted them again, and coated them with melted butter. She then dressed the squares in cloth for storage. As was butter, cheese was a relatively common item in New England households, with up to 30 percent of inventories showing evidence of this relatively perishable product. Cheese presses remained a staple of domestic holdings throughout the colonial period. William Partridge, a Salisbury resident, owned "a churne, 1 firkin, a cheese press & 2 old tubbs," in addition to "five milch cows." He was a fairly typical New England farmer who died with a modest estate.

The most clever aspect of cheese making involved the preparation of a coagulating agent called rennet. Rennet comes from the mucous membrane of a suckling calf. Colonists often referred to it as a "bag" or the "maw." Glands within the maw continued to secrete rennet after the calf died, allowing the farmer to take full advantage of an otherwise bad situation. "If the stomach is preserved from putrefaction," instructed one manual, "this fluid [rennet] retains its coagulating quality for a considerable period." Accordingly, dairymaids routinely removed the rennet-saturated maw from a dead calf and preserved it in salt. After the maw sat in a salting tub for several days, the dairymaid hung the bag from the barn rafters to dry it out. The maw eventually hardened into a solid mass that "will retain the same property for an indefinite period." The dairymaid simply cut a small chunk from it and soaked the piece in warm water. The rennet-laden water would then be poured into the warm curd to help coagulation. Rennet thus could be available to work its magic throughout the year.

Beef and Pork

Initially, as we have seen, there was no shame in hunting. As settlers staked their claims and built their farms, they took a page from the Native American book and derived their flesh from all sorts of wild game, including "deer, bear meat, partridges, gray squirrels, and rabbits, all of which, as well as fish, were plentiful in that new land." Coastal residents regularly bought fresh fish from peddlers on the windswept docks along the coast. Hard, salted cod remained available throughout the year.

Be that as it may, true and proper Englishmen domesticated rather than hunted their protein. Early difficulties notwithstanding, beef cattle—the "dry herd"—came to thrive in New England's expansive salt marshes and meadows. As with milk cows, one reason behind the rapid propagation of cows involved the towns' active efforts to implement policies designed to organize and protect them while promoting their growth. Robert Stanton of Dorchester, for example, assumed the task of keeping the town's oxen and steer from May to October. According to his contract, he agreed to make "their walke or place of feeding on the other side of the river," and to "goe forth with the said oxen and steers halfe an hower by sonne, and bringe them to their appointed place or pen so called about sonne sitting every night, that so the owners may have them there if they please to send for them." This form of "common herding," which was a direct transplant from English husbandry, gradually prevailed over free-grazing habits. It wasn't long before towns achieved complete self-sufficiency in their cattle supply, often breeding enough to export to their southern neighbors. In 1634, William Wood noted that Dorchester, Roxbury, and Cambridge were "well stored" with cattle. Edward Johnson cited several towns with ratios of four dozen families to several hundred head of livestock. By 1725, 95 percent of wealthy families from one Massachusetts county owned salted meat and/or "fat livestock." Less privileged families kept pace, with 70 percent of the poorest residents still owning salted meat and/or livestock, and middle-class families having a 91 percent rate of ownership.

Casual references to beef supplies hide a transformation that most consumers today have the luxury of ignoring: the slaughter. During the first decades of settlement, when colonists consumed the vast majority of the beef that they produced, slaughtering usually took place locally—that is, in a farmer's barnyard. Farmers bartered the task of slaughtering as a service provided in exchange for other goods or services. In Andover, Massachusetts, Francis Faulkner commonly slaughtered his neighbors' cattle in a room adjoining his barn in exchange for a portion of the meat removed from the carcass. After setting aside some meat for his family, he sold dozens of pounds of salted beef to his neighbors. In an exchange with a farmer named Thomas Barnard, as recorded in Barnard's account book, Faulkner accepted homespun shirts and "britches" for slaughtering two of Barnard's dry cows.

Growing demand for beef pushed these practices to a new level. Down in the West Indies, the land was so consumed by sugar production that there was little room to graze. The resulting dearth of cattle, however, was just fine with enterprising New Englanders. As West Indian orders for local beef increased during the last quarter of the seventeenth century, several larger and more consolidated slaughterhouses emerged to accommodate the growing demand. One rarely associates colonial New England with cattle drives, but as Salem and Boston became critical slaughterhouse centers, farmers routinely became temporary cowboys, moving their herds on an overland journey from pasture to packinghouse. The prominent Pynchon family of Connecticut would routinely drive cattle down the Connecticut River to Warehouse Point in New Haven. The slaughterhouse there packaged and salted the meat for Thomas Pynchon, who would then sell some of it locally and ship the rest to the West Indies. Less prominent Connecticut farmers had to drive their cattle to Massachusetts for slaughtering and packaging. Farmers regularly made overland journeys from places such as New Hampshire and Maine, while others in Milford, Connecticut—a prominent place for raising livestock—took a seagoing route around Cape Cod.

While cattle were often loaded up and moved, pigs moved themselves. "Of all the quadrupeds that we know," John Mills wrote in *A Treatise on Cattle*, "the Hog appears to be the foulest, the most brutish, the most apt to commit waste wherever it goes." In case anyone misunderstood his sentiments, he added that "all its ways are gross, all its inclinations are filthy, and all its sensations concentrate in a furious lust." This prevailing opinion on the pig didn't undermine its success in colonial America. New Englanders always preferred beef, but they could hardly afford to share Mills's biases. It was an inauspicious beginning for the relationship between settlers and swine, if for no other reason than the fact that hogs seemed particularly apt at eating settlers out of their food supplies. In 1633, the Massachusetts government had to decree that colonists could feed hogs only corn that was too damaged for human consumption, lest the beasts deplete the region's reserves during a difficult time. Hogs multiplied so quickly and eagerly that settlers couldn't prevent them from rummaging through freshly planted vegetable gardens and fields, however durable their fences. Hogs, moreover, were more susceptible to disease than cows or horses, and they routinely rooted up alewives that farmers had packed into the soil to fertilize their cornfields. Court records from the colonial era teem with evidence of hogs' unique ability to destroy fences and, with them, peaceful neighborly relations.

But there was, after all, that "furious lust." Despite their considerable drawbacks, hogs became a vital aspect of New England's diet. For all the havoc they wreaked on the built environment, hogs not only bred rapidly but held their own against wolves, foraged for their own acorns, and, in some cases, fattened themselves while roaming distant islands (for example, Hog Island), only to be retrieved when the farmer's knife was honed. Hogs were critical when it came to extending meat supplies throughout the entire year because, on the frontier, beef ran low even in the best of times. Household inventories show enormous supplies of beef during the winter, after the fall slaughter, when most of the meat was salted and stored in oak barrels. These supplies usually diminished by summer, however, forcing colonists to eat pork (or, worse, mutton). In a theft case tried in 1677, John Knight testified that he confronted the defendant about his stolen meat. According to the court records, "He asked what meat she had in the house, and she replied that maybe she had forty pieces of pork and four or five pieces of beef. He asked her what they had lived on all winter if they had so much [beef] left now." Pork, in short, was never central to the New England diet, but it became a necessary supplement to the more highly valued beef. The abundance of pork in New England is evident in one scholar's finding that pork went from an average household holding of 120 pounds in 1710 to 200 pounds by the early nineteenth century.

Growing and Co-opting Indian Corn

In 1636, just as the Puritans were pouring into New England and scrambling to establish farms, this is what English herbalist John Gerard had to say about Indian corn:

It is of hard digestion, and yieldeth to the body little or no nourishment. We have as yet no certaine proofe or experience concerning the vertues of the kinde of Corne: although the barbarous Indians, which we know no better, are constrained to make a vertue of necessity, and think it a good food: whereas we may easily judge, that it nourisheth but little ... a more convenient food for swine than for man."

Such was the prevailing English view of Indian corn, not to mention Native American culture in general. It was a problematic attitude, however, given that settlers immediately learned that wheat "came to no good" when planted in New England's obstinate soil. Indian corn, by contrast, "answears for all." "Food for swine," Gerard wrote—and few disagreed. As deeply entrenched as this opinion was, nobody could afford to take this culinary chauvinism seriously, and, in spite of the colonists' effort to become thoroughly English in their foodways, Indian corn became the exception. In fact, it was the most common grain to appear in New England inventories for the first two hundred years of the colonies' existence. It became central to the New England diet alongside vegetables, beef, pork, butter, and cheese. Settlers gradually mixed other grains into their fields of Indian corn, including barley, wheat, and rye. But Indian corn was and remained the norm. By the eighteenth century, residents of the town of Hingham, Massachusetts, harvested upward of 11,000 bushels a year, with some farmers producing an astounding 200 bushels annually with oxen and plows. The southern regions of Massachusetts seemed especially primed for extensive corn production. Residents of Cape Cod fertilized fields with crabs to grow corn. Some farmers subsequently harvested yields of 150 bushels of corn from as little as six acres of land. The technique recalled the Boston farmers who fertilized cornfields with salmon and alewives, a Native American habit that also served the English well. More than two-thirds of seventeenth-century inventories in Middlesex County, Massachusetts, showed ownership of Indian corn. Less than one-third of the residents, by contrast, owned wheat or rye. Indian corn clearly dominated the New England diet.

If the New Englander was going to adopt the native grain, however, he was going to do so on his own terms. Corn would work as long as it didn't upset the goal of replicating the agricultural ways of the homeland. For one, aside from the occasional use of fish as fertilizer, the English settler wasn't going to adopt the Native American method of growing it. For the Native American, planting grain meant burning underbrush and scattering a wide array of seeds in a roughly cleared field. For an Englishman, planting grain required something much more precise. He typically labored for weeks, felling trees, removing stumps, and burning them into fine ash. Once he meticulously cleared the land, growing Indian corn was a relatively simple task. No matter how tired the soil, farmers could plow and cross plow and then furrow and cross furrow at four-foot intervals, thereby effectively preparing the ground for neat rows of seed. They planted at the furrowed intersections and waited for the corn to arrive. Once the seeds sprouted, farmers made small mounds with dirt around the stalks and dug smaller furrows with a hoe between the maturing rows of corn. These methods killed cover weeds and created space to plant a few beans and pumpkins, thus providing extra food while discouraging future weeds from sprouting. Whatever method employed, farmers generally waited until the ears had filled with hard kernels before they cut and cured the stalk and leaves (which could provide up to a half ton to the acre of rich fodder). After harvesting the ears, farmers and their sons would then endure several days of husking. Joshua Hempstead, a New London farmer, recorded in his diary that he had "finished cribbing the corn"—that is, hauling it in a bin to his barn, where he and his son worked until ten o'clock at night husking it.

Once corn became an established element of the English diet, farmers began to conservatively incorporate more traditional grains. Rye, oats, and wheat increased throughout the eighteenth century, even as Indian corn continued to dominate. Rye and oats grew more prolifically than wheat, which—for all its centrality to the English diet—remained a novelty, even for the wealthier classes. A Connecticut farmer from the late eighteenth century recalled that "wheat bread was reserved for the sacrament and company; a proof not of its superiority, but of its scarcity."

The English also reasoned that if they continued to use the native grain, it would, in a sense, become less native. To help overcome the cultural association of corn with Native Americans, settlers incorporated Indian corn into a number of traditional English practices, almost as if to dilute the grain's foreign origins. Settlers "Anglicized" corn by brewing beer with it.

They mixed it with small amounts of rye to make "Rye and Injun" bread. John Josselyn evoked English practices when he "boyle[d] it upon a gentle fire till it be like a Hasty Pudden" and ate it with cow's milk. They used corn as a substitute for flour when they dusted beef with it before frying the meat. Perhaps most important, they paid taxes in Indian corn, an act that no Native American ever remotely considered.

Due in part to these efforts to Anglicize Indian corn, New Englanders came around to the foreign crop with surprising resilience. "I could not eat the bread made from ye maise," wrote a New England woman in 1632, "but now I find it very good." John Winthrop Jr., as we saw at the outset, became an avid supporter of Indian corn, delivering an elaborate speech to the skeptical Royal Society of London on the grain's inherent virtues and versatility. He described in vivid detail his preferred method for making corn bread, a procedure that required the cook to stir the corn into a thin batter, spread it on a wooden palette, place it on the floor of a hot oven, and add successive layers as the bottom layer cooked. John Josselyn remarked in 1699, "It is light of digestion, and the English [that is, the New Englanders] make a kind of Loblolly of it to eat with Milk which they call Sampe." Corn production progressed to such an extent that New England could afford to give the rest of colonial America a chance to savor the grain. By 1700, merchants were systematically exporting it down the coast. Right after settlement, New England depended on Native Americans and Virginians for much of its Indian corn. But by the late seventeenth century, with Virginia growing tobacco almost exclusively, the relationship was reversed. On a small shallop from Boston to Virginia in 1711, for example, merchants loaded 690 bushels of Indian corn. Even by the early nineteenth century, it was hard to find a New England farm that did not grow corn for market sale. The "barbarous Indians," any honest New Englander had to admit, were definitely on to something. They would, however, have been unable to acknowledge as much because they had so thoroughly incorporated Indian corn into their traditional agricultural system that they regarded the once foreign grain—however myopically—as an English crop. In such subtle ways did New England farmers accomplish the founding task that few would have initially thought possible: feeding themselves English food.

The Big Picture

New England settlers became self-sufficient in the familiar ways of home through the careful execution of basic agricultural tasks. Naturally, settlers throughout British America also undertook these practices, but nowhere else were these components of English agriculture carried out as thoroughly or consistently. Without slaves or indentured servants, and without a staple crop consuming their resources, New England families bred livestock, cultivated kitchen gardens, made cheese and butter, slaughtered animals, and grew Indian corn, rye, and wheat. A ready supply of vegetables, herbs, and fruits; a range of dairy products; and several kinds of fresh and cured flesh reflected New England's impressive and unique achievement. These products were essential to survival and tangible proof of New Englanders' dedication to their homeland. These pious residents provided their own food with meager resources on a rugged frontier. Despite the region's fall from its religious ideals throughout the colonial era, its transition toward abundance must be counted as one of its greatest accomplishments. The achievement of self-sufficiency became critical to the region's colonial and early American development, not to mention the relative good health of its residents. New England successfully replicated an English agricultural model that made its culinary world very familiar.

What, in the end, does this accomplishment tell us about the origins of American food? The contrast with the West Indies is instructive. It suggests, for starters, that the origins of American cooking are deeply rooted in radical regional distinctions. It would be hard to imagine more opposite scenarios for providing food than the way in which it was done in New England and the West Indies. The West Indies depended heavily on ingredients and methods from West Africa, relying especially on the knowledge conveyed by slaves, who quickly became a large majority on the British islands. Slaves, in turn, drew not only on the traditions of home but also on the ingredients and methods pioneered by the local inhabitants. This cross-cultural interaction resulted in a cuisine linked to fishing and to cultivating tropical crops in small gardens around which a few goats and pigs might have foraged. Food in the West Indies was acquired as much as it was cultivated, and, as a result, shortages and malnutrition were common realities of daily life when imports failed to arrive or garden crops were wiped out by a hurricane. Domesticated animals and sprawling fields of grain were rarities. Sugar dominated, controlling the fields and shaping the nature of the region's culinary habits. Sugar ensured that the region's cuisine would be based on an extreme kind of adaptability. Settlers—white, black, or red—had little choice in the matter.

New England, a region also settled and established by English migrants, countered this system in nearly every way. From the outset, residents built farms and pursued economic activities that would eventually make New England a fair replica of England. Native Americans offered a stark alternative to food provisioning, and, out of dire necessity, the English settlers temporarily entertained their methods, scattering many different seed types in half-cleared fields, hunting and fishing for food, and foraging when necessary. The cultural bridge that formed between the Native Americans and the English settlers, however, proved to be a rickety structure that collapsed as soon as settlers built their English-style farms. While the English did accept maize into their diet, making it the most popular grain grown in the region, they otherwise downplayed the Native American fare in exchange for beef, pork, garden vegetables, and herbs that imparted a distinctly English imprimatur to their food. Demographically speaking, New England—lacking as it did slaves and immigrants from other parts of Europe—remained overwhelmingly white, overwhelmingly English, and overwhelmingly drawn to its inherited foodways.

In representing two extreme examples of regional foodways in British America, New England and the West Indies offer two models of culinary development. As we move on to examine the food practices in the remaining three historical regions of colonial British America, it's helpful to think about them in the context of these models, seeing them as nodes between two very distant poles. At this point in the story, we must allow these two extremes—one based on traditionalism, the other based on adaptability—to coexist. At the same time, though, we must also stay tuned to how these radically different approaches to producing food intermingled throughout the rest of colonial British America to define other regional foodways. We'll start with that region that fell right in the middle: the Chesapeake Bay region.

The Best Yo

CHAPTER 3

NEGOTIATION

Living High and Low on the Hog in the Chesapeake Bay Region

You can get *high class* and talk about "sweetbreads" and "organ meats" and stuff, but they're all down there with the chitlins anyway. They're all cleanin' and digestin' and filterin' too.

Tim Partridge, quoted in Burkhard Bilger, *Noodling for Flatheads*

BONES CAN RAISE SOME INTERESTING QUESTIONS. In 1981, archaeologists excavating Monticello, Thomas Jefferson's stately home, didn't really know what to make of the scattered cows' feet they kept discovering buried in the walls of the kitchen's dry cellar. What were these bones saying about the past? Wouldn't these feet, like other inferior cuts of meat, have been tossed to the slaves? Why would members of a household that normally dined on choice cuts of meat stoop to scrape gristle from a cow's foot? Why didn't they eat pigs' feet, too? Why did all the pigs' feet land in the slaves' dry cellar? Couldn't these bones rattle out an explanation?

Sometimes they do. A glance into popular English cookbooks of the time reveal an affinity for pies and puddings made from calf's-foot jelly. These items were certainly standard dishes among Virginia's elite, and, although we cannot say with complete certainty, Jefferson very likely indulged his taste for calf's-foot jelly with some regularity. This discovery is more than a neat connection. It provides a symbolic entrée into the mysterious and convoluted world of the cooking and eating habits of the Chesapeake Bay region. When masters sent pigs' feet down to the slave quarters while keeping the cows' feet for the maid to render into English puddings and pies, they drew a critical line between slave and white cooking. That line, of course, provides nothing more than a convenient starting point, but it's one that takes us in the direction of understanding cooking habits in the Chesapeake Bay—a region that combined aspects of both the New England and West Indian models, and a region where some folks ate high on the hog and others, low.

The Defining Qualities of the Chesapeake Bay

As was the case throughout colonial British America, cooking habits in the Chesapeake Bay revolved around the region's cash crop and the workforce required to grow and process it. Virginia and Maryland eventually developed into a single slave society, and, as in the West Indies, people of African descent shaped its foodways. But we mustn't forget about those Virginia pies and puddings and the cultural values they represented. In the West Indies, the white population remained a small minority removed from the extensive black culture evolving under its nose. In New England, whites dominated numerically and culturally with nary a slave in sight. The situation in Virginia fell in the middle. For one, unlike in other slave societies, whites in the Chesapeake always remained a sound majority, usually comprising around 60 to 70 percent of the overall population. Second, tobacco—the cash crop that came to dominate the Chesapeake—necessitated more systematic interaction between whites and blacks than rice or sugar ever did. On most tobacco plantations, whites had no choice but to work closely with slaves if they hoped to turn a profit on what proved to be a lucrative but temperamental crop. Third, slaves rarely, if ever, labored without constant vigilance. Tobacco fields teemed with paranoid white overseers who kept potentially rebellious slaves within their nervous purview. There was, as a result, little time or space available for slaves to cultivate traditional cultural and culinary practices (which was also quite unlike the situation in West Indies). Fourth, the demands of tobacco were constant and unrelenting. Much unlike their counterparts farther south, whites granted slaves scant time to grow their own food and trade their own goods. Chesapeake slaves might have had the inclination, but they never enjoyed the opportunity to cultivate inherited culinary habits as thoroughly as did their counterparts in other British American slave societies. In the Chesapeake Bay, not unlike New England, whites generally called the culinary shots. As a result, the English culinary heritage was a definite goal to shoot for, albeit a much more distant goal than in New England.

None of which is to say that slaves were helpless victims. When it came to their diet, they insisted on retaining some measure of authority. Masters naturally mulled over the same economic concerns as slaveholders did throughout the Americas. On the one hand, chattel needed the strength to work. On the other, they reasoned, wouldn't it be nice if that nourishment could be provided on the cheap? Driven by this blunt calculus, they forged a somewhat ad hoc method of feeding slaves. Masters improvised by combining weekly rations of imported or locally produced food with table scraps from the big house, supplementing this allotment with modest plots for slaves to cultivate their own crops and raise their own livestock, in addition to a little free time to fish and hunt. Compared with the opportunities in the West Indies, the chances for slaves to maintain and disseminate an African American style of cooking were few and far between. At the same time, however, whites worked in such proximity to slaves and existed in such relatively high numbers that cross-cultural culinary influences were inescapable. The pigs' feet and cows' feet should always remind us that Chesapeake slave owners determined to an important extent the limits and opportunities inherent in the slave diet. Whites generally ate what they wanted and what they could afford, while slaves choked down the leftovers.

On many occasions, though, the meager space allotted to slaves allowed them some flexibility to shape their diet around inherited African traditions. A smattering of evidence makes the case that African American and African slaves took advantage of this window of opportunity to develop culinary habits distinct from the dominant white cultural traditions. The Chesapeake style of cooking, in the end, was an ongoing process of negotiation between distinct cultures separated ultimately by skin color but mediated by many other differences as well. The story that the pigs' and cows' feet tell us is by no means a simple one, but it offers insight into a regional culture that combined both the traditionalism of New England and the adaptive attitude of the West Indies. As such, it illuminates yet another British American culinary subculture.

Native American Food Habits in the Chesapeake Bay

But we're already ahead of the story. While blacks and whites would eventually play the most critical roles in determining the Chesapeake's cooking habits, they responded to culinary practices initially pioneered by the region's Native Americans. In the West Indies, as we have seen, Native Americans suffered from smallpox and other European diseases to which they lacked immunity. Those who didn't succumb to deadly pathogens played an important role in influencing the way slaves cooked and ate, but their overall influence waned with their numbers. In New England, Native Americans assisted the English settlers during their first years of settlement, but, with the exception of Indian corn, they also diminished as a source of culinary influence once the English built their farms and became self-sufficient. The

Eastern Woodland chiefdoms that dotted the Chesapeake landscape, by contrast, practiced cooking traditions on which the original inhabitants became dependent for a much longer period of time. Unlike their New England counterparts, the Chesapeake's first settlers lacked the religiously inspired will to build farms and replicate English agriculture. Driven more by the profit motive and plans for a staple crop than by a desire for godliness, they pragmatically turned to Native Americans for food and cooking practices. Native Americans, after all, spent the vast majority of their day obtaining and preparing food. The English arrivals, by contrast, spent the vast majority of their day searching for nonexistent pockets of gold and silver, dreaming up ways to become rich quick, and generally avoiding the tedious chores of building farms. This disparity, and the subsequent dependence that resulted, couldn't have been more obvious to both groups. The settlers' most critical goal was thus initially to ensure that they continued to get their food from the locals. Their lives depended on it.

What evolved was no love-fest, but the earliest Chesapeake settlers couldn't afford to immediately indulge in the cultural chauvinism practiced by their New England neighbors. Initially at least, a diplomatic balance had to be achieved with the Native Americans, who held the upper hand when it came to food and cooking. It didn't hurt that the Native Americans were eager to showcase their methods, demonstrate their dominance, and talk trade. And the English, for their part, were equally eager to adapt, sample the local fare, and barter. The English also knew that they had an upper hand when it came to technology. In terms of variety, durability, and capability, their weapons and farming implements surpassed anything that the Native Americans owned. Cautiously, and perhaps against their better judgment, the English were ready to make these tools available in a mutually beneficial game of barter. Upon this logic—the logic of survival—did these cultures initially, if reluctantly, agree to cooperate.

An early example of the resulting interactions comes from a group of Jamestown colonists who set out to explore the land that they planned to exploit. All we know about the author of this particular tract is that he was an English lawyer named Gabriel Archer. He and his party traveled from May 21 to June 22, 1607, the same year the English arrived to settle Jamestown, England's first permanent colony. Noting in his travelogue how "we were entertayned with much Courtesey in every place," Archer went into great detail about native cooking and eating habits. Ascending the banks of the James River, Archer and company met a Native American "with two women and another fellow of his own consort" who "followed us some sixe mile with a baskets full of dried oysters, and mett us at a point, where calling to us, we went ashore and bartered with them for most of their victualls." Later that day, they encountered the group again. "Now," wrote Archer, "they had gotten mulberyes, little sweet nuts like Acorns, a very good fruite, wheate (corn), beans and mulbeyes sodd together." The travelers entered the river in canoes and, forty miles later, had another encounter with Native Americans. "Heer we found our kind Comrades againe," Archer wrote. "His people gave us mullberyes, sodd wheate and beanes, and caused his weoman to make Cakes for us." As the men prepared to leave, the chiefdom's king "appointed 5 men to guyde us up the River, and sent Postes before us to provide us victuall."

The guides were indispensable, but the extra provisions proved unnecessary. Everywhere Archer and his men went they were greeted with generous displays of Native American fare. The motivations for such munificence were many, but the most common reason pointed to the diplomatic advantages that might accrue to Native Americans embroiled in wars of their own. The Englishmen, for their part, seemed open to new ways, uncommitted as they yet were to this strange new world. A week later, the men lounged on the bank of the James River, high on a hill, and admired a Native American man as "he sowes his wheate, beane, peaze, tobacco, pompions, gourds, &c." The man recognized the white observers and "caused his weomen to bring us vittailes, mulberyes, strawberryes, &c." After a visit with the famous Powhatan, the travelers met with the Arrohatoc chiefdom, an occasion for which the chief "sent for another Deere which was roasted." The men dined on venison, which they deemed delicious, and then the chief "caused heere to be prepared for us pegatewk-Apyan, which is bread of their wheat made in Rolles and Cakes." The "wheate" to which Archer referred was probably the tuber "tuckahoe," which, like cassava, the Native Americans dried and milled into a grainlike consistency. It might also have been Indian corn. In any case, the men enjoyed it. "We had parched meale," Archer wrote, calling it "excellent good." The men appreciated the "mullberryes and strawberryes new shaken of the tree" while being especially impressed when their host "made ready a land turtle, which we eate."

The next stop was at "Queen Apumatecs bowre," a village belonging to a woman described by Archer as a "fatt lustie manly woman." When the men rowed to shore and anchored, the Native Americans eagerly received them, bringing "bread new made, sodden wheat and beans, mulberyes, and some fish undressed." The men dug into the impressive spread, but it proved "more then all we could eat." Fives miles down river, at "king Pamaunches

The Town of Secota, *ca. 1585*

Native Americans in the Chesapeake Bay area developed a balanced, seasonal, and seminomadic method of providing food. Although highly idealized, this engraving by Theodor de Bry (based on a drawing by John White) depicts the important role that providing food played in Native American cultures.

houses," the Englishmen were yet again entertained and enthralled with a feast. Archer recounted a scene that had "the people falling to Daunce, the weoman preparing vitailes." He noted how "some boyes were sent to Dive for muskles." Later during the same visit, after surveying the agricultural habits of the Native Americans, Archer wrote that "the platt of grownd is bare without wood some 100 acres, where are set beans, wheate, peaze, Tobacco, Gourdes, pompions, and other things unknown to us in our tongue."

Archer did more than simply enjoy the Native Americans' food. He also studied their patterns of production, obtained a general sense of their agricultural calendar, and took stock of certain cooking techniques. "In March and Aprill," he learned, "they live much upon their fishing wears; and feed on fish, Turkies and squirrels." By May and June, "they plant their fields; and live on most of Acornes, walnuts and fish." Occasionally "some disperse themselves in small companies, and live upon fish, beasts, crabs, oysters, land Torteyses, strawberries, mulberries, and such like." July and August saw the Native Americans feeding on "roots of Tocknough [tuckahoe], berries, fish, and greene wheat." From September until mid-November, "the chief Feasts and sacrifices . . . they have plenty of fruits, as well planted as naturall, as corne greene and ripe, fish, fowle, and wilde beastes exceeding fat." Archer's description of bread making especially reveals his interest in Native American cooking methods:

The manner of baking bread is thus. After they pound their wheat into flowre, with hote water they make it into paste, and work it into round balls and Cakes; then they put it into a pot of seething water: then it is sod thoroughly, they lay it on a smooth stone, there they harden it as well in an oven.

The focus on culinary detail stands to reason. These men, after all, were on the verge of colonizing a region with a cohort of male settlers plucked from the lesser gentry and endowed with minimal agricultural or cooking experience. One imagines that they paid very close attention to such procedures, and that they did so with open minds, growling stomachs, and a grudging penchant for peace.

A Closer Look at Native American Food Preparation

Fascinating as they are, Gabriel Archer's sober observations are inevitably tainted by the fact that Archer and his mates were strangers whom the locals tried to impress. How did these Native Americans cook on a daily basis when no one else was around? As mentioned, the Eastern Woodland Indians, like all Native Americans, dedicated the bulk of their time and energy to providing food for their village. What did this monumental task entail? As a few hundred Englishmen, illiterate in the ways of the kitchen, began to settle at the head of the James River, how were the original inhabitants structuring their days? Beyond what he wrote for posterity, what did Archer overlook as he traversed the landscape in search of valuable natural resources?

Despite his awareness that the Native Americans ate different foods during different seasons, Archer—like all Englishmen—lacked a fuller appreciation of their relationship with the environment. Numbering around twenty-four thousand and organized into thirty tribes headed by a powerful chief named Powhatan, the Native Americans in the Chesapeake region followed a seasonal cycle similar to that of the New England tribes. They did so, however, in a very different setting. The bay opened into a mesh of rivers, tidewater flats, and tributaries that abounded in game, fish, and edible plants. The region's five main rivers marked the interior like an open hand with fingers extending inland for about one hundred miles before ending in waterfalls. Native Americans moved in and around these rivers to fish, hunt game, and garden. Winter found them living in relatively large villages composed of a couple of hundred people who spent their days hunting and gathering. Come spring, they dispersed into smaller groups to fish and scavenge wild tubers from the rivers and tributaries. Summer brought the villagers back together to cultivate the familiar triad of beans, squash, and corn. Fall sent them scattering again into the woods to hunt fowl and deer. This constant spin of the culinary cycle led to very little surplus and, between seasons, ample scarcity. Well fed as he was in the flush months of May and June, Archer didn't foresee the cycle's stingier turns.

He also failed to appreciate the prevailing division of labor. Native American women took responsibility for ensuring that the chiefdom stayed as well fed as possible. They planned their workday carefully, organized themselves into groups that best distributed skills, and tackled the environment with the same strength and intensity as husbands and sons. Women cultivated crops, processed meat that the men hunted, and foraged for berries and nuts. A typical workday began at the crack of dawn. One group of women would weed the recently planted cornfields. Another would plant new fields. An Indian cornfield was about an acre in size and thus relatively manageable with a few field hands. The year's supply of beans, corn, and nuts from the last harvest would have been very low, so another group

Native Americans planting crops

This engraving by Theodor de Bry (based on a drawing by Jacques Le Moyne de Morgues) shows European-looking Native Americans planting crops in a European manner, with neat furrowed rows. In reality, however, Native Americans practiced a style of agriculture that the English settlers dismissed as wasteful and sloppy.

would forage for roots and herbs. Yet another would check the nets for fish and traps for game. They did all this work before breakfast.

Breakfast was, at least from the English perspective, a fairly sporadic and unpredictable operation. Leftover stew from the previous evening sat on the slow fire. Meat was rarely left over, so breakfast was often vegetarian. Women and girls pounded tuckahoe into flour and made bread with it while others fetched spring water to start a fresh stew over another fire. Boys arrived from gathering expeditions to enrich the stew with mussels, fish, or any other fresh meat they might have caught that morning. Mothers sent sons to fetch fuel. Women might roast some fish to eat with bread and throw any remains into the simmering stew. Some breakfasts were ample, others scarce. It all depended on what happened to be hunted and gathered on that particular morning. The only safe bet was that, after eating, they had to go back to work to ensure that they could keep eating. The women who were weeding would arrange for a couple of boys to stand and act as scarecrows in the cornfields. Other boys would head into fallow fields and practice their marksmanship on raccoon, possum, or deer. As they took aim, the boys had to be careful not to hit the group of women who gathered berries and greens in the same fields. After a few hours of this work, they took another food break.

The stew's contents varied throughout the day, depending on what the women foraged, the men shot, the boys pulled from the river, and the girls ground into meal. By the afternoon, however, chances were pretty fair that the men would have hauled home the kill that the women could summarily butcher and add to the pot. Chances were even better that a greater variety of fish and shellfish would be on hand to be gutted and shucked. Shad, herring, and mussels were especially popular catches for the Chesapeake Native Americans. Foragers mixed their greens into the stew and delivered berries to bread makers, who would mix them into the dough along with any foraged nuts. The afternoon was the time to thicken the stew, usually with cornmeal, in preparation for dinner. But when corn supplies ran low, tuckahoe would make do. With bellies a bit more satisfied, it was yet again back to work.

A new party of women workers would now focus exclusively on what was probably the most important job of the day: tuckahoe collection. A tuber that thrives best in marshlands, with its meaty base located about a foot underground, Chesapeake Bay tuckahoe required a lengthy canoe trip and strong arms. The afternoon tides were just right for grubbing up these stubborn roots, and John Smith, Virginia's first governor, noted how "in one day a Savage will gather enough for about a week." More realistically, they made this journey several times a week, as tuckahoe was quite heavy and could easily tip a canoe when overloaded. After gathering the roots, the team of women began to process them. Tuckahoe preparation actually began in the canoe on the way home, with some women whittling the rinds and rootlets off the tuber's hard exterior while others rowed back to shore. Many women covered their hands with bear grease to protect them from the sting caused by the root's oxalic acid. At home, the women sliced the tuckahoe into chunks and baked them in an earthen oven to neutralize the acid. Then it was time for the day's absolute worst job: grinding. Tuckahoe is an extremely hard tuber, yielding reluctantly to a mortar and pestle. Nonetheless, the long workday ended with this task.

And the men? Contrary to what most Englishmen perceived, Native American men hardly sat idle while the women toiled. They spent the day hunting geese, duck, and wild turkey. "The men bestowe their times in fishing, hunting, wars, and such manlike exercise," observed John Smith. William Byrd, a prominent Virginian, inadvertently helped sully the lazy Indian myth when he learned how "one of the Indians shot a bear, which he lugg'd about half a Mile." It's as though he neglected to read what he had just written because in the very next sentence Byrd impugned the Native American men for their laziness, only then to reverse course and conclude how "they will undergo incredible fatigues" when they "go to war or hunting." The reason for Byrd's contradiction has much to do with the English perception that hunting was ultimately a leisure activity. In reality, though, such work demanded quickness, agility, and stamina, not to mention prolonged patience. When not away on hunting expeditions, men assisted women by felling trees, cutting meat for drying, repairing homes, and even playing with the babies who were otherwise strapped to the women's hips. Most important, though, they fulfilled their essential role of consistently adding meat to the stew pot. In their more honest moments, even the most culturally insensitive Englishmen had to admit that there was nothing lazy or wasteful about that noble accomplishment.

By any standard, then, Native Americans in the Chesapeake region enjoyed an impressive, balanced food economy. Depending on a wide range of staples, including corn, beans, and squash, Native Americans experienced population growth and an abundance of food. Complementing their staples with fish, shellfish, berries, roots, nuts, and wild game, they also enjoyed good health and relative geographical and political stability. As a result of their heavily agricultural system, they rarely moved beyond the vicinity of the region's five main rivers and, because of a warmer climate, didn't experience the same periods of shortages that the New England Native Americans endured. The Native American foodways that the white settlers encountered and partially adopted were thus quite successful. It was perhaps with some envy that the Virginia planter Robert Beverly observed "the natural Production of that Country," admiring how "the Native Indians enjoy'd without the curse of industry, their diversion alone, and not their Labour, supplying their necessities." Surely they would have disagreed that the provision of food was a pleasant "diversion"—as it was undoubtedly grueling work—but they certainly wouldn't have quarreled with the claim that they provided for their own needs with the region's "natural Production." In many respects, the English settlers in the Chesapeake couldn't help but admire Native American foodways.

It was only when the English started to wean themselves from the Native Americans' cyclical economy and pursue full-throttle tobacco planting that these two very different cultures stopped interacting peacefully and decided that it was time to kill each other.

Conflict Between Native Americans and Virginia Settlers

The English who settled the Chesapeake Bay region shared the locals' enthusiasm for the region's natural gifts and, by extension, the Native Americans' foodways. "Heaven and earth never agreed better to frame a place for man's habitation," wrote John Smith in 1608. The Reverend Daniel Price generated a torrent of compliments, saying that Virginia "was not unlike . . . Arabia for spices, Spain for Silks, Netherlands for fish, Babylon for corn, [and] Pomona for fruit." It provided, he continued, "*whatsosever commodity England wantesth.*" Robert Johnson, a grocer visiting Virginia in 1609, called it "*a very good land*" and surmised that "*if the Lord love us, he will bring our people to it, and will give it us for a possession.*" Virginia was "an earthly paradise" destined to "make them rich." The sheer abundance in his midst led Edward Waterhouse, a financial backer of the Virginia settlement, to argue that the English should "blast the savages off the face of the earth, since their removal would, among other things, help conserve the native deer and turkies."

Not surprisingly, Waterhouse made this suggestion from London. Had he been on the ground in Virginia, he would have clearly seen that such a policy would have been tantamount to suicide. Ever reluctant to "turn husbandmen," the initial settlers in the Chesapeake region depended heavily on Native Americans for their early food supply. Their laziness, moreover, hardly went unnoticed. Whatever problems the young colony might have suffered, the founding organization—the Virginia Company—wrote, was due to "an idle crue . . . that will rather starve for hunger than lay their hands to labor." What the company needed, it explained, was "laborers, mechanics, farmers, and craftsmen" to establish an independent society. The goal, as the founders came to realize, involved replicating the practices of the English woodland and pasture farmers—that is, tending grain, a vegetable garden, cattle, and sheep while using the remaining time to weave, mine, and pursue small handicrafts. In other words, practice the lifestyle that New Englanders would soon embrace. And again, if they were lucky, perhaps make a little cash along the way.

The problem was that nobody was terribly interested in doing the kind of work that yielded food. The reasons behind the colony's initial inability to feed itself in a land of rich soil, bountiful woodland, and teeming rivers and seas are, to put it mildly, baffling. Every resource seems to have been in place for a smooth transplantation of old ways to a new environment. The most plausible explanation for its immediate failure to become even moderately self-sufficient involved the colony's poor organization, especially with respect to its attempt to grow food. Rather than grant each settler a homestead and allow him to work the land as an independent owner, the Virginia Company chose a communal arrangement of land distribution that dampened the spark of private enterprise. Ralph Hamor, one of the colony's earliest settlers, suggested this problem when he wrote, "When our people were fed out of the common store and labored jointly in the manuring of the ground and planting corne, glad was the man that could slippe from his labour . . . neither cared they for the increase, presuming that howsoever their harvest prospered, the generall store must maintain them." Add to this assumption the fact that colonists—many of whom came from the lesser gentry—lacked the most basic agricultural knowledge and it's not hard to see why the early Chesapeake Bay settlers turned to the Native Americans for their food.

But the English, as flexible as a man like Gabriel Archer might have been, became increasingly distraught with such dependence, especially when Native Americans made comments such as "we can plant anywhere . . . and we know that you cannot live if you want [lack] our harvest, and that relief we bring you." It was such a tone that infuriated the Englishmen enough to cause Deputy Governor George Percy to organize a raid on Native American villages and, remarkably, "cutt downe their Corne growing about the Towne" in 1610 before the English had built anything as simple as even a kitchen garden. The violent act had distinct culinary consequences, leading one desperate Englishman to chop up his wife, salt her down, and grill her for dinner. Others dug up graves in order to eat the corpses. Needless to say, the initial transplantation of old cooking and eating habits to the New World was not going as the Virginia Company had planned.

But, of course, these were extreme events. When they weren't burning villages or practicing cannibalism, the English settlers and the Native Americans honestly attempted to establish a fairly reliable and rational system of trade based on symbiotic interests. Immediately after the settlers built their roughshod homes, for example, the Virginia Company pleaded with them not to offend the Native inhabitants. For his part, Powhaten, the leader of the region's tribes, summarily encouraged his people to approach the English with minds open and arms bearing gifts. Guns, according the Virginia Company, were to be used only to prevent aggression and not to instigate it. The English, as the Native Americans saw it, could become first-rate allies in the tribes' many territorial disputes with northern chiefdoms. For these reasons, both groups embraced the chance to trade.

It seemed like a good plan. Unbridgeable cultural differences, however, soon disrupted the peaceful flow of exchange and set these cultures on a collision course. Although the English had to depend heavily on the Natives for food, they were ultimately unable to respect their methods of producing it. Whereas the New Englanders condemned the Native Americans for periodic stretches of scarcity, the Chesapeake settlers seized on the fact that women worked the fields. This perversion of proper English work habits eventually undermined whatever cultural respect the English might have potentially had for the Native Americans. Nothing, in fact, could have grated more offensively against English cultural standards of civility or traditional notions of honest agriculture than women toiling, outside, to reap what men never sowed.

Virginia's settlers rarely missed a chance to hold forth on the matter. Succumbing to Montaigne's discriminatory assessment that "savages have no occupations but leisure ones," Smith reasoned that Virginia would be a heaven on earth "were it fully manured and inhabited by industrious people," implying that the Natives lounged around all day, traipsing in the woods and following their bliss wherever mystical spirits moved them. Native American men might have spent their days hunting and fishing, but as the Englishmen mistakenly saw it, according to settler William Strachey, "they place [these activities] among their sports and leisures." William Byrd wrote in the late 1720s that "the little work that is done among the Indians is done by poor women, while the men are quite idle, or at most employed only in the Gentlemanly Diversions of Hunting and Fishing." "When all their fruits be gathered," wrote another settler, "little else they plant, and this is done by their women and children." The opinion was pervasive, and it seriously compromised the cultural interaction that was under way. The danger for the English settlers should have been more evident: whereas the New Englanders could afford this chauvinism because they had successfully established their own farms, the Chesapeake settlers, who had not achieved a similar accomplishment, disparaged the Native Americans at great risk to their food supply.

Tensions between Native Americans and the Chesapeake settlers heated up, simmered, and then boiled over into violence. George Thorpe, a Member of Parliament who had once entertained hopes of a peaceful biracial society in Virginia, perhaps best summarized the diplomatic basis for the eruption that occurred in 1622. "There is scarce any man amongst us," he said, "that doth so much as afforde [the natives] a good thought in his hart and most men with their mouth give them nothing but maledictions and execrations." These maledictions and execrations didn't go unanswered. On March 22, the Native Americans unleashed a brutal and masterfully coordinated assault on their English neighbors. The uprising devastated Virginia, resulting in the slaughter of 347 English men, women, and children; the death of George Thorpe; and the end of any chance for genuine cultural and culinary exchange between the Native Americans and the English settlers. Blood ran too heavily to restore stability. In his own mind, Smith quickly relegated the Native Americans to a position where they "now must justly be compelled to servitude and drudgery." But the Native Americans had no such plans. They would move west rather than submit to such a fate.

Which was just fine with the English because, by 1622, they happened upon a solution. It was a crop that would demand unlimited and unoccupied land, indirectly solve their immediate food problem, justify the importation of hundreds of thousands of African slaves to the Chesapeake Bay, and shape the future course of the region's foodways. They had discovered tobacco.

The Tobacco Boom

Well, they didn't actually discover it. One of the hidden benefits to come from an otherwise disastrous attempt to settle Roanoke Island back in the 1580s was the knowledge that Native Americans grew and smoked this "stinking weed" called tobacco. Within weeks of establishing the first settlement in Jamestown, settlers—who duly noted that the Spanish were capitalizing on Europe's intensifying taste for tobacco by cultivating a West Indian strain of the crop—tried with little success to grow what they universally condemned as a disgusting habit. As they saw it, tobacco was useful for little else than lubricating social life in taverns and inns. Nevertheless, it could also free them from their economic bind. So they toyed with this strange crop, trying out a patch here and there. But they had little hope.

In 1616, however, a settler named John Rolph planted tobacco seeds that he had obtained from the West Indies, and the results boded well. So well in fact that a year later the English settlers were able to ship an experimental cargo of cured tobacco to England, where it sold at an impressive rate. Over the next several years, scruples about the weed's immoral connotations dissipated like smoke rings into thin air as settlers came to see tobacco as the unexpected gold for which they had been so assiduously searching. Throughout the 1620s, Virginians eagerly dedicated more land to the cultivation of tobacco—diversification be damned. As early as 1623, a wary settler scoffed at the rapid transition to monocultural production. "Nothing is done in anie one of [the plantations]," he wrote, "but all is vanished into smoke (that is to say into Tobaccoe)." Few listened. Yields per man varied, but estimates suggest that an individual laborer could produce five hundred pounds of tobacco a year, often pulling in £200 in exchange—a considerable sum. At these rates, tobacco was primed to become what sugar had become for the West Indies: the region's economic, social, and cultural lifeblood. The place would never be the same again.

The Fine Art of Growing Tobacco

Tobacco took off in the 1620s, and, although it was a precarious crop subject to market fluctuations, it had become the region's undisputed king by the 1640s. As such, it dictated how Chesapeake Bay residents lived their lives. As with sugar in the West Indies, we must understand the crop's specific demands in order to grasp the deepest roots of the culinary consequences to emerge from it.

Late December or early January was the time for planters to set seeds in specially manured beds that had been further enriched with wood ash. Careful planters kept these beds small (no more than a quarter of an acre) and separate from one another by enough distance to limit contagion should disease break out. They also purposely overplanted. During this initial phase of production, according to one tobacco grower, "an experienced planter commonly takes care to have ten times as many plants as he can make use of." After placing the seeds in the beds, the planter then protected them from frost by covering the beds with a canopy of debris and branches. He could then pray for growth, cross his fingers, and turn his attention to other farm-related chores. The seeds would not be ready to transplant until early April, the time when most planters judged the tobacco sprouts sturdy enough to withstand removal to the big field.

Transplantation demanded the utmost finesse and patience. The process took several months. At this early stage, leaves were "about as large as a dollar" and thick enough to be opaque. Their roots, however, grubbed deeply enough into the beds to make their complete removal that much more challenging. Experienced planters tried to hold off removing the plants until a soaking rain loosened the soil and minimized the risk of snapping the stiff plants just above their roots. "When a good shower . . . happens at this period of the year," wrote one farmer, "the planter hurries to the plant bed, disregarding the teeming element." While waiting for the rain to arrive, workers headed into the fields to make small tobacco hills (mounds made with cupped hands), leaving a tiny hole in the middle for the seedling. After placing seedlings into the tobacco hills, planters gently tamped the mound around the thin stalks and watered them. Ideally, transplantation would end in May, but, as one farmer explained, fields were rarely planted "until the *long season in May*, which (to make use of an Irishism) very frequently happens in June." Tobacco, in short, was a hard crop to keep up with.

The summer months centered on coaxing the reedy stalks into maturity. Unlike sugar, tobacco is a crop that, once established, demands constant attention. Summer was the time to prune the plants. The appearance of eight leaves on a plant signaled that it was ready to be "topped," a procedure that kept the plant from flowering, thereby further directing nutrients into the fattening leaves. In response to being topped, however, plants stubbornly sent out small shoots called suckers. Another potential drain on a plant's nutritional intake, suckers had to be removed as well, a job made especially noxious by their location at the stem's base. Weeding, topping, removing suckers—these jobs shaped the contours of life during the long, hot summer on the tobacco plantation.

The next step turned planters into nervous, temperamental men. No matter how cocksure the planter, cutting tobacco leaves invariably exposed him to the high risk of emasculating his entire crop. The gamble—and it was one that planters very frequently lost—pitted the desire to keep the plants rooted as long as possible in order to maximize their ripeness against the fickle arrival of the inevitable fall frost that could wilt them into compost. Playing it safe, however, had its problems as well because cutting the leaves too early led to overly moist leaves that cured badly and rotted when packed. Further challenging the planters' quest for a bumper crop was the more daunting reality that nobody really knew what a ripened tobacco plant looked like. Each planter tended to rely on some quirky combination of folk wisdom, science, intuition, and experience. Richard Henry Lee instructed growers to look for the telltale "spots appearing on the leaf." Another "expert," however, urged planters to action when "the leaf feels thick, and if pressed between the finger and thumb will crack." And yet another insisted that "the tobacco, when ripe, changes its colour, and looks grayish." Whatever the methods employed, the vagaries of personal judgment ultimately determined when a planter sent his workers

into the field to hack off the ripened leaves. If all went well, no harvest celebrations followed because tobacco, like sugar, called for extensive and immediate processing.

As the leaves aired out, workers labored by torchlight into the wee hours removing the thickest arteries from the leaves in order to maximize the quantity that planters could pack into a hogshead barrel. One might think that packing tobacco would have been a soothing task that allowed the mind to wander. To the contrary, it posed its own unique challenge. Shippers charged by the hogshead rather than by weight. A well-packed hogshead normally weighed in at about one thousand pounds. Stuffing it to such a density, however, assumed that the cooper had constructed a superior barrel, an assumption too often proved wrong by the explosion that occurred after the greedy addition of a just few more leaves. Prizing, as the packing process was called, required an elusive combination of intuition and experience. Finally, nobody in his right mind was going to carry these hogsheads down to the river. They were instead rolled to a warehouse on the banks of one of the region's five rivers, where they awaited an English ship to bring the load to London. Even today, throughout the Chesapeake Bay, "rolling roads" mark a landscape with twists and turns that pay tribute to the crop it once nurtured.

The establishment of tobacco as a cash crop imposed on the English settlers a cycle that dictated the most basic patterns of daily life. When they finally sent their hogsheads to London, a full fifteen months had passed, a new crop of seedlings were being dropped into freshly hoed tobacco hills, and any hope of taking a breather had been dashed by an agricultural cycle that brooked no rest. Planters necessarily thought in terms of overlapping seasons. Explaining tobacco to a new plantation manager, planter Richard Corbin said, "To employ the Fall & Winter well is the foundation of a successful Crop this Summer: You will therefore Animate the overseers to great diligence that their work may be in proper forwardness and not have to do in the Spring that ought to be done in the Winter." He concluded, "There is business for every season of the year."

Curing and prizing tobacco

Processing tobacco for shipment was even more time consuming than growing it. The routines that tobacco dictated came to dominate the pace of life in Virginia and Maryland.

Unfortunately for the Native Americans, it was also a cycle that, unlike their own, didn't so much renew itself as demand more space to spin. As tobacco swallowed the landscape, economy, and culture of the Chesapeake Bay, the ceaseless nature of tobacco farming came to preoccupy the mind of every enterprising planter. The nature of that preoccupation, the gist of the ongoing concern, was similar to the very thought mulled over by sugar magnates in the West Indies and farmers in New England: labor. It was now the Chesapeake Bay's turn to answer the question that every region of British America would eventually face: Who would work the fields? As in New England and the West Indies, the answer to that question would have important consequences for the region's eating habits.

From Servitude to Slavery

The obvious and most visible choice was the Native Americans. With the Chesapeake population now stable enough both to grow some of its food along the New England model and to import the rest from England and New England, the Native Americans seemed good for nothing else. John Smith, as we've seen, urged his peers toward this solution, arguing that the Native Americans "be compelled to servitude and drudgery." The planter John Martin, who recognized that the Native Americans had special ag-ricultural talent, complimented their potential "to worke in the heat of the day." A moment's reflection, however, quickly reminded these men that Native American servants were out of the question as a reliable labor source. Decades of interaction, much of it violent, as well as the Native Americans' deep knowledge of the surrounding environment and their practice of a radically different economic system, disqualified them for such a role. Many English planters considered it, a few did so seriously, but rarely did anyone follow through.

The enslavement of Africans was another option. The Virginians knew about slavery through the Spanish and Portuguese examples and, later, through the example of their English peers down in the West Indies. "It would not have been surprising if slavery had developed swiftly in Virginia during the booming 1620s," writes one authority on the subject, "when tobacco prices were high enough to inspire the same overpowering greed that moved the Spaniards on Hispaniola." The arrival in 1619 of a few Af-ricans on a Dutch trading ship thus might have seemed to some the timely harbinger of an imminent embrace of slavery. But, as it turns out, the time wasn't yet right.

Certain conditions rendered slavery unsuitable for the early Chesapeake tobacco plantations. The blacks who disembarked from the Dutch ship—along with about five hundred other blacks who came over in the next two decades—didn't enter a brutal race-based labor system but, rather, an ambiguous place in a nascent society still quite ambivalent about skin color. The most notable limitation to the wholesale adoption of slavery was cost. For all the European demand, and for all the rage that café life was becoming, tobacco wasn't sugar, and the returns that tobacco planters earned didn't yet allow for a serious investment in slave labor. Adding to the slaves' prohibitive cost was the lack of well-established shipping routes from Africa to the Chesapeake region, a transportation disadvantage that placed planters out of that loop frequently circled by traders traveling the Middle Passage farther south. Complicating matters even further were planters who were none too keen to negotiate with yet another group of "strange" people—Africans—whose way of life seemed, from their Anglocentric perspective, just as "savage" as that of their unpredictable neighbors. These factors would later diminish, but throughout most of the seventeenth century, they effectively delayed what would later seem like the timeless marriage of tobacco and slavery.

While discouraging slavery, these limitations established the preconditions for indentured servitude. This solution would quickly bridge the labor gap and define working life throughout most of the seventeenth century. In fact, even if slavery and Native American servitude had not posed the problems that they did, indentured servitude would most likely have dominated anyway. The logic behind it was inexorable. While labor demands were chronically high in the tobacco-booming Chesapeake, England was suffering something of an unemployment problem. London and Bristol swelled with itinerant, idle laborers. Men and women caught in the unforgiving grinds of land consolidation and urbanization desperately sought work. A generation earlier, these people would have labored on or possibly even owned small farms, but now they toiled as hired hands without opportunity for upward mobility. Land ownership for these people—the touchstone of individual worth at the time—was out of the question. As these landless day laborers became a visible minority, enterprising merchants did what enterprising merchants were born to do: they merged supply and demand. By the late 1620s, as a result, thousands of servants were placing an X on "indentures"—a type of labor contract—and traveling to Virginia to work in tobacco fields for an unknown and often unforgiving master. Theoretically, the arrangement worked to the benefit of both parties. According to a standard indenture contract, the servant promised his master four to seven years of loyal service in exchange for a fifty-acre plot of land and a modest "start up" package—usually a shovel, seed, and some clothes. Throughout the seventeenth century, the vast majority of migrants to the Chesapeake Bay region came over as indentured servants.

Although many of these servants followed through on their contracts, took their land, and became successful planters, the success stories were far too rare to be called typical. A large minority of servants, in fact, died before their contracts expired. Interestingly, most died during their last year of service. Observations from the time leave little doubt that the sheer and largely unregulated brutality of the work accounted for this sad trend. The prevailing opinion in England was that Virginians "abuse their servants there with intollerable oppression and hard usage." A woman examining a runaway girl servant found that "she had been sore beaten and her body full of sores and holes." The girl had been abused by her mistress with a rake. Another servant remarked upon the indignity he felt when being bartered like prized cattle or, as he more accurately put it, "like a damnd slave." Opportunity and oppression thus mingled in the Chesapeake Bay, and, even in a part of colonial British America where the average age of death was about forty-five years, Englishmen and -women continued to scrawl their illiterate Xs on that lonely "signature" line and take the plunge, hoping to beat the odds.

As indentured servitude effectively turned the Chesapeake Bay region into a sprawling tobacco culture, two interrelated developments emerged. First, black workers trickled into the region and worked as neither slaves nor indentures. Having not come from England or with an indenture, they found themselves caught in a kind of legal limbo. They arrived, forged haphazard contracts with white masters, enjoyed some but not complete legal protection, and, in exceptional cases, worked their way up the social and economic ladder to own land, hire their own indentured servants, and become planters in their own right. Rare as this accomplishment was, it happened, and thus reminds us that tobacco initially dominated a culture that was not yet forged along clear racial lines. Most blacks not only worked alongside whites, but caroused with them socially, too. As the case of Katherine Watkins shows, the carousal could be quite intimate. After claiming that John Long, a mulatto servant, "put his yard into her and ravished" her, another witness defended Long, saying that Watkins made the moves on him, having "kissed him and putt her hand into his codpiece." Of course, most interactions between whites and blacks were hardly so lascivious. Crouching in the fields and complaining about their lot in life as they removed suckers from plants, or bemoaning the length and ambiguity of their contracts, were more typical of racial interaction at the time. But the mundane could easily slip into the scintillating, and when it did, blacks and whites stood shoulder to shoulder through a range of experiences that, however gently or oddly, circumscribed their collective identity as the region's permanent downtrodden. Poverty was poverty, no matter the shade of one's skin.

Which brings us to the second social development critical to slavery's emergence. Poor whites were becoming visibly and vocally discontent with their situation in the Chesapeake Bay. Throughout the century, they gradually came to see themselves as a distinct underclass subject to the fickle whims of the powerful planters. Even those indentured servants who "succeeded" and claimed their land found themselves farming hardscrabble soil on a distant frontier plagued by Native American raids, bad access to rivers and food imports, and poor communication with their supposedly representative authorities back east. Interior farms produced tobacco of a lower grade that made it to market too late to tap demand at its peak. Their cornfields and gardens were the first to be burned by angry Native Americans. The government routinely turned a deaf ear to their distant concerns. It seemed as though their sacred rights as Englishmen had disappeared, along with their dignity, profits, and precarious sense of political participation. So in 1676, when a disgruntled gentleman named Nathanial Bacon organized a violent rebellion against the elite planters and the government they monopolized, poor whites turned out in earnest, armed, to express their anger. Although in no way a successful rebellion, Bacon and his men managed to raise enough hell—they held up the governor at gunpoint, looted a few stores, and burned Jamestown to the ground—to give the elite planters pause. And it was during that pause that the leading figures of the Chesapeake Bay colony thought long and hard about the prospects of a full-blown class war—prospects they were none too pleased to endure. It was then that they asked themselves a pointed question: How can we defuse the tension that inspired Bacon's Rebellion?

They asked this question at an opportune moment. By the 1670s, England's economy had improved considerably, making it much harder to attract indentured servants to work the plantations. As the price of an indentured servant spiked, however, that of a slave plummeted. Fueled by the booming West Indian sugar economy, the transatlantic slave trade had also reached something of a fevered pitch. With the steady growth of the tobacco economy in the Chesapeake, along with the cod industry in New England, international merchants were systematically threading an east coast loop into their travel routes. Just as the logic of indentured servitude in the 1620s had been unassailable, so it was in the 1670s with the transition to slavery. Planters devoured slaves, importing them from West Africa by the thousands. As their numbers increased, a critical distinction began to quietly—and then not so quietly—make itself known. Servants were white. Slaves were black. Race was not yet, as noted, a divisive aspect of social life in the mainland colonies. But some began to wonder: What if it was? The subtle logic behind the transition to black slavery in the Chesapeake Bay operated in the deep psyches of the white elites. "But for those with eyes to see," writes Edmund Morgan, "resentment of an alien race might be more powerful than resentment of an upper class." Another historian has called slavery "an unthinking decision." However, it didn't take

Advertising tobacco

This English advertisement depicts a Native American smoking a planter's tobacco, thus suggesting that it was indeed "The Best York River" tobacco available on the market. The English both consumed and re-exported tobacco throughout Europe.

long for elite planters to think that one way to make even the poorest and most dispossessed of whites feel empowered would be to render them legally (and thus socially) superior to a specific class of lowly workers. Lowly workers, of course, who were singled out by their black skin color.

Thus the course of social and economic life came to be divided by race. By the 1690s, the line was drawn, etched in stone, in fact. No matter how poor a white person was, there was always a black man somewhere lower on the ladder to assuage his anger and stroke his ego. And it was a ladder that whites could climb but blacks, held in place by codes that defined them as chattel, couldn't touch. Unlike the situation in the first half of the seventeenth century, a black man wasn't going to pull himself up into freedom and gain a taste of economic power. There was, with the advent of slavery, no more ambiguity in the Chesapeake's social structure. With a clear racial distinction set, with that basic human injustice called racism given formal and enforceable legitimacy, planters imported slaves by the hundreds, the thousands, and then the tens of thousands. The Chesapeake Bay quickly became a society where almost half of its residents were enslaved Africans, Afro-Carribeans, or, eventually, African Americans. It became, at its core, a slave society.

And that sad development was crucial to the region's foodways.

The Foodways of Slaves in the Chesapeake Bay

The culinary experience of slaves responded first and foremost to the incessant demands imposed by tobacco. As a crop allowing almost no downtime, it kept slaves tethered to their tasks from sunup to sundown for at least six and a half days a week. Unlike their West Indian counterparts, Chesapeake masters couldn't afford to grant their slaves a full day and a half off to cultivate their own crops, raise their own livestock, fish, hunt, and trade in markets. Tobacco wouldn't brook such diversions. So they had to feed them. Slaves, therefore, depended to a much greater extent than they did in the West Indies on rations doled out by the master. From a nutritional perspective, this reliance wasn't necessarily a bad thing. The ample evidence of slave malnutrition in the West Indies is largely absent in the Chesapeake. We should also recall that masters in the Chesapeake had a much greater economic incentive to keep their slaves healthy. Tobacco, as profitable as it was, never generated the cash returns that sugar commanded. Masters couldn't afford to view their slaves as disposable commodities who were easily replaced with only a fraction of the plantation's profits, as they could in the West Indies. Slaves had to be relatively well nourished; otherwise, a planter's earnings—the be-all and end-all for a slave owner—would fall as limp as his precious brown leaves.

Whites thus generally dealt with the slaves' diet. Throughout the seventeenth century, planters in the Chesapeake had forged a diet that relied on myriad sources. As we've seen, Native Americans provided early guidance on how to produce food locally, and the planters turned to extensive corn production as a result. It was an adaptation that would prevail until the 1730s, when the big planters began to mix wheat into their tobacco crops in order to diversify their economic base. Tobacco profits allowed the Chesapeake planters to import not only manufactured goods and, later, slaves, but also many foodstuffs from England, including wheat, barley, ale, a little beef, and vegetable seeds. Additionally, although to a much lesser extent, Chesapeake wives and servants pursued those provisioning tasks that were central to the life of a New England family, depending on kitchen gardens for produce, locally raised pigs for pork, cattle raised locally or imported from New England for beef, dairy made at home or sent from Pennsylvania, and rice from Carolina. None of these sources singlehandedly dominated the ways in which Chesapeake families obtained their food, but they all added up to something of a provisioning system, even if it felt, at times, unsystematic. Families would often resort to a meal called "the mess." As the term implies, anything available went into this dish, and in the Chesapeake this amalgamation more often than not included Indian cornmeal, syrup, pork, salt meat, and greens. The dish evoked a range of traditions: English, Native American, and, with its similarity to one-pot stews, African. It's a meal that we might best recall when trying to understand the complicated foodways of the Chesapeake Bay region and the culinary interaction between whites and blacks.

Because it was relatively easy to grow and harvest, Indian corn became a staple of the Chesapeake slaves' diet. The Native American crop, and the techniques that Native Americans bequeathed to the English settlers, provided a relatively cheap and nutritious way for masters to maintain their workforce without sacrificing too much land and labor in the process. Commenting on the slave diet in 1732, William Hugh Grove observed that slaves "are allowed a peck of Indian corn per week." Indian corn, even more so than wheat, according to one farmer, "nourishes labourers better, and brings a far better increase," a development that planters strongly encouraged given that slave codes allowed them to claim proprietorship over their chattel's offspring. The planter Robert Carter noted that slaves "who are not fed with animal food" received a "common allowance" of sixty bushels of Indian corn a year. Corn's nutritional value in the slave's diet became especially evident when the region began to grow a substantial amount of wheat in the 1730s. This diversification not only lessened the planters' sole reliance on tobacco, but also made wheat more readily available for slave rationing. William Byrd told a story about how after he made his slaves eat wheat, they "found themselves so weak that they begged to allow them Indian Corn again." George Washington also fed his slaves wheat, only to find that "the Negroes, while the novelty lasted, seemed to prefer Wheat bread as being the food of their Masters." It didn't take long, however, before "they soon grew tired of it." Washington thus advised, "Should the Negroes be fed upon Wheat or Rye bread, they would in order to be fit for the same labor, be obliged to have a considerable addition to their allowance of meat." Although the slave owners may not have made the connection at the time, slaves from Africa would have been completely familiar with Indian corn, which West Africans had adopted in the sixteenth century. Why they rejected wheat, a thoroughly English staple, confounded those same owners.

Although the rigors of tobacco cultivation required high levels of protein, most Chesapeake masters provided slaves with only the most modest amounts of meat. Jefferson noted to an overseer that he would need "about 900 lbs. [of pork] . . . for the people, so as to give them half a pound-a-piece once a week." However inadequate supplies were, slaves came to expect these allotments as a matter of course. When one plantation manager failed to follow through on a promised ration of pork, the work gang that he oversaw drew up "a grate petition . . . for some meat." Chances are good that what the slaves ended up getting from the master wasn't an especially impressive spread. One visitor to a Virginia plantation noted how masters gave slaves a small amount of heavily skimmed milk, a slab of "rusty bacon," and a few chunks of salt herring. Masters constantly tried to link their provisions to incentives for slaves to do more work. Landon Carter took the rare step of paying slaves in beef when they killed crows in his tobacco fields, giving them a half-pound of meat per six crow heads. Rarely did he grant a ration of meat outright, preferring instead that slaves buy salted pork by working overtime. Only as a reward for an especially productive day of work would he hack off one or two small pieces of pork to bring to the quarters as a "gift."

It will come as little surprise that slaves received decidedly inferior cuts of meat. When masters gave or sold their slaves pork, beef, and mutton—the most common bones found in archaeological excavations—they usually provided nothing more than the heads, vertebrae, feet, and ribs. Archaeological evidence from Jefferson's plantation demonstrates that pork ribs and sternum were the most popular cuts of meat doled out to the slaves. Excavations have also uncovered a high proportion of carpals, tarsals, and mandibles. Larger and choicer cuts have been found in slave quarters, but only because slaves often ate the gristle off bones from cuts already consumed up at the big house.

Masters worked hard to achieve a sinister kind of balance. On the one hand, they wanted to feed their slaves as little as possible; on the other, they had to keep them healthy. If the balance tipped too far toward frugality, theft would often result. This response happened frequently on Virginia's Kingsmill Plantation, where archaeologists have found wine bottles adorned with the master's seal stashed in the slaves' root cellar, along with long bones from a cow's hindquarters. Masters frequently complained to their overseers about pilfered hams from the smokehouse, and they willingly granted slaves' padlocked compartments in order to create an individual rather than a collective sense of ownership, thereby making it harder to hide purloined goods. How to minimize theft remained a tricky challenge that every owner struggled to overcome. Nonetheless, as annoying as theft was to a master, it was a response that reflected an attempt on the part of slaves to supplement and maintain at least some control over their own diet. Theft notwithstanding, it didn't take long for slave owners to realize that there was a potentially profitable advantage to be gained in this desire. Indeed, whether they did so to avoid starvation or diversify their diet, slaves began to ask for and receive brief pockets of time to hunt and fish. A slave might fake sick and go fishing, hunt in the middle of the night, or make deals with the overseer to get off the plantation for an hour or two and check his homemade traps. We really don't know how or when, but we do know from the bones they left behind that slaves caught and ate squirrels, opossum, turkey, deer, turtles, cats, ducks, geese, chickens, partridges, and all manner of fish. Masters, for their part, quickly came to see that it was in their interest to keep an eye on but also to wink at this "extracurricular" activity. Power and disenfranchisement were never as complete as we might assume. Slaves capitalized whenever they could.

Literary references to slaves obtaining their own food are rare, but a couple of examples support the ample archaeological record. One of George Washington's slaves "asked the lent the use of the sein" to catch fish. A slave owner named Richard Parkinson praised his slaves' ingenuity, noting how "partridges [were] chiefly taken by negroes who have a device for snaring whole coveys in a box." James Gordon commented on how his slaves killed sixty-five pigeons in a single outing, while another master urged his overseer to allow the slaves a bit of hunting time so as to "prevent the people from oustering." The faunal remains from the Willcox slave cabin on Virginia's Flowerdew Plantation offer further evidence that slaves chased at least some portion of their food supply. Catfish, sturgeon, striped bass, and gar composed the bulk of the slaves' fish consumption, which accounted for about 17 percent of the overall meat they consumed. As they did elsewhere, slaves on the Flowerdew Plantation caught their own rabbits, rats, squirrels, opossum, and raccoons. In addition to their domesticated fowl, they shot and cooked mallard and crows. Turtles, snapping turtles, oysters, clams, and mussels confirm their access to the James River for extra supplies of food. The presence of hooks, lead shot, and gunflints help to further complete an admittedly blurry picture of slave provisioning. A similar spread of wild game, fish, and hunting equipment found on other plantations suggests that the Willcox slaves weren't alone. Whether through the threat of insubordination, theft, or a basic desire to determine their own diet, slaves throughout the Chesapeake retained some power over what they ate, however small that power may have been.

In addition to hunting and fishing for their own food, slaves occasionally kept their own gardens. While the size and dimensions of these plots remain impossible to state with any real accuracy, we do know that they were common and substantial enough for slaves to build root cellars to store vegetables. Normally, they built these cellars directly in front of fireplaces in order to prevent the vegetables from freezing. Although few and far between, references to slave gardens lend some insight into their role in the slave diet. A traveler to Virginia in 1762 described the slaves' "small houses or huts, much resembling poor peasants thatched houses, to which they have little gardens, and live in families separate from each other." Thirty years earlier, Hugh Grove had observed that masters encouraged slaves "to plant little platts for potatoes or Indian peas and Cimnells (squash), which they do on Sundays or at night." Jefferson noted how slaves cultivated a kind of sweet potato, adding that they especially enjoyed the potato-pumpkin. In 1781, William Feltman commented on how slaves grew "great quantities of snaps and collards." Pollen and seed analysis reveals evidence of peas, corn, cherries, peaches, beans, pumpkin, and watermelon. Many of the plants that slaves cultivated were popular in West Africa as well, including yams, peanuts, rice, and dried beans. The presence of these crops in slave gardens indicates that slaves may have taken full advantage of these plots not only to diversify their diets but to do so in a way that preserved the culinary traditions of home.

But, again, the opportunity was scarce because the vast majority of a slaves' diet ultimately came from the master's rations. The abundant evidence available from Monticello, Thomas Jefferson's home, lends compelling insight into the specific kinds of meat that slaves received. The Dry Well, the place where slaves routinely tossed their remains, is perhaps the most detailed microcosm we have of the slaves' otherwise hidden culinary world. Domestic pigs were the most popular species found in the cellar, comprising about 30 percent of the overall identifiable fauna. Pigs were slaughtered when they were eighteen to twenty-four months old, an indication that they had been killed for the primary purpose of smoking them into cured hams. As always, slaves supped on the dregs. Cranial fragments, lumbar vertebrae, ribs, and sternums dominate the remains. Although it comprised only 5 percent of the findings, beef was the second most popular meat eaten by slaves. Jefferson's slaves were unique in receiving even a sporadic supply of beef. Other plantation owners never fed it to slaves. But, then again, Jefferson butchered oxen after they had been worn down as beasts of burden, thereby ensuring that their meat would be tough and sinewy (unlike the tender meat on yearlings or calves) and thus not suitable for the big house. Sheep were a small but nonetheless important part of the slave diet. They were especially common at Monticello, and Jefferson tended to slaughter them at a young age, perhaps around six months. Again, slaves rarely saw the finer cuts. Instead, they made do with the cast-offs, which explains the preponderance of lamb jaws scattering the dry cell, as well as a single horse, a mule, a four-year-old deer, and many examples of wild game and fowl, including duck, opossum, rabbit, turkey, and quail. Slaves at Monticello also appear to have kept a few domesticated chickens.

Not only does the archaeological evidence from sites such as Monticello tell us what some slaves cooked, but it also suggests how they cooked it. Bone fragments found in slave cellars on several plantations support the reasonable expectation that, as they did in Africa and the West Indies, slaves cooked their meals in a single pot shared by slaves throughout the entire quarter. We suspect that this method was indeed the norm because, for one, few of the bones were charred, as they would have been had slaves spit-cooked them over an open fire. On Monticello, only 2 percent of the cow bones, 12 percent of the sheep bones, and not a single pig bone show signs of charring. Slave butchering techniques, moreover, suggest that cooks chopped bones to fit inside a particular pot. This chopping was anything but clean, as bones were trampled, smashed, hacked, and splintered in order to fit into a quarter's stew pot. A single rib found in the Monticello slave quarters had twenty-one cuts, five chops, three saw marks, and one shear mark. A single foot showed evidence of five cuts and four shear marks. Most bones, not surprisingly, had their marrow extracted. Slaves rarely, if ever, hacked meat into uniform cuts and joints for roasting. Animal bones from Jefferson's slave quarters were frenetically hacked with four or five different instruments, including chops, saws, and shears. While some butchery marks reveal an effort to reduce the size of a cut for the stew pot, others indicate that slaves were hacking at the bone to get all the meat off it, and perhaps get to the marrow.

Slaves' cooking equipment was at best adequate enough for simple preparation and presentation. In addition to an iron pot, many slave families owned a frying pan and an iron kettle for cooking. Occasionally, slaves obtained more advanced cooking utensils such as brass pots, beer barrels, pot racks, and pothooks. In terms of eating utensils, slaves usually possessed bowls and jars (instead of plates), coarse ceramic serving spoons, and larger earthenware and gourd bowls. As with the food itself, most of the slaves' utensils were owner cast-offs. Although certainly not representative, 11 percent of the ceramic vessels from George Washington's slave quarters, and 20 percent from Jefferson's, was composed of Chinese porcelain plates, bowls, and teacups. A visitor to Mount Vernon, Washington's home, noted the widespread poverty in the slave huts, but couldn't help but observe that "in the middle of this poverty some cups and a teapot." Washington doled out stoneware to his slaves in one large delivery, usually after making a new purchase for himself, as he did in the 1770s when he bought a set of Josiah Wedgwood creamware. Eventually, even some of the creamware trickled down to the slave quarters. Absent from the archaeological evidence at Mount Vernon and elsewhere are large storage or preparation vessels, thus indicating that slaves did not, aside from their root cellars, store large quantities of food. No matter where their food came from, a hand-to-mouth culinary existence for slaves was and always would be their norm.

The Dietary Habits of William Byrd

Whites had a fundamentally different cooking and eating experience in the Chesapeake Bay region. In contrast to their chattel, they ate high on the hog. And they did so by achieving a rough approximation of English eating habits not unlike that in New England while incorporating uniquely colonial aspects dictated in large part by the slave society they had established. White Chesapeake settlers never attained the self-sufficiency that New Englanders achieved. In fact, because of their dedication to tobacco, they often imported much of their food from their neighbors to the north or even England itself. Neither did they "Anglicize" their food to the extent that New Englanders did. Their initial reliance on Native Americans, their original migration as single men from relatively impoverished backgrounds, and their lack of a deep spiritual affiliation with the homeland predisposed them to be more open-minded than New Englanders when it came to accepting foreign or comparatively crude foodways. By the same token, white Virginians and Marylanders never became as flexible in their cultural tolerance as did their cohorts in the West Indies, where sugar controlled the economy far more aggressively than did tobacco in the Chesapeake. As we've seen, masters in the Chesapeake determined their slaves' diet, whereas the opposite situation prevailed in the West Indies. The unique economic and social conditions in the Chesapeake Bay established the preconditions for a system of food preparation that reflected aspects of both the New England and West Indian models. Ultimately, though, it became a model all its own. Hints of how that model evolved are evident in the extensive diary of a Virginia planter named William Byrd.

William Byrd of Westover was a successful tobacco planter and member of Virginia's early-eighteenth-century aristocracy. He was also something of a character. Born in Virginia, Byrd enjoyed the privilege of studying in England, where the Felsted Grammar School taught him, among other things, the cultural norms of English foodways. As an adult living in America, he kept a meticulous and vividly honest diary (it was originally encoded) that chronicled, among other comings and goings (including his vigorous sex life), what he ate on a daily basis between 1709 and 1712. His entries lend insight not only into how white Chesapeake settlers ate compared with their slaves but also into how the Chesapeake diet took on regional distinctions that made the Chesapeake a unique place on colonial British America's culinary map.

The diversity of Byrd's diet was impressive. Consistent with the English diet that was his heritage, he ate a lot of beef. In October 1709, for example, he supped on beef ten times, including boiled beef, roast beef, and, on one occasion, dry beef. He was none too happy about the last option, noting, "I reproached my wife with ordering the old beef to be kept and the fresh beef used first, contrary to good management, on which she was pleased to be very angry." His love for beef didn't preclude the consumption of many other cuts. Throughout the year, his diet regularly included more earthy fare, such as chicken, blue-wing duck, geese, turkey, mutton, venison, sausage, bacon, lamb, pork, partridge, wild duck, and pigeon. Preparations varied, but most of the time the meat was either boiled or, slightly more often, roasted. Nevertheless, Byrd does mention a "fricasse of chicken," "hashed pork," "fried pork," "minced veal," "fried chicken," "mutton pie," "blue wing pie," "chicken pie," "fricasee of veal," and "mutton cutlets." Byrd combined his desire for a diversity of meats with the equally strong desire to hunt for sport and would thus regularly venture into the woods to shoot his own game. "I took my gun and endeavored to shoot some partridges," he wrote on March 22, 1711 (and then admitted, "and could not"). Later he told how "Mr. Graeme and I went out with bows and arrows and shot at partridge and squirrel." The experience provided "an abundance of diversion but we lost some of our arrows." The luxury of eating the choicest cuts from a variety of animals didn't preclude an appreciation for organs or other "lowbrow" dishes. Byrd spoke approvingly of cooked brains, "tongue and udder," tripe, a calf's head, and sweetmeats. He even ate squirrel. Meat was regularly available, and, on more than one occasion, Byrd experienced a sensation that we can be sure his slaves never experienced: eating too much meat. "I resolved to eat no meat today," he wrote in March 1711, "and so I dined on potatoes and butter." A week later, he remarked after a big meal, "I was not very well because I had eaten too much."

Like any good Englishman, Byrd ate his garden vegetables and fruit. However, without the existence of extensive gardens, as in New England, he did so relatively infrequently. The vegetables that Chesapeake residents consumed were never as varied or as ample as they were in New England, nor were they as foreign to inherited tastes as those eaten in the West Indies. "I ate nothing but beef," Byrd wrote in a typical entry. In another: "I ate nothing but fowl for supper." And yet another: "I ate nothing but fowl and bacon." Every now and then, though, and perhaps a couple of times a month (and only in the spring and summer), Byrd ate vegetables alongside his meat, and the vast majority of it was asparagus, turnips, or lettuce. On April 6, 1709, he ate "fish for dinner and a little asparagus." Three days later, he had "nothing but cold roast beef and asparagus for dinner." Not until April 24 did he eat more vegetables in the form of "fish and asparagus." During the next month, he ate "a good supper of mutton and asparagus," "red herring and sallet [salad] for dinner," "mutton and sallet for dinner," "mutton and green peas for dinner," and "roast chicken for dinner and green peas." By December, though, Byrd mentions not a single instance of eating vegetables, enjoying only "some apples" for his roughage. None of this is to suggest that Chesapeake housewives didn't *try* to plant an English-style garden. Byrd's son remarked how kitchen gardens aimed to include "all the Culinary plants that grow in England." It's just that the time, labor, and land wasn't available to maintain the kind of gardens that New Englanders were taking for granted by the eighteenth century. Tobacco wouldn't allow it.

Small gardens usually meant small orchards, and fruit in general was equally sporadic in Byrd's meat-rich diet. But occasionally, in addition to apples, Byrd ate cherries, raspberries, pomegranates, watermelon, strawberries, and other fruit. The potential to grow fruit was huge, but, again, in a tobacco culture, it was never realized as fully as it might have been, a failure that frustrated fellow planter Robert Beverly no end. The fruit trees that Chesapeake residents did grow were "wonderfully quick of growth," and the "almond, pomegranate, and fig ripen there very well." Nonetheless, Beverly continued, "there are not ten people in the country that have any of them in their gardens, much less endeavor to preserve any of them for future spending or to propagate them to make a trade." Perhaps it was their relative scarcity that led Byrd in June 1710 to indulge in a rare delivery of fresh fruit from New England, after which he found "my belly out of order."

More often than not, milk was on hand to soothe it. Dairymaids must have been as busy on Byrd's plantation as they were in New England because Byrd's diet revolved heavily around milk, eggs, and butter, as well as the occasional piece of cheese. Byrd regularly ate boiled milk for breakfast, a "meal" that he considered central to strong digestion. Upon hearing that his friend Major Harrison was "indisposed in the breast," he explained how he "persuaded him to enter into a milk diet." On January 23, 1712, Byrd "said my prayers and because I could get no milk I ate some hashed beef for breakfast." By the end of the day, however, fresh milk had become available, and he had "nothing but boiled milk for supper." Milk was perceived as so critical to health that Byrd would eat pancakes for breakfast only when "my wife tempted me to eat some." Otherwise, it was boiled milk. Eggs were also very common. While most were used in custards and puddings, eggs were also cooked directly. After walking three miles with a friend on a pleasant March afternoon, Byrd "returned and ate some bacon and eggs for dinner." It was a combination he was quite fond of, eating it as he did about every couple of weeks. Bread and butter was a year-round staple. When a doctor came by the house to check on Byrd's "giddy" head, Byrd served him "bread and butter and tea for breakfast." The regularity with which Byrd used butter is hinted in his entry about how "I ate some green peas for dinner and was out of humor because the butter was melted oil." On a March evening, he relaxed and "read the *Tatler* and ate some bread and new butter." Cheese was more of a luxury and usually combined with some form of alcohol, as it was in February 1711, when "at night we ate some bread and cheese and drank some punch and were merry."

Fish occupied a much smaller place on the Chesapeake settlers' table than it did on the tables of the West Indies, but Byrd ate it often enough. Perhaps once a month, he would note something along the lines of "I ate fish for dinner." (He did this, for example, on July 30, 1710, after which he recorded this exciting turn of events: "In the afternoon my wife and I had a little quarrel which I reconciled with a flourish [that is, sex]. Then she read a sermon in Dr. Tillotson to me. It is to be observed that the flourish was performed on the billiard table.") Robert Beverly remarked, "As for fish . . . no country can boast of more Variety, greater plenty, or of better in their several kinds." He mentioned bass, carp, drum, herring, mullet, needlefish, alewives, perch, pike, plaice, rock, shad, sheepshead, sturgeon, trout, whiting, eels, lampreys, crabs, oysters, cockles, and mussels. For all of the purported abundance of seafood, though, meat-loving Chesapeake Bay residents ate it in moderation. Fish, in fact, usually accompanied other meats, as it did on an August afternoon in 1711 when Byrd ate "two small fish and some roast mutton and ate pretty heartily" and in October 1709, when "I ate fish and goose for dinner." One particular benefit of fish was that it was available all year round. In December 1709, he wrote, "I ate fish for dinner which we catch in great quantity." Byrd was lazy about naming the precise kind of fish he ate. On one occasion, however, does he specify, writing, "I ate fish for dinner, which they called trout." He often ate oysters and, on one occasion, "ate some crab for dinner." For the most part, though, fish and seafood took a back seat to beef, pork, and wild game.

Byrd's diary, finally, reminds us that the Chesapeake region was not completely self-sufficient in its food supply. To a significant extent, the region relied on New England and England for its beef and grain, or went without. The wholesale dedication to tobacco resulted in frequently erratic harvests, as Byrd noted in 1709 as he traveled from plantation to plantation surveying his neighbors' yields. After having his customary cup of hot milk for breakfast, Byrd "rode to Kensington where there is a very poor crop." From there, he "waded over the river, stepping from one rock to the other and so got to Burkland where John Blackman has little to show for this year's work." After eating a plate of bacon and eggs back at his house, he "proceeded to walk to Byrd Park where [there] was the worst crop of all." In December 1709, Virginia's governing council considered "taking the protection of[f] corn but agreed not to do it." That same month, Byrd attributed the unseasonably "tempting" weather to "God continuing it for the service of those that have little corn." Wheat was not always available at subsistence levels either, a condition that led Byrd on numerous occasions to trade Indian corn in its stead. "The boatwright was affronted," he once explained, "that I gave him pone instead of English bread for breakfast and took his horse and rode away without saying anything a word." While large planters such as Byrd did a better job of providing their own beef, they had shortages as well. "Honey and milk and mush might very well content [Virginians] in these summer months," Robert Carter wrote to a friend, as they "have no meat this time of year." Indeed, they had to rely on New England for much of their "dry" beef as well as live cattle. One farmer's accounts showed the following purchases in 1671: "seaven cowes & heifers the heifers 3 yeares old & one yearling heifer . . . two steares one five the other 3 yeares old & one yearling bull . . . one fatt calfe." He paid for these beasts as most Chesapeake farmers paid for their imports: with tobacco.

White Foodways in General

As in New England, the Chesapeake diet worked to mimic the ways of England. But at the same time, with an economic and social reality so different from that of the motherland, it also responded to local circumstances. Byrd's obvious affinity for roast beef, on the one hand, clearly reflected his cultural heritage and dominated his culinary decisions. Wild game and fish, on the other, remained strong supplements to a diet that could not, in a staple-producing region, reliably replicate the meat and vegetables habit of the homeland. Resources—land and labor—were far too preoccupied with tobacco to pursue a self-sufficient and thoroughly English diet. This balance between Old World and New was constantly undergoing renegotiation. In the end, though, it led to a few distinct culinary habits in the Chesapeake Bay, habits that distinguished it not only from England but also from other colonial societies.

To an outsider, the most notable characteristic would have been the region's deep love of pork. For all of Byrd's attraction to beef, most Chesapeake cattle were lean and tough compared with those up north. Regionally produced beef tended to be stringy and dry, primarily because Chesapeake cattle roamed free and stayed thin rather than sitting idle in small pastures or getting fat on stall-fed grub. One observer even suggested that Virginians drain their "noble marshes" to make as "fine Pastures as anywhere in the world" capable of nurturing tastier beef. But such measures were unnecessary with hogs. Beverly observed how "hogs swarm like Vermine upon the earth." Skilled foragers traditionally unburdened by a pen, hogs foraged and became fat according to their own natural resources, unlike in New England, where they were penned by farmers intent on rigid order. "They run where they list," Beverly continued, "and find their own support in the Woods, without any Care of the Owner." Late fall was the time to slaughter hogs, and cooking manuals helped ensure that methods used to treat and preserve them became common knowledge. According to Mary Randolph, hogs had to be salted "before they get cold." The back bone had to be removed, saltpeter had to be rubbed "on the inside of each ham," the feet had to be cut off "above the knee joint," and the ears, jaws, and nose had to be removed. More often than not, pork was roasted. According to cookbook author Hannah Glasse, the following rules were to be obeyed: "When you roast a loin, take a sharp penknife and cut the skin across, to make the crackling eat the better. . . . The best way to roast a leg is first to parboil it, then skin it and roast it; baste it with butter, then take a little sage, shred it fine, a little pepper and salt, a little nutmeg and a few crumbs of bread, and throw these over it all the time it is roasting." An Englishman visiting Virginia wouldn't necessarily have found pork strange, but he would have been shocked by its centrality to the region's diet.

Another aspect of the foodways that distinguished the Chesapeake from other regions of colonial America was its liberal and often idiosyncratic manner of seasoning food. New Englanders primarily stuck to flavoring English food with typically English garden herbs—mainly sorrel, marjoram, sage, and thyme. Deep Southerners incorporated African, Middle Eastern, and Caribbean spices into dishes normally accustomed to these seasonings—especially stews and other one-pot meals. Chesapeake Bay settlers, however, combined foreign spices such as nutmeg, mace, and cloves (all of which were plentiful in the West Indies) with traditional English food. One popular dish had the cook "take a sirloin of beef, or a large rump, bone it and beat it very well, then lard it with bacon, season it all over with salt, pepper, mace, cloves, and nutmeg." Glasse's salmon recipe instructed cooks to "score the side pretty deep, that it may take the seasoning, take a quarter of an ounce of mace, a quarter of an ounce of cloves, a nutmeg, dry them, beat them fine, a quarter of an ounce of pepper beat fine, and an ounce of salt." Her roasted fowl recipe called for "a good deal of parsley chopped fine, a little sweet herbs, some mace, pepper, salt, and nutmeg." These spices, of course, were used throughout British America, and throughout England as well, but they were used more consistently, and incorporated into more conventional English cooking methods, in the Chesapeake Bay, thereby adding to its distinct culinary flavor.

Because the Chesapeake Bay planters weren't fully self-sufficient in their food supply, and because they didn't grant their slaves enough freedom to produce their own food, the region was especially vigilant about preservation, especially of meat. Significantly warmer weather than New England's also made this task that much more important. One French visitor to Virginia became tired of eating meal after meal of salted meat. "The summer heat," he wrote, "restricts them to this diet, for fresh killed meat must be consumed within twenty-four hours else it will spoil." He went on to note how "the people here have a special way of curing them that consists of salting and smoking them." Combining preservation with their appreciation for heavy seasoning, Chesapeake housewives mixed the preserving salt with hickory ash and brown sugar. Once salted, meat was either taken to the smokehouse or brined. Brining was an English procedure, described by one English manual in these terms: "Get a thirty gallon cask . . . and put some pitch in it to prevent leaking. . . . Put into it one pound of saltpeter powdered, fifteen quarts of salt, and fifteen gallons of cold water, stir it frequently, until dissolved, throw over the cask cloth, to keep out the dust; look at it often and take off the scum." The meat was ready in ten days, but could be stored in the brine for weeks. If housewives wanted to preserve meat even longer through brining, they could remove the meat from the brine after a month, dust it with bran, and hang it in the coolest and driest place they could find. "After the wet season," one manual advised, "take them down and lay them in the sun."

Just as smoking meat required massive amounts of fuel, brining it took massive amounts of salt, which Chesapeake farmers imported from either England or Spain. Such dependence, however, meant that salt was not always available when it was time to slaughter. When this shortage happened, residents employed a Native American method of curing meat without salt. A backcountry resident named Nicholas Cresswell, who was traveling in Kentucky in 1775, described this "peculiar" process in some detail: "The meat is first cut from the bones in thin slices like beefsteaks, then four forked sticks are stuck in the ground in a square form, and small sticks laid in these forks in the form of a gridiron about three feet from the ground." The meat was then placed on the rack above a fire and "turned until it is done." Cresswell continued, "This is called jerking the meat. I believe it is an Indian method of preserving meat. It answers well, where salt is not to be had, and will keep for a long time if it be secured from the wet."

Pickling and potting were also options that housewives often explored. Smaller cuts of meat and some fish didn't lend themselves to smoking or brining, but were well preserved when pickled. Pigs' feet, ox palates, and oysters in particular were best preserved when placed in stone or glass jars of spiced vinegar. "Make fresh pickle often," advised Elizabeth Raffald, an English cookbook writer, "and your meat will keep a good long time." Housewives also employed an English method of brining whereby they stewed the fish or shucked shellfish in a saucepan with water, mace, salt, and pepper. Then they allowed it to cool and added pale vinegar at the end to give the fish "an agreeable acid." Potting was a popular method used for fowl and some fish. After seasoning the flesh "according to your palate," housewives baked the animal whole, cooled it, drained off the gravy, and packed it into an earthenware pot. The key to potting was to then effectively seal the pot's crevices with clarified butter. Some cooks used this method for beef and venison, too. To do so, however, meant that they had to beat the flesh in a mortar until it became "a fine paste." Then, after allowing it to cool, they pressed it into a pot, sealed it with butter, and kept it in a cool cellar. Housewives simply opened the pot and sliced off a piece for supper, usually garnishing it with fried parsley. Pork, finally, also could be potted, but a better method of preserving pork was to treat it like beef or venison and then "pot" it in gut casings. The combination of pork's popularity with the region's predilection for preserving meat helps explain why the result—sausage—became especially popular in the Chesapeake region.

In addition to Virginians' love of pork, seasoning practices, and dedication to preserving food, another way that Chesapeake food distinguished itself from slave foodways and other regional ways of eating had to do with the Virginia elite's taste for turning meals into lavish affairs. One benefit of eating high on the hog in a wealthy, predominantly white, staple-producing region was the not infrequent opportunity to conform to English expectations of elaborate dining. Full cuts of meat, access to ample cookware and cutlery, and relatively affordable kitchen servants and slaves allowed such an approximation at a select few Chesapeake tables. As one historian has remarked, "Virginians dined; New Englanders merely ate." Another explains that dining "was a fine art in Virginia." Dining rooms were often the most important space in the house, and men and women entered them on their best behavior, in their best attire, and only after careful grooming. Tables and sideboards displayed silver engraved with the planters' initials. When Philip Fithian, a Virginia family's resident tutor, failed to appear for dinner one afternoon, he suffered the consequences of the upper class's more formal dining expectations. He recorded the fallout in his diary: "I took a whim in my head and would not go to dinner. My head was not dressed, and I was too lazy to change my clothes. Mrs. Carter, however, in the evening lashed me severely." Meals among the elite in other regions of British America were far less rigid in their expectations, pretensions, and presentation. Conditions in the Chesapeake, however, afforded better-off planters the chance to ape their English superiors, and they didn't hesitate to take advantage of these opportunities when they arose.

A final distinguishing element of Chesapeake's foodways was the emphasis on the occasional bacchanalian blow-out. Again, the relative riches that accrued to owners of tobacco plantations allowed for a controlled amount of uncontrolled extravagance. A visitor to William Fitzhugh's Virginia plantation in 1686 captured the tone and tenor of these often impromptu affairs. He wrote, "We rode twenty strong to Colonol Fichous but he has such a large establishment that he did not mind. We were all of us provided with beds, one for two men. He treated us royally, there was good wine and all kinds of beverages, so that there was a great deal of carousing. He had sent for three fiddlers, a jester, and a tightrope dancer, and they gave us all the entertainment one could wish." Feasts in the Chesapeake often recalled the carnivaleque atmosphere in West Indian and African markets. On some plantations, slaves were granted special feast days when the master was willing to pay for it, and their affairs could often extend over the course of an entire weekend. As the elite did in England, planters saw to it that on harvest days even the poorest whites had access to beef, bacon, pudding, and beer. Food and celebrations, after all, went hand in hand. Needless to say, New Englanders brooked no such nonsense.

The Big Picture

Once again, we can best understand the overall nature of Chesapeake foodways by quickly revisiting our two other culinary cultures. As far south as one could go in the British colonies was the region most unlike the mother country: the West Indies. A staple crop, slaves, and slave and Native American foodways dominated life in these islands. Whites there were so much in the minority, as well as so intent on making a huge profit and going back to England, that they made little effort to replicate the ways of the homeland and instead accepted the foreign diet as an aspect (and not necessarily an unpleasant one) of doing business in the Caribbean. Wild game, pork, lots of fish and shellfish, as well as many Native American and African foods dominated the exciting and diverse diet of this region. On the other end of the British Empire was New England. As the name suggests, this region did an exceptional job not only of replicating the cultural habits of the homeland but also of doing so on its own, without imports. This region lacked a staple crop dictating the allocation of resources. With the vast majority of the settlers there being white, with slavery almost nonexistent and servitude relatively low, and with the family being the most basic economic and social unit, New England established a culinary model that stressed the essentials of a traditional English diet: meat, vegetables, herbs, and fruit.

If the West Indies and New England represented the extremes, the Chesapeake Bay region fell right in the middle. Like the West Indies, it had a staple crop, slaves, and a white population intent on getting rich and living like English gentry. Like New Englanders, though, its residents planned to stay, populate the land with families, and replicate the ways of England as best they could. This amalgam of cultural imperatives meant that the Chesapeake Bay was always stuck in an ongoing process of negotiating the culinary influences of whites, blacks, and Native Americans. And with blacks comprising 30 to 40 percent of the population, and Native Americans having far more of an early influence than in either of the other regions, the Chesapeake Bay managed this negotiation in a far more balanced way than did New England and the West Indies. Whites in the Chesapeake may have eaten high on the hog while blacks ate low, but they both ate from the same hog. In the same fashion, Native Americans may have been pushed to the fringes of society early on, but their influence lingered strongly. To extend the metaphor, the hog from which blacks and whites ate was fed with Indian corn, a Native American crop. Such were the myriad connections and influences that allow us to call the Chesapeake Bay region a land of culinary negotiation. As we will see in the case of South Carolina, not all regional negotiations were so balanced.

CHAPTER 4

WILDERNESS

The Fruitless Search for Culinary Order in Carolina

The most nutritious, the most easily digested, and at the head of four-teen hundred varieties, stands Carolina Rice.

Louisa Cheves Smythe Stoney, *Carolina Rice Cook Book*

ONE WAY TO APPRECIATE Louisa Stoney's insight is to think about hoppin' John. Popular to this day, it's a dish that Carolina slaves popularized and thrived on in their quest for subsistence. For all its longevity, though, it's also a dish whose exact composition, origin, and name remain shrouded in the mystery typical of food forged on the frontier. Hoppin' John underwent constant change. While we know that it essentially consists of rice and beans in some combination, it has (depending on who's doing the talking) been variously concocted to include cowpeas, red peas, small black peas, and calavances, as well as Crowder peas and whipperwool peas. A recipe from 1814 called for "calavances, or red bean, and black-betty . . . the bean of the former is red, the latter black . . . both are wholesome food, of which the negroes in general are very fond." Other recipes asked for some combination of bacon, fried sausage, ham, onion, mint, red pepper, filé powder, cured pork, pork jowls, ham hock, or "cabobs of minced meat (mutton)." Some cultures traditionally served hoppin' John ingredients on the same plate but kept the rice, beans, and meat separate from one another, further adding to the confusion about what makes hoppin' John what it is. A popular Cuban version of the meal required "California pink beans" and "red kidney beans." A Cajun variation demanded salt pork and ham and still parades under the name jambalaya.

Hoppin' John's versatility further confounds its origin. Some scholars identify it as a strictly West African dish carried to the colonies by slaves from the Congo. Others, however, plausibly suggest an Islamic origin, noting that Senegalese and Nigerian Muslims cooked hoppin' John with jerked beef rather than the verboten pork. Yet another popular theory highlights the influence of the Seminole Indians, as runaway slaves living among the

Florida Native Americans may have adapted the dish to Seminole practices, particularly with respect to the incorporation of beans. Even the dish's name has been subjected to a rash of theorizing, ranging from a variation on the French *pois de pigeon* to an elision of *bahatta kachang*—the latter word being a Madagascar-based term for "pea" and the former a Hindi word for "cooked rice." How did hoppin' John come from either of these phrases? No one truly knows. In the end, we're left to conclude that hoppin' John's authenticity comes from its versatility and, in a sense, its mystery. Wherever and whenever it traveled, it embraced change.

Which is precisely the point. The confusion, diversity, flexibility, and myriad flavors that characterize hoppin' John make it an appropriate metaphor for Carolina's open-ended foodways. Indeed, Carolina's cuisine stood apart—and fundamentally so—for all these qualities. New England effectively developed a stable cuisine of abundance that closely adhered to English tradition. The West Indies threw tradition and stability to the wind and accepted an almost entirely foreign, largely slave-based cuisine. The Chesapeake drew on both the New England and West Indian culinary models to balance inherited traditions with the measured negotiation required by a slave society. When we try to situate Carolina within this culinary spectrum, it falls as it does geographically—somewhere between the Chesapeake and the West Indies. In deciding specifically where it falls, though, the most critical point to remember is that Carolina was a slave society. As the ambiguity and freestyle composition of hoppin' John suggest, Carolina foodways adhered much more closely to the West Indian, and specifically the Barbadian, example of cooking and eating. As such, they followed an unusually liberated and tolerant approach to food in a place that looked very little like home.

Given the fact that Barbadian migrants composed a large part of Carolina's founding population, such an influence stands to reason. Again, as we've seen, land became scarce in Barbados during the second half of the seventeenth century, pushing many planters to pack up and relocate to Carolina, a region that Charles II had granted in 1662 to eight persistent English proprietors who promised ample financial returns for the mother country. Inspired by cheap land and expensive dreams, Barbadian Englishmen soon trickled into the region. They brought with them ambitious plans for large plantations, the slaves to work them, and a kind of cultural flexibility well suited not only to eating hoppin' John but to contending with the overall demands of yet another frontier settlement.

Barbados, with its vast slave majority (about 60 percent in 1670, and 90 percent by the 1770s), was the most un-English of the English colonies in America. In transplanting their profit-driven, acquisitive-minded culture of plantation agriculture to Carolina, settlers from Barbados ensured that whatever kind of society eventually evolved on the southern coast of North America would be a society that flouted tradition. It would, if the Barbadians had any say in the matter, become a place where every aspect of life bowed to the domineering force of the large plantation, and thus a place that tolerated radical breaks with the cultural conventions of the mother country. The most obvious break was, of course, slavery. This diversion from the English way of life allowed the region's food pioneers to indulge in a kind of culinary free-for-all. Hoppin' John was a small but symbolic manifestation of that indulgence.

"Slaves Without a Staple" and the Rise of the Cattle Industry

Carolina might have been a slave society, but it was a slave society with a critical difference from other slave regions of colonial America. The Chesapeake and West Indian planters didn't undergo a transition to slavery until well after they had established a dominant staple crop. Carolinians, however, had the opposite experience. To have a plantation society, of course, required having a staple crop, something that the Barbadian migrants had every intention of acquiring. Nevertheless, when the Barbadian settlers arrived in Carolina, no one knew exactly what that crop would be. Cautiously optimistic that sugar might do well in such a swampy coastal clime, they purchased slaves in Barbados and brought them to Carolina. Quickly, however, settlers learned that the region's ubiquitous low coastal swampland, packed deeply with wet sand, was perhaps the one place in the world where sugar wouldn't grow. Thus despite a "speedy peopling of the place," about one-third of which "peopling" was done by African and Barbadian slaves, no crop for the underemployed slaves to work emerged. There was nothing yet available for the bound labor to transform into regional wealth, power, and prestige for their masters. One proprietor remarked that things were "very hard with us" because "wee cannot employ our servants [slaves] as we would." The need for a staple crop preoccupied the minds of many a planter for obvious reasons, but as they searched for a solution to the staple dilemma, these planters also suffered the added burden of finding a way to keep the colony economically viable. Not to mention their slaves productively engaged. In no time, the absence of a staple became a colonywide concern.

Fortunately for the once-and-future planters, they found a primed market in the region they had just left. Barbados continued to pursue sugar production so comprehensively that its need for food and fuel remained at a premium. This hungry export market just off the coast helped alleviate Carolina's uncertainty about not having a staple crop to exploit. Finding an export trade, though, was only half the battle. While the security of a guaranteed market certainly pushed the Carolina settlers to undertake productive endeavors, it paled next to the more pressing demand that settlers find a way to feed themselves. Throughout the 1670s, the colony's proprietors forestalled the food problem by systematically importing food from England. Without healthy settlers, after all, the English investors had no colony. This subsidy, however, was a temporary measure, and one with which the financial backers quickly grew impatient. Those who migrated from England, in fact, were soon advised to bring with them at least eight months' worth of food. A newcomer in the 1680s recalled how it became the colony's "whole business . . . to clear a little ground to get Bread for their families." Daily rations from the government soon shrank to a measly pint of peas per person. The governor, in a moment of desperation, had to admit that "wee have but 7 weekes provision left . . . the country affording us nothing." A visitor to the colony reported that settlers lacked the essentials: "cattle, company, and good liquor." As much as 10 percent of the colony was soon on the verge of starvation.

Potential starvation was a situation that the New Englanders and Chesapeake Bay settlers would have understood quite well, and the solution was clear to anyone with mouths to feed. A concerted effort to produce food locally had to be undertaken. Such a supply would feed not only Barbadians, but also the locals, especially the newcomers who were arriving without the suggested eight months' worth of food. With the proprietors finally putting their collective foot down in the mid-1680s, there was no other option left. Carolina, like every other settlement, would have to figure out a way to feed itself.

America's culinary history is full of ironic twists, and this is a fine example: the proprietors turned to their slaves. The colony's very basic need to provide its own food pulled underemployed slaves into the guts of the region's incipient system of food production. Slaves might not yet have had a staple crop to grow, but masters found ways to otherwise employ them in the production of food for local provisioning and, after that, Barbadian exportation. Cattle, it turns out, was the best way to kill two birds with one stone. Carolinians had been forced to import barreled beef from England and live cattle from Virginia in a vain attempt to fulfill their substantial meat demands. The reality of that trade, however, was that it was prohibitively expensive, leaving most settlers to do without. Initially, the colony's proprietors naturally encouraged the virtues of self-sufficiency, goading settlers to follow the New England model of raising cattle and adhering to the traditional rounds of pasturing, milking, and slaughtering. The problem with this sage advice, though, was partly cultural: the Carolina settlers, in essence, nurtured much grander visions. They had come to Carolina to become big-shot planters, not yeoman farmers like their more sober New England counterparts. "Our design," said one settler, was "to have planters there and not Graziers." Moreover, and perhaps most important, with so many white settlers having sown their agricultural oats in the harsh fields of Barbados, they knew very little about grazing cattle on large expanses of land and even less about keeping cattle in stalls, as was done in England and New England. Their model of success, in short, was the sugar-plantation owner, the agricultural superstar, not the lowly New England farmer. They didn't want to spend their days keeping track of a bunch of cows. They wanted the sweet benefits offered by a staple.

Not so the Barbadian slaves. These men and women hailed from cattle-grazing regions throughout West Africa. They fully understood the challenges of grazing cattle in large pastures. Africans from the Gambia River region, in fact, had done so for centuries, becoming not only superb grazers but also fine horsemen with exceptional herding skills. The solution was obvious. Within a decade, Carolinians were importing Gambian men for the express purpose of raising cattle. By the late 1680s, plantation investors were regularly relying on slaves to nurture and raise large herds of cattle for local consumption and export. European visitors remarked on the cleanliness practiced by slaves working dairy cattle while also complimenting the region's supply of butter and milk. One Virginia widow said of her deceased husband that he "did formerly transport Severall Negroes out of this Colony of Virginia, into Carolina, did there settle them upon a plantation, together wth some Cattle." Slaves kept track of cattle on large expanses of land while riding horseback late into the night and corralling the animals into "cowpens" that they had built at periodic intervals throughout sprawling pastures. Bills of sale for land in Carolina frequently included a herd of cattle along with the skilled slave who kept them. One settler sold a fifty-acre plot with a herd of cattle and a "Negro man by name Cato." Another planter sold "134 head of cattle [and] one negro man." And yet another, "a stock of Cattle . . . said to be from Five Hundred to One Thousand Head. . . . Also a man used to a Cow Pen and of good character." William Bartram, a visiting horticulturist, found that his hosts were "superintenting a number of slaves . . . that were milking the cows." Some have gone so far as to surmise that the term "cowboy" may have come from these very men.

Carolina's culinary history thus began with the paradox that the region's cattle supply thrived due to the efforts of slaves. In 1674, a settler remarked that "cattell . . . begins to be plentiful." Thomas Newe, another planter, noted eight years later how "severall in the country have great stocks of cattle and they sell to new comers that they care not for killing." In 1687, an official could report that the "chief subsistence of the first settlers being by hoggs & cattle they sell to the New-Comers." Three years after that remark, the governor wrote, "The New Settlers have now great Advantage over the first Planters, being they can be furnished with stocks of cattle and corn . . . at reasonable rates." In 1682, a planter named Thomas Ashe wrote how "it is rather to be admired than believed; not six or seven years past the Country was almost destitute of Cows, Hogs, and Sheep, now they have many thousand head." Thomas Nairne, a Swiss traveler, explained, "It was [once] reckon'd a great deal to have three or four cows, but now some people have 100 head, but for one man to have 200 is very common." In his guide to Carolina, John Lawson speaks of "a Bermudian, being employ'd here with a boy, to look after a stock of cattle and hogs." Clearly, slaves were working the expansive, free-range pastures with productive results. The colony's masters were, as a result, finally eating beef.

Not only were white Carolinians now eating beef, but no longer could anyone say, as the king did back in 1666, that "Barbados and ye rest of ye Caribee Islands . . . have not food to fill their bellies." Although planters remained impatient to get down to the real business of finding a staple crop and starting "to rayse a plantacon," they were now forced to admit, as the Reverend John Urmston observed, that "the planter here is but slave to raise a provision for other colonies." His comment is perhaps overstated. Even so, the reality on the ground in Carolina was that the region was almost single-handedly provisioning the fresh meat supply of the West Indies. As it did so, those fabled "slaves without a staple"—the real slaves—were playing a founding role in shaping the region's foodways. The white planters, for their part, were at least enjoying ample supplies of fresh beef as they continued to search for a way to become inheritors of the Barbadian tradition of getting rich by working very little.

Not everyone was comfortable with the arrangement. The single-mindedness with which white settlers pursued their mission irked men such as Gideon Johnson. Johnson, a missionary to the region, minced no words when he said that "the [white] people here are the vilest race of men upon the earth, they have neither honour, nor honesty, nor religion to entitle them to any tolerable character." Damn these men, he and his ilk reasoned, for not working their own farms. But in the end, the charge never stuck. These incipient plantation kings continued to be just that as long as they lived in an environment where, as Nairne observed, "no body is obliged to beg or want for food." And for this fortunate development, they might have, but never did, thank their slaves.

Native American Trade and Foodways

The demand for beef thus kept the slaves engaged while their masters searched for a remunerative crop on a par with sugar, but meat wasn't the only commodity required for sustenance and export. Nor were slaves the only group to have a founding influence on the region's foodways. Northern colonies, and many Europeans, demanded deerskins and furs to produce textiles. Carolina abounded in both, and, desperate as settlers were to find a commodity, they jumped into these trades as a way to make ends meet during this difficult and uncertain transitional period. Thomas Nairne, for example, listed scores of goods that Carolina was soon able to purchase from England in exchange for deerskins and furs sold by settlers to England. His list included cloth, "nailes of all sizes," gloves, pewter dishes, grindstones, drinking glasses, brass and copper ware, quilts, hats, pins, and needles, among many other small manufactures. In essence, the material goods that Carolinians couldn't produce on their own (but desperately needed in order to survive) were initially acquired through the rich offerings of the forest's bounty. It was a bounty, though, that Carolina whites—lacking basic farming skills, woefully unfamiliar with a strange environment, and, again, seriously intent on becoming plantation farmers—were ill prepared to reap.

The Catawba Nation, however, composed as it was of scattered Piedmont tribes, knew the land intimately. The Native Americans had ample experience catching the elusive animals that could keep the white settlers' trading plans alive. And sure enough, between 1699 and 1714, Carolina exported to England no fewer than an average of fifty-four thousand buckskins a year. Nairne observed how "one hunting Indian has yearly kill'd and brought to his plantation more than a 100, sometimes 200 head of deer." In exchange for these skins and some furs, the English gave the Piedmont hunters, according to English observer John Lawson, "Guns and Ammunition, besides a great many other Necessaries." Trade ebbed and flowed as settlers found their geographical bearings, but it eventually became systematic enough for the colonial government to pass laws approving treaties designed to regulate Anglo–Native American exchange. "There must be," the Carolina legislation explained, "some convenient time given ye Traders to gett in their debts without oppression to the natives." The colony's governing body also asked that "a Judicious man be sent Among the Indjans to inspect into the Regularities of the Traders." An alliance with the Westo tribe in 1674 offered, according to one historian, "the first opportunity for an important source of skins." It was reflective of the kind of trade, he continued, that "for the first 20 years . . . was the [region's] most significant commerce." Through these developments, Native Americans and the Anglo settlers became increasingly bound by tight cords of reciprocation.

The Native Americans weren't naïve about matters commercial. A long tradition of trade, in fact, informed the economic arrangements they forged with the English. Southeastern Native Americans had been swapping goods with one another for centuries. Indian tribes received from their inland neighbors oak and hickory products, flint, turkey and grouse feathers, animal skins, and medicinal roots in exchange for dried fish, salt, deerskins, shells, and medicinal plants gathered from the coastal swamps. When the English showed up on Roanoke Island in the 1580s, the Native Americans there viewed them as yet another tribe with whom to do business. Without much ado, they forged something of a common ground in the universal language of trade, exchanging deerskins for copper goods, hatchets, knives, and other metal goods that the Native Americans had started to acquire from the Spanish twenty-five years earlier. The English, for their part, were often mystified by the Natives' application of such goods, as was Arthur Barlowe when a Native American chief took a "bright tinne dishe" and "clapt it before his breast, & after[ward] made a hole in the brimme thereof, & hung it about his necke." Ultimately, however, it mattered little to the Europeans if Natives bore holes in dishes or hung them as pendants around their necks as long as they proved willing to acquire skins in exchange for "trafficke for trifles"—like wampum. Barlowe, for example, got down to business immediately, recalling how "a day or two after [arriving], we fell to trading with them, exchanging something we had for Chammoys, Buffe, and Deere skinnes." Upon these initial trades followed "a great store of people, bringing with them leather, corrall, divers kinds of dies very excellent, and exchanged with us." When the English showed an interest in fur, the basis for a viable trade already was in place.

It's probably not giving away any surprises to say that the rise of trade between Native Americans and Carolinians was a prelude to its demise. As was true throughout British America, the English nurtured commercial bonds with Native Americans only as long as it was economically advantageous for them to do so. Nevertheless, much more so than in the Chesapeake or New England, the persistence and intensity of the trade that transpired between whites and Native Americans heightened the influence that Native Americans had on the foodways of the Carolina region.

The Piedmont people, after all, had much to teach. They followed impressively calculated cycles of growing, hunting, and gathering that had defined their culture for centuries. In the most general respects, these established methods were not altogether unlike those of their Algonquin neighbors to the north, but there were important differences. As with all

Native Americans cooking in earthen pots

The relatively "wild" nature of the Carolina economy before the discovery of rice brought English settlers into regular contact with Native Americans, introducing the English to new foods and new ways of preparing them. Carolinians seem to have been especially receptive to these changes in their diet.

Native American cultures, food was taken wherever it was found and in whatever quantity happened to be available. The Native Americans were adept at predicting and marking patterns of availability. They reinforced the coherence of nature's rhythms through designations like "herring month" for March, "turkey-cocks gobble" for April and May, "strawberry month" for June, or just *gogi* (the warm season) and *gola* (the cold season). Southeastern Native Americans built base camps along timber-rich riverbanks from which they journeyed into the surrounding territory to undertake elaborate foraging and hunting expeditions. William Bartram remarked on how the Natives located their villages in places where it was "convenient for procuring game" and where "a large district of arable land" adjoined. If such a plot of land wasn't readily forthcoming, the Native Americans would "find a convenient fertile spot at some distance from their town" to which they traveled to check on crops when they weren't hunting, gathering, processing, and cooking.

Archaeological investigations confirm contemporary observations. Maize contributed to at least half the calories consumed by the Piedmont people and their ancestors. Fish satisfied at least a quarter of their protein requirements, keeping most Native Americans in the region "well nourished and reasonably healthy." Native Americans diversified their diet with wild game, especially beaver and turkey, as well as venison for the village's elite members. They foraged for acorns and hickory nuts, from which they processed nut oil and nut flour. "Little barley," sunflower seeds, hazelnuts, chestnuts, walnuts, and pecans were popular, as were squash, may grass, plums, cherries, blueberries, blackberries, and grapes. Compared with the Eastern Woodland Indians in New England, the Piedmont Natives were more sedentary in their habits and thus knew the landscape that much more intimately. As James H. Merrell writes, "Living in one place year after year endowed a people with intimate knowledge of the area. The richest soils, the best hunting grounds, the choicest sites for gathering nuts or berries—none could be learned without years of experience, tested by time and passed down from one generation to the next." And so it was with the Piedmont, a people who had become accustomed to interacting with a variety of other tribes and, as such, were hardly opposed to sharing their ways with this new arrival, even if he was—with his white and hairy skin—one of the strangest foreigners they had ever encountered.

The white man in Carolina was similarly open to ideas. He was no New England prude intent on becoming a self-sufficient farmer in the rigid mold of the homeland. To the contrary, the Carolina settler lived on the edge, and the edge was no place for a conservative yeoman intent on practicing a balanced system of mixed farming. The Carolina migrant was a preindustrial wildcatter awaiting his chance to strike it rich with a staple crop. His counterparts had done it in the Chesapeake with tobacco and slaves, and in the West Indies with sugar and slaves. The Carolinian had the slaves, but, by the 1690s, almost thirty years after the colony's inception, he still lacked the staple. Until he found it, until he could have more control over his own material circumstances, he had no choice but to make do with deerskins, beef, timber, and a few other local commodities that would sustain tight relationships with Native Americans and slaves. Unprecedented as these relationships might have been for all parties involved, they exposed English settlers to Native American foodways frequently enough for them to admit what New Englanders never could: Native American crop choices and hunting habits made tremendous sense.

John Lawson's Exposure to Native Foodways

Perhaps no single contemporary account better captures the intimacy with which the Carolina settlers interacted with Native Americans and their foodways than John Lawson's gripping tale of trade and travel throughout Carolina. Lawson, an English visitor to Carolina in the early eighteenth century, published a fascinating account of that colony called *A New Voyage to Carolina*. Notable for a number of reasons, his book spoke sharply, intelligently, and often quite humorously about Native American foodways, thereby providing unprecedented insight into the cooking and eating practices that the English encountered and, in many cases, eventually accommodated.

Setting out from Charles Town on December 28, 1700, with "six Englishmen, three Indian-men, and one Woman, wife to our Indian guide," Lawson hoped to learn the rudiments of backcountry exchange, as well as a thing or two about the local environment and culture. After a day of journeying, with appetites raging, things got off to an inauspicious start: "We sent out Indians to hunt, who brought us two deers, which were very poor, and their Maws full of large Grubs." In the morning, the food hadn't improved, at least from the English perspective, a perspective within which mangy deer killed while digesting their food wasn't readily accommodated. "At our return to our Quarters," he wrote, "the Indians had killed two more Deer, two wild Hogs, and three Racoons, all very lean, except the Racoons." Later that afternoon, though, the options finally became more palatable as the Englishmen discovered that "these parts being very well-furnished with

Native Americans smoking a variety of fish and game

Native Americans relied heavily on fish and wild game in their diet. Their methods of catching and cooking it were not lost on English observers, who adopted many of their techniques.

---

shell fish, Turtle of several Sorts . . . with other Sorts of Salt-water Fish." As they rowed sixteen miles down the Santee River, Lawson marveled over "the Oyster-banks, which are innumerable in the Creeks and Bays." He was especially impressed with "some Sewee Indians firing the Canes Swamps, which drives out the Game," allowing the hunters to "kill great Quantities of both Bear, Deer, Turkies, and what wild creatures the parts afford." Indeed, in time, he started to become downright upbeat about the culinary possibilities.

After a grueling eighty-four-mile hike up the coast and into the woody interior, the party came to a trading post, described by Lawson as "an Indian hut," where they sat to eat. "We were entertain'd," he enthusiastically wrote, "with a fat boiled Goose, Venison, Racoon, and ground Nuts." After dinner they continued their journey, affording Lawson a view of the broad and low savannas from which these foods came. "They were plentifully stored," he explained, "with Cranes, Geese, and the adjacent Woods with great Flocks of Turkies." The English party traded easily with the Native

Americans they encountered. Meetings were generally free from tension and, with a couple of notable exceptions, mutually beneficial. "This day we traveled about 30 Miles," Lawson explained, "and lay at Night at a House that was built for Indian Trade. . . . Such Houses are common in these Parts, especially where is Indian Towns, and Plantations near at hand."

That night they reached "Scipio's Hutt," but found it empty. Nevertheless, "the Indians allowing it practicable to the English Traders to take out of their Houses what they need in their absence," they took "a great Store of Indian peas, Beans, Oyl, Thinkapin nuts, Corn, barbacu'd Peaches, and Peach-Bread; which Peaches made into a Quiddony, and made up into Loves like Barley-Cakes." Everyone seemed more than pleased with the stash until, "being very intent on our cookery," they managed "to set the dwelling on fire." It was only "with much ado" that they "put it out, tho with the Loss of a Part of the Roof." As to how the returning Native American reacted to the mishap, Lawson is uncharacteristically silent.

After several more days of travel, during which the Native Americans foraged and hunted wild game, the party took a break. It's unclear from Lawson's description where they rested, but it seems that the men made their way back to the coast, because Lawson mentioned that they "had a very large swamp to pass over" near the house where they sojourned. It was here that Lawson discovered "the tallest Indian I ever saw, being seven foot high" and known "for his great Art in Hunting." Elaborating, Lawson described a technique that many Indians used to shoot deer. Like a mascot for a football team, the hunter placed on his head "the Head of a Buck, the back part of the Horns being scrapt and hollow, for Lightness of carriage." Other deceptive touches included deerskin "left to the settling on of the shoulders" and the disguise of fake eyes, which "are made to look as if living." And then "the hunter puts on a Match-coat made of Deer's Skin, with the Hair on, and a Piece of the white Part of a Deer's Skin that grows on the Breast, which is fastened to the Neck-End of this stalking Head, so hangs down." As a result of these "habiliments," Lawson continued, "an Indian will go as near a Deer as he pleases." Native Americans perfected this disguise to the point that one disguised hunter occasionally shot another. When they managed to avoid that mishap, however, they could be assured of ample rewards. "He that is a good Hunter," Lawson couldn't help but notice, "never misses of being a favourite among the women."

For many more weeks, Lawson traveled, traded, and ate with Carolina's Native Americans. Eventually, he and his group once again came across another empty Native American trade house, this one overrun with vermin, and proceeded to help themselves to "Indian Maiz and peas, which are of a reddish colour, and eat well." The party's dependence on Native Americans for their food never diminished throughout the trip. After meeting up with the "Congree Indians," to whom they were led by "Santee Jack, a good Hunter," the party had "a good supper with the scraps of the Venison we had given us by the Indians, having kill'd 3 Teal and a Possum; which Medly all together made a curious Ragoo." The next afternoon, as the men admired a ridge of mountains etched into the horizon, "our Indian going about half and Hour before us, had provided three fat Turkeys e'er we got up to him." This wasn't a bad catch, although, as Lawson explained, "near the Sea-board, the Indian kill 15 Turkeys a Day; there coming out of the Swamp (about Sun-Rising) Flocks of these Fowl, containing several hundred in a Gang, who feed upon the Acorns."

After the visit with the Congrees, as the men traveled between local villages, Lawson's guide continued to demonstrate his hunting prowess, killing "more Turkeys and two Polcats, which he eat, esteeming them before fat Turkeys." They reached the next village after several days of foraging. Given the feasts they enjoyed, it's no surprise that Lawson could attest that "we were never wanting of a good appetite." In addition to "a heap of Indian grain," the party found "good store of Chinkapin Nuts . . . Likewise Hickerie Nuts, which they beat betwixt two great Stones, then sift them, so thicken their Venison-Broath therewith." When both these nuts were "made into a meal," they provided the basis for "a curious Soop, either with clear Water, or in any Meat-Broth." Lawson especially enjoyed a meal of loblolly "made with Indian Corn, and dry'd Peaches." Later, he noted how the Indians, after laying out their collection of deerskins and furs, "immediately" enticed them with "stewed peaches and green Corn, that is preserved in their Cabins before it is ripe, and sodden and boil'd when they use it, which is a pretty sort of Food," not to mention "a great increaser of the Blood."

Once this trade meeting ended, the party again moved on, subsisting for several days due to "a pleasant River, not very large, but, as the Indians told us, well-stored with fish." When they reached the next village, the men were ushered to "the State House, wither we were invited by the Grandees." "As soon as we came to it," Lawson explained, "they placed our Englishmen near the King, it being my fortune to sit next to him." The house, as Lawson described it, "is as dark as a Dungeon, and as hot as one of those Dutch-Stoves in Holland." As the men sat down to the feast, dutifully prepared by "a Woman employ'd in no other business than Cookery," they "brought in great force of Loblolly, and other medleys, made of Indian Grain, stewed Peaches, Bear-Venison, everyone bringing some Offering to enlarge the banquet." Traveling the next day, the men discovered a Sapona Indian who came from a town that had "more than 100 Gallons of pigeon Oil, or Fat; they using it with Pulse, or Bread, as we do Butter." Lawson, with great fascination, observed how the Native Americans caught so many pigeons, describing how they "take a light and go upon them in the Night, and bring away some thousands, killing them with long Poles, as they roost in the Trees." The next morning, Lawson wrote, "we got out breakfasts; roasted acorns being one of the dishes." In a meal that, by this point, had become somewhat of a staple, Lawson appreciated how they "beat them into Meal, and thicken their Venison-Broth with them; and oftentimes make a palatable soop."

Throughout his account, Lawson was reluctant to express any sense of English superiority over the Native Americans with whom he traded and lived. Granted, he made the occasional ethnocentric remark, as he did when he chided his guides for using lead ore "to paint their Faces withal" and remaining "wholly ignorant" about a land so obviously "design'd by Nature for the Production of Minerals." Or when he contemplated a valley of timber and concluded that "were it cultivated we might hoped of a pleasant and fertile a valley as any our English in America can afford." But for the most part, he stood in respectful admiration of the manner in which the Native Americans strategically organized the land around their dietary needs, even if he failed to see the connection between the logic of that organization and the food he ate.

But as the journey came to an end, Lawson couldn't help but indulge in a moment of sanctimonious superiority. Lavished throughout his trip with native offerings, he delivered a speech to a group of traders, a meal spread before them, in which, as he explained, "I concluded, with telling them, that we receive nothing here below, as Food, Raiment, etc., but what came from that Omnipotent Being." Indeed, he told them, it was "God Almighty" who "rewarded him with all the delightful pleasures imaginable." The traders, he explained, "listened to my discourse with a profound silence" before they ate. As they took in this speech, however, one can't help but wonder if, during that long pause, the Native Americans considered putting Lawson's theological assertion to the test. For the very next day, as a parting gesture, they prepared a special feast, "a dish in great fashion among the Indians." The dish was the most unusual yet: "Two young Fawns taken out of the Doe's Bellies, and boil'd in the same slimy Bags Nature had plac'd them in, and one of the Country Hares, stewed with the guts in her Belly, and her Skin with the Hair on." It was the only meal that Lawson could not have possibly attributed to the Almighty, leading him to evoke another virtue altogether. As he explained to his journal: "This new-fashioned Cookery wrought abstinence in our Fellow-Travelers."

Carolina's Recognition of and Adaptation to the Native American Environment

The gut stew notwithstanding, the ongoing trade relationships between the whites and the Native Americans, a relationship vividly suggested by John Lawson's great adventure, predisposed the English settlers to accept and adjust to the region's comparatively uncultivated state without much of a fuss. Indeed, with minimal reluctance, the English integrated themselves into the region's wilderness and, as far as contemporary accounts go, appreciated the food they could wring from it, no matter how it was wrought or how unusual it was. More overtly than settlers in any other region in British America, Carolina denizens—with respect to food—went native.

We can perhaps best glimpse the transferal of food habits through fish. The Carolina Native Americans relied heavily on shad, herring, and salmon for their daily sustenance. Lawson admired how "the herrings in March and April run a great way up the rivers and fresh streams to spawn," adding that "the savages make great Wares, with hedges that hinder their passages only in the middle, where an artificial pound is made to take them in, so that they cannot return." An Englishman named John Brickell observed how "the civilized Indians" were "making Weares to catch fish . . . after a method peculiar to the Indians only." William Bartram explained how "one of our Indian young men, this evening, caught a very large salmon trout, weighing about fifteen pounds." He was especially admiring of the way in which the trout was caught: "The Indian struck the fish, with a reed harpoon, pointed very sharp, barbed, and hardened by the fire." After he impaled it on the reed, the fish "darted off with it, whilst the Indian pursued, without extracting the harpoon, and with repeated thrusts drowned it, and then dragged it to shore."

So there was nothing domesticated or civilized about it. Nevertheless, these fish, and the methods used to catch them, became "a necessary of life" for Englishmen, too, especially as they continued to stubbornly resist the work of yeoman farming and doggedly hope for a staple. "For a small

Native Americans preparing a feast

Carolina traders often found themselves in the position of having to eat foods entirely foreign to their palate. The nature of economic life in early Carolina, however, required settlers to have a relatively open mind about the foods that they were willing to eat.

---

consideration," Brickell explained, the Native Americans agreed to teach a group of Englishmen how they built their weir. The English, for their part, listened carefully and then ran with it. "By the middle of the eighteenth century," one historian writes, "migratory fish were recognized as an important source of food for white families who had established themselves . . . in the Carolinas." A memorial from 1771 referred to "many poor familys who Depended on said fishing for a great part of their living, it being well known that No River of its size in the provence afforded greater Quantity of Excellent Shad and other fish." James Glen, an obsessive list keeper, catalogued the following fish as central to the emerging Carolinian diet: "mullet, witing, black-fish, rock-fish, sturgeon, porgys, trout, bream, and many other sorts of flat fish, likewise oysters, crabs, shrimps, and sometimes turtle." Bartram, too, kept an impressive list of his own. "The great devouring trout and catfish are in abundance," he promised, as were "the golden bream or sunfish, the red bellied bream, the silver or white bream, the great yellow and great black or blue bream." In turning to the region's rich supply of fish as a basic dietary staple, the English were abandoning traditional English practices for an adopted Native American one and, in the process, setting the region's culinary development on a course that it would never completely abandon.

The English were equally eager to adjust to Native American methods of growing and preparing Indian corn. Glen, in the 1740s, may have considered himself a proper Englishmen, but he spoke with evident pride and authority about the intricacies of growing Indian corn. Noting that it "delights in high loose land," Glen went on to explain that "it does not agree with clay, and is killed by much Wet." For those hoping to try their hand at planting Indian corn, he demonstrated a competent knowledge by advising that "it is generally planted in ridges made by the plow or hoe, and in holes about six or eight feet from each other." Imposing a distinctly English opinion on this native crop, he said, "It requires to be kept free from weeds." A primitive approach, however, was often unavoidable and not to be eschewed. Noting that "there are no Wind-Mills in this Province . . . and not above two or three Water-Mills," Bickell explained that "the common method that the Planters use to grind their Corn is with Hand-Mills, which almost every one of them has." The English in Carolina were similarly quick to follow the Native Americans' lead and practice their slash-and-burn agricultural practices rather than fence off land, plow it, and plant in neat rows like New Englanders.

Indeed, like the Native Americans, many English settlers initially worried little about the backbreaking work of clearing forests to plant corn. George Milligen-Johnston wrote that "the Indian corn, or maize, is of most general use." William De Brahm suggested how whites slipped into the grooves left in the landscape in order to grow Indian corn. He explained, "Although most new fields remain for a long time lumbered with the bodies of Trees for one or two years, this does not however hinder the Planters from cultivating clear spots; mean while, the Places thus covered with the Bodies of Trees, improve in Goodness of Soil." Glen alluded to this tendency when he mentioned that "there are dispersed up and down the Country several large Indian old fields, which are lands that have been cleared by the Indians, and now remain just as they left them." Of course, there were many times when modest amounts of land absolutely had to be cleared. But here, once again, the whites avoided such an onerous task and set their slaves to do it. As with cattle, moreover, the slaves may have had experience in this line of work from their lives in West Africa, where they traditionally set fields afire to clear them. De Brahm described how "at Sun-set all the Slaves leave their fields and retire to their Cottages to rest an hour; then all hands are turned out to lopping and fireing, which they continue until 9 o'clock at night." Either way, Indian corn became central to the diet in Carolina, and it did so with absolutely none of the cultural baggage that hung around New England's neck like the proverbial albatross.

The enduring impression that Native Americans left on the English settlers in Carolina is further evident in the English reliance on wild game. Lawson spoke approvingly about the virtues of catching food in the wild, a sentiment that also never would have passed muster on a New England farm, or back in England, where proper food ultimately came from domesticated sources. But hunting, as he perhaps overstated it, was not only a boon in the effort to achieve subsistence but also an honest means toward social betterment. Noting that Carolina was "a place affording many strange Revolutions in the Age of a Man" and a place where those of "despicable Beginnings" might arise to "very splendid Conditions," he explained that "a Quest for game" was central to that advancement. It was, after all, a quest that was "as freely and peremptorily enjoy'd by the meanest Planter, as that is in the highest dignity, or wealthiest in the Province." No matter how poor one was, as long as he was also "master of his gun," he would enjoy "as good a claim to have continu'd Coarses of Delicacies crowded upon his Table, as that is master of a greater purse."

And so, driven by a desire for satiation and status, Carolinians fired away. Milligen-Johnston observed how "in the Woods and Fields, are Plenty of wild Turkeys of a large Size, Geese, Ducks, Doves, Pigeons, Partridges, Hares, Rabbits, Raccoons, Possums & likewise a beautiful species of Deer." Thomas Nairne marveled at the "great Variety of wild Fowl, as Turkeys, Geese, Ducks, wild Pigeons, Partridges, Brants, Sheldrakes, Teal." Glen noted that "the wild Beasts which the Woods of South Carolina afford for Profit . . . are, Rabbets, Foxes, Raccoons, Possums, Squirrels, wild Cats, Deer, Elks, Buffaloes, Bears, Tygers, wild Kine, and wild Hogs." Luigi Castiglioni, an Italian visitor to Carolina in the 1770s, found it curious that "the master of the house where I was staying had spent the whole morning deer hunting." Bartram, who had traveled sixty years earlier, could have related. While "in the company of the overseer of the farm," he found himself "piloted . . . through a large and difficult swamp; he in chase of a deer, and I towards Darian [his travel partner]." Of course, this wilderness, and the often frenetic efforts to take game from it, wouldn't have been news to the

Native Americans, who had relied on it as a source of food for centuries. But for the English, who traditionally conceptualized hunting as a sport, it was indeed a novel and often bemusing fact of material life. As well as one that they eagerly adopted.

Carolina settlers were also especially quick to accept the hunting techniques of their Native American guides. Throughout the summer, they followed the indigenous example of driving deer into remote areas with fire. "From the animal's incapacity to exert speed under such circumstances," wrote William Eddis, "great multitudes of them were annually slaughtered and their carcasses left in the woods." When Europeans wanted to hunt at night, Native American methods also served the purpose well. Much like hunters today will "shine" a deer with a bright light, colonial hunters made torches from pine limbs, paralyzed the deer with the blazing light, and felled them as they stood in a daze. Night hunting had its advantages, but on too may occasions hunters would accidentally blow away a cow, thereby exposing the danger of both hunting at night and allowing cattle to roam free. Their method of catching pigeons similarly adhered to Native American practice. Bartram recounted how a group of servants "came home with horse loads of wild pigeons, which it seems they collected in a short space of time at a neighboring Bay swamp." The men, he explained, "furnish themselves with poles or staves" with which they "approach the [pigeon] roosts." Wielding the same kind of blazing pine torches used to hunt deer, the hunters scared the birds from their perch, "whereby multitudes drop off the limbs to the ground." The rest "are beaten off with the staves, being by the sudden consternation, entirely helpless, and easily taken and put into the sacks."

The free-range grazing practices that the slaves pioneered with livestock became standard practice in Carolina and, in so doing, served to bolster the region's comparatively uncultivated image. Glen explained how "South Carolina abounds with black Cattle, to a Degree much beyond any other English Colony." This accomplishment, he explained, was "chiefly owing to the mildness of the Winter, whereby the Planters are freed from the Charge and Trouble of providing for their Cattle, suffering them to feed all the Winter in the Woods." Nairne described how "we have likewise Hogs in abundance, which go daily to feed in the Woods, and come Home at night." A Huguenot, Louis Thibou, wrote home to France in 1683 about the Carolina way of life, mentioning that "the cattle feed themselves perfectly well at no cost whatsoever . . . and they give you a calf every year, which is a good profit costing no more to feed a lot then a few; you feed them by the thousands in the woods." One drawback of allowing cattle to roam free in the woods, of course, was that it cut down on the supply of dairy products. Bartram spent an evening "at a cow-pen" and was entertained with "plenty of milk, butter, and a very good cheese of their own make." He seemed particularly pleased with the dairy-based meal, as "it is a novelty in the maritime parts of Georgia and Carolina." In New England and, to a lesser extent, the Chesapeake, the availability of dairy products marked a family's success, but Carolinians remained content to accept this touchstone of English cuisine as a "novelty." Indeed, in most descriptions of food from this region, milk, butter, and cheese are rarely mentioned.

Not only did settlers praise and adapt to Native American and slave habits, but they were similarly quick to recognize the comparative inadequacy of European crops in native soil. In Carolina, Johann Martin Bolzius explained, "they also have lettuce, but here it rots before we can get seeds." He added that "white carrots and radishes grow very well, but our people do not know how to grow yellow carrots, spinach, red beets, and onions." By contrast, "many kinds of vines grow wild and have sweet and sour berries; [t]here are also many blueberries and raspberries, small and large chestnuts, large walnuts, all kinds of acorns, and a kind of medlars, which are very sweet and tasty when good and ripe." Bolzius held out hope that European crops could eventually find a home in Carolina's environment, noting that "European grain . . . is cultivated in Carolina and Georgia and grows . . . rather well." Nevertheless, it was "the native crops such as Indian corn, beans, rice, and potatoes [that] grow best and most plentifully." He explained how, with Native Americans, only four acres "require one bushel of Indian corn and barely ½ bushel of Indian beans" to yield "100 bushels of corn [and] 4 bushels of beans," not to mention the "large number of pumpkins, melons, and cucumbers" that will grow among them.

The contrast to English crops was unmistakable when "one bushel of barley yields about 8 bushels" and "one bushel of wheat . . . or rye, yields about 12 bushels." The "wheat up towards August" might "turn out nearly as good as in Europe," but its "thick hull does not yield really white flour," as in other regions. Plus, "wheat often suffers greatly from mold and rust," unlike Indian corn, and, as Bolzius continued, "I am afraid that the correct time and method of planting has not been properly understood." One also had to avoid the traditional wheat because "threshing of wheat and rye is a very troublesome affair," and, if not done at the right time, "little flies get in and riddle it with holes." How cumbersome it was to contemplate, much less grow, when "for Indian corn, beans, and pumpkins one just makes holes in the earth, 6 feet from one hole to the next, and after that prevents the grasses from growing."

In all these ways—the reliance on wild game and fish, the free-range grazing of cattle, the appreciation of Native American agricultural practices, and the willingness to forage—Carolina settlers in search of a staple gravitated in the direction of Native American and slave practices. To be sure, there were those who found the abandonment of traditional English ways—even under the pressing circumstances of a frontier economy—to be a gross dereliction of cultural duty. The Reverend Charles Woodmason, for example, found as late as the 1770s that many Carolinians were, to his prim horror, "living in a state of Nature, more irregularly and unchastely than the Indians." But most settlers, at least as far as we can judge from their behavior, agreed with the enthusiastic assessment of Bartram, who declared after frantically chasing a deer through a swamp: "Was there ever such a scene of primitive simplicity!" Perhaps there was, but for white Carolinians, for men and women still searching for a staple and deeply engaged in systematic trade with the Native American inhabitants, it stood to reason that they would make a virtue of primitive simplicity.

The Yamasee War

For all its persistence, the connection between Native American trade and culinary influence diminished throughout the eighteenth century. As mentioned, the trade that prevailed so productively between the white settlers and the Native Americans presaged a fall that finally came on April 13, 1715. Earlier in the month, two Carolina traders engaged with the Yamasee Indians reported the dire news that "the Creek Indians had a design to Cut off the Traders first and then to fall on settlements." Thrown into a panic, Governor Charles Craven quickly dispatched a team of diplomats from Charleston to "hear and redress their complaints and grievances." But the move proved too little, too late. A day after the diplomats arrived at Yamasee headquarters, the tribe unleashed an all-out attack on the English colony.

The Yamasees raged against the occupying regime until the middle of June, pushed the Carolina boundary back to the coast, and in the process allied with several neighboring tribes, including the Lower Creeks, who were equally eager to see the English colony reduced to rubble. The English, however, were in no mood to go gently. They mustered their powerful forces and fought back with bloodlust. Exploiting the neutrality of many Upper Creeks and the Cherokees, they lured them into the English fold, beat back the Yamasee uprising, and defused what historians agree was "one of the most significant events in southern colonial history." Indeed, the war did nothing less than end the systematic trade that had transpired between the English and Native Americans for more than forty years, not to mention precipitate the demise of several coastal tribes while forcing others deeper into the interior.

The reasons for the uprising were many. The most obvious cause had to do with the arrogant and aggressive behavior of the English traders. There were, for example, the ongoing practical jokes that the English played on the Native Americans, such as sending messengers on three-hundred-mile trips to deliver letters that contained nothing but insults to the recipients. More troubling, however, was the growing habit of interfering with the Native Americans' agricultural system and food supply. Routinely, the English would allow their cattle to trample Native Americans' cornfields without offering redress for the damages. One settler, for example, witnessed English traders "killing their hoggs[,] fowls and go to their plantations take what they please without leave." The traders would swagger "into their cornfields and gather corn and pease . . . and take them." The Native Americans could deal with these matters through diplomacy, and more often than not, they did. When the traders started to violate their women after violating their fields, however, opportunities for any resolution diminished significantly. One witness "heard [the traders] brag to each other of debauching their [Indian] wives sometime force them once see it myself in the day time." There was also the economic reality that the Native American traders owed debts to the English in the form of hundreds of thousands of skins, a massive number of pelts that merchants needed to sustain their highly profitable exportation to England. The debt was so high, in fact, that the English began to consider the policy of punishing debt with enslavement.

And it was when these considerations came to fruition that the primary reason for the Yamasee War emerged. Beginning in 1701, the Carolinians started to systematically enslave Spanish-allied Native Americans. By 1710, the English had captured around ten thousand Native Americans, selling most of them as slaves to New England and West Indian buyers. The Yamasees, who owed Carolina merchants one hundred thousand skins, were critical to the Native American slave trade. Throughout the first decade of the eighteenth century, they joined the English in their Native American raids, playing a critical role in enslaving thousands of Apalatchees and Choctaws, while ensuring the profitable loyalty of the Carolina traders.

But the profit motive behind that loyalty ended when the deerskin trade diminished for a reason so obvious that nobody saw it coming: there was a shortage of deer. And when the deer supply began to shrink, the Yamasees became, from the English perspective, effectively useless. And when they became useless, they fell prey to the traditional, aggressive Carolinian tactics, tactics that left them little choice but rebellion. A combination of overhunting, the loss of forest shade (as trees were felled), and competition with foraging hogs and cattle for "nuts, grasses, and roots" reduced the number of deer significantly enough for the English to start seizing and enslaving the wives of Yamasee traders in order to cover their debts. In April 1715, when the tinderbox of tension exploded, the Yamasees looked invincible, killing four hundred Carolinians, burning buildings, driving off livestock, and destroying any crops under cultivation. This strong showing, however, proved temporary. Ammunition eventually dissipated and, with it, the Yamasee culture. And while the influence of Native American foodways on the Carolinians would never completely disappear, it would, with the end of a routinized trade, decline substantially, opening the way for Carolinians to embrace other culinary influences.

A hint of one such influence is perhaps best glimpsed in the strangest bit of evidence regarding the Carolinians' defeat of the Yamasee Indians. The victory against the Native Americans was, as a contemporary noted, accomplished not only with the support of the Cherokee Indians but also with the help of a Carolinian army consisting of "600 whites . . . and 400 Negros." Confirming the slaves' role in the battle, a letter sent from Charlestown in 1715 said that these men had a job "to protect the Settlements till the crops are all got in & then march to fight the enemy where they can find them." By 1715, slaves were obviously doing more than grazing cattle and felling trees, and their owners must have been somewhat reluctant to put them to a military use. Their reluctance, in fact, would have been well understood by the planters who had quietly emerged to dominate the Carolina economy by 1715. These were planters who initially knew very little about what they were doing until their slaves ironically showed them how to grow the crop that made them rich. Agricultural life had changed so dramatically in Carolina that, in sending slaves to battle, planters risked losing the labor source that had the expertise and manpower to help them fulfill their dreams of establishing a plantation society. The risk was so immense because slaves no longer lacked a staple. Indeed, by 1715 they had rice. And with the Native American threat minimized in the interior, that crop could once and for all expand to its fullest and most lucrative potential. Carolina could finally go from being "a colony of a colony" to being a slave society able to hold its own against the economic powerhouses to the north and south. The culinary implications of this development were equally momentous.

Slaves, Rice, and Power

Precisely where and when Carolinians first grew rice in exportable amounts remains lost in the murky historical record. That slaves played a skilled role in systematically growing that crop, however, is undisputable. When English settlers tried to grow rice in the 1680s, their efforts came to naught. One writer explained, "The people being unacquainted with the manner of cultivating rice . . . many difficulties attended the first planting and preparing it." At the same time that the English, in their desperate search for a "vendible commodity," were struggling to grow rice, however, West Africans were managing a bountiful rice industry. Growing this delicate grain was nothing new for them. African farmers had been cultivating rice since 1500 b.c. and had developed an expertise in producing both African and Asian varieties. It didn't take long for Carolina planters to draw on their expertise.

Methods varied, but one technique that West Africans practiced with particular success bode especially well for Carolina's coastal planters. An English slave ship captain described the method as perfectly crafted for the "flat low swamps" that dominated the Lowcountry. He then elaborated that "they have a reservoir that they can let in what water they please, [on the] other side is a drain out so they can let off what they please. . . . When the rice is ready for cultivating they turn the water off till their Harvest is over then they let the water cover it and let it stand three or four seasons." The West African influence on Carolina rice cultivation was thus, according to an authority on the subject, "a decisive one." The connection was hardly lost on the Carolinians, who acted quickly. One planter wrote that he "directed the Agents in Africa to send a few, full grown Men . . . as have been used to the trades of that country, believing they will soon become useful and handy in a new plantation." He could never have known how right he was.

In becoming "useful and handy," slaves in Carolina never missed the chance to exploit their knowledge to soften the repeated blows of slavery's iron fist. Carolina slaves, as we have seen, enjoyed a relatively rare opportunity to travel extensively beyond the vigilant reach of overseers and masters. Their work in the cattle and timber industries afforded them a chance to roam the countryside at will, form relationships with slaves from other plantations, preserve their cultural heritage, and practice inherited skills instead of the numbing monotony of field labor. Alone, or in small groups, they also capitalized on their relative mobility to establish connections with Native Americans. As with whites, slaves seemed eager to learn from the original inhabitants. "The common idea," reported *American Husbandry*, "is, that one Indian, or dextrous negroe, will, with his gun and netts, get as much game and fish as five families can eat." The slaves' familiarity with the idiosyncrasies of the landscape, honed in large part through their familiarity with the Native Americans, elevated many of them to the status of commercial guide. John Lawson explained how a doctor "sent his Negro to guide us over the head of a large swamp." A visiting missionary mentioned that "as soon as I arrived in the Parish several Parishioners persuaded me to buy Negroes ... for it would be impossible for me to go through the Parish between the woods without a guide." Guiding was a position that slaves achieved nowhere else in British America. It's a telling testimony to Carolina's comparative openness.

In movement and environmental knowledge there was power, and as slaves harnessed it, they had no intention of letting it diminish with the onset of massive rice cultivation. Fortunately for the slaves, rice not only was a crop with which they had traditional experience, but was conducive to their expectation of relative "independence." Understanding the paradox of how rice—the very crop that led to Carolina becoming 60 percent slave-based—supported a modest level of slave autonomy requires some insight into its cultivation.

"The only Commodity of Consequence produced in *South Carolina is Rice*," James Glen wrote in 1761, "and they reckon it as much their staple Commodity, as *Sugar* is to *Barbadoes* and *Jamaica*, or *Tobacco* to *Virginia* and *Maryland*." In very general terms, slaves working in South Carolina's agricultural system played a role similar to that of slaves laboring throughout British America. Johann David Schoepf summarized it well when he explained that "rice is raised so as to buy more negroes, and negroes are bought so as to get more rice." The same could have been written just as easily for sugar and tobacco. Upon closer scrutiny, though, there was a critical difference with rice, a difference with profound implications for slaves and the influence of African culture in Carolina. Unlike tobacco and sugar, rice was a durable plant that, once the intricacies of the plantation were aligned, required frequent but simple operations for its upkeep. Simple operations, in turn, meant that masters did not have to hire overseers—an often belligerent and surly lot—to monitor the slaves' progress.

Planters began the rice cycle in January by ordering their slaves into the swamps to remove stumps and trees. By April, slaves were ready to plant, a process that lasted until June. Planting involved more than just sowing seed; it also required leveling the ground to control flooding, repairing irrigation banks, and clearing drains and ditches to keep the water flowing evenly. Heavy, backbreaking work it certainly was, but—and here is the critical point—it was work that needed little supervision. Slaves sowed by making holes in the ground with the heel of their foot, dropping in the seed, and covering it with the ball of their foot. Europeans tried to impose trenching techniques on the slaves, but the "heel-and toe" method prevailed. June to early August was occupied with three rounds of hoeing, the second of which required slaves to clear any weeds growing around the roots of the rice. Again, very hard work, very repetitive—but not especially demanding of managerial oversight. To the extent that there was a break, it came in September, when slaves' main tasks included repairing equipment, laying roads, making barrels, and releasing the dammed-up water to flow into the rice fields. A particularly unfortunate slave might find himself in a field, "up to [his] knees and waist in water, continually hollowing and beating any sounding things" to frighten birds. Harvesting began in late September, when the pace intensified considerably. Slaves gathered the rice stalks into stacks, or "ricks," and piled them in a storage barn. They threshed and winnowed throughout October, enjoying the opportunity to socialize before the rigors of the next two months. Indeed, the final step, which was "the severest work the negroes undergo," was pounding. So grueling was this labor that some planters, according to one observer, "pay dear for their barbarity, by the loss of many."

So the work was cyclical, brutal, boring, and relentless. But, again, the point here cannot be overstated: rice cultivation demanded minimal supervision, especially for a people who had grown it for centuries. Masters were happy to save on the cost of managers. Slaves were happy to have the cost spared. The logic made a certain amount of sense. But there is, of course, a critical missing ingredient in this scenario. Indeed, the rationale behind this arrangement begs an important question: What was the incentive for slaves to work? If the overseer wasn't hounding them with the whip, why toil? Masters, for their part, had considered this question carefully, and the answer they came up with had powerful implications for the course of the lives of the slaves, their chance to pursue inherited cultural norms, and, thus, the nature of Carolina's cuisine.

The answer that masters came up with was called tasking. A "task," according to one planter, was "105 feet long and will save a great deal of time in Laying out the field, and do it with more exactness." Another identified it as a quarter of an acre. The designation became so common that land advertisements often described acreage in terms of the number of tasks it contained. When a plot was divided into tasks and farmed out to teams of slaves, "a field in a day or two will be completely drean'd." As intended by the planter, it was, as one historian notes, "a system of routine which would work with more or less automatic regularity without [the master's] own inspiring or impelling presence." In an advertisement for a "light made, industrious, and well-disposed" slave, the owner noted his penchant "for doing his task soon."

What ultimately made the system work was the built-in incentive for slaves to complete their task as quickly as possible. When a team of slaves completed an assignment, the rest of the day belonged to the slaves to do as they pleased (within, of course, the confines of the slave codes). "His master," explained Daniel Turner, "feels no right to call on him." The preacher George Whitefield wrote how "several of the negroes did their work in less time than usual, that they might come hear me." The planter Joseph Pilmore explained to a friend that his slaves were hanging around the docks because they "had finished their task." Slaves, according to another observer, finished their tasks "by one or two in the afternoon, and have the rest of the day for themselves." John Drayton, discussing the slaves' tasks, remarked on how they "are diligent in performing them, and have the rest of the day for themselves." This organizational scheme became so well established that when a master violated it, he often reaped the scorn of his neighbors. As one Carolina planter put it: "The daily task does not vary to the arbitrary will and caprice of their owners, and although [it] is not fixed by law, it is so well settled by long usage, that upon every plantation it is the *same*. Should any owner increase the work beyond what is customary, he subjects himself to the reproach of his neighbors, and to such discontent amongst his slaves as to make them of little use to him."

Such informal pressure helped solidify the task system as *the* method of organizing slaves in Carolina. In so doing, it simultaneously helped establish the most important precondition for the Carolina slaves' relative culinary autonomy. As we shall see, the most interesting way that slaves used their free time was in the cultivation and preparation of food.

Slave Provision Grounds in Carolina

The cultivation of their own crops by slaves during the free time that the task system afforded them made a strong impression on white observers. Johann Bolzius explained that "they are given as much land as they can handle" and that "they plant for themselves also on Sundays." Hans Trachsler, a German visitor to Carolina, noted the slaves' system of self-provisioning by explaining how "these people are worth a high price because they are much more able to do the work and much cheaper to keep in food and drink than the Europeans." Visiting a Carolina plantation, François-Alexandre-Frédéric, duc de La Rochefoucauld-Liancourt, wrote that slaves "were at liberty to cultivate for themselves as much land as they choose." John Drayton confirmed the prevailing viewpoint when he saw "slaves in their own private fields, consisting of 5 or 6 acres of ground, allowed them by their masters . . . for their own use and profit, of which the industrious among them make a great deal." A missionary to Carolina remarked on how "there are many planters who, to free themselves from the trouble of feeding and clothing their slaves allow them one day in the week to clear ground, and plant for themselves as much as will clothe and subsist them." Much more than in the Chesapeake region, and very much like the situation in the West Indies, slaves in Carolina clearly enjoyed the chance to pioneer their own foodways.

Compared with that in the West Indies, though, the life expectancy of slaves in Carolina was much higher. The opportunity to make lasting cultural decisions was, accordingly, substantially greater. Evidence indeed suggests that slaves worked hard to incorporate West African traditions into the food they cultivated and ate. The emphasis on West African culinary habits may have become especially strong in Carolina because, with masters importing slaves skilled in rice cultivation, the connection to home would not have been diluted by the Barbadian layover, as it was for the initial Carolina slaves. Furthermore, as historian Peter Wood points out, "The West African and Carolinian climates were similar enough so that even when flora and fauna were not literally transplanted, a great deal of knowledge proved transferable." Again, though, we have no choice but to put our ultimate faith in the observations of European witnesses. Should we take them at their word (and there seems no reason not to), these men had much to say. Maurice Matthews mentioned the popular place of Indian corn in the Carolina diet but also noted, "Guiney Corne grows very well here." John Lawson, in an extensive list of Carolina provision crops, mentioned "Guinea Corne, which thrives well here." Explaining that Guinea corn did not grow prolifically, Mark Catesby assured readers that it was "propagated, and that chiefly by negroes, who make bread of it, and boil it in the manner of firmity. . . . It was first introduced from Africa by the negroes." Evidence emerges in other accounts as well. Many address the importation of "guinea fowl" and "guinea melon," and there's even a reference to a "guinea worm" as one of the African pests infesting Carolina corn crops. Luigi Castiglioni mentions the slaves' cultivation of "an annual herb with mallowlike flower . . . brought by the negroes from the coast of Africa and is called okra by them."

Reflecting their extensive backcountry interaction with Native Americans, slaves leavened their West African diet with a number of Native American methods of food acquisition. The Native American tendency to forage, hunt, and fish, as we have seen, influenced the scavenger-like attitude that the entire colony adopted toward food. Slaves weren't exempt from this influence. John Brickell explained how slaves "on Sundays . . . gather Snake-root," while Richard Ludlum described how "two or three slaves will gather as many spontaneous Plants in one day, as will another Day plant Ten acres." Janet Schaw, a visitor to Carolina, noted that "Negroes are the only people that seem to pay any attention to the various uses that the wild vegetables may be put to." Slaves routinely shot and ate opossum, deer, rabbits, and raccoon. A master who lost his slave described him in a runaway advertisement as "very expert in hunting," while another master guessed that his own missing slave "lost himself (while hunting)." William Bartram, as we've seen, witnessed slaves come "home with horse loads of wild pigeons." Archaeological evidence suggests that as much as 90 percent of a Carolina slave's meat came from wild species.

Carolina slaves further supplemented their diet with ample amounts of fish. As in the Caribbean, slaves and Native Americans borrowed from each other liberally when it came to fishing techniques. In Carolina, slaves built dams out of reed hedges to trap "an abundance of fish, which in a friendly manner distribute to one another, being by that means continually supplied." Lawson told a story about "some Negros and others that can swim and dive well, go naked in the Water, with a Knife in their Hand, and fight the Shark, and very commonly kill him." Another Carolina resident watched slaves poison a creek to "catch great quantity of fish." The English imperative to bound the land with fields and fences might have prevailed in the northern colonies, but down in Carolina, where the infrastructure of traditional agriculture was lacking, it paled next to the more urgent demand that settlers and their chattel scavenge for their sustenance. And although slaves would have thought little of it as they hunted, foraged, and fished for their supper, the Native American influence strongly informed such behavior.

But all was not undomesticated for Carolina slaves. The convergence of inherited and adopted methods of obtaining food was especially evident in the plots that slaves cultivated on the master's plantation grounds. These plots, reminiscent of the plots allotted to slaves in the West Indies, integrated the task of cultivating rice with the closely related job of provisioning the plantation—slaves and masters alike—with subsistence foods. This agricultural activity was a source of special fascination for Johann Bolzius, who left a vivid description of its operation. Slaves planted potatoes in March, an activity that "keeps all Negroes busy," requiring them to plant potato pieces in "long dug furrows, or mounds." Once they completed the potato planting, slaves turned to Indian corn. "A good Negro man or woman," he explained, "must plant half an acre" in a day, a task demanding that "holes are made in the earth six feet from one another, and five or six kernels put into each hole." Only when the potatoes and corn crops were planted did the slaves move to the master's most valuable land and begin planting rice. After hoeing "furrows for rice planting," they "sow and cover the rice in the furrows." Then it was immediately back to the provision grounds, where slaves "start to clean the corn of the grass." Confirming that the task system carried over to provisioning, Bolzius added that "a day's work is half an acre, be he man or woman, unless the ground is too full of roots." While the rice sprouted, the slaves, taking a page from the Native Americans, "plant beans together among the corn" while their children weeded grass in "the potato patches." Then back to rice, whereupon "they start for the first time to cultivate [be-hauen], the rice and to clean it of grass." At this stage of the provisioning cycle, the task system really kicked in. "A negro must," Bolzius continued, "complete a ¼ acre daily." By this point, it was about mid-May.

Slaves interspersed the cultivation of rice with a second cleaning of the corn. "A little earth can be put around the stalks like little hills," he wrote, while "some young corn is pulled out and only 3 or 4 stalks remain." And while they were working among the Indian cornstalks, they made sure that "little earth is laid on the roots of the beans, all of which the Negros do at the same time." In the meantime, they also planted pumpkins ("which are also planted among the corn") and white beets ("in good fertilized soil"). Then it was back to rice, which demanded two more cultivations, followed by another cultivation of corn, after which, finally, "the work on rice corn and beans is done."

Food produced by slaves while working their assigned rice tasks kept both masters and slaves well fed. Another category of provisioning, however, followed rhythms distinct from those of the rice tasks. This activity remained solely for the benefit of the slaves and further ensured that they would not require masters to import food for their upkeep. To achieve the goal of relative self-sufficiency, slaves, according to Bolzius, "are given as much land as they can handle." And handle it they did, planting "for themselves" extra corn and potatoes, in addition to peanuts, melons, and bottle pumpkins, which were used for drinking vessels. "A good slave" might plant ten acres of corn and potatoes "if the land is new and good." From September to March, the slaves subsisted on potatoes, "small unusable rice," and Indian corn. In the summer it, was mostly "corn and beans."

Tedious as this diet may have been, slaves seem to have excelled at providing it. George Milligen-Johnston noted how Indian corn was their "chief sustenance." David Ramsay agreed, saying of corn that "the negroes of Carolina give it a decided preference." Another observer remarked that peas were "one of the principle foods of the Negro, who prefers them to rice." Whatever food they preferred, slaves grew enough of it to lead Janet Schaw to mention how well slaves used "their little piece[s] of land." She added that they grew vegetables "much better than their masters." Brickell wrote that slaves "are very industrious and laborious in improving their plantations." Luigi Castiglioni went on extensively about the slaves' cultivation of the sweet potato. "It is tilled," he explained, "by the negroes in April." In addition to corn, rice, beans, and pumpkins, archaeological excavations have unearthed evidence of peach pits, walnuts, and grape seeds. Here, too, the Native American influence seems evident.

For all the abundance of grains, vegetables, and fruit that slaves grew in their "little piece[s] of land," domestic animals were virtually nonexistent. For meat, they depended on their masters, and their masters proved to be less than reliable—if not completely negligent—suppliers. One slave overseer mentioned that slaves "never had any meat except at Christmas." Excavations show almost no proof of domesticated beef or pork. "If a master wishes," Bolzius explained, "he gives them a little meat when he slaughters," but otherwise "their food is nothing but Indian corn, beans, pounded rice, potatoes, pumpkins." Slaves may have pioneered the Carolinian technique of cattle breeding, but they in no way reaped the benefits of a meat-rich diet. André Michaux perhaps summed it up best. Masters, he said, "never give [slaves] meat." One safely assumes that this reluctance extended to other foods, too.

Nonetheless, slaves were willing to sell their masters whatever they might need. "They sell their crops," Bolzius wrote, "and buy some necessary things." Granted, they were already producing under the task system some of the food that masters were eating. The experience of selling surplus produce on the market was rare, but every now and then, when the stars aligned and the crops did especially well, slaves found themselves in a position to bargain. Lawson recalled when a slave approached him while he was traveling on the Carolina coast. "At noon we went on shore," he wrote, "and got dinner near a plantation. . . . We went up to the house, but found none at Home, but a Negro, of whom our Messenger purchas'd small quantity of rice and tobacco." If they weren't growing food for masters, or selling food to masters, they often were cooking for them. "A Negro woman who is useful in the house," Bolzius wrote, "costs 35 to 37 pounds." A male field hand went for £28. The conclusion was probably so obvious that few white Carolinians recognized it, but the fact remained: the reality of their culinary lives was molded by Native Americans and slaves alike.

The Culinary Attitudes of a Carolina Horticulturist

Eliza Lucas Pinckney understood. In her most notable role, Pinckney was a highly intelligent botanist who pioneered the fine and profitable art of growing indigo throughout the South. At the same time, she was a South Carolina woman living among scores of slaves who described her typical day like this: "In general then I rise at five o' Clock in the morning, read till seven, then take a walk in the garden or field, see that the servants are at their respective business, then to breakfast." What she ate unfortunately went unrecorded, but, as was the case with most whites in Carolina, even those of the elite, her diet was forged in a region whose culinary framework was largely cobbled together by Native Americans and slaves. So thorough was the role that these groups played in shaping the Pinckneys' diet that Eliza's culinary duties had been relegated to whimsical experimentations undertaken for both her own curiosity and that of her haughty London peers. Hence she wrote to a "Dear Mrs. B": "O! . . . I have planted a large fig orchard with design to dry and export them." Admitting that she was "far gone in romance" for entertaining such a scheme, she assured herself by recalling that "your Uncle I know has long thought I have a fertile brain at scheming." Although he might indeed have been correct in that opinion, Eliza had to concede, "I own I love the vegitable world extremely." How could she therefore possibly resist such "an innocent and useful amusement"? So off she went to fail miserably at the cultivation of figs.

Pinckney accomplished a lot, but her correspondence shows how elite whites could afford their amusements. This world was one in which slaves were extensively cultivating provisions, a place where whites and slaves had learned a culinary tip or two from the Native Americans, and a region where the white inhabitants had long ago learned the value of adaptation to a new set of culinary conditions. The traditional English culinary order achieved in New England and strived for in the Chesapeake seems to have generally eluded Carolina. The provisions reaped from the Carolina slave plots and the bounty plucked from the wilderness endlessly fascinated Pinckney not only because of its novelty but also because she shared her region's tolerance for that novelty. Unlike William Byrd, the snobbish Virginian who lamented the region's diversion from the foodways of the motherland, Pinckney reveled in Carolina's comparatively uncultivated foodways while enjoying its abundance. If elite denizens such as Pinckney, who actually had a choice, tolerated the region's relative lack of cultivation, we can safely assume that the rest of Carolina's white population shared something of a similar attitude.

"The country abounds with wild fowl, Venison, and fish," she wrote to her brother in May 1742. "The turkies are extremely fine, especially the wild, and indeed all their poultry is exceedingly good; and peaches, and Nectrons and melons of all sorts extremely fine." Her enthusiasm for the local fare pushed her to send samples of it home to her friends and family in England. To her former governess in England, she proved her point that "their pork exceeds any I ever tasted anywhere" by sending her "a kegg of sweetmeats." To another friend, she delivered "some peach trees and our Country potatoes" and some "Negroe pepper." In May 1759, she wrote to a friend back home, "There is no such thing at this time as a wild Turkey to be got alive, I have laid out for some young one[s] and hope to send them still before the summer is out." She did, however, "hope you have received the Summer ducks I sent by the Penguin."

The Big Picture

Eliza Pinckney lived in a region where food had departed dramatically from that of the homeland and where little effort was made to replicate what other regions saw as a lost heritage. When she wrote, "I was very early fond of the vegetable world," she was referring not to the familiarities of England but to the New World crops that most Carolina families relied on their slaves to grow—including pumpkins, gourds, beans, potatoes, and sweet roasting ears of corn. As exemplified by hoppin' John, whites in Carolina avoided a standard recipe and instead allowed for a radical kind of culinary flexibility. Oats yielded to maize and became grits. Porridge became clabber, a meal reflecting the relative scarcity of fresh milk, made as it was with milk of the curdled variety. Beef, while available due to the efforts of slaves, paled next to the more readily abundant pork. Wheat bread gave way to griddle cakes.

Potatoes and rice were popular starches. And so on. It was a place, in short, where a traveler could describe the standard meal as a wooden bowl of milk and mush flavored with bear oil, and nobody would second-guess him.

Needless to say, many English settlers complained, lamenting the loss of "proper" foodways. The minister Charles Woodmason described "all the cooking of these people" as "exceedingly filthy and most execrable." Documenting one journey, he wrote, "I stayed up all Night by the Fire, quite tired and spent, having not made what could be called a meal for some days—Nothing but Indian Corn meal to be had—Bacon and Eggs in some Places—No butter, Rice, or Milk—As for Tea and Coffee they know it not." As an explanation for why the clergy in Carolina were having such a tough go of things, he cited "the different Meats, Drinks, and Methods of Living of what they've been accustomed to in England. All which is diametrically opposite to their usual Methods." How could a true Englishman survive when "these people eat twice a day, only. Their bread, of Indian Corn, Pork in Winter and Bacon in Summer—if any Beef, they jerk it and dry it in the Sun—So that you may as well eat a Deal Board"? One woman visiting Carolina thought that the solution to the region's "civilization problem" might be found in good old hard work. She admonished that "the ground will bear thistles only while your indolence permits it," noting how "the fruits also will be harsh while you allow them to remain in a state of nature." The "hand of industry," she explained, sounding like a New Englander, "improves even the choicest gifts of heaven." Little did she understand that in Carolina, "the hand of industry" was too busy with other matters—like managing accounts for the rice that slaves were growing.

No region accepted this reality as easily and enthusiastically as did Carolina. Unlike the offended visitors, Carolinians knew their culture well, and two aspects of it struck them with particular force. First, as one resident observed, they knew that "the concerns of this Country are so closely connected and interwoven with *Indian* Affairs . . . that I thought it highly necessary to gain all knowledge I could of them." And, second, they understood equally well Samuel Dyssli's comment that "Carolina . . . looks more than a negro country than a country settled by white people." There was, given the powerful pull of profit, no choice but to accept change, however radical. The white settlers and the American offspring they bore were committed to America, ready to adapt, and prepared—like hoppin' John—to base tradition on change, and, in stark contrast to a man such as Woodmason, they had no intention of going home. They had gotten a taste of the Carolina frontier. And, as far as we can tell, they were content.

CHAPTER 5

DIVERSITY

Refined Crudeness in the Middle Colonies

Variety is the soul of pleasure.
Aphra Behn, *The Rover*

THE HEART OF A PIG seems like an odd place to start looking for the heart of a regional cuisine. It's at that precise anatomical spot, however, where we can find at least one of the many key ingredients that went into scrapple, a hard cornmeal-based "pudding" that became an ideal way for Middle Colony residents to transform pig scraps into a future meal. Pennsylvania and, to a lesser extent, New York popularized scrapple because the dish reflected the imported culinary traditions of the Pennsylvania Dutch, the German immigrants to colonial British America who poured into the colonies after 1715. These newcomers, moreover, didn't stop with the heart of the matter. Cooks incorporated the pig's ribs and liver, too, and then mixed in cornmeal, buckwheat flour, sage, salt, and pepper for good measure. Pork broth provided the stewing liquid for the meat scraps, and, once the mixture had become a mush in a hefty pot, the cook slowly worked in the meal and seasoning, stirring constantly for about thirty minutes and adding hot water to keep the mixture moist. After achieving a consistency akin to that of mashed potatoes, the concoction was poured into molds and placed in the cellar or outside to cool. Once the mixture set, scrapple could be eaten in its immediate form, baked, or fried. Any way it was cooked, it provided a stick-to-the-ribs dinner option, especially when served with maple syrup and stewed apples, as it so often was.

There's something intriguing about Germans preparing a traditional meal using (in part) Native American ingredients on farms sprawling across colonial British America. But such was the cultural flexibility inherent in American food. Just as the other regions of colonial America developed distinct ways of cooking and eating, so did the Middle Colonies. Scrapple suggests, but hardly captures, the complexity of these practices. In the most general terms, the region's food production falls between the extremes. Whereas every other region had or did not have a staple crop, the Middle Colonies *sort of* had one: wheat. Whereas every other region had or did not have a slave-based labor source, the Middle Colonies *sort of* had one, with a combination of whites and slaves working the land. Whereas every other region had or did not have a competent level of self-subsistence, the Middle Colonies *sort of* had it, with the backcountry and the urban areas forming a kind of mutually beneficial relationship that fostered self-subsistence over a much larger geographical area than the single New England town.

In other ways, though, the region went to unmatched extremes. With the budding cities of New York and Philadelphia thriving on the coast, the Middle Colonies were the most urbanized region of British America. With its relatively mild climate, fertile soil, and Quaker-inspired religious tolerance, this region was also the most attractive destination for non-English whites, mainly Germans, Dutch, and Swedes. Finally, with its extensive networks of backcountry trade and, again, Quaker-inspired tolerance, the Middle Colonies nurtured relations with the Native Americans that—while not *always* peaceful—were at least steady enough to remain intact throughout most of the colonial era. For these reasons—that is, its ability to reach extremes and fall between them—the Middle Colonies is the most difficult of the colonial regions to pin down. Like a loaf of scrapple, it can be sliced in too many different ways to summarize with a single description.

Challenges notwithstanding, I'll approach the culinary character of the Middle Colonies through an overview of four influential developments: the powerful cultural presence of the Quakers, the ongoing interaction between whites and Native Americans, ethnic diversity, and the influence of wheat as the region's "staple crop." Together, these key aspects of the region's character frame a cuisine that might best be described as having a refined crudeness, a quality that blends aspects from New England, Virginia, and Carolina to create—not unlike scrapple—something at once familiar and unique.

Quakers and Their Food

In 1682, the ship *Welcome* carried William Penn and one hundred other Quakers from England to the expansive colony that would soon become the namesake of the pious proprietor. As a testament to Penn's considerable charisma and the rich fertility of the land he received, ninety shiploads of settlers—most from the Society of Friends—followed in the *Welcome*'s wake as it survived its first dreadful journey across the Atlantic. The tens of thousands of Quakers and their sympathizers who settled the region that became the Middle Colonies brought with them a well-developed culinary philosophy as coherent and powerful as their system of religious beliefs. Unlike the Puritans, whose cooking habits consciously evoked the ways of the homeland, Quakers concerned themselves less with what they ate than with their attitudes while eating it. They were a people who made a virtue of frugality while making frugality more elaborate than anyone could have imagined. Penn once remarked, "Frugality is good, if liberality is joined with it." In making this claim, he suggested just how far his people would go to keep their food simple, basic, and modest. To be sure, the Quakers' influence on daily life in the Middle Colonies would decline throughout the eighteenth century, especially as non-Quakers poured into the area and made it home. But the initial culinary stamp that the Quakers left on the burgeoning society that they established never fully faded. Some would say that it's still there.

William Penn, a man who evidently dined on a steady diet of pithy aphorisms, perhaps best articulated the precise nature of the Quakers' collective culinary attitude. Men and women, he wrote, should never "live to eat," but rather "eat to live." Even when "recipes of cookery are swelled to a volume," the temperate Quaker must choose to "have wholesome but not costly food." Penn frequently referenced the proverb that "enough is as good as a feast" while impugning "the luxurious eater and drinker who is taken up with an excessive care of his palate and belly." The best medicine for "a good stomach" wasn't rich food but instead "industry and temperance." The world was rife with temptation and "luxury has many parts," he wrote, but the imperatives were firm for the earnest Quaker: "drink when thou art dry" and never abandon the truism that "all excess is ill." Penn wasn't alone in these sober sentiments. George Fox, the founder of Quakerism, dismissed culinary indulgence as an especially pathetic example of "pampering the lower self." He admonished his followers to shun "feastings and revellings, banquetings and wakes." "Revelling" was to be avoiding, but leveling—at least with respect to food—was to be celebrated. One pious Quaker wondered how anyone could live "in excess of apparel and diet" when "your brethren want food and raiment." Through these beliefs, Quakers strove to take the pleasure out of eating and keep the act of feeding oneself and one's family, in the words of David Hackett Fischer, "exceptionally plain and simple." These people were, as Penn suggested, liberally frugal.

The natural environment surrounding these upstanding ascetics, however, knew no frugality. The landscape that settlers to the Middle Colonies exploited in their quest to make a new and supposedly simple life for themselves yielded a cornucopia of wealth. As the Society of Friends exercised what proved to be a formidable work ethic, the land yielded its riches with surprising generosity. Writing home to a friend one year after Pennsylvania's founding, Thomas Paschall admitted that "provisions are somewhat hard to come by in some places," but, at the same time, he couldn't get over the natural and cultivated abundance thriving in his midst. "When we came into Delawarebay," he wrote, "we saw an infinite number of small fish in sholes, also large fish leaping in the water." In a rambling account, he mentioned "great stocks of cattle," "Gardens with all sorts of Herbs, and some more then in England," and "very good butter and cheese, as most in England."

Two years later, Penn (who admittedly had an interest in exaggerating the region's natural wealth) gushed over how Pennsylvanians had quickly become a people with "Houses over their heads and Garden plots, Coverts for their Cattle, and increase of stock, and several enclosures of corn." English culinary expectations were, he explained, easily met in the Middle Colonies. The "Corn and Roots that grow in England thrive very well," he wrote, as did "Wheat, Barley, Rye, Oats, Buck-Wheat, Pease, Beans, Cabbages, Turnips, Carretts, Parsnups, Colleflowers, Asparagus, Onions, Charlots, Garlick and Irish Potatoes." Fish matched this variety and quantity of garden produce. Penn claimed that "whales roll upon the coast," "sturgeon play continually in our rivers," "shads . . . are of the bigness of our largest carp," and the "rock[fish] are somewhat Rounder and larger." The existence of these plentiful fish, in addition to "the diligent application of People to Husbandry," enthused settlers who were soon able "to pay with the provisions of [their] own growth." Materialistically, the world they were sowing and reaping, fishing and hunting allowed them to "live comfortably." Even more than in New England, prosperity came relatively easily to the first Quakers who farmed Pennsylvania's soil, fished its rivers, and hunted its forests.

For all of Penn's self-interest in promoting images of abundance, other settlers with a less direct stake in sparking immigration offered comparable accounts of the region's early success. In 1686, Nicholas More aimed to counteract "the evil Reports that I do understand are given out by many enemies to this new colony." He took grave offense at the occasional characterization of the Middle Colonies as a place where "the Land is so barren, the Climate so hot, that English Grain, Roots, and Herbs do not come to Maturity." "How untrue," huffed More, as he went on to describe how "our

The Quakers Unmasked, *1691*

This drawing pokes fun at the Quakers and their rigid ways. Satire aside, their frugality and powerful aversion to indulgence helped influence the foodways of the Middle Colonies.

Lands have been grateful to us, and have begun to reward our Labours by abounding crops of Corn this year." He glowed over "the abundance of good fresh pork," beef, butter, wheat, rye, and "Corn this Year in every Plantation." His own experience proved the point. In addition to "twelve Acres of Indian Corn," he explained how "I did sow both Wheat and Rye, at which many Laughed, saying That I could not expect any Corn from what I had sowed, the Land wanting more Labour." But he proved them wrong, bragging that "yet I had this year as good Wheat and Rye upon it, as was to be found in any other place." In addition to these grains, he "had a good Crop of Barley and Oats" and took pride in his "Hopp-Garden . . . which is now exceeding full of Hopps at which all English people admire."

More evidently had a lot of company, as letters from the period abound with similar assessments. James Claypole, a merchant: "I have never seen brighter and better corn than in these parts, especially in the County of Chester. . . . Fish is plentiful." Robert Turner, another merchant: "Things prosper very well, and the earth brings forth its encrease." James Harrison, a Quaker minister: "The Peach-Trees are much broken down with the weight of the Fruit this Year. All or most of the Plants that came from England grow. . . . Cherries are sprung up four and five foot. Pears and Apple grafts, in Country Stocks, and in Thorns, are sprung three and four foot. Rasberries, Gooseberries, Currans, Quinces, Roses, Walnuts and Figs grow well. . . . Our Barn, Porch, and Shed, are full of Corn this year." Mahlon Stacy, a settler: "The cranberries [are] much like cherries for color and bigness . . . an excellent sauce is made of them for venison, turkeys, and other great fowl, and they are better to make tarts than either gooseberries or cherries."

It's tempting to dismiss these positive assessments as tall tales designed to drum up interest in a nascent colonial venture. In the case of Pennsylvania, however, the enthusiasm was simply too consistent and comparable in tone to be characterized as the misconstrued views of pie-in-the-sky promoters. The fact was that settlers in the Middle Colonies were sitting on a culinary gold mine. And, as their testimonies suggest, they knew it.

In the face of this obvious and elaborate natural wealth, the staid Quakers stuck to their culinary philosophy of simplicity with impressive tenacity. Their simplicity was perhaps most evident in their habit of boiling their food. Much of this tendency was merely an extension of English habits. Most Quakers came from an area of northern England known for boiling as its primary way of cooking. Hence the Quakers could avoid the temptations of taste—the gustatorial satisfaction of frying and the delicacy of slow roasting—in exchange for a blander culinary method that nourished without indulgence. "In the country," explained Quaker John F. Watson, "morning and evening repasts were generally made of milk, having bread boiled therein, or else thickened with pop-robbins—things made up of flour and eggs into a batter and dropped in the boiling milk." Boiled puddings and dumplings became labeled "Quaker Food" as pot-puddings and apple dumplings evolved into staples of the Quaker diet.

Reflective of their frugality, Quakers not only boiled their meals but went to extremes to extend their ingredients. Avoiding waste at all costs, they did whatever it took to prevent spoilage, including taking the unique step of dehydrating their food. Cream cheese, which resulted from an extenuation of an Old World Quaker practice, owed its existence to a procedure that had the cheese maker heat cream and allow it to curdle over the course of several weeks, during which time the water was periodically squeezed from the curds until the mass solidified. Quakers dehydrated fruits and vegetables in a similar manner, slowly cooking the produce to reduce it and then adding sugar and spices to make what they referred to as butter or cheese. Apple butter, pear butter, and plum butter kept for ages. Meat could be treated likewise. Dehydrated beef probably tasted about as good as it sounds, but what mattered to the Quakers wasn't taste but longevity—the stuff lasted for more than three years. They called it "Quaker gravy."

"We eat so moderately," Edward Shippen wrote, "that the whole day seems like a long morning to us." The Quakers were hardly alone in the Middle Colonies, and as non-Quakers poured in to take advantage of the region's natural abundance, they came to develop foodways that didn't necessarily contradict Shippen's assessment. Peter Kalm's visit to the Middle Colonies brought him into regular contact with a manner of cooking among non-Quakers that he found heavily seasoned with Quaker habits. "Care was usually taken that there should be no waste," he wrote about a meal he had with a Dutch family in New York, "so that when all had eaten not a bit of porridge should remain." The porridge was evidently anything but scrumptious. As Kalm remarked, "After the porridge one ate bread and butter to hold it down." Dinners also avoided lavishness. "For dinner," Kalm continued, "they rarely had more than one dish, meat with turnips or cabbage; occasionally there were two [dishes]." He was impressed with how "they never served more than was consumed before they left the table." On another occasion, again in New York, Kalm said of the Dutch there that "they are careful not to load up the table with food as the English are accustomed to do." John Woolman, a Quaker minister, knew that his people were fortunate to live in a land of plenty, but at the same time he admonished them never to take for granted the region's natural wealth. Quoting Habakkuk, he explained how the proper Quaker was to eat and live as though everything were on the verge of extinction, "as if the fig tree shall not blossom." Evidently, others heeded such wisdom for, to an extent, the Middle Colonies practiced culinary habits that avoided ostentation and indulgence, despite every opportunity to do otherwise.

Native Americans and Foodways in the Middle Colonies

For all the impact of the Quakers on the region's eating habits, they ultimately became a minority of the population who, by virtue of their own tolerance, ended up blending their beliefs into a wide range of cultures and culinary influences. As in every other region, another significant factor shaping the culinary habits of the Middle Colonies was the ongoing interaction that the region's settlers nurtured with the Native Americans. This influence was, in many respects, a genuinely powerful distinguishing factor in the region's complex culinary development. The other regions of colonial British America witnessed the demise of white–Native American relations much earlier and faster, usually through a violent event. In the West Indies, for example, it was primarily smallpox. Relations in New England came undone in 1676 with King Philip's War (if not earlier, with the building of farms). The Chesapeake Bay had its Native American bonds severed with the massive raid of 1622. Carolina's white–Native American interaction unraveled in 1715 with the Yamasee War. But the Middle Colonies avoided comparable conflicts until 1754, maintaining relatively civil relations with the Native Americans until the outbreak of the Seven Years' War.

In addition to the deferred demise of this relationship, the Middle Colonies was a region of British America with an especially rich and geographically expansive backcountry. Settlement and agricultural practice—driven by rapid natural increase and immigration—spiraled outward from the eye of Philadelphia like a hurricane. Constant diplomatic negotiations kept at bay the conflicts that wracked other regions. Nevertheless, the press of settlement heightened the whites' extended dependence on the Native Americans for basic information about their new world. If they weren't going to fight each other, they would have to learn to achieve some measure of peace. Food, as we'll see, was always an element of that critical education.

The intricate ties that bound whites and Native Americans in the Middle Colonies before 1754 were enhanced by two other factors. First, the Iroquois Five Nations—the major Native American presence in the region—proved to be an unusually powerful and unified ally covering a wide swath of the western frontier. Among other roles, they effectively protected the settlers from hostile incursions or retaliations from the Chippewas, Hurons, and Ottawas. The Iroquois, in turn, relied heavily on English weapons to devastate the Native Americans to the north while monopolizing access to the beaver-pelt trade, which interested the newer white settlers back east. Unabashed about wielding power for their own benefit, the Iroquois helped the Middle Colonies acquire vast tracts of land from less formidable but land-rich tribes, most notably the Delawares, who were otherwise downright hostile to the prospect. Second, in addition to their established presence, the Iroquois were eager to trade with the white settlers in order to improve their own diplomatic and military position vis-à-vis other groups, not to mention improve their material standard of living. In exchange for furs and skins, they happily took from Dutch and English traders clothing, brass pots, knives, jewelry, iron ax heads, rum, wampum beads, woolen blankets, and a variety of other necessities and baubles. With the tragic exception of rum, the Iroquois had an obvious knack for incorporating these items into their own material culture in a way that strengthened their traditions. Raw materials obtained from Europeans were used for Native American crafts, brass pots were reworked into finger rings and armbands, wool shirts were worn to protect their traditional garb from rain and snow, and so on. However the Iroquois used these imports, the crucial culinary factor was that they and their neighbors found ample opportunity to share time, money, information, and many, many other things.

Not the least of which was food. The Iroquois lived more or less communally. They took shelter in rectangular longhouses that extended up to two hundred feet in length and were periodically interrupted by hearths with vent holes cut into the roofs. Living in close proximity within a compact space was conducive to a cooking style that allowed Native Americans to "boile in one kettle, eat out of one dish, and with one spoon, and so be one." Like Native Americans throughout North America, a clear gendered division of labor sent men into the woods to hunt protein, while women generally stayed near the village to grow and tend vegetables. Young men chased game over vast areas, while older men and children fished. Women of all ages processed game; maintained patches of corn, beans, and squash;

and foraged for nuts, berries, roots, greens, and small animals that sometimes pulled them several miles distant from the longhouse. The hunting and gathering basis of this food system, frequent wars with neighboring factions, and Native Americans' heightened susceptibility to outbreaks of European diseases inevitably meant infrequent but nonetheless painful food shortages. After one raid, a group of Iroquois found themselves, in the words of one European, "severely straitened for want of provisions, which they were unable to carry with them by reason of their sudden flight." When these mishaps, or when nature itself, imposed such limitations, however, the Native Americans were quick to help one another make ends meet. "A whole village must be without corn, before any individual can be obliged to endure privation," one Frenchman observed.

The rarity of these shortages spoke to the precisely calculated and well-honed provisioning system that the Iroquois developed to meet material needs. The culinary imperatives of the Iroquois boiled down to the essential tasks of horticulture and hunting. After men girdled trees to open small fields in the dense forest, women planted a combination of beans, corn, and squash on dirt hills made on the forest floor. Beans crept up the cornstalks, using them as natural poles, while the squash spread out under shade provided by the corn leaves. Women hoed fields only twice after planting. When the first maize seeds appeared, women gathered a sample, soaked them in a decoction made from ground roots, and left the concoction in the fields to intoxicate crows that would otherwise eat the corn. The plot belonged to an entire village, whose women worked the fields and harvested the crops together. Men worked in a similarly communal fashion as they hunted, although their activity took them far from home for long periods of time. Large hunting parties drove deer into enclosures and killed them with bows and arrows or trapped them in snares. Bears and other animals were driven off cliffs, if such "deadfalls" were available. Pigeons and beavers were especially valued for their taste, but any flesh was literally fair game. Once the Native Americans caught and killed animals, they ate them quickly and they ate them all. Preservation, because of the Native Americans' seminomadic existence, was rare. With the addition of edible wild plants, fish, greens, and edible tubers, the Iroquois who interacted so regularly with the white settlers in the Middle Colonies rooted their eating habits in wild game, beans, squash, and corn. And while their methods of providing food were far more stable and systematic than those of their more itinerant forebears, they were still relatively "wild" compared with the practices of the white settlers in their midst.

No matter what white settlers imagined, however, the reality of life on the ground in the Middle Colonies—a reality dictated mainly by trade and continued western settlement—subjected them to Native American culinary influences, agricultural practices, and hunting habits on a regular basis. Traveling through New York, Peter Kalm observed a scene in which "the native had killed a great number of roe deer and hung up the flesh on all sides to dry. . . . At the fire's edge sticks were set in the ground perpendicularly and at the tip of these sticks were meat for cooking." Kalm and his traveling companions might have found the scene comparatively uncivilized, but he nonetheless concluded his account by writing that "after we bought a little of the meat of the roe deer we continued our journey." In Albany, he noted the popularity among the whites of eating squash and pumpkins. Describing first the Native American approach to these foods, he wrote, "The Indians do not raise as many pumpkins as they do squashes. Some mix flour with the pumpkins when making porridge . . . others add nothing. They often make pudding and even pie or a kind of tart out of them." When the English or the Dutch in New York got their hands on pumpkin, it might be "cut into halves, the seeds removed, the two halves replaced [put back together] and the whole put into an oven to roast." Once roasted, "butter is spread over the inside while it is still hot so that the butter is drawn into the pumpkins after which they are especially good eating." They could also be boiled. "It was customary," wrote Kalm, "to eat them this way with meat." But his most favorite way to prepare squash was the following: "They boiled them first in water, next mashed them in about the same way we do turnips, then boiled them again in a little of the water they had first boiled in, with fresh milk added, and stirred then while they were boiling." His assessment? "What a delicious dish it became!"

Kalm wasn't alone in his exposure to Native American culinary habits. The minister Henry Muhlenberg was another traveler who meandered throughout the Middle Colonies and encountered his fair share of local food habits. Describing his "noon meal" at the house of a Dutch justice of the peace, Muhlenberg explained, "He treated us to bear meat." Later that evening, he was somewhat taken aback to find himself "right in the thick of the forest" where he and his companions "saw a bear, which took flight from us," and then "several wild Indians" who, much to his relief, came in peace. After crossing the Delaware River into Pennsylvania, the men stopped at an inn where, Muhlenberg noted, "we were fed on *raccoons*, the American fox or badger, and pumpkins." With great enthusiasm, Thomas Paschall explained, "I have Venison of the Indians very cheap," and "we had bearflesh this fall for little or nothing." Of the bear, he said, "It is good food, tasting much like Beef." William Penn highlighted the settlers' early reliance on native produce when he recalled how, in 1685, "the Old Inhabitants supplied us with most of the Corn we wanted." Ample evidence suggests that this dependence continued throughout the colonial era. In the 1760s, for example, backcountry traders routinely remarked on the role of Native Americans in their own quest to obtain food. "Game is always to be found," said David Zeisberger, as long as "the Indians plunge into the woods and shoot a deer, a turkey-cock, or something else." George Croghan, another trader, wrote, "All . . . kinds of wild game are extremely plenty," so much so that "a good hunter, without much fatigue to himself, could here supply daily one hundred men with meat." A traveler might not have to even stop to eat, as long as he was willing to allow nature to be his serving plate. "The gooseberries being now ripened," wrote John Bartram, "we were every now and then tempted to break off a bough and divert ourselves with picking them, tho' on horseback."

Because of the mutually beneficial nature of the Native American–Anglo relationship in the Middle Colonies, Native Americans with whom settlers interacted often showed an eager affinity to share their food. Whites continually remarked how Native American generosity was an almost habitual reaction, a perception confirmed by one Native American, who said, "If we had but one loaf of bread when we met each other in the Woods, we would cut it in two and divide it one with the other." Bartram's experience suggests that the assessment was no mere boast. Native generosity was "so punctually adhered to, that not only what is dressed is immediately set before a traveler, but the most pressing business is postponed to prepare the best they can get for him." Granted, the proffered fare wasn't always what the whites might have ordered up at a Philadelphia or New York tavern. A common sentiment among many whites, in fact, was that anything "grown in the woods"—that is, anything that wasn't processed in the kitchen—"did not have much taste." Colonists cringed, for example, when plates were "licked by the dogs in lieu of washing" or when lice and entrails were added to the simmering stew. One Iroquois expressed surprise when he met a Pennsylvanian who "could eat Indian fare," as not all of them "were able to." But many, especially traders and new settlers in the backcountry, had no choice in the matter and, like one Mr. Clous, adapted under the mundane duress of dire necessity. When a group of traders sat down to a meal of "Ind.n Corn Aquash & Entrails of Deer," the spread proved to be "no Hardship for Mr. Weiser who experienced the like before, [but] was a great one to Mr. Claus who never saw Such eatables made use of before by Mankind." The hapless initiate "was pretty well pinched with hunger before he could persuade himself to taste them."

Much as in early Carolina, where the trade relationship between the Native Americans and the white settlers thrived (at least before 1715), Native Americans had a powerful impact on the foodways of the Middle Colonies. Their "constant application of the mind to observing the scenes and accidents which occur in the woods," as one missionary put it, imbued the Native Americans with a "practical acquaintance with the country that they inhabit." These were people who obviously knew the environment inside and out and, as a result, became an invaluable resource to the Pennsylvanians and New Yorkers who were trading and settling farther and farther from the coast, in the wilderness, on the distant periphery. "I cannot," a young George Washington wrote, "conceive the best white man to be equal to them in the woods." Knowing better than to try to compete with that knowledge or, as men did in the Chesapeake, respond to it with hostility, the Middle Colonists accepted it.

In so doing, they established the essential preconditions for an atmosphere of culinary tolerance that, not unlike Carolina, remained open to a relatively rough, frontier-influenced style of gathering, cooking, and eating food. Reverend Andrew Burnaby noted that the "province *in its cultivated state* affords grain of all sorts, cattle, hogs, and a great variety of English fruits." Even in 1759, however, parts of the Middle Colonies retained the rough demeanor of frontier life, leaving Burnaby to remark how "the waters afford various kinds of fish" while the "elks or moose deer" were similarly plentiful. Philadelphia may no longer have been "a wild and uncultivated desert, inhabited by nothing but ravenous beasts," but the same couldn't necessarily be said for the rest of the region. Dr. Alexander Hamilton, a sophisticated urbanite who traveled throughout the colonies in 1744, came face to face with the region's predilection for rough simplicity when he stopped to eat with a ferry keeper on the Susquehanna River. "It is kept," he wrote, "by a little old man whom I found at vittels with his wife and family upon a homely dish of fish without any kind of sauce." The man asked Hamilton to stay, "but I told them I had no stomach." In actuality, the doctor was starving. But the atmosphere wasn't quite up to snuff. "They had no cloth upon the table," he explained, "and their mess was a dirty, deep, wooden dish which they evacuated with their hands, cramming down skins, scales and all. They used neither knife, fork, spoon, plate, or napkin because, I suppose, they had none to use." Hamilton, assessing the experience, "looked upon this as a picture of that primitive simplicity practiced by our forefathers."

The good doctor thought the scene to be a rare one. In point of fact, though, he was witnessing a rather common culinary standard of living practiced by a great many Middle Colonists who resided along the rivers that extended deep into the frontier, away from the more civilized coastal towns, ending in forested regions where Native Americans continued to have an impact on those who chose to live and work and cook and eat in the wilderness the Native Americans once completely controlled.

Ethnicity and Food in the Middle Colonies

Native American control of the wilderness, however, was not permanent. Between 1700 and 1775, colonial America grew from 250,000 to 2.5 million residents. Two-thirds of this expansion came from natural increase. Due in large part to the fact that white Americans were feeding themselves so well, colonial families reproduced at an impressive rate, leading to an average family size of about eight children. Not only ample food but also cleaner air, extensive land, and a relatively dispersed population helped fuel and sustain population growth. These factors reduced infant mortality, prevented the spread of disease, heightened fertility, and extended life expectancy.

But natural increase wasn't alone in accounting for a near doubling of the colonial population every twenty-five years. The other third of the population's overall growth came from immigration. During the eighteenth century, patterns of immigration looked much different from those in the seventeenth century. Many of the settlers who were marrying and bearing a brood of children were voluntary immigrants from non-English countries. About 150,000 Scotch-Irish immigrants from Northern Ireland, about 80,000 Irish and Scottish immigrants, and about 100,000 Germans joined thousands of Jews, Swedes, and even Frenchmen and -women in weaving intricate ethnic threads into the once thoroughly English tapestry that draped across colonial America. To be sure, not all these immigrants settled in the Middle Colonies, but thousands enough did to make the region—one that, not incidentally, was partially founded by the Dutch before England took New Amsterdam from Holland in 1664—the most ethnically diverse in British America.

Too often the story of American food uncritically celebrates the culinary contributions of America's ethnically diverse white immigrants without examining the precise nature of cultural integration. It's an understandable impulse. After all, there's something quite exciting about the preservation of non-English cultural (and especially culinary) habits that persist to this day. America's love of "authentic" foreign cuisines remains unmatched. We like to think that foreign food can stay completely foreign in America—a pure and unadulterated reflection of the Old World. But, in reality, the transfer of cultural and culinary habits to British America was never quite as direct or intact or smooth as we might hope. One of the most exceptional characteristics of colonial British America, in fact, was its ability to absorb non-English immigrants while simultaneously allowing them to selectively preserve and adopt culinary practices to a very British society. In other words, cultural adaptation—including the preservation of foodways—required constant negotiation rather than a single transplantation. This assessment held true much more for non-English whites than for Africans, who were more isolated from the dominant culture and, most important, couldn't freely participate in it. Ethnicity definitely mattered, and ethnic culinary contributions certainly had an impact on the Middle Colonies, but—in the end—the transfer of Old World culinary habits mildly seasoned the region's foodways without permanently changing its flavor.

The main reason for the cautious transferal of culinary ways from Old World to New had to do with the fact that the British methods of farming, trading, and working the land shaped economic life on the ground in ways that made cultural preservation very difficult. Extensive farming based on grain, wheat exports, livestock, and dairy production—mixed in with small-scale processing ventures—proved too convenient and profitable a system for foreigners to forgo in favor of more traditional farming practices. Which is not to say that non-English settlers completely adopted English habits. The Middle Colonies, yet again, found a middle ground. A few examples of the region's evident ethnic and culinary diversity should keep us from overstating the considerable power of the dominant English culture. Through them, we can appreciate the significant extent to which the diversity of the Middle Colonies left its mark on the region's eating habits, without fully characterizing the region.

Few visitors to the Middle Colonies overlooked the ethnic and religious diversity in their midst. The topic seemed to be a matter of constant conversation. Dr. Alexander Hamilton found himself one evening "att a taveren with a very mixed company of different nations and religions." "There were," he elaborated, "Scots, English, Dutch, Germans, and Irish; there were Roman Catholicks, Church men, Presbyterians, Quakers,

Newlightmen, Methodists, Seventh day men, Moravians, Anabaptists, and one Jew." The motley table of men ate and drank English fare in an English tavern and found common ground in a discussion about "politicks and conjectures of a French war." It perhaps stood to reason that the only group to remain aloof from the convivial scene was the Quakers, the original white inhabitants of a region that, decades after its founding, swarmed with men and women of different beliefs and backgrounds. "A knott of Quakers," Hamilton continued, "talked only about the selling of flower and the price it bore." While a few of them "touched a little upon religion," Hamilton concluded, "their blood was not hot enough to quarrell."

Hamilton wrote in 1745, but even sixty years earlier the diversity of the region had been apparent. "The people are a Collection of divers Nations in Europe," William Penn explained. "As, French, Dutch, Germans, Sweeds, Danes, Finns, Scotch, Irish, and English." Of the last group, he said, "they are equal to all the rest." By 1760, Andrew Burnaby could accurately write that the Middle Colonies were a place composed "of different nations, different languages, and different religions," so much so that "it is almost impossible to give them any precise or determinate language." As to religion, "there is none properly established; but Protestants of all denominations, Papists, Jews, and all other sects whatsoever, are universally tolerated."

Whether or not the same could be said for food was another question altogether. Some, like Hamilton, thought the English-inspired fare quite superior to non-English offerings. His rather comic experience at the dinner table of yet another ferryman, this time while journeying through New York, introduced him to Dutch food, or at least this one man's version of it. He was less than impressed: "I dined upon what I never had eat in my life before—a dish of fryed clams, of which shellfish there is abundance in these parts." His first gaffe as this new culinary experience unfolded was an ecclesiastical foul. After noting that the family "observed a manner of saying grace quite new to me" (they were "hanging down their heads and holding up their hands for a half minute"), he proceeded to sit "staring at them with my mouth choak full." After "this short meditation" came to an awkward end, the diners "began to lay about us and stuff down the fryed clams with rye-bread and butter." Hamilton quickly became impatient with the whole affair, explaining how "they took such a deal of chawing that we were long att dinner, and the dish began to cool before we had eat enough." The Dutch woman evidently noticed that the meal had become cold as well. "The landlady called for the bedpan," Hamilton wrote with some astonishment. "I could not guess what she intended to do with it unless it was to warm her bed to go to sleep after dinner," he surmised. But, regrettably for Hamilton at least, "I found that it was used by way of a chaffing dish to warm our dish of clams." The denouement to this less than auspicious introduction to the foodways of the Dutch was nothing if not appropriate: "I stared att the novelty for some time, and reaching over for a mug of beer that stood on the opposite side of the table, my bag sleeve catched hold of the handle of the bed pan and unfortunately overset the clams, at which the landlady was a little ruffled and muttered a scrape of Dutch of which I understood not a word except mynheer, but I suppose she swore, for she uttered her speech with an emphasis."

Hamilton's account notwithstanding, it's hard to determine the extent to which the Dutch preserved their culinary tradition. They conventionally relied on potatoes, vegetables, and meat—a combination certainly not unachievable in New Amsterdam and the Hudson River Valley. Their diet worked well in a frontier environment because soup, especially *ertensoep* (split-pea soup) and *bruinbonensoep* (brown-bean soup), was a common Dutch meal, usually accompanied by rye bread and bacon. Peas, bacon, beans, pork, and rye were all available from the rich bounties of farms skirting the Hudson. The Dutch ate a steady diet of gruel, or pap, made from tapioca, rice, oatmeal, and semolina mixed with buttermilk. They relied on regular servings of shellfish (especially mussels) and herring. Other common dishes included *boerekeel met worst* (cabbage with sausage), *stampot* (mashed potatoes mixed with vegetables and greens), and *speculaasbrood* (a kind of spicy biscuit). Fried raisin yeast bread, apple turnovers, and raisins were all very popular as well. Again, the evidence is scanty, but the nature of these ingredients; the absence of any particularly intricate cooking techniques in the Dutch diet; the settlement pattern of the Dutch, many of whom lived in relatively close quarters on estates granted to landowners who were known as patroons; and their access to regional markets all bode well for their transferal of Old World foodways.

Peter Kalm was equally sensitive to the region's broad culinary offerings but, perhaps because of his Swedish heritage, showed a bit more tolerance toward Dutch food. His tolerance also may have been due to his general sensitivity to all diversions from mainstream English eating habits. He noted, for example, that "the Jews never cook any food for themselves on Saturday, but that it is done the day before" and that "the majority of the Jews do not eat pork." These restrictions, however, "do not trouble the conscience of the young people when on their journeys, for then they eat whatever they can get, and that even together with the Christians." He admired how the Native Americans "catch a large number of small eels of nine or twelve inches in length, and all the dexterity needed for their capture is to go below the cataract and feel around with the fingers in the cracks, holes, and crevices of the wet rock, find them and grab them." Noting the Native Americans' intense reliance on fish, in fact, motivated the Swedes "who then came over" to settle "near bays and rivers, where they had good opportunities for fishing." A temporary landlady of his impressed him with a culinary range that drew on German and Native American foods. When she "prepared to-day an unusual salad which I never remember having seen or eaten"—a salad made of shredded cabbage, vinegar, oil, and butter—Kalm declared the dish to have "a very pleasing flavor [that] tastes better than one can imagine." He found her way of preparing Indian corn—a method that cooked the entire cob before removing the kernels—"especially suitable for cooking and eating."

So whereas Hamilton demonstrated a wry tendency to mock the Dutch, Kalm found their foodways to be particularly pleasant and refreshingly simple. "They are careful not to load up the table with food as the English are accustomed to do," he explained, adding how "they are not so given to drink as the latter." The Dutch, he continued, "are more frugal when preparing food, and seldom is more seen on the table than is consumed, and sometimes hardly that." After living "for almost a week in a house with a good-sized [Dutch] family," Kalm described "the same perpetual evening meal of porridge made of corn meal." Called *sappan* by the Dutch, "it was put into a good-sized dish and a large hole made in the center into which the milk was poured, and then one proceeded to help oneself." Breakfast was equally austere: "they drank tea in the customary way by putting brown sugar into the cup of tea. With the tea they ate bread and butter and radishes." The Dutch even seem to have followed a method of eating these foods, as Kalm watched them "take a bite of the bread and butter and . . . cut off a piece of the radish as they ate." Every now and then, breakfast would include "small round cheeses (not especially fine tasting) . . . which they cut into thin slices and spread upon the buttered bread." While Kalm had certainly never seen the precise likes of this kind of meal, he still "observed nothing unusual about it." If any porridge remained after the evening meal, "it was boiled with buttermilk in the morning so it became almost like a gruel." The buttermilk was often made "more tasty" with the addition of syrup or sugar. Between-meal snacks usually included "some meat left over from the noonday meal, or bread and butter with cheese." Pudding or pie, "the Englishman's perpetual dish," was unheard of in the

Dutch diet. "One seldom saw" it, claimed Kalm, suggesting the Dutch's relative isolation from English ways of eating.

The Dutch weren't the only ethnic group living in the Middle Colonies who were capable of eliciting comments. The Germans were equally adept at drawing attention to their foodways, although probably less successful at preserving them. Henry Muhlenberg, who was of German descent, wrote with considerable excitement about how "our good hostess treated us to a great rarity which had been sent to our host by a good friend from Philadelphia . . . namely, sauerkraut, which to me and my family was like a gift of a costly medicine." In a comment that aptly reflected the challenges involved in preserving the foodways of the homeland, he explained, "Since such things are rare and not easily preserved in this warm climate, the whole family derived great sensual gratification from it, and I cannot deny that I shared in it." Later, he came across a German servant who "ran away from his English master because he thought he ought to have meat every day," while "two others were sitting in jail, having falsely accused their master of making them eat rotten meat." A Hessian officer living in America at the time of the American Revolution remarked how "the way of living with respect to food is very poor. No German stomach can put up with it." Germans made familiar food when ingredients allowed, but, like all Americans, they had to be flexible. After all, as one European visitor to Pennsylvania noted, what the land often afforded could be nothing more thrilling than turnips. Instead of traditional German bread, immigrants often had to make do with bread described as "heavy and sour." Germans might have worked assiduously to re-create and eat a steady and familiar diet of pot roast, dried apples and ham, dumplings, sweet yeast bread, pickled cabbage, apple cake, and scrapple, but—as these comments indicate—conditions and ingredients didn't always cooperate to achieve such a goal. A German-owned inn in eighteenth-century Bethlehem, Pennsylvania, for example, offered a menu of "venison, moor game, the most delicious red and yellow bellied trout, the highest flavoured wild strawberries, the most luxurious asparagus, and the best vegetables." Not bad food, but certainly not German food.

For all the obstacles blocking the pathway to culinary familiarity, though, German settlers in the Middle Colonies managed to preserve at least a recognizable semblance of their traditional eating habits, one that still maintains a grip on the region. Although the most popular cookbook used by the Pennsylvania Dutch wasn't published until after the Revolution, the *Economical Manual of Domestic Arts* suggests the persistence of German cuisine in the colonial Pennsylvania region. Friederike Luise Löffler's impressive collection of homeland recipes includes steamed dumplings, fried flour soup, stuffed noodles, apple butter, and mustard marinades for roasted meat. Other books following in Löffler's wake reminded German Americans about the nuances involved in preparing *dummus* (omelet made with potatoes and bread), *schales* (meatless casserole made with egg, milk, potatoes, and fish), *gumbis* (layered casserole made with noodles), *griewesupp* (soup made with chicken and pork), and *torte* (flat and round cake or bread). Germans in Pennsylvania frequently built raised hearths to foster the process of slow cooking stews and soups, stocks and broths. The ceramic stew pot could sit for hours on the raised hearth and become a willing receptacle for bones, vegetables, flour, and meat scraps. The addition of water and a long simmer yielded a hearty and flavorful liquid that could be added to a roux of fried flour and butter and turned into a meat stew. It was an arrangement that one expert on the topic calls "the essence of frugal cuisine."

More so than the Dutch, who tended to live in close proximity for generations upon generations on upstate New York manors, the Germans gathered no moss. They were constantly on the move throughout Pennsylvania, traversing the colony for more fertile land, better access to markets, and greater opportunities to pursue the fruits of economic gain. Their relative itinerancy precluded the complete transmission of cultural values while predisposing the Germans—as the opening scrapple recipe suggests—toward an adaptive Americanization of their food that underwent constant, if subtle, change. The Germans cooked regularly with dried corn, made dumplings with catfish, baked crayfish casseroles, simmered bog-potato soup, and even thickened soups with wild okra—none of which occurred in the Old World. By cooking these foods and serving them alongside the occasional dish of sauerkraut, *dummus*, or *schales,* the Germans who settled the Middle Colonies achieved a balancing act that reflected culinary life for all Americans, men or woman, white or black, English or non-English.

Wheat

Before 1710, it wouldn't have been altogether wrong to observe that the Middle Colonies were evolving into a larger version of early New England. Settlers, mostly of English descent, had dutifully built solid houses and cleared land, and were soon practicing a version of traditional mixed farming. They shared a set of religious beliefs. A couple of modest urban centers kept both regions integrated into the transatlantic economy. Settlers living in relatively dense counties had strategically formed patterns of local exchange as they moved rapidly toward what appeared to be almost certain self-sufficiency. For a while, it looked as though the Middle Colonies were going to evolve in accordance with the dictates of the New England model.

By 1710, however, social and economic developments were beginning to emerge that would make the comparison with New England moot. The population had exploded, ethnic diversity had become the norm, a wide range of Protestant denominations had complicated the religious landscape, and settlers who had once staked a small claim and pursued a modest profit were now looking elsewhere to stake a larger claim and pursue a fatter profit. The Middle Colonies quickly evolved into a region in which the Quaker influence diminished, town stability yielded to constant internal migration, and the residents realized that the land's fertility was its own subtle kind of mother lode. People were eager to make money, acquire land, and improve their standard of living. So much so that even ethnic bonds strained under the pressure of land acquisition. As two experts on the British American economy explain, "Market considerations were more critical than ethnicity in determining land use, crop choice, farming techniques, and the like." All the preconditions were thus in place for the warm embrace of that touchstone of wealth in British America: a staple crop. The Middle Colonies wanted their version of sugar, tobacco, and rice. They wanted to become profitably tied into the transatlantic world. They wanted their own plantation experience. And they got it, sort of, with wheat.

Much as sugar, tobacco, and rice shaped the general contours of historical development in the West Indies, Chesapeake Bay, and Carolina, wheat—more than Quakerism, Native American influences, or ethnic diversity—similarly shaped the broad course of change in the Middle Colonies. In his master plan for his colony's development, William Penn proposed quaint agricultural villages nestled within well-defined townships near the coast. He intended his arrangement to establish the basis for a community where "neighbors may help one another . . . and that they may accustom their children to do the same." Good wheat fields, however, made good neighbors much in the way that good fences did. Farmers, it turns out, preferred to sprawl across the countryside into distantly spaced, highly decentralized plantations capable of accommodating the extensive agricultural practices that wheat demanded. The primed grain market compelled these responses among the region's entrepreneurially minded population. Throughout the eighteenth century, grain exports to Europe and the West Indies increased steadily, reaching 75 percent of all the goods exported to Europe by 1760. This trade began with the West Indies, where sugar planters whose land was too preoccupied with white gold to make their own food demanded a consistent supply of wheat, flour, and bread. By 1740, commerce shifted to Europe as the Middle Colonies became the primary supplier of wheat and flour to southern Europe, Ireland, and Britain. It was in response to this obvious opportunity for economic gain that the region's population exploded from 15,000 in 1680 to 428,000 in 1760. Settlers, both immigrants and American born, grew enough wheat to help along the region's considerable sprawl, with three towns forming in the 1730s, eleven in the 1740s, and sixteen in the 1750s. Wheat dominated the region's production enough for land prices to keep pace with population change and increasing levels of production. An acre went for 10 shillings in the 1730s, 20 shillings in the 1740s, and 40 shillings in the 1760s. Living standards kept pace. Average inventories rose from £105 in 1730 to £153 in 1750 to £208 in 1760. In many ways, wheat set the Middle Colonies on a steady course of generally healthy expansion.

Wheat production was harder on the land than on those growing it. Farmers and their labor first tilled a field with oxen and plow, making sure to work the "trash" from the previous crop back into the soil in order to help battle weed growth, pests, and diseases. Plowing was shallow, usually enough to create a dusting of friable soil. This technique saved time and prevented overly deep sowing. Farmers then fertilized the soil with livestock manure and treated it further with topsoil that had been irrigated on land lining a local riverbank. Next they either threw seeds across the treated plot or spread them in neat rows. A few wheat farmers may have sown their crops, which took considerably more time, in order to keep birds from eating the scattered seeds while protecting seeds from temperature fluctuation. Scattering them by hand, however, suited most farmers just fine because not only was it less time consuming but sowing seeds too deeply subjected them to pests and soil-borne diseases. To line the seeds in rows or not was also left to the farmer's discretion. Scattering, or "broadcasting," was both faster and more conducive to preventing weed growth, as the randomly but densely spaced wheat plants could effectively choke out incipient weeds. Placing seeds in rows obviously took more time, but it enabled farmers to better focus their seedbed preparations and space their crops at ideal distances.

Once these decisions were made and the seeds sprouted on the prepared acres of land, minimal upkeep was required before harvest—or at least nothing along the lines of the maintenance needed by tobacco. Once it ripened, workers cut the wheat with sickles, bound it into sheaves, and stacked them in a barn. Most of the work involved processing, as threshing the wheat could take much of the winter, followed by several weeks of winnowing the chaff. All in all, wheat was a friendly crop to grow in the Middle Colonies. It thrived in the cool, relatively moist early growing season (March), could be planted without much effort (at least compared with other staple crops), enjoyed an extensive growing season (180 days), and benefited from an easily tillable landscape. Once harvested, it was light, compact, and easily transported and processed.

For all the benefits it offered to the human population, however, wheat delivered a knockout punch to the once fertile soil, which rapidly deteriorated under the crop's burdensome demands after only two or three harvests. Initial yields as high as forty or fifty bushels of wheat an acre declined so rapidly throughout the eighteenth century that, by 1750, farmers were touting eight bushels an acre as a bumper crop. The anonymous author of *American Husbandry* noted that while "good lands yield 25 to 32 bushels per acre; on fields of inferior quality . . . they get from 15 to 25 bushels, and sometimes not so much as 15." The impulse to cultivate wheat more intensively—that is, with assiduous fertilization, improved seeds, and crop rotation—was more a matter of best intentions than agricultural reality. As one historian of Pennsylvania farming writes, "Pleas were voiced to buy improved seed from other areas (and thus enrich what today would be called the gene pool), to rotate crops, and to fertilize grain fields, but before 1800 few farmers sought to improve wheat yields." It was simply easier to gobble up more land, exhaust it, and move on deeper and deeper into the seemingly endless backcountry, which is precisely what settlers did.

The Role of Wheat in Shaping the Region's Foodways

These critical aspects of wheat production—the comparably lower labor demands of wheat (vis-à-vis sugar, tobacco, and rice) as well as the tendency to induce sprawl rather than keep people congregated within tightly knit communities—contributed to three related developments that would collectively help shape the region's foodways. First, wheat became a crop whose cultivation for export nevertheless allowed for substantial agricultural diversity throughout the region. Unlike the West Indies, Chesapeake Bay, and Carolina, the Middle Colonies couldn't in any way be accurately deemed "monocultural." To the contrary, wheat was a staple that allowed farming families to pursue other endeavors in earnest, as they so effective-ly did in New England. Second, wheat turned out to be a crop best worked through family labor buttressed by healthy doses of servant and slave labor. In this respect, the Middle Colonies reflected aspects of both the southern and New England colonies. In striking this balance, farmers developed a labor force that couldn't possibly make a notable singular culinary contri-bution in the way that, say, slaves did in Carolina. Third, because wheat was a crop that was easily transported and processed, mills, merchants, bakers, and shipping firms arose to process wheat into flour, and sometimes flour into bread, and move it all to where it needed to go. The evolution of these businesses helped establish Philadelphia and New York as the most active urban centers in colonial America. The result, in turn, was an unprec-edented level of internal specialization, trade, and dependence between cities and outlying farms that made the region self-sufficient, albeit in a way that required more constant exchange over greater distance. All these factors further influenced what and how the Middle Colonists ate. They can be quickly summarized.

While it dominated the economy and productive cycles of the region's farms, wheat peacefully coexisted with a broad range of mixed-farming activities. According to a register of wills from several Pennsylvania coun-ties, farms produced wheat alongside other grains, including rye, barley, oats, buckwheat, and Indian corn. Widows received pork, beef, mutton, eggs, and butter in their husbands' wills. Inventories from the Middle Col-onies also include garden and orchard produce such as potatoes, turnips, cabbage, and apples. Honey, milk, cheese, and malt are in evidence. This range of products made an impression on contemporaries, but often in a way that indirectly reiterated the popularity of wheat. The presence of barley excited one German settler, but he couldn't understand why more of his people didn't grow it. He blamed the comparative dearth of barley on the fact that "sufficient encouragement has not been given to raise it." Buckwheat sprouted up in small amounts, being the crop of choice for the region's poorest. Peter Kalm recalled seeing Indian corn on almost every farm but explained how it paled in comparison with corn yields in New England, which he thought unfortunate, given that it was "a graine [that] produced more increase than any other Graine whatsoever." Orchards were well established. "Scarce an house but has an apple, peach, and cherry or-chard," one settler wrote. Newspapers offered for sale homes with orchards containing several hundred trees. Gardeners produced potatoes "in great plenty on every farm." Livestock, however, drew mixed reviews. Johann

David Schoepf said that the Pennsylvania farmer "raises enough cattle to over stock the market." According to inventories, pigs were almost twice as common as cows, but their numbers may have steadily declined over the century because pigs in the Middle Colonies didn't forage on islands but, rather, had to be fed grain. Given that an average pig needed about thirty-two bushels of grain a year, one can see why farmers didn't go hog wild. The region's dairy supply was praised by many, while others doubted its availability on the basis that timothy grass—a necessity for decent milk cows—was hardly in existence. One farmer told his servant "not to neglect the timothy seed if he had to Ride a Hundred Miles for it." The boy undoubtedly passed miles and miles of wheat fields before he completed his assigned task.

The point here is that wheat allowed for a measured level of agricultural diversification while limiting that diversification. So, on the one hand, the Middle Colonies continued to look very much like New England, even after the onset of the wheat economy. Its access to garden produce, meat, a variety of grains, dairy products, and orchard fruit suggests strong parallels to New England's regional self-sufficiency and finely calibrated balance of economic pursuits. On the other hand, the Middle Colonies also looked something like the southern regions in that all economic endeavors—to some extent at least—responded to the magnetic pull of a single crop.

The labor arrangement that wheat and mixed farming demanded was, compared with those in other regions, equally hard to categorize. Family labor, as it did in New England, dominated, but not nearly as decisively as in that area. In the Middle Colonies, many other labor options prevailed alongside family labor. Wheat in no way justified the loyal dedication to slavery that sugar, tobacco, and rice required. Nevertheless, the slave population in the Middle Colonies rose from six thousand in 1710 to thirty-five thousand in 1770. Slaves more often than not found a home on a New York or New Jersey farm rather than a Pennsylvania one, and a significant portion of them worked in urban settings. (In 1746, for example, 30 percent of New York City's labor pool was slave labor.) The Philadelphia backcountry, by contrast, was only about 5 percent slave-based during the first half of the eighteenth century. This figure, however, rose during the second half of the century. The Middle Colonies, in essence, produced no staples that required a plantation-style labor force. Wheat farmers in the Pennsylvania backcountry thus never acquired more than two or three slaves at the most—but acquire them they did, if not to work from sunup to sundown, then to represent, as status symbols, the owner's newfound wealth and power. But demand also might have been more agricultural. After all, when the Seven Years' War took a substantial number of servants off backcountry farms to backcountry fields of battle between 1759 and 1762, Pennsylvanians purchased an unprecedented twelve hundred slaves in a three-month period to replace these servants. Slaves never came close to playing a dominant role in the region's economic or cultural development. But their presence served as a constant reminder that the Middle Colonies were a murky reflection of the South as well as the North.

White servants worked alongside slaves on the farms of the Middle Colonies, as servitude played a consistently critical role in shaping the labor force, comprising at times as much as one-third of the region's workers. While the earliest form of servitude was indentured servitude, it was never as harsh as it was in the Chesapeake, and, accordingly, servants had a much better chance of farming decent land once they fulfilled their terms. But indentured servitude became increasingly rare during the eighteenth century as another form of servitude—redemptioneering—became popular. As potential servants saw it, one problem with indentured servitude was that contracts were fixed in England, leaving them no bargaining room with their future masters. As the shippers of the indentured servants saw it, the problem with indentured servitude was that they were liable if the servants became sick on board the ship—a not uncommon occurrence. By the middle of the eighteenth century, as the supply of available English servants diminished, the bargaining power of servants increased. Redemptioneers—very often German—relied on loan transactions rather than contracts. An immigrant borrowed money from a shipper for the trip to America and then, once in Pennsylvania or New York, negotiated a labor contract with a farmer that would allow him and his family to repay the shipper and save enough to purchase his own land with an eye toward starting his own farm. In a region where many farmers needed labor for a couple of months at a time, rather than year round, this arrangement tended to suit the needs of all parties involved.

Other forms of labor included cottagers, tenants, and wage laborers. Cottagers were laborers and their families who were housed in cottages on farms. The owners of the land and the cottages demanded a small rent, paid their cottagers by the day or the week, and granted them many privileges not given to typical servants. The cottage movement took off as a result of expanding farms and incomes among the region's landowning farmers. As profits accumulated, they were much more inclined to sink their money into more land rather than expand their homes to include more servants in the main living quarters, as had traditionally been the case. A cottage out in the field came to seem more economical and piecemeal jobs more efficient. In New York, tenancy became a popular living arrangement and labor option. The original Dutch settlers in New York had established manorial-style estates in an attempt to live like European landlords. These estates lasted well into the eighteenth century, with one surviving until the mid-nineteenth century, despite the English conquest of New Amsterdam in 1664. Although only a superficial approximation of European manors, these patroonships—of which there were about thirty—divided and leased their lands to families who practiced a mixed-farming form of agriculture for both themselves and their landlords. While feudal in name, in effect they served as stepping-stones for young laborers to become independent landowners themselves and thereby served the needs of a wheat-based mixed economy quite flexibly. Wage labor, finally, played a minor but nonetheless useful role throughout the Middle Colonies. Although wage workers never constituted a significant force anywhere in colonial America (due primarily to the relative abundance of land), the Middle Colonies had a diverse enough economy—one that effectively combined industry and agriculture—to support a decent supply of laborers who were willing to shift their jobs on a daily basis and work in many settings.

Thus while family labor along the lines of the New England model prevailed throughout the Middle Colonies, it coexisted with a wide range of other labor forms: indentured servants, redemptioneers, tenants, cottagers, wage laborers, and apprentices. This diversity suited the wheat-based mixed-agricultural system that became entrenched during the eighteenth century while ensuring a broad range of agricultural pursuits beyond wheat farming. As a result, the general labor system of the Middle Colonies—alongside its diverse but staple-oriented economy—did not support the formation of a single, dominant mode of cooking and eating. Whereas slaves played critical roles in shaping food in the South and free families played powerful roles in stressing the importance of traditional food in New England, the workforce in the Middle Colonies was varied enough for everyone to have an impact and no one to dominate. The labor system in the Middle Colonies therefore failed to significantly shape the region's eating habits, at least compared with other regions.

The third factor to emerge from wheat production was the region's distinctive urbanization, a development that sparked an impressive level of internal specialization and, in turn, strongly shaped how the region acquired its food. While Boston had the longtime distinction of being the colonies' most bustling urban center, Philadelphia exceeded it in the 1740s and New York followed in the 1750s. The combination of wheat exports, a diversified economy, and the region's lack of intricate internal rivers (on the level of the Chesapeake), as well as the Middle Colonies' strategic position between the West Indies and New England, predisposed the region to coastal urbanization movements so powerful that Philadelphia could count thirty thousand residents in 1774 and New York, twenty-five thousand. The rise of these conspicuous and dense urban centers helped inspire the evolution of less obvious but nonetheless important urbanized towns such as New Castle, Delaware; Lancaster, Pennsylvania; and Newark, New Jersey. Urbanization revolved around wheat. Unlike tobacco, wheat could be easily and profitably processed on the spot. Millers arose to turn wheat into flour, which inspired bakers to turn flour into bread. These tasks required river travel and access to a port. The milling industry sparked other endeavors, and the urban population soon teemed with merchants, insurance agents, warehousemen, and shipbuilders. These trades had their own "multiplier effects," attracting artisans, doctors, lawyers, and laborers to the urban center like bees to a hive. By the early eighteenth century, cities in the region were thriving.

The unprecedented level of urbanization that swept the Middle Colonies strongly influenced the way the region fed itself. Technically speaking, the Middle Colonies, like New England, did feed itself. It did so, however, through an extensive internal trade that cities facilitated. In essence, the presence of cities allowed farming families throughout New York, New Jersey, Pennsylvania, and Delaware to specialize their provisioning activities in such a way that they did not have to rely so much on local exchange with immediate neighbors, as New Englanders did, but on a more routinized and sophisticated pattern of intraregional trade with towns and counties that they knew in name only. One area within the region would focus on dairy, and others would focus on pork, beef, garden produce, or beer and cider production. Relying on the comparatively efficient systems of roads and ferries in the Middle Colonies, these producers would pay teamsters to transport their produce to urban markets, both large and small. From there, some of the produce would leave port for Europe, the southern colonies, or the West Indies; as for the rest, merchants and traders would eagerly disperse them throughout the region to areas that specialized in other goods. Food products were reabsorbed into the economy by distant neighbors whom the producers never met. This specialization didn't foster the more communal cohesiveness that prevailed in New England. Nevertheless, it did encourage the production of more plentiful amounts of food products that were more efficiently distributed in an increasingly commercialized economy. It was, in short, an arrangement of food distribution that helped the Middle Colonies earn the moniker of "bread basket."

William Penn didn't envision the level of internal specialization and economic progress that the region's farmers, artisans, and merchants achieved. In his earliest account of Pennsylvania, in fact, he predicted the sort of relative self-sufficiency that New England had already accomplished. "The town," he wrote, referring to Philadelphia, "is well furnish'd with convenient Mills; and what with their Garden Plats (the least half an acre), the Fish of the River, and their labour, to the Countryman, who begins to pay with the provisions of his own growth, they live Comfortably." The goals of the settlers, however, would prove to be more ambitious than mere comfortable living. As they later observed, it took more than just the "diligent application of people to husbandry" to feed the Middle Colonies and enable them to turn an ample profit. It took efficient internal movement, coordination, specialization, and trade. Henry Muhlenberg said on one of his journeys that "we have no lack of food here." The reason he cited confirmed the major difference between New England and the Middle Colonies. He wrote that the "country people must carry their produce to the city and receive very little for it." He further observed that "the country people are isolated and do not live near one another." "Their entire wealth," he continued in a remark that further suggested the extent of the region's internal specialization, "consists of cattle and grain." In 1759, Andrew Burnaby remarked on the prevalence of the region's internal specialization when, on a visit to New Jersey, he explained how "there is no foreign trade carried on from this province; for the inhabitants sell their produce to the merchants of Philadelphia and New York, and take in return . . . other necessaries of life." Peter Kalm made a similar observation about commercial arrangements between New Jersey and New York. "The products which came from New Brunswick," he wrote, "were said to be grain, flour in quite large quantities, bread, linseed in considerable amounts, and various utensils. All of these were sent on small sailing boats to New York, which is the only trading center, and to which wares are shipped. New York is situated forty English miles from New Brunswick."

Specialization didn't benefit every area equally, especially if an area lacked transportation capabilities. According to Kalm, the Swedes tended to suffer this fate. "The Swedes who then came over," he explained, "settled near bays and rivers, where they had good opportunities for fishing. Most of them had no horses or beasts of burden, so that when they needed salt, which could not be procured elsewhere then in New York ... they went tither after it, riding in part on oxen and in part on cows, bought salt there and whatever they needed and brought it back home on the backs of the just mentioned animals." The frequency of local trade was enough for the Middle Colonies to stipulate, as Kalm put it, that "the produce of the land, such as wheat, rye, corn, barley, oats, pork, meat ... shall in trade be valid as money." Indeed, such products were the region's collective gold standard, one that allowed it to become such a stable economic powerhouse tightly woven into the transatlantic world.

Kalm was perhaps the most acute observer of how the region's internal specialization shaped the way Middle Colonists thought about and acquired their food. His account teems with references not only to particular foods but also to their availability. "The best cider," he noted, "is said to be made in New Jersey and New York, hence this cider is preferred to any other. I have scarcely tasted any better cider than that from New Jersey." He later recounted how, for all their popularity in the region, "few peas are planted in New Sweden because worms eat them up before they are ripe." A friend's crop planted in 1748 "had been so infested by vermin that hardly a pea had escaped." All of them had been "hollowed out and spoiled." The preferred place to find the best cheese, according to Kalm, was in Pennsylvania. "In New York," he began his short treatise, "several kinds of cheese were made. Most of them appeared in an average, suitable-sized mold, were round, reasonably thick; and some tasted pretty well, but most varieties were poor and manufactured from sour milk." Not so in the next colony over. "Here in Pennsylvania," he wrote, "we got cheese of both kinds, good and bad; but in general better cheese was made here than in any other place in America that I visited." Parts of New Sweden produced notable cheese as well. "The cheese made by the Swedes of Raccoon was especially good. . . . Some of it could rival the English variety," he explained. Eastern Pennsylvania impressed Kalm with a popular breakfast food. "Farmers sow a considerable amount of buckwheat in this locality," he observed. "It is used especially in preparing cakes similar to pancakes (griddle cakes). As these cakes come hot from the pan they are covered with butter which allowed to soak into them." They were typically eaten in the morning "with tea or coffee." The cities offered their own specialties. Kalm became very excited about "some colonists in this vicinity [Philadelphia] [who] made a pleasant beverage of apples" through a process that boiled dried apple peelings and added yeast and bran to the liquid. "One who has not tasted it before would not believe that such a palatable beverage could be prepared from apples," he cheered.

The Big Picture

For all its impact on the region's culinary development, wheat never dominated the Middle Colonies in the way that sugar, tobacco, and rice did the more southern regions of British America. But it may very well be the best lens through which to view the region's overall foodways. Wheat's tendency to sprawl across the landscape, as well the relative ease with which it could be processed, allowed farmers to pursue other agricultural and industrial ventures, required a highly variable labor force to complement family labor, and fostered an intraregional level of economic specialization unseen anywhere else in British America. These factors collectively provided Middle Colonists a chance to pursue a relatively self-sufficient English-oriented diet that was free from any single dominating force. It did so while intermingling with the frugality of the Quakers, the impact of Native Americans, and the mélange of ethnic diversity. Together, all these factors lent the region a distinctive—if hard to identify—flavor.

The wide variety of influences that shaped the Middle Colonial diet, in addition to the fact that no single factor had an overwhelming impact on the region's overall foodways, helps explain the range of contemporary descriptions about the region's food habits. They are hard to characterize, follow no single pattern (or even handful of patterns), and generally seem to have cohered within a framework defined by very different historical preconditions. What you see depends on what perspective you take, what document you crack, or what voice you find the most authoritative. Thus one might come across the following account from the Pennsylvania settler Nicholas More and rightly posit the development of distinctly English habits of providing and eating food:

But to give you to understand the full of our Condition, with respect to Provision in this Province; we had last Fall, and the Winter, abundance of good fresh Pork in our Market at two pence half-penny per pound . . . Beef at the same rate . . . and Butter for six pence per pound; Wheat for four shillings per Bushel; Rye three Shillings; and now all this Summer Wheat is at three shillings.

Next, one might encounter this quotation, taken from *The Journal of John Woolman*—a passage in which he describes how his peers should handle the region's obviously blessed bounty—and appreciate the region's culinary frugality:

When men take their pleasure . . . and so indulge their appetite as to disorder their understandings, neglect their duty as members of a family or civil society, and cast off all regard to religion, their case is to be pitied. . . . Every degree of luxury hath some connection with evil; and if those who profess to be disciples of Christ . . . have that mind in them . . . it is a means of help to the weaker. . . . Though trading in things useful is an honest employ, yet through the great number of superfluities which are bought and sold . . . they who apply to merchandise for a living have great need to be well experienced in that prospect which the Prophet Jeremiah laid down for his scribe: "Seekest thou great things for thyself? Seek them not."

Naturally, the incomparably vivid accounts of Dr. Alexander Hamilton easily suggest a world of ethnic interaction, a veritable melting pot of cultures, as in these descriptions of his food exchanges with foreigners:

I found two strange gentlemen that had come from Jamaica. . . . Our conversation was a medley, but the chief subject was the differences in climates in the American provinces. . . . We dined at Todd's [Tavern], with seven in company, upon veal, beef steaks, green pease, and rasp berries for desert. . . . [Later, in a Dutch home, he observed] They set out their cabinets and bouffets with much china. Their kitchens are likewise very clean, and there they hang earthen or delft plates and dishes all round the walls in manner of pictures . . . they are in their persons slovenly and dirty . . . rustic and unpolished . . . [an opinion confirmed when the hostess] made me a present of dryed tongue.

Finally, one might pay attention to Peter Kalm's accounts of Native American interaction and assume that the Middle Colonies were a region where the original inhabitants shaped the way settlers obtained and ate their food. The aforementioned account of catching eels between the crevices of rocks, in particular, might further that assumption:

A large quantity is gotten this way. Some small native boys tried the method today for my benefit, and returned very soon with a large heap of them. The Indian lads were real daredevils; they walked right out to the very edge of the cataract or river and looked down, where it was not only vertical but where the rock besides had grown worn by the water. They waded a long distance into the water right above the cataract, and then proceeded to approach the falls themselves so close that there was not more than a foot to the outer edge of the cliff where the water spills over from its terrifying height. There stood those rascals, gazing down!

Indeed, one might draw different conclusions about the foodways of the Middle Colonies from each of these examples. And, in a sense, each conclusion wouldn't be necessarily wrong. Each example, in fact, suggests a basic similarity with another area of British America. The Quaker simplicity and desire for English foods certainly evoke the New England model. The ethnic influence hints at the role that African Americans played in molding the eating habits of the South. The Native American impact recalls the ways of Carolina. While these conclusions wouldn't necessarily be wrong, however, they would—as single expressions of the culinary ways of the Middle Colonies—misrepresent a region that cannot be pigeonholed in the way the other regions can. In other words, all characteristics had a tremendous influence on the region but none singularly enough to impute to the region a definitive set of foodways. We might thus call the Middle Colonies a land of diversity, plenty, and refined crudeness. Not coincidentally, such a description applies perfectly to scrapple, the food that—perhaps unjustifiably—defines the region more than any other.

...timore county, about 24 miles from Baltimore town; ... Patapsco river, and about the same distance from a ...od landing on Gunpowder river; there is a fine branch ...ns through it, adjoining to which is a good deal of low, ...h, meadow ground, which may be brought to great ...rfection with little expence; it is well situate for raising ...ck, there being a great range back of it. Any person ...clinable to purchase the aforesaid tract of land, may, by ...plying to the subscriber, examine the title, and know ...e terms of sale.

JOHN GALLOWAY.

Philadelphia, May 21. 1747.

ABRAHAM SHELLEY, Keeper of the Workhouse in Philadelphia, continues to buy ...sorts of fine grey linnen yarn, for which he gives rea-...money; he likewise makes and sells all sorts of fine co-...red thread, hat linings, shoemakers hemp, gives out ...x to good spinners, prints and glazes linnen or callicoe ...r gowns, curtains, or counterpains, cuts logwood for ...ters, and sells good oakum, all at reasonable rates, and ...ans cloth clothes.

N. B. He has a servant lad to dispose of, that has about ...ven years to serve, and is a shoemaker by trade. ☉

Philadelphia, May 21. 1747.

RICE and SOAL LEATHER, to be sold by Capt. Grant, at Mr. Hazard's Wharff.

Philadelphia, May 14. 1747.

To be SOLD,

A Servant Man's TIME, by Trade a Blacksmith, has between Three and Four Years ...serve. Enquire of William Rush, of Philadelphia. ☉

Philadelphia, April 30. 1747.

JUst imported, and to be sold by Nathaniel Allen, jun. in Front-street, near Market-street, a ...rcel of Carolina reed, fit for stay-makers. (T b c t f.)

Philadelphia, April 2. 1747.

...ust imported from London, in the Fortune, Captain Russel,

A Fresh assortment of druggs and me-...dicines, likewise fine broad cloths and shalloons, ...be sold reasonably, with most sorts of varnishes, by ...ichard Farmar, at the Unicorn in Second-street. T

...brings it to John Wood, Wa... ...shall have *Twenty Shillings* re...

...Phila...

WHereas, on the ... ...some person or pers... mothy Scarth, of the North... Philadelphia, broke open his ... lowing goods, viz. A gold ... gold locket, and a pair of ... spoons, and two large silver ... bed linnen, a set of fine hu... ther Things, to the value of ... the person in whose possession ... are, will return the same to ... days from the date hereof, ... asked concerning the same; ... said Timothy Scarth where... ceive *Five Pounds* reward, p...

⊕ TIM...

...Phila...

FIVE PISTOL...

RUN away last night ... of Chester, in Penns... med Sion Wentworth, bor... bout 25 years, by trade a ... inches high, well set, ... look, slow of speech, walks ... had the Small-pox. Had on ... beaver hat, sharp cock'd, ... dark brown broad-cloth coat ... ble breasted, and more worn ... of the buttons worn off, and ... leather breeches, blue yarn ... skin shoes, with holes bur... white homespun shirt, and ... cures him in any goal, or ... may have him again, shall ... reasonable Charges, paid by ...

...Phila...

RUN away on the ... ...subscriber, near Warwic... Irish servant man, named B... of age, a short well-set fellow ... brown hair, if not cut off, ... a felt hat, ozenbrigs shirt ... jacket, without lining, w...

CHAPTER 6

CONSUMPTION
The British Invasion

All the ships of the sea and the sailors in them visited you to trade
with you. . . . [T]hey brought you glory . . . and helped make
your beauty perfect.
Ezekiel 27:9–11

DESCRIPTIONS OF KITCHENS are rare in the historical record, but a visitor
to the Deep South left a vivid one. He was astonished that "wooden benches
were used in place of chairs, one iron spoon answered for the whole family,
and the mother added the sugar to the coffee with her fingers, and tasted
each cup before sending it around to ascertain if it was right. Such things
as andirons, tongs, and washbasins, were considered useless. . . . All the
family, excepting the parents and two sons, were barefooted." The scene
wasn't colonial America, but Mississippi in the early nineteenth century.
It could have, however, been just about anywhere in seventeenth-century
British America.

Even for wealthy colonists, seventeenth-century kitchens, like the run-
down kitchen in nineteenth-century Mississippi, were spartan affairs.
Consider Mark Symmons, a farmer from Ipswich, Massachusetts. His impressive inventory was recorded on April 28, 1659. Despite his substantial
brood of livestock, "fetherbed & boulster & red rug," one "greate chaire &
4 small and too cushions," and a rare grindstone, Symmons's kitchen held
the following items: "one great kettell," "3 small ould ones," "2 old skillets
& a scimer [skimmer]," a warming pan, a frying pan, two iron pots and
pothooks, and a spit. A well-off Salem resident, William Jiggles, registered
an inventory taken exactly two months after Symmons's. He, too, enjoyed
a cache of luxury items, including a silver beaker, a rug, curtains, a feather
bed, a sword, and "bedsteed and hangings." His kitchen, however, contained nothing more elaborate than "iron potts & hangers," "earthen ware,"
one frying pan, and "1 kitle." In Salisbury, Massachusetts, Joseph Peasley
went par for the course in the kitchen department. With an estate valued

at an impressive £143, his kitchen contained simply "one pare of and Irons and 2 spits," in addition to "on[e] iron pot and skelet, pot hokes and flesh hoke." If these homes reflected the ownership of kitchen equipment among the elite, one can safely assume that more common residents cooked and ate with even fewer utensils. Elizabeth Lowle of Newbury, Massachusetts, certainly suggests so. Her sole culinary item bequeathed to "Sister Tappine" was "1 pann." Extreme as her case may have been, she wasn't alone.

Tables, chairs, spoons, forks, knives, serving plates, dinner plates, individual cups, bowls, napkins, tablecloths, serving trays, and other household utensils that we might deem timelessly central to culinary life were in fact rarities for colonial America's founding generations. To an extent, this relative dearth of cooking and eating implements reflected the comparative primitiveness of a frontier culture. The settlers' lack of purchasing power during the first decades of settlement necessitated the acceptance of "primitive simplicity" as an unavoidable condition that pioneers building a society on the empire's rugged frontier had to endure. But the wealthy did accumulate a few luxuries. They just weren't kitchen-related luxuries. The common appearance of elaborate textiles in the inventories of the well-off, contrasted with their seeming lack of interest in the fancier accoutrements of cooking and eating, spoke to a prevailing culinary ethic whereby food played only a functional role in the lives of colonists trying to establish communities in a new world. They needed food to live and work, not to luxuriate in. Although the experience was rare, people *had* once starved in colonial America, and stories of those hardships weren't easily forgotten. While the chances of food scarcity were remote in a land of unparalleled natural abundance, they were evident enough to encourage an attitude toward food that basically made people happy enough just to have it.

Of course, colonists more concerned with status wrung their hands incessantly over the content and quality of their food. New Englanders aimed for a culinary replication of the homeland, while men such as William Byrd snobbishly fussed over the dreadful "mess" that their contemporaries too often stooped to consume. Ultimately, however, the manner in which seventeenth-century colonists cooked food, presented it, and lifted it to their mouths mattered less than how cloth felt against their skin, whether their roof leaked, and if their fence successfully kept out the neighbor's hogs. The evidence on this point is strong. There were plenty of wealthy farmers and merchants in Weathersfield, Connecticut, for example, but only half of them saw fit to own a table before 1670. By 1680, families with several children and a few servants averaged a mere 2.6 chairs. A visitor to one typical home recalled how he "sat down on the bed, for chairs and stools there were none." Another noted in 1650 how he "took up my dinner and laid it on a little table made on the [baby's] cradle head." When weather permitted, diners placed their food on a board and ate in the yard. When inclement, they dumped the meal onto the floor in front of the fireplace, squatted in a semicircle, and dug in. Food was food was food, and, for all the fuss they sometimes made of it, early settlers of all backgrounds ultimately found satiation as long as it stuck to the ribs and nourished.

Such a frontier attitude wasn't permanent. As the colonial American economy grew, and as white colonists began to regard the colonies as stable societies rather than rough-hewn settlements, they did what came naturally and began to replicate the general ways of England. As we'll see with respect to food, they did so through the improvement of kitchens, the acquisition of English goods (including cookware), and a reliance on English cookbooks. While these developments naturally affected different colonists from different regions in different ways, they nonetheless collectively served to lessen the isolation of regional cooking styles and inspire the beginning of a convergence of colonial British American food habits. To be sure, they didn't single-handedly lead to a unique American cuisine, but they pushed Americans a step in the direction of cooking and eating in a similar manner.

The Evolution of the British American Kitchen

Seventeenth-century simplicity had much to do with the diminutive size and rough layout of the kitchen itself. No matter how economically successful the colonial family, no matter how powerful its English pedigree, seventeenth-century British America was no time and place to indulge in elaborate displays of architectural prowess. More pressing tasks beckoned. Fields had to be cleared and planted, fences built, livestock fattened, crops planted, gardens tended. Time and energy were indebted to more immediate tasks. And thus a common seventeenth-century dwelling in the mainland colonies, even for large families, was about a four-hundred-square-foot single-room box constructed of wood, adorned with two small windows covered with wood shutters or oilcloth, and showcasing a large fireplace recessed into a wall—by any standard, an altogether crude abode.

It's also for this reason that, early on, many colonists chose to use the interior fireplace for heating purposes only, building a smaller cooking fireplace outdoors. Peter Kalm, a Swedish traveler to colonial America, explained, "I have not seen an oven in a cottage anywhere." Instead, "it is built separately in the yard, a short distance from the house, and is generally covered by a little roof of boards, to protect it from rain, snow, or storms." More often than not, he claimed, "it is elevated a few inches above the ground so that chickens and other small animals can stand under it when it rains." Indoor kitchens, which were certainly more common than Kalm allowed, were cramped rooms serving a number of other functions, such as storage, reading, or sleeping space. One English traveler, a Mrs. Knight, was horrified when she was sent off to bed in "a little Room parted from the kitchen *by a single bord partition*." A recent immigrant to Delaware found his uncle living in "a Loansome Cottage," which he described as "a small Log House that serves for Kitchen, Parlour, Hall and Bed Chamber." Many probate inventories throughout the colonies refer to a "kitchen bedroom."

The baseness of the colonial kitchen is made more tangible through a brief comparison of similar wealth groups in England and Virginia. Historian James P. Horn's meticulous research on the Vale of Berkeley in England and St. Mary's County in Virginia shows how, among the poorest seventeenth-century English residents, 84 percent owned pewter, while only 53 percent of the poorest colonists did. Boiling and frying equipment was ubiquitous on both sides of the Atlantic, but while 63 percent of the English lower middle class owned roasting equipment, only 24 percent of their colonial counterparts did. An even greater disparity divides these groups when it comes to tables and chairs. Of the poorest in England, 81 percent owned a table or table board. The same could be said for only 7 percent of the poorest colonists. Among England's lower middle class, 80 percent owned chairs, compared with 28 percent of the colonists. Whereas 25 percent of lower-middle-class Vale of Berkeley families owned a warming pan, about .05 percent of St. Mary's lower-middle-class residents did. Although the wealthier classes did a better job of approaching the English standard of living appropriate to their class, they suffered material deprivation on the frontier. As Horn discovered, 41 percent of the upper-middle-class English displayed their polished wares in a cupboard, whereas only 12 percent of their colonial counterparts could do the same. Although sharing similar levels of wealth with their English brethren, colonists lived much more meanly.

The general lack of dining and cooking implements during the seventeenth century, in addition to the minimal cooking space available to store those goods, helped foster the regional culinary distinctions that defined colonial America. Simplicity with respect to food preparation and consumption enhanced regional differences because it necessitated a habit of creative adaptation, pulling white settlers into tighter relationships with the land, the Native Americans, and the labor sources that they exploited. The widespread presence of no other cooking utensil except a single pot helped ensure that what colonists tossed into that pot reflected the flora and fauna of their backyard, the surrounding woods, and the local market rather than some overarching cultural ideal of what food should be. Should a settler have walked north from Carolina in 1680, these regional distinctions would not have blended into a gradual continuum. Instead, they would have impressed the traveler with their stark differences. Populations not only existed in relative isolation, but pioneered regional foodways reflective of that isolation, thus confirming what Benjamin Franklin observed as their "different interests . . . different manners."

This situation began to change by the middle of the eighteenth century, when the rugged simplicity of the seventeenth-century kitchen gave way to more elaborate cooking arrangements. The change was gradual, but it was real, and it had a pivotal impact on the state of American cooking. Due in large part to the agricultural decisions discussed earlier, settlements evolved into societies on the backs of the profits generated by their staple crops. As the colonies matured economically, the material conditions and tools of daily life improved dramatically. A look into a few eighteenth-century kitchens confirms that this slow but significant transformation in material culture didn't leave cooking behind. In December 1771, for example, Samuel Gardner, a Virginia gentleman, left an estate that included among its "kitchen furniture" the following: a damask tablecloth, two brass kettles, a teakettle, a skimmer, a pepper box, twelve brass candlesticks, a gridiron, a spit, a frying pan, two iron pots, fifty-one pounds of pewter ware (spoons and cups), a bellows, a chafing dish, knives and forks, a churn, earthenware, a cheese press, a teapot, cups, a canister, a cream pot, a mustard pot, and a dozen glass bottles. In 1762, a Philadelphia merchant listed a similarly sophisticated stash of kitchen items in his inventory, including a silver spoon, brass candlesticks, six enameled plates, twenty-three pounds of pewter (spoons, forks, knives), six teaspoons, a brass kettle, a China bowl, andirons, a set of pot racks, a teakettle, a saucepan, a "large brass pann," a China plate, six maple rush-bottom chairs, five tablecloths, six delft plates, twenty-two bottles, a tankard, four old pots, two oval tables, a colander, a pepper box, a coffee mill, a chopping knife, a large cedar tub, and bread and cheese testers. In Roxbury, Massachusetts, John Bridge had in his four-room house, which sat on his fifty-acre farm, two brass kettles, a brass pan, a warming pan, two skillets, six pewter dishes, fifteen pewter plates, six porringers, a tankard, a quart pot, a dripping pan, a pastry pan, a chafing dish, a gridiron, two trammels, a spit, andirons, a chopping knife, a ladle, a "flesh fork," iron candlesticks, a table and eight chairs, eleven knives and forks, and "some wooden & earthen ware." Although all of these homeowners were financially successful, none was exceptional in terms of his kitchen creature comforts.

Complementing this explosion in cooking and eating implements were changes in the kitchen's design. Whereas kitchens had traditionally been cramped multipurpose spaces in which competing household activities were carried out, they now expanded into separate rooms designed to accommodate specialized tasks. One must, however, be careful not to overstate this transition. Architectural changes occurred slowly in colonial America, and most families continued to live in one- or two-cell box houses built around the chimney and rarely measuring any more than 600 square feet. Richard Bushman discovered that in Kent County, Delaware—a relatively prosperous region—67 percent of the houses in the late eighteenth century measured less than 450 square feet, and 22 percent of the populace lived in houses that measured between 450 and 600 square feet. A *Pennsylvania Gazette* advertisement from 1743 wasn't at all unusual in offering for sale "a framed and log-house, 20 foot by 23," nor was a *New York Journal* ad in 1771 for "a dwelling house, 2 rooms on a floor." That said, colonial homes did expand in size, however modestly, and the presence of "mansions" among the well-to-do became unmistakable markers on the eighteenth-century landscape. While comparatively few in number, these elaborate and conspicuous displays of wealth served to redefine the architectural standards of the day, encouraging common colonists to update their own houses by adding several dozen square feet in the form of a lean-to or an extra room, or tacking on a garret or a second floor. Merchants and planters used their profits to build homes with brick and mortar in humbler versions of the Georgian styles so popular in England at the time. The elite skimped on little, adorning their homes with sash windows, parlors, stairways with balusters, discrete sleeping areas, hallways, and, of course, larger and better organized kitchens. Less prosperous colonists, in turn, although unable to copy these houses with any realistic precision, proceeded to add rooms, build stairways, plaster ceilings, erect scroll-pediment chimneypieces, and—like the elite—improve their kitchens. Early food traditions in colonial America might have moved from the bottom up, but architectural changes trickled from the top down. When it came to the built environment, few colonists approached the grandiosity of English architecture. Nonetheless, the colonial elite set the provincial trends that the masses followed.

The two met somewhere in the middle. It was this confluence of cultural influences that led to several changes in the design and location of colonial kitchens for white colonial Americans of all backgrounds. In the seventeenth century, if families cooked inside, they typically did so in an expansive hearth surrounded by a smattering of basic cooking utensils dangling from a worn mantle. As we have seen, the kitchen served as a bedroom, place to spin wool and weave, and even reading nook. It was, historians of technology agree, a terribly inefficient arrangement that makes the necessity of a one-pot meal that much more understandable. Indeed, not only was there little room to cook, but most of the fire's heat was sucked directly up the chimney, failing to roast food evenly (much less warm the room) and necessitating the gathering of an acre woodlot's worth of wood every year. In response to these problems, the architectural changes that evolved over the eighteenth century included three major improvements: families moved cooking space into a separate room, improved the quality of the cooking hearth itself, and established small, specialized food-preparation areas. Each change deserves a closer look.

The "suppressed kitchen," as architectural historians call it, became a standard feature of common households. The kitchen might have occupied a number of places in the eighteenth-century house—including outside—but it was rarely located in a central portion of the house. Not only did wealthier families build new houses to incorporate this significant change, but those of more modest means made the requisite alterations as well, both to keep up with the Joneses and to make cooking and eating less cumbersome and crowded affairs. One surviving example of this renovation is Andrew Keyser's early Virginia home. Although precisely when he made these changes is unclear, we know that at some point in the eighteenth century he altered and enlarged his simple house in order to move cooking activities from the main block of the house to a small, newly built area eight feet off the central room. Similarly, the owners of the Hempstead House in New London, Connecticut, turned what was originally a one-room structure, built in 1643, into a two-room home with a large lean-to on the back. The most conspicuous outcome of this remodeling was a brand-new kitchen. However, instead of building a new chimney to accommodate it, the carpenter opened the other end of the existing chimney and made the new room adjoining it into a kitchen. In ways such as these, carpenters throughout the colonies worked to convert homes originally designed for seventeenth-century needs into eighteenth-century examples of a renovated kitchen.

Heating improvements were directly linked to this architectural transition. The wastefulness of the wide-open hearth, an inefficient arrangement made increasingly evident by frequent timber shortages, encouraged colonists to reduce the fireplace width from several yards to several feet. Smaller fireplaces meant that colonists could, if they so desired, specialize by building two fireplaces, using one for heating and the other for cooking. Families also built a smaller cooking fireplace into the same wall with the chimney while keeping it far enough removed to use it as a distinct cooking space. When Benjamin Franklin wrote a treatise on stoves in 1744, he described "large open fires" as an old habit "used in the days of our fathers," noting that "most of these old-fashioned chimneys in towns and cities have been, of late years, reduced." Franklin's solution of incorporating an iron fireplace inside the regular one proved an especially influential development. The smaller iron fireplace—designed exclusively for heating—came equipped with a series of air ducts and chambers that retained the hot air that would otherwise have escaped up the chimney. Drawing on colder air from outside, it then sent the heated air radiating back into the living room. Although not everyone could afford a Franklin fireplace, Franklin's invention was relatively easy to approximate. His iron fireplace not only became popular, but provided a master blueprint for others to tinker with and improve throughout the eighteenth century, the end of which saw the enclosed stove. The widespread acceptance of the heating fireplace was a form of domestic specialization that further helped displace the cooking fire—which did not have to radiate outward to warm the household—into a distinct room. Moreover, the new cooking fireplace, because of its reduced size, could free itself from the cumbersome andirons, bellows, cranes, and trammels, thereby creating space for updated cooking equipment.

A separate kitchen had the added benefit of discrete storage and cooking areas. Although the addition of distinct areas for food preparation was a development enjoyed by only elite families, it set a design standard that families of more modest means would increasingly follow after 1750, when English manufactured goods became more affordable. Houses that substantially expanded did so by adding a second story that matched the blueprint of the first. The addition of a second story, which became a popular option around the 1740s, widened the potential to refine cooking and storage functions. Home layouts started to include areas such as the "kitchen chamber," "larder," "buttery," and "pantry," standard features of English homes but relatively new colonial amenities. Other houses expanded downward. Peter Kalm identified a popular architectural change when he claimed that, by the mid-eighteenth century, town homes were "commonly built in the English manner"—a manner that included a cellar that was "sometimes a kitchen." Cellars with stone floors, serviceable through trap doors, appeared throughout the century and throughout the colonies. They provided space for a number of critical culinary functions. It was in the cellar, for example, where Joshua Hempstead, according to his diary, engaged in such activities as "pickling my meat" and "husking." It was also the place where he "killed my Red Hogg" and "helped salte up ye pork." The cellar, as we have seen in New England, proved to be an ideal place to store herbs, roots, and other garden vegetables.

Other spaces emerged, too. Back in the main room of the house, cooking space might have moved elsewhere, but shelves and cupboards took its place. The shortening of chimney stacks due to smaller and more efficient fireplaces provided room in recesses for recently acquired plates, cups, bowls, and serving trays. On a visit to Albany in 1744, Dr. Alexander Hamilton observed of the Dutch residents, "They set out their cabinets and bouffetts with much China." William Torrey exemplified the quest toward the specialization of cooking space when he renovated his house, built in 1717, to create a separate kitchen, in which he kept "kettles, pans, and skillets, pewter, earthenware, silver cups, and spoons." He also built a cellar, which held "butter and hog's fat," and a lean-to, where he stored cheese. Together, additional rooms, lean-tos, and cellars encouraged cooks to spread out and rethink their range of culinary options.

These three changes imbued the colonial kitchen with newfound importance. It was an importance confirmed by the advertisements that homeowners placed in newspapers when they wanted to sell their estates. In ad after ad, the only specific room routinely singled out for comment was the kitchen. A "plantation in Baltimore," advertised in the *Pennsylvania Gazette* in 1743, describes a "good dwelling place" with separate "kitchen, corn-house, quarters, and stables." The kitchen abutted a garden and "a good bearing orchard." Another ad for a house and lot on the Schuylkill River outside Philadelphia offered not only "20 acres of winter corn" and two orchards but "a good stone house and kitchen." A Maryland plantation sported its own gristmill, "a constant run of water in the driest season," a "good new dwelling house, of two rooms on a floor," and "a Kitchen and other outhouses." Mary Cole offered for sale a New Jersey plantation that conveyed "a Negro woman who understands Country business" in addition to "a new stone house and kitchen." John Large described his home as "having kitchen . . . [with] good conveniences." A *New York Journal* ad mentioned "a large entrance and other conveniences, an excellent cellar, a very good kitchen . . . and kitchen garden, well stocked with fruit and other trees, vegetables, etc." An ad placed in the *South Carolina Gazette* in 1735 offered "in Beauford, a Town Lot . . . with a dwelling house and good brick chimney [and] a kitchen." Ad space wasn't cheap, so to single out the kitchen for an added plug was to confirm its critical place in the home, something that few seventeenth-century settlers could have done.

Few aspects of the human environment shape human behavior as powerfully as consumer goods and architectural space. The transition to the "suppressed kitchen" was thus a critical step toward the convergence of regional foodways throughout colonial America. During the seventeenth and early eighteenth centuries, American colonists owned few consumer goods and lived in meager dwellings dismally spare by English standards.

ON Wednesday the nineteenth of *November* will be exposed to public Sale, for Current Money or Bills of Exchange, at the late Dwelling House of Capt. *Richard Lux*, Deceased, in *Chester-Town* in *Kent* County, all the Estate and Effects of said *Lux*, consisting of divers forts of Houshold Goods, one young Negro Woman fit for Town or Country Business, with a Child about 18 Months old, several good Draught-Horfes, one Cart, one Dray: And alfo the Leafe-Hold of the fame Dwelling Houfe and Lot, (being 22 Years) whereon is a new well built 40 Foot Dwelling Houfe, a Store Houfe, Bake Houfe, Bisket Loft, a Stable and Kitchen, two Ovens, two Bolting Mills, a paled Garden and Yard; all in good Repair. The Sale will begin precisely at 12 o'Clock.

All Persons indebted to the Estate of said *Lux*, are defired to pay their respective Debts at that Time and Place, without further Trouble to themfelves, or

JOHN GALLOWAY, Administrator.

Advertising an American homestead

New and updated kitchens had become selling points for many houses by the eighteenth century, very often being the only room mentioned in advertisements for house sales.

The barriers between settlers and the woods, fields, rivers, pastures, and peoples around them were thin, permeable, and actively crossed. The colonists' intimacy with the wilderness tightly wove them into the coarse fabric of their regional landscapes, limiting their range of culinary decisions while enhancing their dependence on a literal and figurative hand-to-mouth way of eating. Meals quite naturally leaned toward one-pot stews stocked with local fare. Any culinary philosophy that may have existed was one of rugged individualism and radical adaptation.

But by the mid-eighteenth century, the widespread proliferation of consumer goods (especially culinary utensils) joined specialized cooking and storage space to redefine colonial America's culinary potential. To be sure, the one-pot meal persisted, as did wasteful hearths, cramped homes, and the reliance on trenchers and cups as a family's sole dining accoutrements. But increasingly, and quite conspicuously, white colonists expanded and specialized their kitchens, improved their hearths, differentiated cooking and storage spaces, and adorned these areas with efficient and elaborate utensils. The result was that the once regionally diversified nature of American food began to diminish. One might suspect that these changes provided the preconditions for the rise of a uniquely American cuisine. Such a supposition, however, would be premature. Aside from making material life more convenient for tens of thousands of Americans, these changes established the foundation for many colonists throughout British America to do what New Englanders thought they should have been doing from the start: eat like proper Englishmen.

The Rise of English Manufactured Goods in British America

And to do that, they had to embrace Britain. Although Anglophilia was a cultural impulse that came quite naturally to colonial British Americans, our conventional narrative rarely acknowledges the power of this attraction. The American Revolution looms large on America's historical radar screen, so much so that it often crowds out every other contemporaneous development. The Stamp Act, George III, the Boston Tea Party, the Boston Massacre, Tom Paine, Lexington and Concord, and the heroic rise of the flawless founding fathers seem so inevitable in their emergence, so poetic in their advocacy of liberty and justice, so loyally wedded to the rhetoric of equality, that it comes as a shock for many contemporary Americans to learn that during the three decades preceding the American Revolution, the colonies fell in love first and foremost with all things English.

The evidence is hard to miss. In 1755, an anonymous American echoed popular opinion when he wrote that his fellow colonists "do not think themselves aliens, or the less a-kin to those of Great Britain, because parted by a vast ocean, and dwelling in a distant part of the globe." To the contrary, "they insist they are branches of the same British tree, tho transplanted in a different soil." With respect to Englishmen, Americans "consider themselves to be upon an equal footing," an equality that allowed them to "daily extend the power and dominion of *Great Britain*." John Barnard, a New England minister, wrote in 1734 that there was not "a single true New England man" who did not wholeheartedly believe "that the form of Civil Government that is best for us, which we are under, [is] the *British Constitution*." Samuel Keimer described the colonies as "Great Britain itself in miniature," a place where "habits, life, customs . . . etc." were "much the same as about London." Jonathan Mayhew, in 1754, saw "another Great Britain rising in America." As for colonial planters, they "talk[ed] good English without idiom or tone" and "dress[ed] after the same modes, and behave[d] themselves exactly as the Gentry in London." The "magnetick Force of English culture," as Henry St. John, first viscount Bolingbroke, put it, "brought England into the heart of colonial America." Surveying this wealth of evidence, historian Jack P. Greene concludes, "The result was a strong predisposition among the colonists to cultivate idealized English values and to seek to imitate idealized versions of English forms, institutions, and patterns of behavior."

Complementing and motivating America's adoration of all things English was a growing self-consciousness among the colonists about their provincial, frontier status. By the mid-eighteenth century, most white Americans were creole whites. That is, they had been born in America. Whereas their parents and grandparents often had at least some direct recollection of England, and could identify to some extent with the culture they had left behind, American creoles had to confront the troublesome reality that they personally knew virtually nothing of their empire's vital center. They were, as a result, especially eager to demonstrate their affiliation with England, an eagerness that was further manifested when the British looked down on them—which they frequently did—with snobbish denunciations of the colonial lifestyle. The Lord Bishop of Landaff, for example, remarked that the colonists had "abandoned their native manners and religion" in exchange for "the most brutal profligacy of manners." Instead of converting the Native Americans, he continued, they themselves had turned into "Infidels and Barbarians." James MacSparran made a similar case, arguing that the provincials were living in "a State of Ignorance and Barbarism, not much superior to those of the native *Indians.*" The colonists "have generally no Opportunity of Improvement by good education," were often mocked as having undergone "creolian degeneracy," and were constantly subject to "the disintegrating forces which the liberty of a wild country unloosed." J. Hector St. John de Crèvecoeur, who spoke from the American side of the pond, explained that his fellow colonists carving a life out on the frontier habitually indulged in the sort of behavior that fostered a "a licentious idle life," one in which "wretchedness" prevailed. Theirs was a society thrown into "a perfect state of war," a Hobbesian underground of brutish pursuits and unrefined tastes. Needless to say, many creoles chafed under this widespread and unflattering characterization of American life and, to compensate, sought conspicuous ways to reiterate their love of English culture.

Then, as now, nothing is more conspicuous than consumption. What better way, Americans reasoned, to show one's affiliation with the mother country and prove their civilized status than to buy British. During the 1730s and 1740s, driven to a large extent by the logic of this question, colonial America integrated itself into the booming British consumer economy through the purchase of "the latest goods imported from England." This development—as much an expression of an emerging Anglophilia as a quest for comfort—was a fundamental transformation that historians have gone so far as to label a "consumer revolution." The designation isn't overstated. From Maine to Georgia, American demand for consumer goods spiked, and the British, who were in a perfect position to respond profitably and predictably to the upsurge in demand, flooded the market with manufactured durable goods. Throughout all of the British mainland colonies, newspapers swelled with advertisements, stores weighted down their shelves, and "everywhere," according to one merchant, "the pace of business picked up."

This change thoroughly altered American culture. Jonathan Trumball, a Connecticut storeowner, stocked a display of wares in the 1740s that would have been unheard of a decade earlier. Running a contemporary Wal-Mart of sorts, he sold "pepper, lace, gloves, gunpowder, flints, molasses, rum, *Watts' Psalms,* mohair, drugs, tiles, paper, garlix (a kind of cloth), pots, pans . . . cord, pails, needles, knives, indigo, logwood, earthenware, raisins, thimbles, buckles, allspice, tea, buttons, mace, combs, butter, spectacles, soap, brimstone, nails, shot, sewing silk, sugar, wire, looking glasses, tape, 'Italian crape,' 'allam,' pewter dishes, etc." Storeowners, according to one historian of early Maryland, now had "to build substantial brick store buildings

Philadelphia, April 2. 1747.
Juft imported from London, in the Fortune, Captain Ruffel,

A Frefh affortment of druggs and medicines, likewife fine broad cloths and fhalloons, to be fold reafonably, with moft forts of varnifhes, by Richard Farmar, at the Unicorn in Second-ftreet.

Advertising European wares

Importers began to pay for regular advertisements in newspapers throughout the colonies in the 1730s and 1740s.

equipped with more elaborate shelves and counters for display, and chairs, tables, glassware, and teaware for the genteel entertainment of customers." Stuff, in other words, was available for everyday sale, and not just for the elite but for Americans of every status. "At the lowest levels of wealth," historian Lorena S. Walsh writes, colonists "acquir[ed] more of the ordinary amenities families had so long forgone—tables, chairs, bed steads, individual knives and forks, bed and table linens, and now inexpensive ceramic tableware." Every year, in short, an increasing number of colonists were buying an increasing number of consumer goods, and the colonies, in the process, were becoming more and more English in their dress, decoration, architecture, and cooking and eating habits.

The extent of this consumer explosion amazed contemporaries. A German minister visiting Pennsylvania marveled at the wine, spices, tea, china, cookware, and textiles he saw for sale in merchant warehouses, remarking that "it is really possible to obtain all the things one can get in Europe in Pennsylvania, since so many merchant ships arrive there every year." These merchants would routinely take out newspaper ads for hundreds of items, and a single issue might make reference to as many as four thousand different consumer imports. Stores selling these goods proliferated in tandem. One Virginia merchant exclaimed in 1743, "There are 25 stores within 18 miles around me which is 13 more than . . . [in 1740] and 4 or 5 more expected next year from some of the outports [of England]." A Virginia planter surveyed the colonies' consumer habits in 1753 and declared consumer goods "extravagantly dear" to the heart of the American consumer, while members of the Maryland Assembly announced with great urgency: "We want the British Manufactures." William Eddis, an Englishman living in Maryland, noted how "the quick importations of fashion from the mother country is really astonishing." Widespread advertisements for new English goods appeared so often that Eddis quipped, "I am almost inclined to believe that a new fashion is adopted earlier by the polished and affluent American than by many opulent persons in the great metropolis." In 1751, Benjamin Franklin confirmed how "a vast demand is growing for British manufactures," praising "a glorious market wholly in the power of Britain." A very young George Washington admonished his American agent for importing a batch of shabby goods that "could [only] have been used by our Forefathers in the days of yore." He, too, wanted the British manufactures. These comments were music to the ears of insecure colonists struggling to gain cultural legitimacy and acceptance out on the British Empire's remote but increasingly commodified frontier.

And, indeed, these assessments of material accumulation have a clear ring of truth. If, as one historian of consumer culture posits, "material goods themselves contain implicit meanings and are therefore indicative of attitudes," then the consumer revolution that swept across the North American colonies in the 1740s and 1750s allowed colonists burdened by the stereotype of provinciality to express their affiliation with the country they so deeply admired. Franklin observed that Americans before 1763 "submitted willingly to the government of the Crown, and paid, in all their courts, obedience to acts of Parliament." But their loyalty went beyond mere political admiration. Colonists, he continued, "had not only a respect, but an affection, for Great Britain, for its laws, its customs and manners, and even a fondness for its fashions, that greatly increased the commerce." This commerce, fueled by the ongoing production of those crops and goods that made each region of colonial America unique, resulted in the accumulation of objects that stimulated widespread colonial pride in being a vital part of the empire. It was a pride, moreover, that was felt among white Americans of all ranks, both sexes, and in every colonial region. This material convergence in the ways of the mother country was so powerful, so transformative, that on the eve of the American Revolution, when America had never had more creoles in its expanding population, and when America had never been so "American," this imminently independent fringe of the empire had never felt so integrated into, so accepted by, and, paradoxically, so in awe of English culture.

The Consumption of Culinary Utensils

Food was integral to this thoroughgoing Anglicization of colonial life. Although we don't know precisely how much, a large percentage of America's imports during the British invasion were, as eighteenth-century kitchen inventories confirm, related to cooking and eating. Hints abound that goods acquired for the preparation, storage, dispensation, and consumption of food and drink became typical items in colonial kitchens rather than the rarities they once were. Several painstaking, bean-counting studies by social historians present impressive evidence that colonists improved the quality of their material lives by acquiring the now affordable equipment that broadened their cooking methods, improved sanitation, added flexibility and variety to their diet, and turned the once utilitarian act of dining into a more elegant, cosmopolitan, and, of course, English experience.

Insofar as they're available, the numbers tell a story of material improvement. In York County, Virginia, the value of cooking items more than tripled for common residents between the 1720s and the 1750s. During the same period, the county's wealthiest cohort saw its cooking items double in value. In Somerset County, Virginia, ownership of dining utensils rose fivefold during this time, while ownership of cooking equipment increased by 50 percent. Among the middle ranks in one Maryland county, the boom in kitchen and cooking-related equipment was equally impressive. Between 1700 and the 1750s, ownership of table knives increased from 18 to 60 percent; earthenware, from 68 to 92 percent; fine earthenware, from 0 to 20 percent; and tea sets from 0 to 50 percent. A similar transition in material life occurred between the mid-seventeenth and the mid-eighteenth century in southern New England. Ownership of forks rose from 0 to 50 percent among the middling ranks, while evidence of fine earthenware went from 0 to 16 percent; coarse earthenware, from 50 to 67 percent; and silverware, from 9 to 14 percent. While similar estimates aren't available for the Carolina region, the substantial economic growth there after 1720 indicates that consumer behavior followed the booming rice economy. In 1809, looking at Carolina's recent history, David Ramsay correctly observed that "few countries have . . . exhibited so striking an instance of public and private prosperity as appeared in South-Carolina between 1725 and 1775." There's little doubt that culinary consumer goods were part and parcel of that prosperity. The ubiquity and force of this material change is even evident in the 1780s on the Kentucky frontier, where 89 percent of the middling settlers in this very raw environment already had a Dutch oven, a griddle, and a frying pan in addition to a standard pot. One hundred percent had pewter ware, 67 percent had tea equipment, and 70 percent had delft. A survey of eighty customers at a Kentucky store over a two-year period shows purchases for 37 cutlery pieces, 139 dishes, and 84 items of glassware. For the better part of a half-century, the consumption of kitchen goods knew no bounds, except those provided by what England could offer.

This substantial rise in cookware and tableware included items that expanded cooking possibilities. Although the evidence isn't quite as abundant, several hints suggest that many colonists complemented their basic utensils with several specialized cooking tools, including copper pots, posnets, saucepans, stewpans, fish kettles, teakettles, colanders, ladles, skimmers, chafing dishes, coffeepots, and plate warmers. A brief comment on a few of these objects illuminates their potential to broaden culinary horizons.

Copper pots were needed to stew large hunks of meat, such as a rump of beef or a shoulder of pork. Designed with three legs and holding up to thirty gallons, these pots could stand above a pile of burning logs or coals. A removable iron handle allowed the cook to suspend the pot from a hook or crane if the meat required a long, slow cook. Posnets were short basins or porringers with very long handles whose design—geared for cooking over uneven hearths or open fires—hadn't changed since the fourteenth century. Made to hold one to four gallons of liquid, saucepans were containers with a narrow, rimmed opening and a wide bottom to encourage the thickening of reductions. A stewpan cooked meat slowly, concentrating its flavor and enhancing its texture. It differed from a saucepan in having straight sides and a flat lid with a shorter handle. According to one English writer, it was an object "much in vogue, it being convenient for many purposes." Fish kettles were used to steam a fish without bending it, a procedure made much easier by the oval kettle's built-in strainer and lug to lift out the cooked fish. To avoid the sour taste that untreated copper could impart to hot tea water, cooks used teakettles because they had a thin tin coating on their insides. They often held up to twelve quarts of water and came equipped with a spout twisted in a way to make water boil faster than it otherwise would in a saucepan. It's hard to imagine a simpler device, but the colander enhanced kitchen activity to the point that it found a place in

Denis Diderot's *Encyclopédie*. An English writer allowed how the colander left food "pure and cleane" after "dirt runs through the holes." It was a godsend for cooking rice. A cook with a colander could properly adhere to the cookbook instruction to "drain." The chafing dish had a purpose strongly indicating that cooking had definitely become a matter of more than utilitarian concern: its sole purpose, after all, was to keep food warm. As a round pan with a hollow basin set on three short legs and designed "to hold coales of fire" on which meat dishes could be set "till the time of serving them up to the table," the chafing dish was another luxury item that showed how cooking was a task done for more than mere sustenance.

Merchants importing English goods evidently thought so. Colonial newspapers from Charleston to Boston affirmed the increasing popularity of English consumer goods in kitchens throughout the colonies. William Neilson's imports, which arrived in New York on "the last vessels from London and Liverpool," included "knives and forks," "frying pans," "pewter plates, basins, and dishes," "quart, two-quart, and five pint" stewpans, and empty bottles. Neilson's competitor James Rivington offered for sale to "ladies and gentlemen at this season," "tea pots, tea spoons, sugar tongs," "silver plated coffee pots," and "silver handle and other forks in cases, with deserts and spoons." In 1743, John Paul Grimké arrived in South Carolina from London to sell "tea potts, waiters, punch ladles, soop ladles, pepper boxes, milk potts, table and tea spoons, tongs and strainers, small sauce pans." He stressed that these goods were "just imported." A "choice parcel" from London was advertised in the *South Carolina Gazette* as having frying pans, "bakery bells," iron pots, "frying hooks," and cooking tongs. In 1742, the *Pennsylvania Gazette* ran an ad placed by Samuel Neave, who was selling goods "lately imported from London" at his "store near Fishbourne's Wharff." Among many dozens of goods, he offered teakettles, pots, "brass scales," pewter plates, "dishes, basons, porringers and spoons," "water plates," frying pans, "files and rasps," and "knives and forks." At the same time, over on Carpenter's Wharf, Reese Meredith was selling "damask table cloths" and tea chests. The very next season, Neave came back with a new batch of "lately imported" goods, including "tea kettles and pots, coffee mills, bras & iron candlesticks . . . pewter plates," and a "variety of knives and forks." This year, though, his competition was Samuel Perry, who sold from his Hamilton's Wharf store "cutlery and brass ware," "chaffin dishes, gridirons . . . tongs." It was truly, as T. H. Breen has termed it, "an empire of goods." Colonists, for their part, were indulging.

The General Rules of English Cooking

All these factors—the emergence of separate kitchens, a cultural affiliation with all things English, and the widespread availability and affordability of cooking and eating equipment—became the essential preconditions for colonial emulation of English cooking. While current assessments of the English diet tend to disparage it as bland and uncreative, the historical reality is something quite different. In fact, throughout the eighteenth century (and before), English cooking was the envy of Europe. Mrs. Fisher's *The Prudent Housewife: or, Complete English Cook, for Town and Country*, a widely read English cookbook from around 1750, presents an overview of the ideal English diet—a "bill of fare for every month of the year"—that both confirms the culinary patterns delineated in dozens of other English cookbooks and helps explain why this favorable opinion of the English diet prevailed throughout Europe. A number of qualities distinguished English food and defined its character, but what stands out most obviously was its ability to maintain the highest culinary standards while allowing flexibility within those standards. This subtle balance made its adoption by Americans a viable possibility.

The English style of cooking imposed limits that reflected both the seasonal availability of different foods and traditional cultural preferences. In the winter months meals almost exclusively emphasized meat, with little else garnishing the plate. The typical elite dinner consisted of "beef soup made of brisket of beef and the beef served up in the dish" or a roasted turkey "with rich gravy sauce." Chefs might also serve "ach-bone of beef boiled, carrots, and savoys, with melted butter," "ham and fowls roasted— with rich gravy sauce," vermicelli soup, a "fore quarter of lamb," or even boiled salmon "with smelts fried and lobster sauce." Roasted mutton was another popular winter option. *The Prudent Housewife* advised serving it with a "calf's head boiled and grilled, and garnished with broiled slices of bacon, and with brains mashed with parsley and butter, salt, pepper, and vinegar." Supper in the winter might consist of "a hare with a pudding in its belly" served with a "strong gravy and claret sauce," a "hen turkey served with onion sauce," scotch scallops, a roasted chicken with asparagus, and "fried foals in shrimp sauce." Along with several other cookbooks, Fisher's guide also promoted "chickens fricasseed" as a valid winter option.

Spring and summer meals continued to rely heavily on meat, but they now began to incorporate more vegetables. Dinners included roast beef served with potatoes or parsnips and melted butter, boiled beef with carrots and greens, fricassee of lamb with asparagus, and boiled fowls with greens and melted butter. Suppers tended toward ducklings with mushrooms, "beef soup with herbs well boiled," a rump of beef "boiled with summer cabbage," and a "saddle of mutton roasted with a spring salad." Summer meant less beef, more game, more veal and chicken, and even some pork, along with the usual array of herbs and vegetables. Dinners involved a "shoulder or neck of veal roasted, with rich gravy sauce and claret sauce," a green goose with gravy, served with "bacon and greens," a neck of venison with claret sauce, and haddock boiled and served with green peas. For supper, Fisher mentions "chickens or pigeons roasted, with asparagus and artichokes with melted butter," fricassee of chicken with green peas, mackerel boiled with melted butter and herbs, fricassee of young rabbits with gravy sauce, and a "roasted pig, with proper sauce of gravy and brains well seasoned."

Fall meals, finally, had little to no beef, relying instead on game, fish, organs, and—most notably—pies. Dinners included green-pea soup; a leg of lamb with turnips, spinach, and caper sauce; a goose with applesauce and pigeon pie; a "roast tongue and udder"; a "cod's head with oyster sauce, and minced pies"; and a "calf's head dressed turtle fashion." Supper revolved around "boiled pullets with oyster sauce, greens, and bacon"; wild ducks with gravy, onion sauce, and apple pie; fried smelts with anchovy sauce; a hare with rich gravy sauce and minced pies; fresh salmon with "whiting"; and fried trout with anchovy sauce. Although only an ideal seasonal spread, these were the foods that the English elite obtained from a market, prepared in their kitchens, and ate with knives and forks, in chairs, off plates, and on a regular enough basis for them to become something of a cultural standard.

English culinary rules were similarly unyielding when it came to sauces and combinations of ingredients. Sarah Harrison's *The House-Keeper's Pocket-Book; and Compleat Family Cook* describes, in addition to more than seven hundred recipes, the commonly accepted ways of preparing meals and combining ingredients. In so doing, it reveals how the force of tradition played a powerful role in shaping acceptable culinary arrangements. To cite just a few examples, codfish and cod's head had to be served with oyster sauce. Rabbits were always boiled with onions. Roasted tongues and udder were unacceptable without venison sauce. Larks roasted on skewers needed bacon slices wedged between the chunks of meat. Cooks boiled mutton with turnips, pigeons with greens and roots, and venison with cabbage and cauliflowers. Stewing had its own demands, as mutton had to be stewed with "a crust of bread," a nutmeg, an anchovy, and a claret/ale combination for five hours. Wild fowl was invariably stewed with a slice of lemon, "a sprig of sweet herbs," and a claret/water mixture. A hare had to be "beat in its own blood," fried, and then "cut into little bits" before being stewed for two hours with an anchovy, an onion, a turnip, and a claret/ale mixture. Pigeons needed to be fried "a little light brown" in a skillet before being stuffed with veal and bacon and stewed "till tender" with sweet herbs, a lemon peel, an onion, and "three corns of Jamaica pepper and a bay-leaf" in white wine. Pies also followed fairly strict rules. Shrewsberry pie required that "a couple of rabbits" be baked with "rabbets livers parboiled," "artichoke hearts boil'd tender, cut in dice," and seasoned fat pork. A fine egg pie called for—in addition to the yolks of twenty eggs—suet, apples, currants, mace, nutmeg, "half a pint of sack," and a "lump of marrow" to dollop on the top. A "carp pye," to cite a final example among scores of others, commanded a vinegar/water mixture, the "flesh of an eel," slices of "fat bacon" to stuff in the fish's gut, and an anchovy. Even sixty years later, according to cookbooks published in London, these traditions continued to define English cookery.

These culturally prescribed combinations were as much a matter of health as of taste. Thomas Hayes, in *Concise Observations on the Nature of Our Common Food*, built his culinary ideology on the premise that "the great secret of health, consequently of long life, consists in keeping the *blood in a proper state*." Thus we learn (in the pages that Hayes hopes are "not useless") that cucumbers "are very apt to produce flatulency, are of hard digestion, and have even brought off the stomach after forty-eight hours." Relief, however, came in the form of "oil and vinegar," which "check their fermentation." Likewise, lettuce and endive were "most wholesome eaten with vinegar, as it corrects them." Parsley, mint, and fennel were necessary complements to many forms of flesh, but they were "not wholesome eaten in large quantities." Nutmeg, cloves, mace, ginger, and pepper were needed to "take off the spasms arising from the flatulency of our food, and moderate its putrid tendency in the bowels." Gastrointestinal turmoil was similarly minimized with horseradish and mustard, which was "very properly joined both with animal and vegetable food." Vegetables had to accompany meat because, as Hayes put it, "animal food promotes scurvy and vegetables correct it; hence a due mixture of both animal and vegetable food is most wholesome to the constitution."

Even table settings demanded similar adherence to traditional rules and regulations, thereby further defining the fundamental rudiments of English cooking. As might be expected in a country with an established royalty, table arrangements could become unusually intricate affairs. The formal set-up of the standard eighteen-dish spread served at a royal dinner, for example, demanded precise spots for eighteen main serving dishes of varying sizes. Most settings, however, followed simpler rules. "Soup, broth, or fish," explained *The Prudent Housewife*, "should always be set at the head of the table." If these foods were not being served, then "a boil'd dish goes to the head, where there is both boil'd and roasted." Should the cook plan on serving only one "principle dish," it migrated to the head of the table. Two had to be placed equidistant from each other at the head. Should the cook serve three, the two smaller ones had to stand opposite each other and a foot behind the largest main dish. For four, "the biggest to the head, the next biggest to the foot"; for five, "you are to put the smallest to the middle and the other four opposite"; and for six, "you are to put the top and bottom as before and the two small ones opposite for side dishes."

Side dishes had to be arranged in proximity to the foods they complemented. Boiled beef, for example, was orbited by an arc of smaller dishes of cabbage, sprouts, carrots, and a small boat of butter. On a properly set table, mutton would usually find itself surrounded by separate plates of turnips, capers, and melted butter. A leg of pork stood next to parsnips and "pease porridge." Cooks served roasted lamb with "mint sauce chopped" and a bowl of sugared vinegar; roasted rabbit with liver sauce mixed with parsley; roasted pork or goose with "apple sauce and mustard"; and roast beef with plates of horseradish, salad, potatoes, and pickles. In such culturally acceptable ways did English food become English food.

The Inherent Flexibility of English Food

These three factors—the consumption of specific foods at specific times of the year, the conventional pairing of particular meat and fish with particular vegetables, herbs, and sauces, and the traditional arrangement of dishes on the table—helped define English food. If Americans expected to replicate these English culinary habits exactly, however, they would have been doomed to fail. Fortunately, for Americans living on the wild and woolly periphery hoping to indulge their intensified love of British culture, English foodways were as forgiving as they were rigid. While general principles certainly prevailed to shape a distinct national cuisine, the need for English food to adjust to regional conditions within England ensured that culinary traditions were more like vague benchmarks than a set of solidified recipes. Anne Battam, author of *A Collection of Scarce and Valuable*

Recipes, touched on this adaptive quality when she advised the reader to "be assured she can do these [recipes]" because although cooking might be a "strange art," the cook thrives as long as she is willing to "alter the task by the alterations of the compounds as she shall occasion." This built-in openness to modest change proved a critical precondition for colonial America's embrace of English food from the 1740s to the 1760s. It allowed, in essence, the colonies' emerging foodies to gravitate toward English ways, feel as though they were indeed eating like true Englishmen, and celebrate the virtues of the homeland without adhering to every strict detail of English culinary standards.

One way to appreciate the hidden variation within English food would be to look beyond specific culinary terms to the precise ingredients composing them. Take, for example, the salad. "First then to speak of sallats," Gervase Markham explained in *Country Contentments*: "there be some simple and some compound, some only to furnish out the table, and some both for use and adoration." They consisted of "young lettuce" served on everything from "a fruit dish, or chines, scallions, radish rootes, boyled carrets, skirets, and turneps." Simple salads could be served with nothing more than "a little vinegar, oyle, and pepper" or "bean cods, sparagus, and cucumbers served in likewise with oyle, vinegar, and pepper, with a world of others too tedius to nominate." Compound salads were similarly open to interpretation. A meal that was considered "usual at great feasts," the compound salad might include blanched almonds (cut "grossly with a shredding knive"), "raisins of the sunne clean washt and the stones picked out," figs, capers, olives, currants, or "a good handful of the small tender leaves of red sage and spinage." The salad's versatility was enhanced by the fact that the English habitually pickled their lettuces, a procedure that allowed cooks to "set them in a dry and temperate place and use them at pleasure, for they will last all year." While the colonists may not have had enough vinegar to do the same, their widespread adaptation of salads by the mideighteenth century spoke to the ease with which they could construe it as an example of English food, no matter the ingredients that went into it.

Common English cooking methods also highlight the variation within the conventional diet. Consider the fricassee. An old French method of stewing butchered meat in gravy along with root vegetables, the fricassee underwent in the hands of the English something of a transformation. As Markham put it, the fricassee came "to consist of many things." The fricassee migrated so far from its traditional French source, in fact, that the English began to identify it by another French term: *quelquechose*, or "something." Markham instructed readers how "to make a quelquechose, which is a mixture of many things together." The simplest fricassees, he wrote, "are eggs and collops fried, whether the collops be of bacon, ling, beefe, or young porke." In terms of procedure, he continued, "the frying thereof is so ordinarie that it needeth not any relation . . . with butter or sweet oyl," thereby dispensing with the gravy altogether. Another recipe for *quelquechose* opened the dish to any combination of "sweet cream, currants, cinnamon, mace, salt, and a little ginger, spinage, endive, and marigold flowers grossly chopt . . . beat very well together." The cook then fried the mixture in sweet butter and added "pettitoes" that were "very well boiled before you put them into the frycase." As cooks reached the end of this recipe, Markham actually encouraged them to play around with the procedure, noting that "in this manner, as you make this quelquechose, so you may make any other, whether it be of flesh, small birds, sweet roots, oisters, muscles, cockles, giblets, lemons, oranges, or any fruit, pulse, or other sallet herb whatsoever . . . they vary with men's opinions." Just as a "sallet" wasn't a "sallet," so a fricassee wasn't a fricassee. Instead, it was a dish "of many compositions, and ingredients, as flesh, fish, eggs, hearbs, and many other things." Thus pretty much anything the chef wanted it to be, which was a comforting reality for the American cook who was trying to live in English ways.

Popular and pliable as the fricassee was, nothing better epitomized English culinary versatility quite as aptly as the pie. A comparison of pie recipes in several contemporaneous English cookbooks sheds even more light on the overall flexibility inherent in English cooking. Battam, in *A Collection of Scarce and Valuable Recipes*, includes a recipe for "battalia pie" that instructs:

Take some lamb, rabbit, chicken, pigeon, some forc'd meat balls, cosk-combs, marrow, asparagus, and hard yolks of eggs, season all pretty well, and if you have any mushrooms put them in also, and then put in some butter, with some lemon peel, and lay this last with some slices of bacon on top of your meat, then bake it, and when you serve it up, pour through the lid some good gravy, and a very small glass of white wine.

Her account stands in contrast to a battalia pie recipe published in the widely read *Family Magazine* in 1741:

Take two small chickens, two squab pigeons, two sucking rabbits; cut them in pieces, season them with savoury spice, and lay them in the pye with two sweet-

breads sliced, as many sheps tongues, one shivered palat, a pair of lamb stones, with savory balls and oysters; lay on butter and close the pie: put it to a lear.

The same level of variation can be found in popular recipes for artichoke pie. Battam advised:

Take twelve artichoke bottoms boil'd tender, the yolks of twelve eggs boil'd hard, three ounces of candied orange, lemon, and citron peel, half a pound of raisins ston'd, a blade of mace, a little nutmeg sliced, a quarter of a pound of sugar, put these in your pie with a half a pound of butter, and lay the sweetmeats uppermost, and when it comes out of the oven put in a half a pint of sack, and as much cream.

And *Family Magazine:*

Take the bottoms of six or eight artichokes boil'd and sliced; season them with sweet spice, and mix them with the marrow of three bones with a few gooseberries or grapes, upon these lay some dates, yolks of hard eggs, citron and mace, then cover these with butter; bake, and pour in hot wine.

Pies weren't the only dishes that encouraged a creative approach. Even a traditional procedure such as roasting a mutton neck could be widely interpreted. *Family Magazine* instructed cooks to "draw it with parsley and roast; when it is most enough [done]; dredge it with salt, white pepper, and crum bread, serve it with gravy and juice of an orange." But Battam advised:

Bone a neck and breast of mutton and having taken off the skin, strew upon it some pepper, salt, nutmeg, lemon peel, crumbs of bread, and sweet herbs, beat six hard eggs with six ounces of butter, then roll it together like brawn, and roast it, sprinkling it with the aforementioned ingredients; serve it up with fry'd oysters, and horse-radish, with a good strong gravy underneath.

A classic meal such as blood pudding also left much to the chef's discretion. Markham insisted that one needed to use the "blood of an hogge whilest it is still warme," while Battam suggested soaking oatmeal with the hog's blood and adding cream and white bread. The British might have considered food such as battalia pie, artichoke pie, roast mutton, and blood pudding timeworn markers of a national cuisine, but these iconic meals were anything but uniformly understood or practiced.

The widespread ownership of multiple cooking utensils allowed the English to prepare and serve discrete dishes in precise combinations, but it didn't keep them from relying on a one-pot meal of their own: pottage. Technically, pottage was simply a stew of meat and vegetables. In reality, however, it was an excuse to throw anything and everything that may have been available into a single pot and stew it for hours on end. A couple of examples convey the flexible flavor of this freestyle dish, one that Americans well understood and that easily adapted to the less equipped colonial kitchen. "If you will make pottage of the best and daintiest kind," wrote Markham,

you shall take mutton, veale, or kid & having broke the bones, but not cut the flesh in pieces, and washt it, put it into a pot with faire water, after it is ready to boile, and is thoroughly skumd, you shal put in it a good handful or two of smale oat-meal: and then whole lettice of the best and most inward leaves, whole spinage, endive, succory, and whole leaves of colafl—or the inward parts of white cabbage, with two or three onions, and put all into a pot and boyle them well together till the meat be enough, and the herbs so soft as may be, and stir them oft well together: and then season it with salt and as much verijuice as will only turn the taste of the pottage; and so serve them up covering the meat with the whole hearbs, and adorning the dish with sippets.

Another recipe advised:

To make the best ordinarie pottage, you shall take a rack of mutton cut into pieces, or a leg of mutton cut into pieces, for this meat and the joyntes are the best, although any other joint, or any fresh beef will likewise make good pottage; and having washt your meat well, put it into a cleane pot with faire water, and set it on the fire, then take violet leaves, succory, strawberry leaves, spinage, langdabeefe, marigold flowers, scallions and a little parsley and chop very small together, then take half so much oat-meale well-beaten as there is hearbs, and mix it with the hearbs, and chop all well together; then when the pot is ready to boyle, skum it very well, then put in your herbs, and so let it boyle with a quick fire, stirring the meate oft in the pot, till the meat be boiled enough, and that hearbs and water are mixed together without any separation, then season them with salt and serve them up.

Other pottage recipes called for potato roots, turnips, "forepart of a fat pigge," quail, partridges, chickens, larks, sparrows and "other small birds," prunes, raisins, currants, and blanched almonds, to name just a small sample of ingredients. Pottage was a meal, in short, consistent with a frontier philosophy of flexibility and thus ready to cross the Atlantic to the British Empire's most unrefined frontier and find a new home.

A final aspect of English food that predisposed Americans to Anglicize their diet was measured but enthusiastic tolerance of the English for foreign influences. Markham described a way to make a "principall dish of boild meate which is esteemed in all of Spaine." Battam's directions for dressing an ox-cheek called for "Jamaican pepper corns," and her recipe for a stewed rump roast demands "some toasts of French bread." She stewed a "neck of mutton" with French turnips, dressed asparagus "the French way," offered a "Dutch sauce for any fish," and routinely specified "Seville oranges," "Spanish onions," and "Naples biscuit grated." *Family Magazine* directed its readers how "to make English hams like those of Westphalia, in shape and taste," to make sausages "equal to those brought from Bologna," to pickle French beans, and "to bake a French bread." For Americans well versed in the art of adjusting to a welter of ethnic culinary influences ranging from Europe to Africa to the Caribbean to the Native American backcountry, England's openness to other cultural influences further eased the effort to cook and eat like "true" Englishmen.

The New Art of Cookery

The defining qualities of eighteenth-century English food—qualities that blended tradition with flexibility—migrated from England to America through a number of avenues: word of mouth, novels, plays, and newspapers. Most important, however, they came to America through cookbooks. From the 1740s to the 1760s, Americans not only craved and consumed British durable goods, textiles, and architectural innovations, but also demanded the written recipes directing metropolitan cooking trends. Precisely how many cooks ended up buying cookbooks remains impossible to determine, but we do know that the book trade grew exponentially during these years. We also know that dozens of cookbook titles arrived in the colonies during the British invasion, and that several of them became popular enough for early American publishers to eventually update and print revised editions for a growing American market.

Hannah Glasse's *The Art of Cookery Made Plain and Easy*, for example, was originally published in 1742 in London, with new editions coming out in 1747 and 1796. The book did well enough in America between 1742 and 1804, however, for an Alexandria, Virginia, publisher to put out an

American edition in 1805. Richard Briggs's *The English Art of Cookery* documented his culinary innovations as chef of the Globe Tavern. The book was initially published in Dublin, but Briggs's edition for Americans, *The New Art of Cookery, According to the Present Practice*, came out in Philadelphia in 1792. Thomas Hayes's *Concise Observations on the Nature of Our Common Food* was a London publication that shaped a generation of American cooks before being brought out by a New York publisher in 1790. The American market for English cookbooks became demanding enough for many authors to publish their books simultaneously in America and England. Susannah Carter did just that, publishing her very popular *The Frugal Housewife, or, Complete Woman Cook* in New York and London in 1772. A Boston publisher put out the second edition of her book in 1803. Not all cookbooks found an American publisher, but they continued to arrive as imports, pushing Americans to find room on their shelves for titles such as *The Prudent Housewife, The House-Keeper's Pocket-Book, The Compleat City and Country Cook, England's Newest Way in All Sorts of Cookery,* and *English Housewifery*, to name only a few.

Endowed with renovated and new kitchens, equipped with a wider range of serving and cooking implements, and enamored with British culture in general, colonial women not only were eager to follow the recipes in these coveted books, but also wanted to use those recipes to demonstrate their adherence to another significant trend: the growth of English-style hospitality in America. Whenever they found themselves in a colonial kitchen, English visitors to America began to take note of the quality and familiarity of American food. When a group of visitors stopped in at a Virginia home, they found "the house keeping much better than the house." While the house "consisted of one dirty room," the "landlady" compensated for external appearances when she "made us amends by providing a supper sufficient for a Battalian." A visitor to a North Carolina home complimented the "great many provisions and fruits" he found in the cupboard. An English traveler to Virginia complained that he missed his beloved English artichokes but noted with approval how "the Gentry sometimes rayse a few and have very lately tried the Brochili. Cucumbers and cymnells . . . are in request, especially cimneles, at gent[leman's] tables." On Cape Fear, a North Carolina woman not only kept eggs, poultry, and butter, but—according to "a lady of quality"—"even descends to make minced pies, cheese-cakes, and little biskets." Sally Fairfax, from Virginia, reported how her mother spent the afternoon making "6 mince pies, & 7 custards, 12 tarts, 1 chicking pye, and 4 puddings." Cooking in order to impress meant that the preparation of food was no longer, as one cookbook put it, "a bare piece of Housewifery." It had grown "into an art." The English visitors, for their part, seemed pleased with the transition.

Examining English cookbooks sold in America, even those that were eventually published by American presses, poses something of a research problem. It's impossible to tease out which—if any—of the recipes were geared for Americans, thus complicating the question of whether Americans earnestly followed them. The one exception to this rule would be William Parkes's addendum to Eliza Smith's *The Compleat Housewife, or, Accomplished Gentlewoman's Companion*. When he published Smith's book, Parkes excluded "ingredients or Materials for which are not to be had in this country," selecting only those recipes "useful and practicable here." Exceptions aside, the vast majority of the remaining recipes were appropriate for English cooks. It thus almost seems safe enough, given all the supporting evidence, to assume that American cooks, who were undoubtedly limited by the availability of ingredients, nonetheless attempted to approximate as best they could the English recipes in the English cookbooks sold in America. Of course, there's always the chance that American women did not adhere to the British recipes, buying the British books for no other reason than to display as a demonstration of their connection with the metropolis. But when the American edition of Glasse's *The Art of Cookery Made Plain and Easy* includes a section on "a modern bill of fare" detailing the ideal menu throughout the year—and it's a menu that in almost every way conforms to the standard eighteenth-century English menu—it still seems safe enough to conclude that, indeed, Americans had been approximating English cookery for decades.

The First "American" Cookbooks

What we need to place our assumption beyond a reasonable doubt is a detailed and exclusively American cookbook that relies heavily on standard eighteenth-century English recipes. The most obvious candidate would be Amelia Simmons's *American Cookery* (1796), routinely touted by food historians as "the first American cookbook." Pursuing the understandable question of what exactly makes this cookbook American, other than the fact that it was published in America, food historians have highlighted recipes that incorporate Indian corn and pumpkin, as well as directions for a "spruce beer." But do those qualities really make it American? Aside from the fact that the English had been cooking with these ingredients for more than a century, the question of the book's American focus is ultimately undermined by the fact that corn, pumpkin, and spruce beer comprise only a tiny proportion of the overall ingredients and recipes in the book. As it turns out, at least 95 percent of the recipes are of direct English derivation—most of them coming in fact from Susannah Carter's *The Frugal Housewife*. Recipes revolve around the classic English meat dishes, including roast beef, roast lamb, fowl smothered in oysters, stuffed leg of pork, dressed calf's head, a variety of pies, puddings, and preserves. *American Cookery* might be American in name, but in content it's as British as battalia pie and a warm stout beer.

Simmons's real influence wasn't so much to pin down an American style of cooking as to collect a reservoir of British American tradition. There was nothing cutting edge about cookbooks at the time. The eighteenth- and early-nineteenth-century examples examined here, in fact, were downright reactionary. Americans by 1796 had diverged substantially from the English tradition of cookery, almost obviating the contemporary value of Simmons's book. But—and this is the crucial point—the formal cookbooks that Americans published after 1796 captured the trends from a recent era, the 1730s to the 1770s, in a way that allows us to look into them as a fair approximation of what cooks were doing in their kitchens during these years.

The other valuable quality of Simmons's book was that it spawned a series of local American cookbooks. Lucy Emerson's *The New England Cookery* is the most impressive and telling example. It was impressive in its thoroughly English character and telling in its adherence to Simmons's work. The book deserves a careful analysis because of its unusual clarity and depth. Strange as it seems, we can learn a lot about British American food between 1730 and 1770 from an American cookbook published in New England in 1808.

New England Cooking: Ingredients

We look to New England cooking as the most reflective of American cooking at mid-century because it was New England that led the charge to Anglicize the region's culture and its cooking habits. To be sure, the vast majority of recipes that brought New England ingredients together in the colonial kitchen were spread by word of mouth, inherited through obscure oral traditions, and thus evaporated like water from a boiling kettle. Lucy Emerson's tour de force, however, is a delightful exception. Her manual serves our purpose well because it offers a concrete example of how New England's local traditions converged with the influences of the British invasion to produce the most Anglicized food in America. The cultivation of a garden, the fattening and slaughter of cattle, the grinding of grain, the drying of herbs, and the constant rounds of churning butter and pressing cheese joined these relatively elaborate cooking instructions to change the nature of New England cooking, making it more like both England's and, at the same time, British America's.

When it came to fresh and flavorful food, Emerson brooked no diversions from the English standards. Her careful stipulations closely followed the advice detailed not only in Amelia Simmons's *American Cookery*, but also in Hannah Glasse's *The Art of Cookery Made Plain and Easy* and Richard Briggs's *The English Art of Cookery*. When cooking salmon obtained from a neighbor or a merchant, she warned, "strictly examine the gills—if the bright redness is exchanged for a low brown, they are stale." Shad, she continued, did best with a few days of rest. "I have tasted shad," she explained, obtained "thirty or forty miles from the place where caught and really conceived that they had a richness of flavor, which did not appertain to those taken fresh and cooked immediately." Most saltwater fish, she wrote, "are best fresh from the water, though the Hannah Hull, Black Fish, Lobster, Oyster, Flounder, Bass, Cod, Haddock, and Eel may be transported by land many miles" before being cooked. When buying fish from a local fishmonger, she cautioned that "deceits are used to give them a freshness of appearance, such as peppering the gills, wetting the fins and tails, and even painting the gills, or wetting with animal blood." When choosing fish, Emerson explained, "your smell must approve." When it came to freshwater fish, "none so well afford taste in cookery as the salmon trout." "They are," she advised, "best caught under a fall" because "at the foot of a fall the waters are much colder than at the head." Perch, she wrote, "are notable pan fish, the deeper the water from whence taken, the finer are their flavors." Eels were best dealt with by "salting, peppering, and drying in the sun." She preferred them "broiled and moistened with butter." Again, every one of these details—as well as those that follow—can be found in an English manual. British Americans, however, were increasingly coming to find such information useful.

Meat and fowl called for the same vigilant attention to freshness and flavor as did fish. Emerson insisted that "the large stall-fed ox beef is the best, it has a coarse open grain and oily smoothness." To test for freshness, the cook should "dent it with your finger" in order to see if it "will easily rise again." If "the dent remain . . . it will be rough and spongy." The meat from a cow, Emerson told her readers, in a rare comparison with an American food, "is generally more tender and juicy than the ox, in America, which is used to labor." Indicating the continued importance of wild game in the New England diet, Emerson taught cooks what to seek in a variety of undomesticated birds. In a goose, for example, a cook should look for a yellow bill and fragile bones that snap easily. Woodcocks "ought to be thick, fat, and flesh firm, the nose dry and the throat clear." Partridges, "if young, will have black bills, yellowish legs; if old, the legs look bluish; if old or stale it may be perceived by smelling at their mouths." Pigeons, finally, have "red legs, blackish in parts, more hairs, plumper." Briggs, the English chef, advised his readers to seek "pale legs" and to "loosen a vent" to test for freshness. Emerson, and Simmons before her, obviously listened carefully.

Emerson kept on equally sharp eye on her vegetables. She encouraged cooks to use potatoes with smooth skin, arguing that they were "the most mealy and richest flavor'd." The potatoes "cultivated from imported seed on sandy and dry loamy lands are best for table use," although "the red [potato] will produce more in rich, loamy, highly manured garden grounds." As for onions, "the high red, round and hard onions are the best," and "the smallest are the most delicate." Emerson appreciated that "onions grown in the richest, highest cultivated ground, get better and better year after year on the same ground." Beets came in best when grown "on light gravel grounds—the red is the richest and best approved." She warned against white beets, admonishing their "sickish sweetness, which is disliked by many." Parsnips "are richer flavored when plowed out of the ground in April, having stood out during winter." Yellow carrots, she continued, "are better than the orange or red." And with carrots, size mattered. One should seek samples that were "middling siz'd, that is, a foot long and two inches thick at the top end." Thin carrots, however, "are good with veal cookery, rich in soups, and excellent with hash." She advised cooks to find asparagus that were six inches in length and "cut just above the ground" rather than below the surface. Of the three kinds of parsley that grew in New England, "the thickest and branchiest is the best." She especially enjoyed parsley that had been grown among onions or placed "in a bed by itself." Radishes had to be "salmon colored." The best lettuce was "purple spotted and free from bitter." Cabbages grown in old ground "have a rankness." And, last but not least, there's garlic, of which Emerson betrayed the common English sentiment: "though used by the French, [it is] better adapted to the uses of medicine than cookery."

Fruit, finally, didn't escape her scrutiny. As for pears, cooks should seek "the large bell pear—the yellowist is the best." Hard winter pears were well suited for making sauces and for baking. Summer pears were "a tolerable dessert" improved "in this country, as well as other fruits are, by grafting and cultivation." Apples had the most wholesome associations, she opined, and "ought to be more universally cultivated." Currants led to a fine-tasting jelly "and are easily grown from shoots trimmed off old branches, and set carelessly in the ground—they flourish in all soils." Black currants "may be cultivated," she advised, but not until they were dried out "and until its sugars are propagated." Her discussion of fruit capped a longer discourse on the ingredients that not just New Englanders, but all Americans, were starting to incorporate more formally and consciously into their increasingly Anglicized diet after 1740.

New England Cooking: Techniques

Once assembled in the kitchen, the meat, herbs, vegetables, and fruit underwent a variety of transformations in the hands of the colonial cook that closely followed techniques described in the best-selling English cookbooks sold throughout the colonies. The most common cooking techniques were the classic ones (boiling, roasting, and frying), and, reflecting the material transformation caused by the British invasion, Lucy Emerson's descriptions assume that those from even the humbler ranks owned a spread of cooking implements unheard of a hundred years earlier.

Boiling flesh required chefs to follow a few standard rules. Emerson advised cooks to "be very careful that your pots and covers are well tinned, very clean, and free from sand." It was critical that chefs ensured that boiling water remained boiling at a consistent pace while the flesh was submerged in it, "otherwise you will be disappointed in dressing any joint though it has had proper time over the fire." Salted meat entered the water when it was still cold, while fresh meat went in after the water reached a boil. Most books suggested about fifteen minutes of boiling per pound of meat. Boiling recipes ranged in complexity. On the one hand, a recipe could stick to the basics, as did Emerson's for "boiled beef or mutton":

When your meat is put in, and the water boils, take care to scum it very clean, other wise the scum will boil down, stick to your meat, and make it look black. Send up your dish with turnips, greens, potatoes, or carrots. If it is a leg or loin of mutton, you may also put melted butter and capers in a boat.

On the other hand, boiling dinner could demand a series of intricate steps. Consider the following:

Wash and clean your Salmon very well; then score the side pretty deep, that it may take the seasoning. Take a quarter of an ounce of mace, the like quantity of cloves and nutmeg . . . add an ounce of black pepper and an ounce of salt. Lay the salmon in a napkin and season it well with this Seasoning of spices and salt, cut some lemon peal fine and some parsley also, which throw or strew over the fish, and in the notches or scores on the side, put about a pound of butter rolled in flour. Roll it up tight in the napkin and bind it about with twine. Put it into a fish kettle, just big enough to hold the fish . . . and a quart of wine, a quart of vinegar, and as much water as will just boil it. Cover your kettle close and set it over a quick fire. . . . [S]tew until you are ready. Turn your salmon out of the napkin it was boiled in. . . . Garnish with butter. Horse-radish is the best sauce for this dish.

One imagines that the latter was less popular than the former. But even with simple boiling recipes, adhering to specific details was critical. "To boil veal," Emerson explained, one had to keep in mind that "a knuckle of veal will take more boiling in proportion to its weight than any other joint, because the beauty is to have all the bristles soft and tender." Reflecting the proper English pairing of ingredients, she advised serving the dish with "parsley and butter; or with bacon and greens." A leg of pork "must lie in salt for six or seven days" before boiling and "requires much water to swim in over the fire." She suggested serving it with "buttered turnips, carrots, or greens." Venison tasted especially good when the cook boiled it with "some turnips, young cabbages, and beet-roots." She advised, "Lay your venison in the dish, dispose the garden things around it, and send to the table." Simple as it was, the drawback with boiling meat was that the cook could not control the flesh's interior texture. One cannot easily boil something medium rare.

Boiling vegetables might seem to be too basic a procedure to require written directions. Not so for Emerson. Preparing asparagus required the cook to "first cut the ends off about six inches from the head and scrape them from the green part downward very clean." After soaking them, she was to tie them into small bundles and throw them into a shallow pan of water after it boiled. "By overboiling," she warned, "they will lose their heads." Beans "require a great deal of water," and "it's best to shell them just before they are ready to go into the pot." Emerson advised cooks to "put them in with some picked parsley and some salt." When they appeared to have completely swelled with water, she wrote, "they are done enough." She called for a garnish of parsley and a ladle of warm butter. With respect to green peas, she required just a little bit of water, "not much more than will cover them," and the addition of "a few leaves of mint." When much of the water had boiled off, the cook was to "put in a piece of butter as big as a walnut, and stir them about." She garnished, as she so often did, with parsley.

As kitchens and kitchen equipment became more sophisticated, chefs chose roasting more often than boiling. Roasting enabled cooks to control the extent to which their meat cooked and to impart more flavors through stuffing. As with boiling, roasting techniques varied with the different sorts of flesh under fire. Beef, for example, demanded a "brisk hot fire," cooked for about fifteen minutes per pound, and required constant basting with salt and water. Emerson insisted that "rare done is the healthiest," not to mention "the taste of this age." Roasting mutton had to be done "more gently than beef." Because the meat was less flavorful and had a tougher texture, Emerson advised the cook to hide it in a mound of "potatoes, beans, collisflowers, water-cresses, or boiled onions, caper sauce, mashed turnips, or lettuce." Veal, by contrast, had a more tender consistency than beef or mutton, a quality that led Emerson to urge cooks to "lay it some distance from the fire a while to heat gently." It needed frequent basting in its own juice and quick cooking—"a fifteen pound piece requires one hour and a quarter roasting." Lamb had its own demands. Emerson began by basting the flesh with melted butter and dusting it with flour (likely made from Indian corn) before setting it on the spit. "Before you take it up," she explained, "add more butter and sprinkle on a little salt and parsley shred fine." She served it with "a nice salad, green peas, fresh beans, or a collis-flower, or asparagus." Roasting pork, finally, was no different from roasting beef, but every now and then the cook might opt to roast an entire pig. It wasn't a job for the squeamish:

Spit your pig, and lay it down to a clear fire kept good at both ends: put into the belly a few sage leaves, a little pepper and salt, a small crust of bread, and a bit of butter, then sew up the belly. Flour it all over very well [with Indian corn]. . . . When you find the skin is tight and crisp, and the eyes are dropped, put two plates into the dripping pan, to save what gravy comes from it: put a quarter of a pound of butter into a clean coarse cloth, and rub all over it until the flour is quite taken off; then take it up into your dish, take the sage, etc. out of the belly, and chop it small; cut off the head, open it and take out the brains, chop, and put the sage and brains into a half pint of good gravy, with a piece of butter rolled in flour; then cut your pig down the back . . . cut off the two ears . . . take off the underjaw, cut it in two, and lay one upon each side; put the head between the shoulders, pour the gravy out of the plates and into your sauce, and then into the dish.

Hence roasting could—as every English cook knew—be a contact sport.

As this recipe also indicates, cooks regularly adopted the English practice of using stuffing when they roasted. To stuff a leg of veal, Emerson directed the cook to "take one pound of veal, half-pound pork (salted), one pound grated bread—chop all very fine." She then added "a handful of green parsley," three eggs, pepper, and butter. "Cut the leg round like a ham," she wrote, "and stab it all with holes, and fill it all with holes and the stuffing." The cook then salted and peppered the roast, dusted with milled Indian corn, and roasted. Her stuffed beef recipe followed a similar course. She stuffed a fourteen- to sixteen-pound round with the following concoction: "one and a half pound of beef, one pound slat pork, two pounds of grated bread—chopped all fine." She rubbed the stuffed beef with salt, pepper, butter, thyme, and summer savory. While roasting the beef, the dedicated cook placed three pots of boiling water underneath the skewered beef in order to keep it moist. Emerson included a recipe for stuffing and roasting a "turkey or fowl" as well. She began with "one pound soft wheat bread, 3 ounces of beef suet, 3 eggs, a little sweet thyme, sweet marjoram, pepper and salt," and proceeded to "fill the bird therewith and sew it up and hang down to a steady fire." The cook basted often and roasted the bird until "steam emits from the breast." With the bird drippings, the cook made gravy by adding a pound of butter to the grease. She then dusted the bird with flour and basted with the thickened gravy. When the chest steamed, she served the bird with boiled onions and cranberry sauce. She noted, however, that others "boil and mash three pints of potatoes, wet them with butter, add sweet herbs, pepper, salt." We might imagine that such decisions, given the work behind these ingredients, weren't made lightly.

It took copious amounts of butter, but the smell and taste of fried flesh was (and still is) unmatched. It was, moreover, simple—demanding less experience and delicacy than roasting. New Englanders fried meat with gusto. Veal cutlets were a popular option. They required the cook to cut veal into steaks "and fry them in butter." To further enhance flavor, she "made a strong broth with the scrag end, boiled with two anchovies, some nutmeg, some lemon peel, and parsley shred, and browned with a little burned butter." Into this broth went white wine and the cutlets. After thickening with "butter rolled in flour," the cook "strewed on much salt" and served immediately. For frying beef, Emerson took the leanest cut and "beat it with the back of the knife," after which she fried the steaks in "just enough butter that will moisten the pan." As the gravy cohered, she poured it into a separate pan, all the while frequently turning the steaks over a gentle fire. To make the sauce, she advised, "put to the gravy a glass of red wine, half an anchovy, a little nutmeg, a little pepper, and a shallot cut small." Following "two or three little boils," she then seasoned with salt "to the palate" and poured it over the steak. Oysters, finally, were a preferred New England item to fry. Emerson's recipe was simple and, in its own way, elegant:

You must make a batter of milk, eggs, and flour; then take your oysters and wash them; wipe them dry, and dip them in the batter, then roll them in some crumbs of bread and a little mace beat fine, and fry them in very hot butter.

A modest people, the New Englanders were generally loath to dwell on their sensual pleasures, especially for the historical record. But as a people accustomed to working to provide their own ingredients, and as a people who achieved an unprecedented self-sufficiency during the first half of the colonial era, they must have found the taste of fresh oysters to have been one of the kitchen's especially rewarding pleasures. Not to mention a tasteful confirmation of their successful adoption of English cookery. In overcoming their prudence and indulging their tastes more than the dictates of Puritanism had once allowed, New Englanders were leading the way for Americans throughout the colonies to take the step of living, thinking, and cooking like the British, their proper permanent ancestors. The other colonies, to varying degrees, followed New England's lead in making these cooking techniques increasingly standard aspects of a less regionalized culinary landscape. As a result, an "American" way of cooking—however tentatively—began to cohere.

The Big Picture

The first American cookbooks, as Lucy Emerson's *The New England Cookery* especially indicates, had their immediate roots in English cookbooks dating well back into the 1730s and 1740s. The adherence to strict rules combined with the moderate flexibility that defined English food appears throughout not only Emerson's cookbook but dozens of others printed and sold in America well after the Revolution. As we'll see, however, the reality of culinary life on the ground in 1796 (Amelia Simmons) or 1808 (Emerson) had advanced in a far more American direction than Simmons's and Emerson's books remotely suggest. These women, in short, did a much better job of codifying for an elite American market the cooking habits that the English had been practicing for more than a century than reflecting the pressing reality of the culinary moment. If we can accept this strong possibility, then we might also accept the argument that these cookbooks indicate that Americans had begun to adopt the British culinary habits as early as the 1730s, an adoption that led to a more unified way of cooking.

White, free Americans living and cooking between 1730 and 1770 could pursue the very British culinary measures that Simmons and Emerson later codified because they had enthusiastically adopted new kitchens, utensils, British attitudes, and sense of metropolitan hospitality. Despite their persistent regional variations, colonial Americans were increasingly ready to take on the challenge of proving their allegiance to the dominant cultural heritage through the everyday decisions they made in the kitchen. All these factors—from kitchens to cookbooks—imposed a modest level of culinary coherence on a regionally diverse patchwork of colonial cooking habits. What colonists drank as these changes occurred only smoothed this gradual interregional convergence.

CHAPTER 7

INTOXICATION

Finding Common Bonds in an Alcoholic Empire

Man, being reasonable, must get drunk;
The best of life is but intoxication.
Lord Byron, *Don Juan*

IN 1714, when Judge Samuel Sewall entered a Boston tavern and "found much company," he warned the unruly throng of revelers to call it a night and return home to their families. Sewall had recently gotten an earful from a group of ministers who insisted that drinking habits in Massachusetts had become so dissolute that clergymen should be housed across the street from each of the town's drinking establishments to monitor the clientele. Happening upon this scene of carefree indulgence, Sewall—with these ministerial complaints still ringing in his ears—made an ad hoc Puritanical plea for moderation. The results weren't encouraging.

"They refused to go away," he wrote in his diary. Not only did they scoff at the otherwise respected judge's presence, but they "said [they] were there to drink the Queen's health, and [that] they had many other healths to drink." Undeterred by their persistence, Sewall continued with his admonishment. This time he was mocked. "[They] call'd for more [drink]," he wrote, "*drank to me.* . . . Mr. John Netmaker drank the Queen's health *to me.*" Rejecting a proffered cup of ale, Sewall replied that he "drank none," a response to which "Mr. Brinley put on his Hat to affront me." After threatening to send the drunken mob to jail, Sewall ended the evening by telling them "if they had not a care they would be guilty of a riot." At that, the tired and drunken crown had a final laugh a Sewall's expense, drank yet another round to his good health, and, finally, dispersed.

Intoxication has proved to be an irresistible human experience. The fortuitous recognition that airborne yeasts could convert sugar into carbon dioxide and alcohol was made well before the Mesopotamians domesticated barley in 8000 B.C. and possibly before humans even figured out how to bake bread. The strong pull of inebriation owes its magnetism to a variety of emotions and desires. Since time immemorial, humans have gotten drunk to have fun, escape, socialize, feel a temporary release from strictures of reason and convention, avoid boredom, transcend the dull limits of sobriety, rebel. Should colonial Americans have forgone alcohol, should they actually have listened to Sewall, it would have contradicted one of history's most reliable and universal culinary behaviors.

Coexisting with every alcoholic binge, however, was a vocal and passionate opposition. Every tavern bash has had its Sewall. As drinking exceeded the extent of its English practice on the open frontier of colonial British America, voices of moderation and even abstinence harangued Americans to sober up, or at least drink less. Whatever solace alcohol might have provided for the average tavern tippler, Cotton Mather, who recognized its value in very moderate amounts, otherwise dismissed it as a substance that would "overwhelm all good order among us." The "votaries of strong drink," he continued, "will grow numerous" and "make a Party against every thing that is Holy, and Just, and Good."

Although we might think otherwise, voices of protest were hardly limited to New England. In Georgia, when James Oglethorpe established his colony of convicts, he tried (unsuccessfully) to ban rum after learning that workers hired by the colony to carry out government contracts were spending their days in a drunken stupor. The *Pennsylvania Gazette* called taverns "a pest to society." The Philadelphia physician Benjamin Rush went so far as to publish a "Moral and Physical Thermometer" that matched alcoholic beverages with various ailments. While water, at 70 degrees, induced "health" and "wealth," grog, at –30 degrees, led to "lying" and "sore and swelled legs." Gin, way down at –52 degrees, left an individual "melancholy" and prone to "burglary." Punch had the unfortunate drawback of causing "tremors of hands in the morning," not to mention "peevishness" and "debt." Whatever his mood or financial condition, every tippler was bound to have his temperature taken by a teetotaler.

Most tavern-crawlers, however, were of a mind to tell Rush where he could stick his thermometer. Colonial Americans had no intention of moderating their boozy ways, and contemporaries routinely remarked on the less than temperate habits of British Americans. A visitor from Sweden noted "a general addiction to hard drinking." John Adams blamed "the ruin of half the workmen in this Country" on distilled spirits, asking, "Is it not mortifying . . . that we, Americans, should exceed all other . . . people in the world in this degrading, beastly vice of intemperance?" Another observer witnessed what he called "a nation of drunkards." In his famous sermon

"Wo to Drunkards," Increase Mather carried on about "the brutish sin of drunkenness," a vice that had "become a prevailing iniquity all over the country." One need only casually browse colonial court records to discover that, for all the hyperbole booming through these condemnations, copious alcohol consumption was a way of life in the colonies. Drunkenness, violence, flouting authority, and carousing into the wee hours of the night hardly undermined the colonial project, but these activities persisted nonetheless in the face of constant griping from men displeased with alcohol's deleterious affects. Many a modern genealogist has had his hopes of ancestral nobility dashed upon finding that the only place his colonial forebears appeared were in the local court records as persistent, pathetic drunks.

Colonial Americans drank more aggressively than their English counterparts. The frontier, with its ruggedness, lack of regulation, and palpable sense of raw opportunity, remained free from the customary social and legal strictures that tempered, however mildly, drinking habits back home. Sure, one could crack open any set of English court records and find infinite equivalents to the booze-soaked rabble-rousing of the colonists. But given the sense of urgency behind the colonial temperance screeds, and given the greater popularity of hard liquor in America (as opposed to cider and beer), it seems safe to conclude that alcohol consumption in the colonies was unique. A Georgia gentleman might not have been exaggerating when he wrote, "If I take a settler after my coffee, a cooler at nine, a bracer at ten, a whetter at eleven, and two or three stiffeners during the forenoon, who has a right to complain?" Statistics from 1790 suggest that the complaints would indeed have been few. The average white American older than fifteen years consumed almost six gallons of pure alcohol a year. What this means is that he imbibed thirty-four gallons of beer and cider, five gallons of distilled liquor, and about one gallon of wine. These figures are *averages*. Factor in nondrinkers, and the amount spikes to astonishing levels for the active drinkers. We lack comparable figures for England, but—to put this consumption in perspective—the average American today drinks less than half the amount of his colonial forebears.

Are we to conclude that colonial America was an incipient nation of drunks? Not at all. Interestingly, alcohol consumption never became the pervasive moral problem that it supposedly became in the nineteenth century, when middle-class women led a powerful and well-organized temperance movement to moderate its ill effects. Despite the shrillness of the opposition's rhetoric, despite the linguistic evidence of more than 150 slang terms for inebriation, and despite the strikingly high per capita consumption of distilled spirits in colonial America, Americans seemed fully capable of handling their booze with remarkable poise. All things considered, most colonists took a measured, rational, and healthy approach to alcohol. Benjamin Franklin, a close friend of Benjamin Rush, spoke often and approvingly of alcohol's benefits, noting, for example, that there was no "good living where there is not good drinking." Few, if any, spoke of alcoholism or mentioned a drinking problem or worried openly about alcohol abuse. The controlled consumption of alcohol had much to do with the fact that drinking wasn't taboo. Women and children joined adult men in beer and cider consumption; colonists drank in family and community settings; excessive indulgence was allowed in moderation at funerals, militia drill days, and court days; the introduction of drinking at a young age fostered a useful appreciation of alcohol's dangers; and the popular association of alcohol with medicine was strong enough for even a Puritan as devout as Increase Mather to admit that alcohol could, properly used, be "a Creature of God."

Faced with the greater opportunity to drink excessively on the fringe of the British Empire, most Americans responded by drinking excessively on the fringe of the British Empire. To drink occasionally to excess was an act in which the colonists certainly indulged, but as their 3 percent annual economic growth rate suggests, these men, women, and children handled their booze well. They had, as their tradition demanded, mastered "the art of getting drunk."

Alcohol and Food

Mastering that art had a critical impact on the way Americans ate. In the most general terms, it helped spark a vibrant coastal trade in food that built itself on the back of the explosive rum trade while rum, in turn, diminished the cultural impact of Native Americans. The centrality of alcohol in colonial British American life—driven partly by that mysterious urge to feel intoxication—might have inspired excessive fears of disorder, but it also helped further the convergence of America's once disparate regional food habits. Just as alcohol could bring people out of their shells, it could do the same for regions. None of the connections between alcohol and food are immediately obvious, but they nevertheless begin with a simple decision: that of the British American settlers to provide beer and cider for themselves and their families.

Early on, reflecting the inherited English culture, beer and cider became the most popular drinks of choice in colonial America. Most of these drinks were initially made at home, and they served to tighten cultural connections to the homeland even as regions began to develop distinct ways of cooking and eating. As farmers throughout the colonies specialized, however, the will and the capacity to produce beer and cider domestically, on individual farms, significantly decreased. And as it did, colonists increasingly relied on taverns to produce and serve not only beer and cider but also a range of distilled drinks—most notably, rum. The establishment of the colonial tavern was a very English thing for English settlers to do. In so doing, though, they created an institution that would take on far more roles and have a much larger cultural and culinary impact than it did at home in England.

The significance of taverns to the development of American food cannot be overstated. Although nobody ever became wealthy by running a tavern, and while taverns remained the domain of the "lesser" classes, they flourished as one of America's most culturally influential businesses. They fostered a deep sense of community, offered an increasingly itinerant population a warm and welcome place of comfort, transformed the consumption of food and drink from a private to a public activity, and provided the essential context for food and drink to mix with (increasingly heated) political discussion. Taverns were unusually democratic in the clientele that they served. Men, women, servants, and sometimes even free blacks frequented the local tavern with regularity, and taverns were hardly limited to the big cities, dotting the rural landscape from Georgia to Maine and deep into the colonial backcountry. If a trend intended to become a trend, if it was going to be spread far and wide, it would do so by way of taverns.

Few trends were more evident than the rise of rum as a culturally acceptable drink throughout the colonies. Beginning in earnest in the 1720s, rum came to dominate the tavern menu. In one sense, the rum itself—a very strong drink—was critical in that it severely compromised the cultural impact of a group that once had a powerful influence on regional foods: Native Americans. Alcohol, according to one historian, "killed and impoverished Indians in colonial America." In another sense, rum also factored critically into the history of American food for what it accomplished with respect to trade. The trade in rum, driven primarily by demand from colonial taverns and the local distillers and sugar refiners with whom they contracted, laid the groundwork for the related and increasingly consistent coastal trade in other foodstuffs. Whereas before the 1720s colonial regions attempted to achieve self-sufficiency in foodstuffs (with only New England fully succeeding), they now began to trade systematically with one another. They did so, moreover, not so much from necessity as from a desire to have foodstuffs from around the colonies: beef from New York, cod from New England, pork from Virginia, and beer from Philadelphia. Rum greased the wheels of this trade because it was on the back of its trade that colonial Americans began to bring regional foods together. It was a crucial, if indirect, step toward the convergence of an "American" food—a convergence that would come to fruition in the political ideology that began to cohere in the 1760s and finally mature in the aftermath of the American Revolution.

Beer

Rum eventually dominated, but it initially followed the lead of more provincial, humble, and less intoxicating beverages. Letters home from the first colonial settlers suggest that they cared about nothing except their beloved beer supply. One Virginian, Thomas Studly, complained in 1607 that "there remained neither taverne, beer house, nor place of relief." He offered the opinion that "had we beene as free from all sinnes as gluttony, and drunkenesse, we might have been canonized for saints," adding, with much disappointment, that "our drinke was water." Two years later, the situation hadn't much improved, leaving the governor of Virginia to advertise for two brewers on the grounds that "there are about three hundred men there more or less; and the majority sick and badly treated, because they have nothing but bread of maize, with fish; nor do they drink anything but water—all of which is contrary to the nature of the English—on which account they all wish to return." A settler in Plymouth spoke earnestly about "desiring a small can [container] of beer" and described how a group of settlers sick with scurvy were treated with beer that the governor had obtained from England. Up the coast in the Massachusetts Bay Colony, William Wood remarked on New England's pure water but added, "I dare not prefer it before a good beer." Richard Mather attributed the health of recent arrivals to their ship's "good and wholesome beer and bread," some of which was left over when the ship landed. In a letter home to future New England migrants, Francis Higginson, Salem's minister, compiled a list of "things which were better for you to think of there than to want them here," among which "malt for drink" was an important item. John Smith promoted Virginia as a place where "few of the upper planters drinke any water; but the better sort are well furnished with . . . good English Beere." Every English settler would have understood the beer-soaked nature of this correspondence.

The ubiquitous focus on beer reflected the English settlers' intimacy with the beverage that their countrymen had been brewing and adoring since the third century. Alcoholic drinks were generally considered to be safer than water, much of which was polluted throughout Europe. Alcohol, however, was also perceived to be inherently beneficial on its own merits. According to the conventional wisdom, it was essential for health, keeping away chills on a cold evening, aiding digestion of fatty foods, making hard work easier to endure, and generally helping fortify the constitution. Alcohol was, as one English cookbook writer put it, critical to keeping *"blood in a proper state."* Beer became an ideal frontier beverage, thus making particular sense for the colonies because it was cheaper and easier to produce than distilled spirits, requiring less equipment, time, and precious labor. Additionally, beer was what the settlers were most inclined to drink immediately after landing, given that the English ship-provision industry had a long tradition of outfitting merchants with "ship's beer." The transition to life in a new world—with the immediate production of beer—would have been mitigated by the continued presence of the beverage that the settlers drank at home and in transit.

Perhaps more than any other factor, however, beer prevailed as the founding beverage of the colonies because of its versatility. At its core, beer is the product of the fermentation of cereal malt infused and decocted with water. To have beer, a few simple events had to happen: cereal had to be dampened to cause germination, dried or heated to halt germination (leaving malt), mixed with water to make a mash, strained and cooled (leaving wort), and, finally, introduced to yeast. Hops weren't necessary to the process, but their addition technically turned ale into beer (at least according to the traditional definition of both drinks, a tradition that may have become meaningless by the seventeenth century). Manuals printed idealized versions of the brewing procedure. In *The New Art of Cookery, According to the Present Practice*, Richard Briggs eschewed "all the various branches of brewing" in favor of the most traditional brewing method "necessary in a large family." His directions called for the highest quality barley, a copper pot with legs that placed it exactly six inches above a fire, a two-door airtight cellar, the coldest river water obtainable ("such as it is soft . . . and easily insinuates itself into the malt"), several mashings, precise steeping times, and the finest hops. His recipe brooks few deviations from the tried-and-true methods. Settlers, however, were happy to toss tradition to the wind, adapt to life on the colonial fringe, and feel little compulsion to follow brewing customs with any exactitude. Beer allowed them to do so.

Because beer was nothing if not adaptable. Other English cookbooks, in contrast to Briggs's, included instructions that assumed the inevitability of

Beer Street, *1751*

As reflected in this engraving by William Hogarth, the English considered beer a beverage that connoted health and productivity. Along with cider, English colonists brewed it as a matter of course, drank it daily, and used it to lubricate social life in ordinaries and taverns.

Gin Lane, *1751*

William Hogarth's counterpart to *Beer Street* reveals the popular perception that beverages harder than beer had a deleterious effect on society. In British America, as rum became increasingly popular, many critics feared that mass debauchery and cultural decline would occur. To an extent, they did, but more for Native Americans than for white settlers.

variation from traditional brewing standards. Hannah Glasse, for example, included recipes for "middling beer" and "small beer"—weaker and quicker versions of "strong beer." She made suggestions for brewers who "intend to keep your ale a great while" by allowing for "the softest and clearest water you can get" rather than insisting on river water. Casks needn't be scalded, as the purists demanded, but rather brushed with a "little birch broom." Tubs could be used interchangeably to make wine as well as beer, and if, as a result, the beer soured, it could be rendered potable by throwing in "a piece of chalk as big as a turkey egg" or a "quart of oat-meale." Colonial settlers, in their quest to provide beer domestically, eagerly capitalized on this tolerance for flexibility. We have seen how John Winthrop brewed beer with corn. "The English have found out a way to make very good Beere of this graine," he informed the Royal Society. Although the Royal Society might not have caught his drift, his fellow settlers certainly did. Speaking of the numerous virtues of maize, one Virginian wrote, "Wee made of the same in the Countrey some mault, whereof was brued as good ale as was to be desired." Another Virginian went so far as to claim that he actually preferred Indian corn beer to English barley beer.

Beyond using corn, colonists adjusted beer to frontier conditions in several other innovative ways. The beer consumed on ships coming to America was a dark drink made from barley malt and flavored with ample hops—the familiar stuff. But the beer consumed in the colonies was more likely to have been brewed with anything from wheat, oats, persimmons, and pumpkins to Jerusalem artichokes. According to one surviving recipe, "The fruit, seeds and all, was crushed, mixed with wheat bran, then baked in cakes. As occasion arose, the cakes were soaked in water and the beer brewed." Hops grew naturally in America, but access was often difficult and, relying to some extent on imports, colonists didn't start growing them on poles until the eighteenth century. To compensate, they would frequently flavor beer with sassafras, spruce, and other English garden herbs. A verse from the 1630s drove home this powerful point of adaptability, reminding colonists:

If barley be wanting to make into malt
we must be content and think it no fault
for we can make liquor to sweeten out lips
of pumpkins, and parsnips, and walnut-tree chips.

Few colonial Americans found fault in stretching the definition of beer to such unaccustomed, however unpoetic, limits.

Several surviving recipes reinforce the liberal interpretation that home brewers applied toward this beverage they deemed absolutely integral to human health and happiness. (Small beer on Benjamin Rush's "Moral and Physical Thermometer," by the way, was equivalent to "happiness," while porter ensured "strength and nourishment.") When serving as a colonel in the Virginia militia in 1739, George Washington recorded the following small beer recipe in his journal:

Take a large Siffer [sifter] full of bran hops to your taste.—Boil these 3 hours then strain out 30 Gallns into a cooler put in 3 gallns molasses while the beer is scalding hot. Let this stand till it is little more than blood warm then put in a quart of yea[s]t if the Weather is very cold cover it with a blanket and let it work in the cooler for 24 hours then put it into the cask—leave the bung open till it is almost don[e] working—bottle it that day week it was brewed.

A brewer from Providence known in the region for a "beer famous throughout the countryside" scribbled down this recipe for a friend:

One ounce of senna tree [the dried leaves], chicory or celandine, one handful of red sage, or large quarter pound shells of iron crushed into small pieces. Take ten quarts of water, steep [boil?] it away to seven; and a quart of molasses. Wheat bran baked hard [into a cake]. One quart of malt, one handful of sweet barm [yeast]. Drink as soon as it is fermented.

A final example from Virginia on the eve of the American Revolution shows one of the more rugged manifestations of colonial beer. It was made with green cornstalks. The brewer, Landon Carter, explained:

The stalks, green as they are, as soon as pulled up, were carried to a convenient trough, then chopped and pounded so much, that, by boiling, all the juice could be extracted out of them; which juice every planter almost knows is of as saccharine a quality as almost anything can be, and that any thing of a luxuriant corn stalk is very full of it; . . . after this pounding, the stalks and all were put onto a large copper, there lowered down in its sweetness with water, to an equality with common observations in malt wort, and then boiled . . . after that it is strained, and boiled again with hops.

In such extemporaneous ways did colonists work to ensure that one of their most sacred cultural traditions—brewing—survived transatlantic transplantation. And, indeed, they seem to have succeeded—albeit with qualifications. Throughout the seventeenth century, most colonial Americans consumed beer on a regular and perhaps even daily basis, much as they had done back in England. As their food habits assumed regional distinctions, their beer-drinking habits transcended those differences, providing a rare spot of commonality for all colonists. Few would have had a chance to notice the similarity, however, because beer production continued to be domestically based throughout the seventeenth century.

Consider the situation in New England, where the structure of the brewing industry reflected the status and development of brewing throughout the colonies. There, between 1630 and 1660, the vast majority of brewing occurred at home on a small-scale level. Between 1635 and 1655, 60 percent of Massachusetts inventories, for example, showed evidence of home brewing. The scale of these home operations was modest enough for the average amount of malt recorded in these inventories to weigh in at just over two bushels—barely enough to brew a few dozen gallons of small beer. Home brewers also lacked specialized equipment, a situation that led them to do things such as mash and cook in the same kettle. They lacked coolers, copper pots, and malt mills and, as a result, improvised in ways only left to the imagination. Standard English brewing manuals warned brewers of the mishaps that would inevitably ensue if they didn't use the proper equipment and follow exact rules. Their beer would turn out "ropy," assume a "crankish taste," become "curdy," or "grow flat and dead." Ropy, crankish, curdy, flat, and dead beer, however, was better than no beer. For most of the seventeenth century, settlers made do with minimal equipment and small batches of homemade brew whose taste too often confirmed the common assumption that brewing was indeed as much mystery as art. Life on the colonial periphery, however, tolerated little snobbery.

The "Ordinary" and the Expansion of Drink Menus

Toward the end of the seventeenth century, colonial brewing remained a relatively decentralized activity, but less so than it had once been. Throughout the colonies, families and planters spent the century specializing their economic activities. They turned land, labor, and capital over to cultivating rice, wheat, and tobacco; cod fishing; timber harvesting; fur trapping; and other endeavors. As they did so, most families dropped brewing from their long list of productive activities, leaving a select few to pick up the slack by beefing up their brewing operations and tapping the emerging regional market. This subtle shift in the structure of supply and demand may have gone unnoticed at the time, but its most conspicuous outcome did not. The decline in home brewing quickly led to the establishment of a new colonial drinking establishment called the ordinary.

It was a place that few tipplers could pass without at least a brief visit. Usually run by a woman, the ordinary took home brewing to a level sophisticated enough to require a license from the town government. An ordinary was no tavern, however. Instead, it was a place that brewed, stored, and served a slightly larger amount of beer than the home brewer typically cooked up, all the while doubling as the proprietor's home, depending exclusively on family labor, serving only a few patrons at a time, usually lacking an official name, and offering neither room nor board. In New England, evidence of home brewing dropped to one-third of all households after 1665, but at least two licensed ordinaries appeared in every town. The quality of the brewing equipment in these ordinaries increased considerably, as did the quality of the beer. By the end of the seventeenth century, most colonists were more likely to wet their whistles with a tankard or two of "3 penny beer" from the local ordinary than gulp down the small beer brewed at home.

As satisfying a repast as it proved to be, beer wasn't enough. Although no one could have predicted it at the time, the local demand for beer—a logical extension of English culture—set off a chain of events that eventually would have important implications for the convergence of America's foodways. The connection is hardly immediate or obvious, but the rise of the ordinary was a critical link in the chain because it led to the proliferation of a loyal clientele, who, in turn, intensified efforts among ordinary owners to meet its growing demand for other alcoholic beverages—for instance, cider.

As apple orchards matured from Carolina to Maine, patrons called on ordinaries to provide cider alongside beer. Ordinary owners responded by building rudimentary presses and doing whatever it took to make enough cider to meet local demand. The transition to cider was another way that colonists bucked the trend toward culinary regionalism with the colony-wide perpetuation of an English tradition. Cider, too, was old. The Druids had the distinction of introducing cider to England, while the Romans and Normans improved apple varieties, to the great benefit of an industry that, by the seventeenth century, had become a basic aspect of life in Mother England. Like beer, cider was relatively cheap and easy to produce. Orchard keepers and gardeners began to grow smaller crab-apple varieties because their tannin levels far exceeded those in apples produced for eating or cooking. Kitchen gardeners grafted apple varieties to create apples that were not only high in the essential tannins but also imbued with more acid and natural sugar. (Modern growers call them bittersharps.) After harvesting the bittersharps, cider makers—usually ordinary owners—crushed the apples into a pulp called a pomace, which they laid on the corkscrew press over a bed of straw. The press extracted the unfermented juice, or must, which went directly into vats or wooden casks for fermentation. Wild yeast in the apples converted sugar into alcohol, and, as that chemical process occurred, it was up to the cider maker to determine when to intervene and filter the must. Early filtering yielded sweeter cider that was lower in alcohol content. Late filtering (after about three months' worth of fermentation) produced hard cider that was much higher in alcohol content. The proliferation of cider presses in inventories, as well as evidence of purchases of cider presses in farmers' account books, suggest that the most obvious obstacle to producing large amounts of cider—the press—was being regularly hurdled by a population of colonists intent on complementing beer with cider.

Unlike beer, the cider produced in the British colonies closely resembled the cider produced in England, primarily because the apples were so similar to those in England. The widespread and very creative resort to substitutes generally didn't have to occur with cider production, and it may be for this reason that cider consumption actually outpaced beer consumption in colonial ordinaries by the end of the eighteenth century. Nevertheless, cider produced in the colonies became readily available not only because the demand for it remained constant and its quality fairly consistent but also because, like beer, it was a forgiving beverage to produce, allowing significant room for error and correction. It, too, was an exceptional frontier beverage.

When cider became overly acidic, according to Richard Briggs's cookbook, the cider maker could mix milk with "two pounds of calcined oyster shells" and "whisk it well together with four gallons more of the cider, and apply it to the hogshead." After a good stir, "it will immediately discharge the acid part out of the bung." Another common problem with cider, especially in regions with relatively new apple trees, was its frequent oiliness. Oily cider resulted from variations in the apples used to make the cider, "for the juice of fruit that is not ripe will seldom mix with ripe juice in fermentation." Achieving uniform ripeness, however, was especially difficult with new trees in a new setting, and thus colonial cider too often turned out to have a "disagreeable, foul taste." One correctly suspects that colonists tolerated cider that tasted "off" on more occasions than their English counterparts. However, they could, if they so wished, correct the oiliness by mixing milk with "salt of tartar" and "sweet spirit of nitre," adding the mixture to the tainted hogshead of cider, and letting it sit for fifteen days. The oily cider would sink to the bottom, and all the cider maker had to do was drain out the cider from the top, or "rack it," taking care to "observe when it runs low, to look to the cock (the draining tube), lest any oily part should come up." Solutions such as these—solutions entirely in keeping with the flexibility of American food and drink—made it much easier for ordinaries to incorporate cider onto their expanding menus.

A third beverage that seventeenth-century colonists began to demand from the ordinary was brandy. Like beer and cider, brandy required minimal equipment to make, relied on readily available ingredients, and tolerated a range of production techniques—qualifying it as yet another frontier beverage. Brandy is a drink distilled from fruit. Although the ancients very likely enjoyed concentrated wine, brandy's immediate origins are in the sixteenth century when Dutch traders realized that it was cheaper to evaporate water from wine before shipping it and then adding it back to the distillate when they reached their destination. They soon discovered, however, that the concentrated wine had a seductive flavor all its own. They initially called it *brandewijn*, and, later, as the French began to make cognacs, it evolved into brandy. But brandy could be made from more than just grapes, as the colonists, who began to construct backyard stills called limbecs, quickly realized. Thomas Paschall wrote home in 1683 to mention the abundance of "wild plums and grapes" growing across the Pennsylvania landscape, noting that "most people have stills of Copper for that use." Apples, blackberries, pears, cherries—anything the colonists grew in their orchards—could theoretically be distilled into simple, tasty, and highly alcoholic drinks collectively known as aqua vita. Brandy had the added advantage of keeping longer than both beer and cider. And even if he lacked a limbec, an ordinary owner could approximate a still by cobbling together a device that included a container to boil the liquid, a condenser to capture the vaporized fermenting beverage, and another container to collect the condensate. The condenser could be as simple as a thick piece of wool that could catch the distillate and hold it until the "distiller" squeezed it out with his bare hands. An overview of stills listed in colonial inventories suggests a wide range of devices, ranging in worth from a modest 10 shillings to a not so modest £5.

Court records from New England paint a vivid picture of this expansion in the ordinary's menu. In the 1640s, the vast majority of ordinaries served beer and beer alone, but by the 1660s and 1670s, they had expanded their menu offerings considerably. John Sorla had his license renewed for the year in 1670 but now added a "license to draw liquors for a year." John Gould applied for and received a special license "to draw cider and liquors for six months." The effort among cider and liquor sellers to maintain their legislated market share could be intense, a sense of protection confirmed by Caleb Kimball's condemnation of Michael Cross for "selling cider by small quantities contrary to law." A town lacking a cider-selling ordinary would often petition the court to acquire one, as "several inhabitants of Marblehead" did when they filed a request for John Cope "to keep an ordinary and draw beer and cider." Demand for cider and brandy became constant enough for towns to grant licenses to retailers who, in turn, sold their product "out of doors" to ordinaries. Theophilius Baily, to cite just one example, "was licensed to sell strong waters out of doors, according to the request of the selectmen of Lyn[n]." It was in these ways that ordinaries in colonial America, which had begun by serving a humble tankard or two of beer, expanded their production throughout the seventeenth century to include cider and brandy, and, in so doing, keep their clientele happy.

Drunkenness and Its Scapegoat

Recall, however, that every expansion in alcoholic consumption had its Samuel Sewall. These new beverages may have been ideal frontier drinks commensurate with the available ingredients, technology, and labor in the colonies, but they grated against the will of the more conservative community leaders. While the varied offerings undoubtedly pleased most residents and travelers alike, they evoked plaintive concerns among colonial governments intent on preserving order in the precarious new settlements sprouting up on the equally precarious frontier. Most noticeably, the rise of stronger alcoholic beverages such as cider and brandy led to a rise in conspicuous drunkenness, so much so that colonial leaders began to turn their ire as much toward ordinaries as they did toward drunkenness itself. Indeed, the court records tell a story of growing discomfort with both inebriation and, significantly, the decentralized venues in which it acted up.

Court cases documenting drunkenness run literally into the thousands, but a few deserve mention. One evening of alcoholic debauchery among a group of men in a Salem ordinary suggests that the growing concerns about public drunkenness weren't altogether unjustified. After a full hearing on the case, the court fined Charles Turner "for scurrilous speeches and tippling" after he confessed that he had been drinking "for three hours or more." His defense—that he wasn't in any way drunk—ran counter to a Mr. Pester's assertion "that Turner staggered." Turner's reply: the "floor was uneven." The excuse didn't work, but Turner wasn't going to go gently. After receiving his sentence, he "complained of Daniell Owls for drinking" as well. Evidence was initially shaky on Turner's accusation against Owls, but he claimed that "Owls came in as if he was drunk and went to bed in a quarter of an hour." Any lingering doubts about his state of drunkenness, however, were completely diminished when Thomas Oddingsol, to the most certain horror of the jury, testified that Owls had "eased his stomach in the chimney before going to bed." Disgusting as his gesture was, the party raged on. Pester also tattled that Samuel Archer, who insisted that he did not drink "unto drunkenness," had "smelt of beer," and that Archer and his friend William Allen "had been drinking strong water at Mr. Johnson's" on the day of their military training. Such scenes severely worried the more virtuous souls trying to impose order in a new world. Their ability to overcome these problems goes a long way toward explaining why the social order never crumbled. Drinkers drank, opponents complained, and others sought legal redress, but through all the bickering, a balance of sorts was achieved. The casualty, however, wasn't booze per se but the ordinaries that served it.

The crackdown was anything but subtle. Voices emanating from the benches and pulpits of New England, a region with a special penchant for social control, rang the shrillest. The Ipswich court, for example, licensed Stephen Hasscot to "sell liquors" but to supply only "his own boats for a year," stipulating that "he did not allow it to be drunk in his house." Quartermaster Perkins renewed his license to "keep an ordinary . . . to draw liquors," yet he had to do so under the new demand that "no townsmen drink in his house," thus limiting the hard stuff to outsiders. These kinds of strictures became increasingly common as the seventeenth century progressed. Charles Grover, the constable of Gloucester, Massachusetts, deposed that "William Vinsonne had been chosen by the town to keep the ordinary and to sell wine." When Vinsonne asked the court to confirm him, it did so, but clarified that "he was licensed to keep an ordinary, but not to sell wine." In 1670, John Gould "had his license to sell cider and liquors renewed . . . but not to suffer townsmen to drink liquors in his house." Through such measures, town governments took steps, as Cotton Mather put it, "to punish all the vices which disturb the good order and repose of human society." In such ways did they also work to lessen the influence of ordinaries that "do daily and frequently draw and sell by retail wine, cider, and all other liquors at their pleasure without control." Faced with the proliferation of ordinaries serving drinks more potent than the relatively innocuous small beer, magistrates vowed to inspect all ordinaries and enforce the laws. An earnest bunch, we can be assured that they meant it.

Again, a major cause for this response was the ordinary. "There is no place more overrun with wickedness, sins so scandalous, openly committed in defiance of law and virtue," William Penn wrote. The council of Pennsylvania apparently agreed, noting that "as for ordinaries, we are of the opinion that there are too many in this government, especially in Philadelphia, which is the great cause of the growth of vice." The opinion undoubtedly reflected Penn's sentiment that "all excess is ill: but drunkenness is of the worst Sort. It spoils Health, dismounts the Mind, and unmans Men." Such concerns, however loudly they echoed throughout the colonies, initially fell on deaf ears as ordinaries opened at a rate that outpaced the increasing seventeenth-century population. As they spread, so did the harder beverages, conspicuous drunkenness, and an incipient fear of a social disorder sure to unravel these loosely bound societies. And, thus, the forces of reform mustered to promote an institution that hardly seems a likely candidate to control the abuse of alcohol—the tavern.

The Tavern: An Unlikely Solution to Drunkenness

Despite the periodic Puritan or Quaker rant, colonial leaders were nothing if not pragmatic in their expectations for reform. Nineteenth-century temperance zealots they were not. Magistrates knew quite well that any attempt to prevent or even moderately curb the consumption of hard alcohol was doomed to fail among a population of landowners scattered on the fringe of an empire whose center had its own problems controlling frequent and abusive tippling. A more realistic response, colonial officials reasoned, might be to centralize the alcohol industry even further by encouraging settlers to open larger and more sophisticated drinking establishments while discouraging the proliferation of so many tiny and liberally dispersed ordinaries. Although the transition occurred at different times in different colonies, the overall result was the tavern, or, as it was often appropriately deemed, the public house. The tavern existed as a separate structure from the owner's house, served a wider variety of patrons, could accommodate many more drinkers in a single setting, sold enough alcohol to rely on local wholesalers to supplement its own production of beer and strong waters, dealt extensively with merchants to provide imported drinks, offered meals, and often provided sleeping arrangements.

Adapting to these new roles, the tavern expanded to the point where it differed sharply from the humble ordinary. Patrons walked into a typical tavern to find a dozen or so tables lined with benches, the occasional set of chairs, a large fireplace with receptacles for pipes and tankards, a lean-to kitchen, cupboards, a separate dining room, and, of course, the stone-walled taproom. The grounds around the tavern also reflected a significant diversion from the ordinary. Taverns became popular stopping points for men carrying produce to market, and thus they had to provide space for horses and carts, as well as, according to a visitor to a Lexington, Massachusetts, tavern, "pens for the sheep, and turkeys, driven in flocks, to the roads to the Boston markets." Another tavern between Boston and New Hampshire contained enough space so that "one hundred horses could be stabled in the barns, and two or three cattle could graze around the tavern." An advertisement for a tavern published in a Maryland newspaper in 1745 mentioned that it "has good Pasture and Provider for horses; and keeps a number of horses to let to Gentlemen Travelling to any part of the Eastern Shore, and has Boys to attend them." Another from the *Pennsylvania Gazette* mentioned "a large brick kitchen, and a new brick stable, two story high, sufficient for above a hundred horses, the loft over it will hold 40 or 50 ton of hay." Even backcountry taverns offered their share of amenities. A Carolina tavern provided special rooms for meetings; plates, knives, forks, and spoons; a hand basin; and double beds for a decent night's rest.

From the perspective of colonial leaders intent on maintaining social and economic control, taverns significantly eased the burdensome task of regulation. Theoretically, the rise of taverns as the most conspicuous public drinking establishments helped town leaders enforce regulations such as the one they imposed in 1702 on Elizabeth Russell's tavern. Allowing Russell to sell everything from beer to a variety of mixed drinks, the town magistrates, referring to the landlady, stipulated that Russell could sell her drinks provided she sent her "customers home at reasonable hours, with ability to keep their legs." Such a requirement—that a tavern keeper be held responsible for her patrons—would have been unthinkable under the decentralized ordinary system.

A similar confidence in regulatory mechanisms is evident in Philadelphia's decision in 1704 to revise its licensing laws across the board, demanding that taverns pay a much higher fee than they once did to have the privilege of selling wine and spirits alongside beer. Under the old system, with ordinaries dispersed pell-mell, such an increased charge would have been beyond enforcement and too easily ignored. The regulatory impact of concentrating retail sales of alcohol in taverns can also be glimpsed in the determination of the North Carolina government to license taverns located deep in the backcountry. Spread out as they were, however, the assembly licensed 129 taverns between 1753 and 1775, a figure that might not account for the suspected prevalence of unlicensed taverns but confirms the effectiveness of licensing taverns nonetheless. And not only could the government license taverns, but it could realistically regulate them. In 1764, for example, Peter Johnson's Rowan County tavern came under fire because it "permitted Diverse idle and ill disposed persons . . . at severall Times as well as by night as by day to be and remain in the same house tipling, drinking, and behaving themselves in a disorderly manner." Similar admonishments became commonplace, in part because taverns were bigger targets than ordinaries.

Perhaps most significant, the development of the tavern as the colonies' conventional drinking establishment led to an overall decline of legal drinking establishments throughout the colonies (with respect to population). In the late seventeenth century, Virginia required that no county could license more than two taverns, Massachusetts initiated a successful colonywide program to reduce taverns per capita, and New York allowed no more than three taverns per settlement. Fewer houses hardly meant fewer drunks, but it helped ensure that those drunks would be in one place, that they could be more actively punished, and that the public houses that quenched their thirst could be held to higher standards of behavior.

The consolidation of many ordinaries into fewer taverns had other important social effects. Because taverns were more public in nature than ordinaries, they fostered a higher level of social interaction among people from various classes that had been unachievable under the previously decentralized arrangement. The manifestations of this sociability were many. For one, the advent of taverns created a more sociable context for economic activity. Not everyone was pleased about this change. "Is it not vile," Benjamin Wadsworth opined, that whenever colonists had to make "a bargain, make up accounts, pay or receive a little money . . . they must needs go to a tavern, and solemnize the matter as it were by swallowing a strong drink?" Why, he wondered, "can't tradesmen finish or bring home a piece of work, but must always think themselves wronged, if they are not treated with strong drink?" Whatever the reason, to pass the bottle in a tavern came to be seen as essential to "good fellowship," a popular belief that led colonists to "generally transact all business of this kind in taverns and coffee houses, at a great additional expense, and the loss of much time."

Time lost, however, obscured other gains. In addition to serving as centers of financial transaction, taverns became theaters of social transaction where men from a variety of backgrounds, regions, and experiences performed in ways that reinforced the stable hierarchy coming to shape colonial relations. Social ranks coexisted and interacted in a tavern in very real and often equal ways, but—like a performance on a stage—these interactions were in actuality only a momentary suspension of customary behavior that ultimately reinforced who led and who followed. Games were critical to this process, and taverns frequently offered the chance to indulge in a raucous round of billiards, dice, or cards, or even a bout of wrestling. A French visitor to a Virginia tavern remarked that "at night [there was] Carousing and Drinking in one Chamber and box and Dice in another, which continues till morning

Tavern patrons considering their hands of cards

Taverns had become an important component of colonial social life by the eighteenth century. As designated drinking establishments, they allowed colonial regulators to keep some oversight of drinking habits. At the same time, though, patrons demanded, and received, from their taverns a wider range of thirst-slaking options.

Commonly." Another observed how the customary rules for a good natured brawl encompassed "kicking, scratching . . . biting . . . throttling, gouging [the eyes], dismembering [the genitals]," and how these brawls were "attended with a crowd of people." Men from all ranks and backgrounds joined in these activities, and their participation provided a rare opportunity for property owners to reaffirm their theoretical equality with the lesser ranks while drawing lines in the dirt that those lesser ranks toed often but crossed with peril—opportunities of gouging and dismembering notwithstanding.

Taverns also provided a chance for towns and counties to shorten their poor-relief rolls. If illness, widowhood, or unemployment afflicted an otherwise upstanding citizen, the local court would often help ameliorate that person's misfortune by granting him or her a coveted license to operate a tavern. Reflecting the English tradition that believed, in the words of one historian of the English tavern, "aleselling kept poor men from coming upon the parish," colonial governments put the downtrodden into "such places [taverns] and callings [selling drink] rather than turn them out" on the streets. Potential tavern keepers began to cite both their personal character and the external hardships they had suffered when they went before the court to apply for a license. In 1670, a man who had, by his own admission, once provided "a comfortable livelihood for my family" and had been "careful of my particular calling as a seaman," applied for a tavern license on the grounds that he suffered from a gall- or kidney stone. Another did so on the basis that illness prevented him from "follow[ing] his other calling." Claiming that his family was "in a lamentable distressed condition not having a house fit to live in," a Boston man received a license from the court, which the court granted as "an act of charity." The fear behind this policy of granting licenses to the poor was that the impoverished would lack the good sense required to maintain sober establishments—hence the applicants' frequent stress on personal character. However robust a man's recommendation of his own character might have been, though, it was never enough to convince Wadsworth that the practice was anything but the essence of evil. He railed, "It may be a man has met with losses, or his trade fails, he's become low and indigent; the next thing, he seeks a license to sell drink; and when he has it, possibly many of his neighbors ruin themselves, by being his wicked customers." As with most such protests, however, Wadsworth's plea went unheard, since the poor frequently found a new lease on life behind a tap in a tavern.

A final immediate benefit of consolidating drinking culture into taverns involved their ability to introduce the hinterland to material trends emerging on the east coast and London. In most colonial communities, taverns were the only venues through which rural Americans living beyond the cultural orbit of Boston, New York, Philadelphia, and Charleston were able to participate in the consumer revolution that transformed colonial American society in the 1740s and after. Visitors to backcountry taverns were able to see and use, for perhaps the first time, such amenities as pewter plates and glassware rather than wooden bowls, brass spoons instead of tin, feather mattresses instead of straw, and a novel spread of "baubles" ranging from curtains to pewter chamber pots. An ad placed in a Philadelphia newspaper in 1746 described a backcountry tavern for sale with "4 rooms on a floor, with fire-places in each, and two ditto above stairs, also four good cellars, one of which is a kitchen, and an oven and a sink in it and room for a copper to be hung." An inventory from rural Carolina, surviving since 1766, reveals evidence of walnut chairs and table, embroidered tablecloths, pewter plates, and "fine" towels. The rate at which the styles and trends emanating from London could spread into corners as distant and dark as a Carolina backcountry tavern is glimpsed in the example of a drink called sanger. Invented in a London tavern in 1736, sanger—a mixture of red wine and lemon water—appeared on a menu in a Salisbury, North Carolina, tavern only thirty years later. It seems safe to assume that it wasn't the only metropolitan import that made its way to this tavern and introduced backcountry colonial Americans to a material world beyond the confines of their otherwise provincial colonial outposts.

The Demon Rum and Coastal Trade

As important as these tavern-related benefits were to colonial Americans, they collectively paled next to the tavern's most influential (and overlooked) role—introducing colonial Americans to a drink that would quickly become their beverage of choice: rum. Taverns and the rum trade became mutually reinforcing entities as colonial Americans' taste for the "demon," as it came to be called, dwarfed the consumption of all other drinks. Rum had been trickling into the colonies since the mid-seventeenth century, but conditions conspired to make it the colonies' most popular alcoholic beverage by the 1720s, after which it poured into taverns and, for a few pence, down patrons' throats. The most notable of these conditions was the rise of distilleries in Boston, Providence, New Haven, and Philadelphia—all of which emerged in response to the declining price of Barbadian molasses—and, more directly, the number of established taverns ready to retail the 100- to 200-proof beverage to a preexisting and eager clientele. Distillers correctly assumed that rum was a product that would practically market itself. The first distillery to open in colonial America was a Boston operation in 1700. By 1770, the colonies could boast 141, with 92 percent of them located in the northern colonies. Complementing these distilleries was a boom in sugar refineries, of which there were twenty-four by 1770. These operations never monopolized the colonial market because Barbadian and Antiguan rum still offered stiff competition. Over the century, though, mainland distillers cornered American markets effectively enough to drive West Indian rum out of every market save Charleston. The New England distillers did especially well. In fact, New England distilleries were making and selling so much rum that they were not only meeting local demand, but also exporting about six hundred thousand gallons a year to southern Europe, Ireland, England, and Africa. Supply and competition ran so high that rum—unlike wine and brandy—became a beverage in which all classes could afford to indulge. Between 1722 and 1738, for example, the price of retailed rum dropped almost 40 percent to a mere 2 shillings a serving. When it came to rum, life became a perpetual happy hour for the colonial consumer.

Taverns welcomed rum with throats wide open, and rum, in turn, proceeded to change colonial life in significant ways. For one, rum didn't trace its origins to England. Truly American in its provenance, it was distilled only from the molasses that dripped from West Indian sugarcane. Insofar as the Native Americans never made rum before the arrival of the colonists, and insofar as the English depended on the colonists for its production and importation, rum might be called the first genuine "colonial" product that colonists from north to south, coastland to inland, made into a marker of culinary life on the empire's periphery. During the decades that colonists were embracing all things British, rum was an item that reminded them of at least one essential difference they had from the homeland. In a sense, they "owned" rum. Even more important, rum actually showed how the cultural influence worked the other way as well, with Americans shaping English behavior through their exportation of the beverage to the homeland. While it's tempting to argue that the drink succeeded in weaning colonists from the tastes of England, it's also important to recall the prevailing context of the British invasion, not to mention the continued prominence of beer, cider, brandy, and wine on tavern menus throughout the colonial era. Still, the conclusion that Americans were a people becoming committed to their love of hard liquor cannot be disputed. Rum was a popular object of that new love, a love that collectively endured at least until the American Revolution.

Another quality of rum that stands out as especially important in the colonial context was that it was *not* a frontier beverage. Unlike beer, cider, and brandy, rum required trade, and not necessarily transatlantic trade but intercoastal trade (or, as economists call it, internal trade) as well as back-country–coastal trade. While mainland colonists were processing sugar and molasses, none of them was growing sugar. That reality—an accident of geography more than anything else—pulled together otherwise different regions in ways that only the slave trade had done between the mainland colonies and the West Indies. The most obvious and powerful trade connection with respect to rum emerged between the West Indies and New England, with New England merchants selling cod to the islands in order to help feed slaves and then buying molasses for distillers to turn into rum. Between 1768 and 1772 (years during which concrete statistics are available), the northern colonies sent the West Indies £95,000 worth of fish (and other goods) in exchange for £120,200 worth of sugar and molasses. It's a common opinion that, at this stage, New Englanders then carried out the famous "triangle trade" by making rum and sending all of it to Africa in order to purchase slaves and sell them to slave ships bound for the West Indies. Much of the rum did indeed go to Africa for that very purpose, but a substantial portion of it also stayed at home, where it was sold to local taverns and shipped down the mainland coast to other regions of colonial America. That crucial internal trade carved a wide swath for other goods to follow.

Evidence of this pioneering internal trade can be found, for starters, in colonial newspapers. An advertisement placed by "William Govane, at his house near Annapolis," in a Maryland newspaper in 1745 mentions the sale of "New England Rum, Muscovado Sugar, Mollasses." Just a week later, he spent the money to publish another ad for the same goods in the same paper, but this time with better directions to his shop. When Barbadian prices rose, importers in Charleston looked to New England for rum as well. "Barbados, Antigua, and New England rum" were all advertised by the Charleston firm Wragg and Lamblon in 1743. It would be interesting to know how much of each kind of rum was sold, as the New England rum, which traveled farther, cost substantially less (up to 20 percent) than either the Barbadian or the Antiguan varieties (an especially curious discrepancy given the transportation costs). Comprehensive statistics on the internal rum trade are available from only 1768 to 1772, but we can safely assume that they speak well for the general pattern that prevailed after 1720. That pattern was, to say the least, intricate. Between 1768 and 1772, Massachusetts annually shipped to the Middle Colonies 1,313,273 gallons of "New England rum." To the same region, Massachusetts also reexported 1,026,901 gallons of molasses for Pennsylvania distillers to make into locally sold rum. In addition to Pennsylvania—as well as Newfoundland, Nova Scotia, Quebec, and Prince Edward Island—Massachusetts carried rum to New York (£5,000 worth), Maryland (£11,500), Virginia (£9,000), North Carolina (£4,100), South Carolina (£10,100), and Georgia (£2,700). When these regions wanted to produce their own rum, Massachusetts merchants were more than obliged to provide the requisite molasses to do so. Of that product, New Yorkers bought £13,000 worth; Pennsylvanians, £1,000; Marylanders, £4,900; Virginians, £4,100; and North Carolinians, £2,300. Of course, New England and the other British American colonies had been trading goods on a periodic basis since they were founded, but rum was fatefully adding a much more systematic dimension to that trade.

Massachusetts didn't lead the rum and molasses trade alone. Other northern colonies soon joined it in sending rum, brown sugar, and molasses down the coast to the mainland colonies, thus making the growing web of internal transaction that much more involved. Rhode Island exported £4,900 worth of rum, £11,400 of molasses, and £2,600 of brown sugar. New Hampshire sent off £4,000 worth of rum, £1,800 of molasses, and £600 of brown sugar. Connecticut sold £1,000 worth of rum, £7,600 of molasses, and £2,000 of brown sugar. New York off-loaded £8,100 worth of rum, £2,500 of molasses, and £4,800 of brown sugar. The mainland-destined exports of New Jersey and Delaware were negligible, as were those from the Upper South and Lower South. Nonetheless, Pennsylvania reexported £7200 worth of the £11,500 worth of rum that it had purchased from Massachusetts, while also selling £1,800 worth of molasses and £1,900 worth of brown sugar to other mainland locations. Through such well-traveled paths—all blazed in the name of demon rum—did merchants begin to pull the disparate regions of colonial America into something of a well-tied knot. On Benjamin Rush's famous "Moral and Physical Thermometer," rum was said to have induced "madness." American merchants, however, were more than eager to wet the lips of that mad thirst, a thirst that conveniently led to other hungers—and the fulfillment thereof.

Intercolonial Trade in Food

The prominent Charleston merchant Henry Laurens wrote the words "the sloop arrived this evening and is now unloading" often in his extensive ledgers. The sloop in question was increasingly arriving from somewhere else within America. Only recently have historians, seduced as they once were by the neat logic of the triangle trade, started to pay attention to the more complicated patterns of internal trade that rum and slavery sparked. "Trade among the continental colonies," Arthur Jenson once wrote, "has been treated as something of a poor relation." A look at Laurens's account reveals the need to bring that poor relation back into the fold. Laurens wasn't a prime mover in the rum trade but, rather, one of its beneficiaries, as he traded often in the coastal exchange that rum made routine. To be sure, Laurens earned the bulk of his money by selling rice to southern Europe, but his letters and accounts brim with evidence of an emerging trade in colonial foodstuffs built on the foundation established by the vibrant trade in America's ubiquitous intoxicant. Rum, in short, not only fueled the growth of taverns and tavern life, but established the well-traveled sea-lanes for merchants to ship other goods up and down the Atlantic coast, bringing food from one region of British America to another—no mean development in a society as insular and fragmented as this one once was.

Much of this trade was, of course, borne of necessity. The rules of this new community of exchange were built on the expectation that when one region experienced shortages another would step up and supply the necessary goods. When, in 1762, the Middle Colonies suffered a rare but dismal grain harvest due to a spate of bad weather, Laurens explained how "the loss of their Crops in New York, Pennsylvania, &ca. has induced many people here [in Charleston] to fill up all the vacancies in the holds of their Vessels loaded for America with rough rice to supply the want of their oats." At times, merchants were a bit too eager to meet that demand, as they were when Laurens wrote how "a great deal of Indian Corn has been Ship'd at 12/6 to 15/ per Bushel & as the demand increases even at these high prices I apprehend we may feel a want of it in some parts of our own Country [South Carolina] before the seasons come round again." But for the most part, such transactions proved to be in everyone's interest. After another instance of providing emergency shipments of rice to Philadelphia, Laurens noted that one added benefit to come from that trade was how the "Europian markets will not be overstock'd with rice."

For their part, consumers in Carolina would have found much to admire in Laurens's shipments to Pennsylvania because, as his advertisements proved, he came home with a range of "foreign" goods for Carolinians to purchase at affordable rates. On December 23, 1760, Laurens's company ran an advertisement in the *Charleston Gazette* that read "CHOICE Minisink FLOUR, double and single BEER, and ship BREAD, just imported . . . from *Philadelphia* to be sold by Austin, Laurens, and Appleby." A November 6, 1762, ad reiterates the theme of the previous one: "IMPORTED *in the sloop* Dispatch, Isaac Kelly, *master, from* PHILADELPHIA, BEST Philadelphia double BEER, new FLOUR." Granted, Philadelphia and Charleston weren't worlds away, but for common colonists whose material life was circumscribed by a few square miles at most, the chance to consume these distantly produced mainland products would have been, in its own small way, something of a revolutionary experience, one that coexisted with and often complemented the colonists' voracious appetite for the goods of Mother England.

The shipping schedules maintained by customs officials help round out the story of active internal movement emerging around the 1740s and continuing through the 1760s. Over the course of a typical week in the 1740s, Philadelphia saw ships leave not only for Lisbon, Jamaica, and Barbados, as they always had, but also for such destinations as Newbury, Massachusetts; Boston; Piscataway, New Jersey; Rhode Island; Maryland; and Virginia. It saw ships arrive from Salem, Massachusetts, and South Carolina while watching them depart for Rhode Island and Boston. These arrivals were a relatively recent occurrence, but they were becoming more regular. At the same time, ships entered from Newport, New York, Providence, South Carolina, and Perth Amboy, New Jersey, while departing for New York, Rhode Island, and South Carolina. Trading schedules not only varied, but did so consistently—consistently enough anyway for customhouses to print the prices of commodities unladed from other mainland ships. In November 1742, Charleston residents could have found imported peas at 10 shillings a bushel, corn at the same rate, New England rum at 17 shillings and sixpence a hogshead, milk at £3 a cask, in addition to New York beer, flour, brown bread, ship bread, "middling" bread, and white bread. All these goods reflected the growing extent to which foodstuffs from one colony were becoming available in another. America, insofar as these shipping logs are concerned, was beginning to explore its own backyard.

Gathering evidence from 1768 to 1772, historians have sketched a more definite picture of this critical colonial development. While in no way perfect, these British records do tell us, for example, that New England sent 13,496 barrels of fish to the Middle Colonies annually. In addition to the fish (and, as we have seen, rum, sugar, and molasses), it annually sent 239 dozen poultry, 4,555 bushels of barley, 6,467 pounds of hops, and 339,436 pounds of cheese. In exchange for these goods, many of which Philadelphia merchants reexported, the Middle Colonies sent 5,629 bushels of bran, 28,640,304 pounds of bread and flour, and 51,038 bushels of oats and rye. Another reciprocal trade relationship developed between New England and the Upper South, with New England merchants bringing Virginians and Marylanders 8,494 barrels of beer and 273 tons of hay to feed its horses in exchange for 155,743 bushels of wheat, which, after 1740, Virginia began to grow alongside tobacco. The Upper South traded in the other direction as well, sending down the coast a combination of Indian corn and wheat in exchange for limes, turtles, and yams. The Upper South and Middle Colonies further added to this evolving web of intercoastal trade routes. Virginia and Maryland sent Pennsylvania and New York 443,085 bushels of Indian corn and 9,805 pounds of sarsaparilla, while the Middle Colonies reciprocated with 302 barrels of ham, 13,454 bushels of potatoes, and 290,165 pounds of loaf sugar. The Lower South sent every other colony rice, including 12,155 bushels to the Middle Colonies. Trade within these regions was as equally brisk as trade among them. Maine, Massachusetts, Rhode Island, and Connecticut actively swapped cattle and fish oil among themselves. New York and Pennsylvania sent each other 15,204 pounds of ginger, 21,944 barrels of beef and pork, 22,987 bushels of peas, 403 tons of butter, 9,835 bushels of malt, 1,432,477 pounds of brown sugar, and 183,189 bushels of salt. The world of goods that colonists were getting to know was becoming as much their own as England's.

These figures only scratch the surface of the actual trade. In capturing just those aspects of intercoastal trade large enough to justify measuring, they suggest but ultimately overlook the full extent to which the colonists had started to trade with one another across regional lines, from city to city, town to town, village to village, home to home. Most trades, of course, weren't nearly as systematic as those just chronicled. Instead, they typically included smaller quantities of goods secured in nooks alongside rum, sugar, or molasses and thus going unrecorded. We can be sure, for example, that New York City and Philadelphia sent butter to places other than each other's ports, that the Middle Colonies sent potatoes and ham to regions besides the Upper South, that New England sent beer to areas other than the Upper South, and that the Lower South sent yams to regions besides the Upper South.

In 1783, Thomas Paine looked at America and reiterated a sentiment articulated by the land's first European settlers. "The vastness of its extent," he wrote, "the variety of its climate, the fertility of its soil, the yet unexplored treasures of its bowels, the multitude of its rivers, lakes, bays, inlets, and other conveniences of navigation" made America "one of the richest subjects of cultivation ever presented to any people on earth." In their own regions, their small towns, their own farms, and their vibrant trade with England, colonists spent the better part of a century reaping the benefits of Paine's observation. One significant result of their work, as we've seen, was their development of unique regional ways of providing and cooking food. But this relative isolation began to change after 1720, and, as we've also seen, colonists owed this change, in part, to a new exchange in regional goods. And for that they could first thank taverns, which provided rum. Next, the colonists could thank their eager thirst for this beverage, which helped foster a convergence of different American foodways without withering the economic productivity of a population that had mastered the "art of getting drunk." Or withering their appetites for new kinds of food. For rum did more than support taverns and allow for widespread inebriation—it laid the basis for a brisk intercolonial trade in foodstuffs that, as far as we can tell, was embraced with all due enthusiasm by colonists whose consumer appetites already had been effectively piqued by the infusion of goods from the mother country. The story of alcohol and food in colonial British America might have ended on this positive note had it not been for the fact that rum, while it fueled the many fires of tavern culture and a growing food trade, threatened to snuff out another culture altogether.

Native Americans and Rum

Rum decimated Native Americans. Throughout the colonies, settlers had dealt with the Natives in a variety of ways, and while some ways were more peaceful than others, every transaction between Europeans and Native Americans was, by the mid-eighteenth century, fraught with some level of anxiety. After all, more than a century of turmoil marked by disease; legally questionable land transactions; wars with the English, French, Spanish, and one another; as well as unfair trading practices had worn the Native Americans down to struggling cultures with only the weakest connection to the mainstream Anglo-American society evolving and converging in their midst. Driven to the expanding periphery of the British Empire, Native Americans nevertheless continued to assert themselves through trade, diplomacy, and other alliances—all made possible by the fact that the French maintained western outposts in North America and posed a constant threat to British American security and expansion. Should the English push too aggressively, hedge too much, drive too hard a bargain, the Native Americans could always switch their allegiance to the dreaded French, or at least threaten to do so. It wasn't a threat to be taken lightly. And thus on this peg did the Native Americans hang their culture throughout most of the eighteenth century and, as a result, maintain some measure of cultural and culinary influence over British American foodways, especially in places such as the Middle Colonies and the Upper and Lower South. Rum, however, weakened this influence as it soaked the backcountry after 1720 and ravaged the Native Americans until the end of the Seven Years' War, a war that drove the French out of North America once and for all and thereby diminished, for all intents and purposes, the Native Americans' sustained impact on British American culture.

Natives consumed alcohol—mainly rum—with unusual fervor. More distressing than the quantities consumed, however, was the behavior that it induced. Perhaps the most enduring description of Native American drunkenness comes from an account penned by Benjamin Franklin in 1753. At a treaty negotiation in Carlisle, Pennsylvania, Franklin and his men encouraged the Native American negotiators to "continue sober during the Treaty" by offering to "give them Plenty of Rum when Business was over." This was one promise that the English evidently kept, for later that evening, after the Native Americans had consumed the entire (generous) supply, Franklin recalled "hearing a great noise." Upon investigation, he discovered that they "had all made a great bonfire in the Middle of the Square. They were all drunk Men and Women, quarrelling and fighting . . . running after and beating one another with Firebrands, accompanied by their horrid Yellings." In Franklin's final analysis, the event "form'd a Scene the most resembling our Ideas of Hell that could be imagined." The next day, the Native Americans apologized for their untoward mayhem with an excuse that confirmed the English perception that they hadn't come even close to mastering the "art of getting drunk." The spokesman explained: "*The Great Spirit who made all things made every thing for some Use, and whatever Use he designed any thing for that Use it should always be put to; Now, when he made Rum, he said, LET THIS BE FOR INDIANS TO GET DRUNK WITH. And it must be so.*" Rum, as most Anglo-Americans saw it, seemed to have a better grip on the Native Americans than they had on it.

Nestled in their insulated and relatively safe coastal enclaves, colonial leaders feared the explosive potential of such scenes and reacted by eagerly supporting laws that prohibited the trading of rum with Native Americans. But for the fur and skin traders and diplomats venturing into the back-country and dealing with Natives on a face-to-face level, such legislative schemes were pointless. There was, they believed, no realistic way to regulate the Native Americans' thirst for the demon. "Can it be expected that any law," the governor of Virginia was forced to admit in 1771, "made by the Assemblies to stop the progress of such an abuse that is committed at the distance of perhaps an hundred miles from any magistrate who has the power to punish, can do it?" Doubts arose over more than just the logistics of enforcement. Peter Chester indicated as much when he remarked, "It is often bad enough with white people when they are [drunk] . . . therefore what can be expected from Indians who are void of sense and reason, born in savage ignorance and brought up the same way?"

Whatever the reason, there wasn't a trader or diplomat worth his salt who thought the idea a practical one. Nor did these men necessarily *want* the trade in rum prohibited; more often than not, it was their mission's most useful trump card. "Sometimes," wrote one fur trader, "you may with Brandy or Strong liquor dispose them [the Natives] to an humour of giving you ten times the value of your commodity." One Native American testified as to how rum was employed by less than scrupulous traders, explaining how "Sylvester Garland [a trader] had brought to the settlement of Indians of their nation several Anchors of Rum, to the quantity of about 140 Gallons, & that to induce them to receive it and trade with him, he pretended he was sent by ye Gov[erno]r, and gave one Cask, as a present from him, uppn wch, being entreated to drink, they were afterwards much abused [in trade]." One Moravian missionary carried along a barrel of brandy because it "is by this opportunity to Deale with them."

It would be tempting to tell the story of rum and Native Americans as a simple tale of a good and evil. In a superficial sense, it could easily be regarded as a story of injustice, whereby the English forced the demon rum on a people who wanted nothing to do with it but fell prey to its seductions for reasons that might have had something to do with genetic predispositions. But it wasn't that simple. The fact is that we know very little about why Native Americans drank the way they did, or why they behaved the way they did when under the influence of a beverage they obviously had difficulty controlling. The genetic explanation has been substantially weakened in favor of a behavioral analysis that assumes Native Americans made their own decision to drink and did so for a very specific reason. And that reason was, many agree, one that's common to anyone who abuses alcohol: to escape. As Peter C. Mancall, an authority on Native American drinking habits, writes, "Indians drank at least in part because the world they knew was eroding around them. Whether liquor was supposed to bring power, as many believed, or to make them forget their problems, its effects were welcome at the time. The tragic dimension of the story is not that Indians drank but that their drinking only exacerbated the crises that were besetting their communities."

How it did so bears consideration. Binge drinking—a habit reinforced by the inconsistent availability of rum—fostered a number of detrimental developments for Native Americans who, it should be noted, redefined the act for the average Englishmen. "From the 16th to the 26th we *co[u]ld* do nothing," one astonished trader wrote from western Pennsylvania, "the Indians being Constantly drunk." The most conspicuous impact of this behavior was to transform what was traditionally seen as an orderly and reasonable world into a place of utter chaos and disorder. For all their willingness to trade rum, missionaries found this particular outcome to be especially problematic, noting how when alcohol was sold to Native Americans, "satan seems to have his seat . . . in an eminent manner." Nor were they of the disposition to take lightly what ensued as the bender raged. "In a few days this festival exhibited one of the most ludicrous bacchanalian scenes that is possible to be conceived," wrote William Bartram. "White and red men and women without distinction, passed the day merrily with these jovial, amorous topers, and the nights in convivial songs, dances, and sacrifices to Venus, as long as they could stand or move; for in these frolics both sexes take such liberties with each other, and act, without constraint or shame, such scenes as they would abhor when sober or in their senses." A French visitor was shocked to see, "in full view and to the great horror of all," Native Americans "engaged openly, like wild beasts, in shameful and unspeakable acts with one another." After one alcohol-infused orgy, the Natives, although "sick with intoxication," pawned "everything they were in possession of, for a mouthful of spirits to settle their stomachs, as they termed it." These collective rejections of English civility became common and worrisome enough for even Native American leaders to petition colonial leaders on the troublesome matter of alcohol, as a group of Chickasaws did when they told a colonial official in 1725 that rum had to be kept away because it made their "young men . . . drunk and Mad."

Booze obviously took a sad toll on the Native American family. "A husband will kill his wife," wrote a French observer, "and those women who get as drunk as the men knife their husbands and their children and strangle them without knowing what they are doing." Although hardly a common event, such a tragedy was an extreme reflection of the weakening familial bonds among a people using rum to escape their tragic fate. A group of Native Americans complained to a Presbyterian missionary how "there are some that do at times hire some of our Squaws to go to Bed with them & give them rum for it . . . this thing is very bad, & the Squaws again selling the Rum to our People make them Drunk." They asked the missionary "to advise our brothers against this thing." A family and village's economic security— as flimsy as it may have been—was similarly compromised when drunken Native Americans attempted to conduct business with whites. In Georgia, a rum trader remarked, "The poor Indians . . . when Drunk are easily cheated. After parting with the fruit of three or four months toil, they find themselves at home, without the means of buying the necessary clothing for themselves or their families." A traveler among the Choctaws in 1770s, Charles Stuart, recalled how he saw "nothing but Rum Drinking and Women Crying over the Dead bodies of their relations who have died by Rum."

One could fill volumes with this ponderous commentary of cultural decline. Instances and observations of inebriated Native Americans became so common that Native American leaders eventually initiated a temperance movement of their own. If alcohol abuse had an encouraging aspect it was that, unlike smallpox or white territorial expansion, it could be confronted and theoretically ameliorated. Several prominent Native American chiefs— including those from the Abenakis, Nanticokes, and Piscataways—appealed to colonial leaders to ban completely the rum trade and admonished their tribal communities to lay off alcohol. Other Native Americans who converted to Christianity led an attempt to embrace abstinence and preach the evils of demon rum with godly zeal. Scattered pieces of evidence suggest that these efforts didn't go completely unheeded. David Brainerd, a white missionary, explained how "the power of God" elicited a radical change in the collective drinking habits of the Crossweeksung Natives, turning "drunken wretches" into sober, God-fearing Christians. Christian Native Americans inhabiting the Ohio Valley vowed to ban rum and drunkards from their communities. A broadside written in 1772 by a Native American antibooze crusader named Occom took a poetic angle to the problem:

My kindred Indians, pray attend and hear
With great attention and Godly fear;
This day I warn you of that cursed sin,
That poor, despised Indians wallow in.

Mean are our houses, and we are kept low,
And almost naked, shivering we go;
Pinch'd for food and almost starv's we are,
And many times put up with stinking fare.

Our little children hovering round us weep,
Most starv'd to death we've nought for them to eat;
And this distress is justly on us come,
For the accursed use we make of rum.

A shocking, dreadful fight we often see,
Our children young and tender, drunkards lie,
More shocking yet and awful to behold,
Our women will get drunk, both young and old . . .

For all the passion invested in these efforts, though, stories of Native Americans kicking the habit were too few and far between to be said to constitute anything like a successful movement. The attempt to curb alcohol abuse never approached the impact that white temperance reformers would have on American urban centers in the nineteenth century. Mancall has called the sobriety efforts among the Native Americans a "Sisyphean quest." And, indeed, the rock of inebriation rolled back on these people who had already endured so much, diminishing their sense of cultural identity, their way of life, and, of course, their culinary impact on America.

The Big Picture

Native Americans had played critical roles in shaping regional foodways throughout colonial America. Even as they were pushed to the peripheries of every colony due to the imperatives of white expansion, they did their best to preserve their traditional culture while incorporating the increasing demands of European trade into their seasonal routines. The bitterest item in that exchange—rum—proved to weaken them to the extent that any ability to maintain the defining rudiments of their culture diminished substantially. A writer in the *American Magazine* hinted in 1757 at the gulf that had come to separate the whites and Native Americans when he wrote that "almost nothing has been attempted, to cultivate and civilize the untutored barbarians, whom providence by making them dependent on us, seems to have recommended to our special care." When this gulf widened, and when the Native American cultures clinging to life on the periphery of the British Empire used the bottle to blunt the collective blows that recent history had dealt, they diminished whatever impact they continued to have on American foodways. It is, without a doubt, one of colonial America's saddest chapters.

While rum weakened the Native Americans, however, it invigorated the economy and social life of colonial British America. Here was a drink that necessitated more systematic interaction with the West Indies and other colonial regions, could be said to be authentically "colonial" in character, fostered the growth of taverns, and became a seductive (and cheap) enough product after 1720 to overtake in popularity those once dominant frontier beverages, beer and cider. Americans from all walks of life began demanding rum, and rum, ever versatile and intoxicating, obliged with an effusive outpouring. A Creek Native, delivering a temperance speech to his brethren, might have excoriated the sweet beverage as "the Tyrant," but for white colonists up and down the coast—men and women for whom mastering "the art of getting drunk" was a cultural expectation—it was a benevolent tyrant that orchestrated the movement of new and unfamiliar foods. These foods were not the goods of England but, instead, the stuff made in those other "countries" of colonial British America.

Such a movement of goods, a movement that occurred alongside the evolution of taverns as houses of public interaction, was an essential factor in fostering a convergence of American food, however tentative that convergence may have been. At the same time that colonial Americans were embracing the goods of England, so were they becoming familiar with the culinary terrain of their own backyards. Rice, peas, and yams moved north; fish, wheat, and bread moved south; beer, pork, beef, and potatoes moved in both directions; and, through it all, Americans were getting a better sense of the foodways of their colonial counterparts in other regions. This trend coexisted and complemented the equally dominant trend of colonial Americans embracing all things British. In fact, the existence and negotiation of these foods effectively defined American food from the 1730s to the 1770s.

Precisely what Americans regarded as being truly "American" about their food, however, didn't become remotely evident until the colonists stopped taking small steps toward convergence and made a giant leap. The catalyst for the popular and self-reflective effort to define American food was nothing less dramatic than the American Revolution, an event that allowed Americans to ponder their culinary independence alongside their political liberty.

CHAPTER 8

REVOLUTION

A Culinary Declaration of Independence

How unripe we yet are.

Thomas Jefferson, *Notes on the State of Virginia*

WHETHER HE DID SO out of scientific ignorance or a perverse desire to bully the incipient nation known as America, Georges-Louis Leclerc, comte de Buffon, the famous French naturalist, condemned the landscape across the Atlantic Ocean as entirely unfit to support its inhabitants for any meaningful length of time. Thomas Jefferson, who took grave offense at such a characterization, summarized Buffon's objections to the New World in the following terms:

1. *That the animals common both to the old and new world are smaller in the latter;*
2. *That those peculiar to the new are on a smaller scale;*
3. *That those that have been domesticated in both have degenerated in America; and*
4. *That on the whole it exhibits fewer species.*

Clearly, as Buffon first suggested in 1749, something was fundamentally amiss in the American environment. In his *Histoire naturelle* and elsewhere, he portrayed America as a place where the climate's moisture and chill prevented the growth of beneficial organisms, where the "tremendous struggles of elemental forces" still raged, where thick forestation blocked the sun's warmth, where prolific swamps "replenish the air with heavy and noxious vapors," and where "everything degenerates." It wasn't an assessment that Americans, no matter how vehemently they disagreed with it, wanted to shine a spotlight on. Buffon, after all, was widely respected, and the colonies were struggling to earn cultural respect.

Thus we can only imagine the consternation that ensued when Buffon's gross misrepresentation of America's natural history caught on like wildfire. In *History of Mexico*, Abbé Francisco Clavigero, referring to Buffon, explained how America *"has been . . . and is at present a very barren country*, in which all the plants of Europe have degenerated, except those which are aquatic and succulent." Abbé Guillaume-Thomas-François de Raynal, in 1779, revived Buffon's theories when he described America as a place where "every thing carries the vestiges of a malady" and where "the imperfection . . . of nature is not proof of the recent origin of that hemisphere, but of its regeneration." Bashing the American environment (often through the Native American) was becoming a European sport.

These assessments were further echoed in the opinions of a group of British writers whose justification for upbraiding America was at least more obvious, if no more accurate. In 1767, Adam Ferguson portrayed the American environment as a place with "extensive marshes, great lakes, aged, decayed, and crowded forests . . . that mark an uncultivated country." Ten years later, William Robertson, in his best-selling *History of America*, portrayed the Native American as an inevitable product of the colonies' "coldness and insensibility," qualities that kept inhabitants stuck "in [their] rudest state." Even America's ostensibly greatest asset—its rich soil—failed its inhabitants because of its being *too* fertile, actually leading colonists, according to Robertson, to "decrease its fertility in order to cultivate it." Indeed, it was America's "furious growth of vegetation" that explained why "the different species of animals peculiar to it are much fewer in proportion than those of the other hemisphere." The continent's lack of massive lions, elephants, rhinoceroses, and tigers proved that point beyond a reasonable doubt. Under such circumstances, the animals and, by extension, the people of America were doomed to degenerate to the point of total expiration.

Amateur naturalist that he was, Jefferson couldn't hold his tongue. This widespread opinion, after all, flew in the face of a young nation that had just fought and won a revolution due in large part to its unique ability to feed itself with the productions of its own land and the beasts that fed on its grain and grasses. His *Notes on the State of Virginia* dedicates considerable space, accompanied by several precise graphs, to proving Buffon wrong. In a tone both measured and irate, Jefferson explained that the growth of vegetables in America was a phenomenon beyond criticism. "Vegetables are mediately or immediately the food of every animal," he snipped, "and in proportion to the quantity of food, we see animals not only multiplied in their numbers, but improved in their bulk, as far as the laws of their nature will permit." In response to the criticism that America suffered too many extremes of cold and dampness to support ample animal growth, Jefferson made an "appeal to experience" and noted that in America "a race of animals . . . has been increased in its dimensions by cold and moisture, in direct opposition to the hypothesis, which supposes that these two circumstances diminish animal bulk, and that it is their contraries heat and dryness which enlarge it." Consider the bear, he implored. John Bartram had and, Jefferson recalled, described an average American bear weighing "400 lb." Compare that with the average weight of an English bear (367 pounds), not to mention the wimpy French bear (141 pounds), and thus the claim that "the animals common to the two [continents] are considerably less in America" proved patently false.

This kind of comparison came naturally to Jefferson's encyclopedic mind. "It may be affirmed with truth," he continued, "that in those countries, and with those individuals of America, where necessity or curiosity has produced equal attention as in Europe to the nourishment of animals, the horses, cattle sheep and hogs of the one continent are as large as those of the other." As for hogs: "I have seen a hog weigh 1050 lb. after the blood, bowels, and hair had been taken from him." Should anyone think this hog's size the result of its English stock, he explained how the "hog was probably not within fifty generations of the European stock." The impressive growth rates of American livestock, moreover, demanded little effort. Goats, which had been "much neglected in America," nevertheless "are very prolific here, bearing twice or three times a year and from one to five kids a birth." The same held true for sheep, which averaged around one hundred pounds compared with sixty-two pounds in Europe. After assembling detailed charts comparing the relative weights of red deer, beavers, flying squirrels, hedgehogs, wolves, and even water rats, Jefferson—who found the American varieties of each to be larger—concluded his defense of America's natural cornucopia on the grounds that "with equal food and care, the climate of America will preserve the races of domestic animals as large as the European stock from which they are derived." On this point, he was being modest. Jefferson surely knew that America far outpaced Europe in its natural endowment.

Jefferson also compiled a welter of evidence concerning animals indigenous to America in order to debunk even further the claim that America was destined to degenerate as a result of an inadequate food supply and an intemperate climate. In the brilliant, if somewhat mocking, step of relying on Buffon's own research for his "ground work," Jefferson reminded the "best informed of any Naturalist who has ever written" that, as the

Frenchman's own research proves, "there are 18 quadrupeds peculiar to Europe; more than four times as many, to wit 74, peculiar to America." Acknowledging that large swaths of America "remain in their aboriginal state, unexplored and undisturbed by us," Jefferson noted that "no instance can be produced of [America] having permitted any one race of her animals to become extinct; of her having formed any link in her great work so weak as to be broken." The only viable threat to America's aboriginal creatures, he continued, was "the general destruction of the wild game by the Indians, which commenced in the first instant of their connection with us, for the purpose of purchasing matchcoats, hatchets, and fire locks, with their skins." Of the continent's copious supply of native game, he charged, "it does not appear that Messrs. De Buffon and DiAubenton [Louis-Jean-Marie Daubenton] have measured, weighed, or seen" its species, choosing instead to rely on the accounts of "some travellers."

"But who," Jefferson wondered, in a passage that was as aggressive as he got, "were these travellers? Have they not been men of a very different description from those who have laid open to us the other three-quarters of the world? Was natural history the object of their travels? Did they measure or weigh the animals they speak of? Have they not been so ignorant as to often mistake the species?" Jefferson, of course, intended these questions to be rhetorical, and he appropriately finished his refutation by quoting "one sentence of [Buffon's] book [that] must do him immortal honour: 'I love as much a person who corrects me in an error as another who teaches me a truth, because in effect an error corrected is a truth.'" Jefferson wouldn't have been out of line in expecting a bit of that love.

There's a startling, obsessive, and almost panicked tone to Jefferson's refutation of the eminent French naturalist. And with good reason. In the 1780s, America was in a precarious position. Free but lacking a federal constitution, ill-served by its Articles of Confederation, unable to tax its populace, and mired in a depression induced by the trade disruption with England, the fledgling nation needed the court of international opinion (especially France's) on its side as it moved toward solid nationhood. Not only that, it needed more immigrants and more investors. America might have been a nation in theory, but in reality it was still very much a mere confederation of states, scattered and tenuously connected through fraying tethers. And although Jefferson had made his mark as a first-rate statesman, and Thomas Paine as a first-rate polemicist, the country as yet couldn't look up to the brilliant constellation of James Madison, Alexander Hamilton, and John Jay. National leaders holding the reins of federal government with confidence were a mere glimmer in the nation's eye. For that reason alone, a man with the national vision of Jefferson bristled with anxiety when a man like Buffon, for whatever reason, slung his mud.

But one aspect of the topic that indirectly came under fire—food—was just as important as the nature of the French naturalist's attack. More than historians acknowledge, food and political independence were intimately linked phenomena. Jefferson's hackles were so sharply raised in part because he knew as well as anyone in America that the defining events of the Revolutionary era were related in one way or another to the broad issue of American food. Food, as we'll see, was at the heart of Britain's most egregious taxation schemes, played a pivotal role in providing common colonists an education in revolutionary politics, and established an essential precondition for America's widespread acceptance of a "radical Whig" ideology. Even more important, the pervasive role that food played in furthering the cause of American independence eventually led Americans to make their first collective attempt to describe what their food was all about, what it meant to them, what they thought about it. The answers that they came up with—frugality, pragmatism, honesty, and a lack of pretension—not only articulated the defining qualities of American food for the next two centuries, but also proved critical to America's embrace of a pastoral ideal that reaffirmed the centrality of food production to American life while distinguishing the new nation once and for all from the continent that it would never again call home.

Economic Development and Food

"No Taxation Without Representation." These immortal words became the rallying cry of the Revolutionary generation. They effectively summarized the underlying constitutional principle that had been repeatedly violated by the mother country during the 1760s to raise revenue after the costly Seven Years' War. The mantra forcefully reminds us that disgruntled Americans decided to fight a revolution based in part on the undeniable reality that their English liberties had been systematically abridged. At the same time, on a more basic level, this phrase also obscures the equally important fact that the items being taxed were very often directly related to food and the colonists' ability to produce it and trade it among themselves without interference. Everyday patriots responded as much to abstract principles as they did to the concrete reality of their material lives. The connection among food, local trade, and Revolutionary activity mattered so deeply because if there was one single customary right that white colonists throughout the colonies universally and passionately valued it was their ability to produce and consume their own food and gain access to those foods that they didn't produce. In a very real sense, food was freedom.

Insofar as the colonists aimed to be loyal colonial subjects, this self-reliance on food was exactly how it should have been. England hardly wanted to waste time and money supplying its most peripheral colonies with foodstuffs. Instead, it wanted the colonies to become collectively self-sufficient regarding food and dependent on England for nothing but man-ufactured goods. Throughout their short history, the colonists dutifully met these goals, producing a plethora of food, trading it among themselves, and protesting minimally when Britain discouraged their manufacturing ventures. But, in another sense, what the colonies had gone through to achieve such self-sufficiency made them rightfully—shall we say, defen-sively—proud of the way in which they had fulfilled their prescribed co-lonial duty. With varying degrees of regional success, free colonies took a hoe to hard dirt and built farms to feed their families and, later, produced a surplus to sell in regional markets. These regional markets slowly expand-ed; internal trade pulled the colonial regions together through the charms of sugar, molasses, and rum; the major colonial regions wove themselves into the transatlantic economy through cod, wheat, tobacco, and rice. As these developments transpired, the average free colonists by the middle of the eighteenth century enjoyed something that their ancestors could only have dreamed of enjoying: the ability to eat and drink more or less what they wanted when they wanted it. In exercising this freedom, the colonists had pioneered a way of eating that combined indigenous culinary develop-ments with the more traditional ways of the homeland. Striking this bal-ance was an ongoing process and a hard-earned accomplishment, one that nobody ever took for granted. Jefferson wasn't the only one to guard that privilege with missionary zeal.

Unfettered access to food was, in many respects, a reflection of what historians have only recently come to appreciate as the colonies' especially impressive rate of economic growth. Settlements had grown into societies as the colonial economy expanded by an average annual rate of 3.5 per-cent between 1650 and 1770, "a truly remarkable performance by any stan-dard," according to John J. McCusker and Russell R. Menard, authorities on the topic. It was especially remarkable considering the *English* standard, which was a mere .5 percent over the same time period. Per capita in-come among the free American population over the same period rose from

$572 to $1,043, or .49 percent a year. While the slave-produced exports of sugar, rice, and tobacco accounted for much of this growth and income, the vast majority of the food cultivated in colonial America—perhaps as much as 85 percent—was consumed *in colonial America*. What this statistic means is that the colonists had succeeded in building a dynamic internal economy—one quite distinct from England's—under the long cast of the empire's shadow. It was an economy, moreover, that offered immigrants to America a better chance of living lives of relative material comfort. "That the colonists were able to produce significant food surpluses despite the consumption trends of a rapidly growing population," one historian writes, "is one reason for believing, as most economic historians do, that substantial extensive growth was taking place." The fact that the colonial American population expanded from 1.5 million to 2.5 million between 1754 and 1775, and that their standard of living was on the rise, spoke powerfully to that increased opportunity while making the economic growth rate of the colonies seem even that much more impressive.

The years 1668 to 1772 saw the colonies perform especially well with respect to food production and internal trade. Regions had specialized to the extent that they were now producing and exporting some goods to other regions while choosing not to produce but to import other goods. Webs of dependence evolved, for example, as Connecticut, New York, New Jersey, Pennsylvania, Delaware, Maryland, Virginia, and North Carolina supplied bread and flour to Maine, New Hampshire, Massachusetts, Rhode Island, South Carolina, and Georgia. Connecticut, Pennsylvania, Maryland, and Virginia supplied Massachusetts, Rhode Island, New Jersey, and Delaware with wheat. Corn came to all the New England colonies from every middle and southern colony. Rhode Island, Connecticut, Pennsylvania, Delaware, Virginia, the Carolinas, and Georgia produced ample beef and pork for themselves and for Maine, New Hampshire, Massachusetts, New Jersey, and Maryland. These connections, as already suggested, diminished the regional quirks and trends that characterized cuisines throughout the colonies. They also led to a better balanced diet for a hardworking population whose average annual dietary needs included "2 hundredweight of flour, 11 bushels of corn, and 150 pounds of beef and pork (75 lbs. of each)." In fact, based on the most liberal consumption requirements, Americans—even after overseas exportation—were producing more food than they could consume.

They were also distributing it with relative ease and efficiency, as the case of New England—and Massachusetts especially—demonstrates. For all its success in the seventeenth and early eighteenth centuries in producing all its own food, Massachusetts slightly sacrificed its hard-earned self-sufficiency to dedicate more of its resources to the fish trade. The demands of the cod market drove an economic wedge between coastal fishing towns and inland farming communities. Inland areas continued the relatively self-sufficient habits of their ancestors, while the coastal towns specialized in exporting cod (mainly to the West Indies) and shipbuilding. Ideally, the inland communities would have fed the coastal towns, but they never seemed able to do so reliably. Hence coastal Massachusetts turned to its southern neighbors for the corn, wheat, bread, flour, beef, and pork that enabled it to become a more stable and stronger economy even as it slightly compromised its ability to supply all its own food. Not only did the colony's economy become more powerfully integrated into the transatlantic economy, but, as it did, Massachusetts coastal towns were able to become choosier in the food they ate. Evidence indicates, for example, that they paid more to import pork from North Carolina rather than from New York or Pennsylvania because of its preferred taste. Here indeed was a healthy, interdependent economy that had grown into a fat target to tap for some extra cash. Which is exactly what England did after the Seven Years' War.

Food and Political Tension

It couldn't, however, have chosen a more incendiary way to go about raising cash than through the regulation of food-related commodities. For if any aspect of the colonial economy stood out as a model of efficiency, food production was it—made from scratch, built up from nothing, profitable, reliable. Nevertheless, England forged fatefully ahead as Parliament, pushed by George III and his ministers, started a reign of legislative terror on food products in 1764 with the Sugar Act. This law built on the Molasses Act of 1733, which aimed to provide the British sugar growers with a monopoly in the mainland market by imposing a tax on the sugar, molasses, and rum imported from the French and Dutch West Indies. Smuggling by American merchants soon made the act a dead letter. But now, thirty-one years later, England decided to pass the Sugar Act as a way to enforce the preexisting duty on sugar and reimpose its monopoly on the sugar trade in the colonies. The Quartering Act followed in 1765. It was one of the most onerous of the legislative bombs dropped on the colonies, if for no other reason than it subjected colonial farm produce to random seizures. The Quartering Act specifically required colonial authorities to do nothing less than provide food, drink, quarters, and fuel to the redcoats stationed in their villages (ostensibly for the colonists' protection after the Seven Years' War, but more precisely to exert authority over the colonies). After the Stamp Act in 1765, the Townshend Duties followed in 1767, placing a duty on many manufactured imports, as well as tea. By imposing arbitrary customs collections, these duties also placed severe restrictions on the colonists' ability to trade both at home and overseas. More insultingly, revenue from the customs duties went toward funding more customs officials, spies, searches and seizures, and writs of assistants, as well as the establishment of the Board of Customs Commissioners in Boston—all

British troops docking at Long Wharf

This detail of an engraving by Paul Revere shows the landing of British troops in Boston in 1768, when relations between the American colonies and England were becoming tense.

of which curtailed the brisk and systematic food trade (among, of course, other trades) that the colonists had been enjoying for decades. These measures inspired a widespread, simmering political response.

Acts passed in the 1770s brought the situation closer to a boil. In 1770, things looked as though they might be improving. The Crown repealed the Townshend Duties on every product except—again, just to assert authority—tea. A couple of years of relative peace prevailed because the colonists, who had developed an intense love of tea during the British invasion, were able to buy it from the ever resourceful Dutch smugglers. But the Tea Act, passed in 1773, changed that. Designed to off-load 17 million pounds of tea that the ailing East India Company had accumulated in its bulging warehouses, the Tea Act altered excise regulations to allow the company to pay the Townshend Duty on tea while still undercutting its competitors. In essence, Lord North and his cabinet imposed a direct tax on the colonists by forcing them—if they continued to drink tea—to buy it from the East India Company. The response was the famed Boston Tea Party. In December 1773, a group of patriots dressed as Mohawk Indians dumped 342 chests of East India tea into Boston Harbor. Their action provoked Lord North to impose the Boston Port Act, which isolated Boston from the rest of the trading world until Massachusetts paid for the destroyed tea. At this point, most colonists agreed, the drift toward war became a possibility. Fifteen months later, about twenty miles from where the tea had been dumped, that possibility became reality.

As historians have long pointed out, war erupted because each and every one of the offensive measures—the Sugar Act, Quartering Act, Stamp Act, Townshend Duties, Tea Act, and Coercive Acts—violated the basic liberties that white colonists had come to assume as subjects of the British Empire they so adored. The British measures were clear cases of imposing taxes without direct representation, a blatant transgression of the natural rights preserved in Britain's unwritten constitution and an unfair tightening of the screws after decades of "benign neglect." They were thus a perfectly sound, even noble, justification for rebellion. The colonies' official responses to Britain's twelve-year attempt to reduce their inhabitants to total subservience naturally brim with angry references to "the ruin of our liberties," "the violation of the principles of the *British* Constitution," "the unrelenting Monarch of Britain," "the defence of our common rights," and "the maintenance of our freedom." Colonial patriots further enriched and intensified the official language of rebellion when they evoked "a corrupt and prostituted ministry . . . pointing their destructive machines against the sacred liberties of the Americans, [attempting] by every artifice to en-slave the American colonies and plunder them of their . . . *liberty*." Others thickened the rhetorical brew when they deemed the acts as nothing less than "the ministerial plan for enslaving us," the policies that would "en-slave us forever," rendering them "slaves to the minister of state."

Slavery, of course, meant the absence of freedom. But what, from the perspective of the average colonist, did the absence of freedom exactly entail? What did this concept mean in the mind of the average colonist? These egregious English measures were, as the heated responses suggest, heinous and intolerable examples of the arbitrary abuse of power. It helps to recall, however, that at the same time that these policies tread on the white colonists' most basic constitutional rights, they more immediately stomped on their customary access to material goods—including sugar, tea, and a wide variety of farm produce. These commodities meant more than sweetness, bitterness, and stick-to-the-ribs heartiness. They had come to play critical roles in the society that America had built since 1740. Then, as now, consumer goods didn't have inherent meanings. Instead, as con-sumers, colonists generated cultural meanings when they produced goods, bought goods, and used goods. The consumption of sugar, tea, and other foodstuffs had become, by the 1760s, vivid manifestations of several cul-tural values—values inherent in the concept of liberty and its opposite, slavery. They represented concrete aspects of life, such as the colonists' upward mobility, their increasing sense of choice, and even their identity as British Americans. The widespread acquisition of not only food and drink themselves, but also their visible accoutrements—teakettles, tea chests, china, tankards, bowls, plates, and myriad other manufactured goods—was also a genuinely powerful experience and expression for colo-nial Americans. These goods provided the language and grammar through which they "sparked the production of meanings." They were, as a result, absolutely integral to the sense of liberty that colonists believed was sacred enough to fight the American Revolution to protect.

In the most obvious sense, then, the offensive acts imposed by the Brit-ish had the effect of pushing colonial Americans to build an apparatus for fighting a revolution. They not only dumped tea in the harbor but dutifully formed organizations such as the Sons of Liberty and Committees of Cor-respondence, arranged mass boycotts of British goods through nonimpor-tation agreements, undertook propaganda campaigns, took to the streets to protest violators of the boycotts, tarred and feathered loyalists with glee, and ransacked the occasional British official's residence. Resistance was constant but constantly well ordered, never spilling into the mob violence that even the most radical revolutionaries cautiously feared. Eventually, of course, the patriots came to the conclusion, in the words of Joseph Galloway, that "every spot of the Old World was overrun with oppression," and thus "the logic of rebellion" compelled them to muster their forces and fight. Although historians will disagree over the causes of the Revolutionary War for as long as they write, the basic outlines of the story are as well known as they were once articulated.

A less obvious aspect of the Revolutionary response, however, involves the more subtle justifications that the colonists relied on to inspire their rebellious march toward revolution. Recalling the basic premise that the colonists took great pride in—and were quite defensive of—their ability to produce and acquire the food and drink that they needed and wanted, and recalling that providing and protecting access to that food and drink consumed the vast majority of the average colonist's time, it comes as no surprise that colonists understood British infractions as—perhaps above all else—an infringement on the material conditions of life that they had worked so hard to achieve. Eleven inhabitants from Boston suggested as much when they tellingly declared, "We Look upon [the Tea Act] as unconstitutional *and a Burden*." With so little attention devoted to food in the standard histories of the Revolution, the precise nature of this "burden" warrants a more careful look.

Finding reactions to such a burden isn't especially difficult. It was, for example, front and center in the minds of several Concord, Massachusetts, leaders when, in formulating their official response to the Tea Act, they evoked the toil of their forefathers, who had left to them "a fair inheritance, purchased by a waste of blood and treasure." The British violation of that inheritance, they explained, accounted for their "unhappy situation." The Braintree Resolves, coming out of Braintree, Massachusetts, as a protest against the Stamp Act, similarly described the offensive measures not only in abstract constitutional terms but in concrete materialistic ones too. It was a "burthensome tax," they explained, because it promised to "drain the country of its cash, strip multitudes of their property, and reduce them to absolute beggary." Weighing the consequences of Britain's "violent infringement of our rights," nobody relied more on the time-honored language of rights and liberties than Samuel Adams, but he, too, understood that the matter was fundamentally about defending the material self-interests of the colonists. The heinous measures were "unconstitutional *and* entirely destructive" because "our houses are . . . exposed to be ransacked, our boxes, chests, and trunks broke open, ravaged and plundered by wretches." He cut to the heart of the matter when he identified the acts passed by Parliament as restrictions on "the produce of our own farms," noting how farmers, in order to avoid new ferry customs, had to travel "near a hundred miles by land" when "passing over a river or water of one quarter a mile . . . would have prevented all that trouble." The journey must have reminded many a lukewarm rebel about the true merits of the patriot cause.

Fighting over Food

The conceptualization of political infringements in self-interested terms— and in terms that responded to a population's access to its own food sup- ply—saw its most radical expression in the more than thirty local food riots that raged from 1775 to 1779 alongside the official grievances that fueled the Revolutionary War. Whereas the onerous policies of the British Empire had interrupted the free trade in goods that colonists had come to take for granted, the Revolutionary War erected obstacles even more severe. The resulting scarcity of food both produced locally and imported from the West Indies motivated many merchants to succumb to the unsavory temptation of price gouging. American consumers, however, reacted with an even greater defensiveness than they had honed in the decade before the war when they responded to British infringements on their food sup- ply. As Barbara Clark Smith explains, "Rioters and their allies claimed that confronting merchants in their shops was a patriotic action, much like facing redcoats on the battlefield."

The connection between resistance and food supply was manifestly evi- dent in several incidents. In July 1776, a group from Longmeadow, Mas- sachusetts, blackened their faces, wrapped themselves in blankets, and told Jonathan Hale, a local merchant, about their "uneasiness with those that trade in rum, molasses, and sugar." They explained that "it is a matter of great grief that you Should give us cause to call upon you in this uncom- mon way. . . . We find you guilty of very wrong behaviour in selling at ex- travagant prices." The crowd looked forward to "a Thorough reformation for time to come" and abruptly handed over a list of acceptable prices. Hale dutifully complied within the hour.

Not every merchant succumbed to popular pressure so easily. After the crowd finished with Hale, they paid a visit to Samuel Colton, another Long- meadow merchant whose prices were deemed "detrimental to the Liberties of America." Colton, however, refused to lower the cost of his goods, leading the crowd to confiscate his imports and hide them in a barn. Apparently chastised, Colton "made prayer in publick" and lowered his prices. A week later, however, he raised them. This time the crowd, who claimed to have dispensed with "moderate measures," broke into his warehouse, confiscated his goods, and destroyed his store. They "ransacked it from top to bottom," Colton complained, causing him "great Fear and Terr'r." The goods were hauled over to the town clerk, who sold them at the requested rates. The profits were later offered to Colton, who refused them, out of spite. Undeterred, the crowd simply dropped the cash at his house and left.

In New York a month later, the issue was tea; the rioters, a group of women; and the recalcitrant merchant, Jacobus Lefferts. Lefferts refused to sell his tea for 6 shillings a pound, as the Continental Congress suggested. Pushing his tea at 9 shillings a pound, a rate that the local newspaper said was designed "to make a prey of the friends of the United States by asking the most exorbitant price," he ignored a "committee of ladies" who were protesting in front of his store. He did so, however, at his own peril, for they eventually seized the tea, appointed a clerk, parceled up the tea, and sold it to local inhabitants for 6 shillings a pound. Lefferts, however, wasn't fortunate enough to have the proceeds go his way. Instead, the committee sent them to the county's revolutionary committee.

These cases show how access to food and food-related goods were integral to the most basic material and cultural values that Americans had shaped over the course of their impressive history of economic growth. When seventeen men from Maryland seized salt from an unscrupulous merchant; when a "quarrel for bread" erupted at a bakery in Massachusetts; when crowds in New York seized food wagons; when sixty women confiscated sugar in Beverly, Massachusetts; when Bostonians forced a French baker to make bread for the town; when Virginians announced that "measures by the MOB" would keep prices down; or when Philadelphians armed with clubs bullied shopkeepers to behave fairly, rebellious Americans—especially women—reiterated the popular assumption that political ideology and action reflected Americans' rightful access to the literal fruits of their labor. "The very honey of our bees," J. Hector St. John de Crèvecoeur observed about the American's farm, "comes from this privileged spot." Food, in short, was worth fighting over.

Although the most obvious outbursts over food and access to it erupted in the North, the South's political ideology was also informed by food-related issues. In 1787, between the end of the Revolution and the ratification of the United States Constitution, Americans living in Orangeburg District,

South Carolina, inveighed, "No individual has a Right whereby he may deprive the People in its vicinage of those just Rights & Privileges which as Citizens of a free & independent State they are entitled to." In South Carolina, one angry citizen claimed, "the common rights" of the people were being trampled on, leaving the people "totally cut off from availing themselves of the common rights of mankind." One might guess—given the heft of this rhetoric—that the issues at stake were nothing less than the weighty constitutional matters that James Madison, Alexander Hamilton, and George Mason were hammering out at the Constitutional Convention in Philadelphia during that summer. These words were, however, about fish.

Shad, in particular. This "necessary of life" was integral to the Carolina diet and routinely consumed by whites, slaves, and Native Americans. "Cheaper than bacon," packed with flavor, and emblematic of the region's semisubsistence economy, American shad ascended Carolina's rivers every spring to their upstream spawning grounds. When they migrated, a fish trap, line, or dip-net yielded an ample meal, as adult shad range from three to fourteen pounds in weight. Inspiring the outbursts, however, was the increasing construction of dams for sawmills, devices that abruptly negated "the Benefits and Emoluments arising from a Fishery" and thereby denied residents "a *necessary of life*, which their fellow citizens living upon other water courses 200 miles above the said Mills enjoy in the Greatest plenty." As Americans had done before and during the Revolution, Carolinians responded to the infringement of their customary access to food by fighting back in defense of a right that couldn't have been more central to their political and material freedom. Scores of petitions speak to the colonists' perception that the dams represented a threat as dire as an overt military affront to their independence. Food supply and independence were understood during these episodes as two sides of a coin.

Petitioners around the Edisto River in South Carolina explained that "the keeping open of the River Savannah, is of the greatest importance to the citizens of the back country, as well in consequence of navigation, as the advantages resulting to the citizens generally, by having an annual supply of fishing therefrom." In North Carolina, arguments by relatively poor inhabitants who had every intention to eat rather than sell their fish led to "an Act to . . . prevent the stoppage of the passage of Fish up the Several Rivers therein mentioned." A South Carolina law reacted to petitions from four counties by imposing a penalty of £8 on anyone found guilty of obstructing Big Lynches Creek "by fish dams, mill dams, hedges, and other obstructions" during spawning season. In 1771, as Revolutionary rhetoric heated up, residents of Guilford County, North Carolina, concerned themselves with "many poor familys who depended on said fishing for a great part of their living, it being well known that no River of its size in this province afforded greater quantity of exelant shad and other fish." Again, whether in a Boston tavern or a backcountry courthouse in South Carolina, the protection of food was consistent with the protection of freedom.

The Revolutionary and post-Revolutionary equation of food and political freedom makes even more sense when placed in the perspective of the Seven Years' War. This war, which actually lasted for nine years (1754–1763), was a world war that pitted France, Austria, Saxony, Sweden, and Russia against Great Britain, Prussia, and Hanover. The North American theater saw Britain and France battling for control of the vast colonial territory ranging from the Atlantic to the Mississippi. The fight began over ownership of the Upper Ohio River Valley and intensified into a conflict over whose empire the sun would never set on. England, whose resources were stretched thin as a result of the war's wide geographical range, relied heavily on the colonies not only for military support but also for food. And that's where the internal spat began.

Much as their behavior during and just after the Revolution suggested, colonists were none too eager to part ways with their hard-earned access to material goods, even for their own soldiers and the British regiments fighting the French. A typical weekly food allowance for a British soldier during the war was seven pounds of beef, four pounds of pork, seven pounds of bread, three pints of peas or beans, half a pound of rice, and one-quarter of a pound of butter. Parliament attempted to contract with colonial governments to supply these rations, but more often than not, what the soldiers ended up with was scurvy, an ailment resulting from a lack of fresh meat and vegetables. On any given day, about one-quarter of the soldiers of any regiment might be unable to fight because of disease. Fresh garden produce, milled flour, and recently slaughtered meat were rarely and reluctantly forthcoming from American farmers more intent on supplying their own needs and trading surpluses in preestablished channels of exchange than making contributions to a cause to which many were indifferent. Soldiers were routinely left to eat hard salted pork and stale bread without vegetables. In 1759, the men of the Forty-second Regiment sat down to a dinner of "ship's beef" and bacon "which had been in store since the former war and Biscuits full of maggots, so that after endeavoring to clear them of vermin we used to wet them and toast them." The Deputy Commissary of Stores surveyed the troops' food inventory before an expedition in 1758 and lamented that they had to set out with "mouldy Bisket" and "rusty salt pork" that was "extream bad," with much of it being "rotten and stunk." Writing from Fort Stanwix on the Mohawk River, a commander complained of "having had no Vegetables, or scarcely any fresh provisions during the winter, or likely to have any for some time." From Lake George in 1758, Joseph Nicols remarked, "Our army is very much uneasy with their manner of living. Our allowance at present is only flour and pork . . . we labor under a great disadvantage."

The lack of food supplies began to take its toll on military performance. To prepare General Edward Braddock for his campaign against the French at Niagara and Crown Point, the army arranged to acquire food and other supplies from New York, Rhode Island, Connecticut, Virginia, and Maryland. The governor of Rhode Island tried to rouse his fellow colonies with a pep talk, explaining, "Hence every Government, concerned in the present Enterprise will, I doubt not, proportion supplies according to the value they put upon their religion, their liberty, their estates, and the freedom of themselves and their posterity." He should have had his doubts. New York failed to supply beef. Albany merchants refused to accept notes from other colonies for peas and bread. Maryland and Virginia delivered rations so damaged that Braddock erupted, "They had promised everything and performed nothing." Virginia would release provisions only if they were earmarked for Virginians. Pennsylvania farmers complained about having to travel long distances to exchange farm produce for cash. Many put off their deliveries, leaving Braddock's regiment reduced to half rations. When the governor of Massachusetts tried to impress horses and wagons from local farmers to make an emergency delivery of food, the farmers violently refused. As Braddock moved toward his target, his men were on the brink of mutiny. While he pulled through, it was in spite of the food supply. The British, described by one observer as "a poor pitiful handful of half starved, scorbutic skeletons," defeated the French at the Battle of Sainte-Foy only because the French were "melted down to Three Thousand fighting men, most by Inveterate Scurvy."

The widespread intransigence on the part of American farmers over providing food for British (and, to a lesser extent, American) soldiers was often met with the kind of aggression that only motivated them to protect their food supply even more stubbornly. Soldiers descended on local farms and confiscated apples from orchards, pigs from pens, and cattle from meadows. British redcoats combed over so many New York farms that Albany, which repeatedly noted robberies of "sheep Fowl & Roots of all kinds carried off in the Night," had to post guards around targeted settlements and fine soldiers who wandered off camp after dark. Much to his chagrin, General Thomas Gage spent considerable time responding to complaints that his troops had plundered local gardens and orchards, often at gunpoint. His task wasn't made any easier by the fact that many generals sanctioned these pilferings, as Jeffrey Amherst did when his troops picked clean a Massachusetts apple orchard. Obadiah Harris wrote home saying that he and his comrades were "very mad" at local farmers.

Needless to say, the farmers were none too happy in return. In fact, they responded to raids by practicing the time-honored inflammatory techniques of price gouging and bilking what they could from the government trough. When demand rose among British troops, so did the price of foodstuffs offered to them for sale. Peas that had been selling for 5 shillings a pound suddenly increased to 6 shillings. The cost of bread rose 2 shillings per hundredweight when the soldiers came knocking. As one historian explains, "The lure of war profiteering was greater than patriotism." Profiteering was especially rampant after the Crown officially took over the financing of supplies in 1756. Trusting the laxity in government oversight, colonial leaders filed receipts and were often compensated for goods that had nothing to do with war supplies. Rhode Island, for example, managed to get the Crown to foot the bill for a merchant's shipment of coffee, tea, chocolate, sugar, ham, knives, forks, spoons, and plates—none of which made it to the British soldiers but instead went to Rhode Island cupboards.

British officials didn't find this behavior particularly endearing. To a very large extent, the intolerable policies that flew in the face of American freedom from 1763 to 1775 were, in addition to crass revenue-generating policies, expressions of anger that the British felt toward the colonists for their antics during the Seven Years' War. Thus one of the greatest paradoxes of the Seven Years' War was that, in eliminating the French threat to North American land and security, the British found themselves at odds with their own colonies. On the one hand, the colonies experienced a surge in British loyalty. They were proud to be part of an empire that single-handedly controlled North America; they were eager to continue benefiting from England's traditional willingness to allow Americans to pursue their economic self-interest through transatlantic and intercoastal trade. On the other hand, though, the English were irate at the arrogance and presumptuousness of their colonial subjects. In addition to providing less than impressive supplies, the colonists took advantage of the war to violate trade laws that stretched back to 1651, traded with the enemy when it was convenient to do so, and generally convinced England that it was high time to bring the colonies down a notch or two. Hence the Sugar Act, the Quartering Act, the Stamp Act, the Tea Act, and so on. Historians have described this sudden flip-flop on the part of Parliament and the Crown as a violation of traditional relationships. Again, as the events before and after the Revolution confirm, it was also a violation that transgressed the very item that shaped the social and economic life of the colonists: food.

Food and the Emergence of a Political Ideology

The events of the Seven Years' War, the difficult years of 1763 to 1775, the Revolutionary era, and even the post-Revolutionary period pushed Americans to practice an almost paranoid vigilance over their food supply and material rights. Whether it was through withholding food from British soldiers, rioting over high prices, opposing acts that limited access to sugar, tea, and farm produce from other regions, or fighting to preserve their customary rights to shad during spawning season, landowning Americans reiterated the critical point that they were a people who defined themselves first and foremost according to the land they owned and exploited. Defending land and all that it produced was their political education. It was both that simple and that complex. The land and the produce and profit that they squeezed from it fed their families, allowed them to participate in the market, provided liberal access to foreign and extraregional goods, and generally enabled yeoman farmers to improve their standard of living to an extent that their European ancestors could never have dreamed possible. Remarkably, colonists did this while their numbers burgeoned. If there was any aspect of American life worth gloating over and guarding, here it was.

It was no coincidence, then, that these earnest patriot-farmers—men who only a few years earlier couldn't have been more enamored of their countrymen—now condemned the English in terms that were the direct opposite of how they were coming to idealize themselves. Customs officials, complained James Wilson, were nothing more than "a set of *idle drones.*" Rather than work the soil for an honest living, they existed as "lazy, proud, worthless *pensioners* and *placemen.*" Whereas the upright colonists served the interests of their families and communities, these "baneful harpies" did nothing more than "*serve the ambitious purposes of great men* at home." Colonial landowners were born to till the soil and reap the rewards, but the English in their midst were "born with long claws like eagles," designed to scrape an ignoble profit from others who legitimately earned it with the sweat of their brow. They were "bashaws in their divans," no better than "wretches" of "infamous character."

The colonial character, by contrast, evolved in the more rugged context of the land and thus ultimately responded to the pristine principle of *virtue*. There was, it was thought, nothing more virtuous than making a living from tilling the soil and sowing and reaping its rewards. It was from the act of farming that colonial Americans—in the face of threats to that basic right by the mother country—elevated virtue to something of a secular creed, a national slogan, or a myth to idealize. Making a living from the land, as the colonists came to portray it, allowed the yeoman to practice true virtue, which, during the Revolutionary era, meant the willingness of the individual to subordinate his private interests for the good of the whole.

In embracing that value, if only theoretically, the colonists set themselves up to do something few could have predicted: adopt a coherent political ideology encompassing both virtue and self-interest. In other words, as they struggled against imperial interruptions to their freedom, especially the freedom to grow and catch and shoot and trade what they wanted, the colonists formulated a political theory that blended material acquisition and community interests into a single ideological package. Indeed, as threats to the colonies' food source—and, by extension, their most basic liberties—intensified, and as their characterization of the British officials as lazy parasites took hold, colonists from Georgia to Maine reformulated a version of republican political thought that had its roots in seventeenth-century England: the radical Whig ideology. From that ideology—an ideology that evolved in partial response to materialistic concerns—colonists would go on to recast American culture according to a new set of values, a set of values that would come to define American cuisine well into the nineteenth century and, perhaps, beyond.

When the colonists' adherence to the land and the food it produced inspired their attraction to a hibernating ideology, Americans broke new political ground. Prior to the Revolutionary era, Americans had traced their political ideologies to a variety of sources. Their ideas found precedents in classical antiquity, the Enlightenment, English common law, and even Puritanism. None of these ideologies, however, proved to be universally appealing. As Bernard Bailyn explains, "Important as all of these clusters of ideas were, they did not in themselves form a coherent intellectual pattern." One reason for their failure to "exhaust the elements that went into the making of the Revolutionary frame of mind" has to do with the fact that none of them single-handedly spoke to the ongoing threat to America's material way of life that the British were perpetuating. None of them, in other words, spoke to the collective heart and soul of America's landowning yeoman, the land he worked, and the food he produced on it.

Not so the radical Whig ideology. The gist of this set of political ideas was that corruption—once unleashed—would undermine virtue and send a republic down the dreadful path of tyranny. In England, supporters of the Whig ideology—whose ideas had evolved by the end of the eighteenth century through the vocal opinions of the "country" party—were part of a radical fringe. They effectively kept themselves on the political radar screen, however, by becoming the "Cassandras of the age." They spent the entire eighteenth century growing into a kind of governmental watchdog group over England, and they sniffed out corruption of the sort that led to the laziness that colonists saw in the British officers on their own soil. "Cato," for example, complained in a typical passage how "public corruptions and abuses have grown upon us; fees in most, if not all offices, are immensely increased; places and employments, which ought not to be sold at all, are sold for treble value; the necessities of the public have made greater impositions unavoidable, and yet the public has run very much in debt; and as those debts have been increasing, and the people growing poor, salaries have been augmented, and pensions multiplied." To the non-Whig British, such a tone seemed terribly overwrought. But the message to the average colonist couldn't have been any clearer: without proper vigilance, all of America's hard work would collapse under a systematic corruption that not only was beginning to infect England but was doing so in a way that violated the most basic American principle that the fruit of a white man's labor was his own. None of that fruit belonged to the "idle drones" who didn't work for it. Without vigilance, in short, virtue would wither alongside the colonists' hard-earned freedom to enjoy the material way of life earned by the sweat of their own (and their slaves') brows. Here, then, was a political system with some mass appeal.

But, fatefully, only in America. The problem with the radical Whig ideology in England, and the reason it continued to remain a fringe ideology with only the most radical adherents, had to do with the scarcity of land in England. As a result, a critical mass of landholding citizens able to lend the ideology the necessary weight of public opinion was lacking. A minority of Englishmen owned land and the titles that land conferred. A vast majority, by contrast, worked that land as servants, thus losing out on any claim to the land's productive wealth. In America, however, where up to

75 percent of the white adult male population owned land and, by extension, a political voice, the situation couldn't have been more different or more beneficial to the popularization of the Whigs' message that if people weren't paranoid, they were crazy.

John Norris, an Englishman, recognized this very basic demographic difference between the colonies and England as early as 1712. Speaking of Carolina, he praised it as a place where "any industrious man . . . with his own labor" could do precisely what he could not do in England: "maintain a Wife and Ten children, sufficient with Corn, Pease, Rice, Flesh, Fish, and Fowl." Norris reflected the opinions of William Penn, who similarly promoted America as a place for those who, in England, could "hardly live" to acquire "all Necessaries and Conveniences." Writing about New York, Daniel Denton claimed that men who once could "scarcely procure a living" could depend on "inheritances of land and possessions, stock themselves with all sorts of Cattel, enjoy the benefit of them while they live, and leave them to the benefit of their children when they die." Perhaps the most amazing thing about these promotional characterizations of America is that they generally turned out to be true. America was a place where white people *could* cultivate their own garden and live a better life than they would have back home for the simple reason that they owned good land and had the fortitude to make it yield a profit. Hundreds of thousands of white men had come to realize that, in taking the plunge, they and their forebears had indeed fulfilled something of an American dream. They also came to realize that, in doing so, they were part of a majority, a majority that did not exist in England, and a majority with a potentially powerful political voice.

Thus the idea that Americans had to be vigilant in protecting the virtue on which they built their colonies captivated white Americans. The driving tenets of the radical Whig ideology had been bouncing around the colonies since the 1720s, when two tenacious polemicists named John Trenchard and Thomas Gordon began to publish the popular *Cato's Letters* in American newspapers. By the 1760s, though, especially after the Seven Years' War, this oppositional ideology, according to Bernard Bailyn, "was devoured by the colonists." So thoroughly was it consumed, in fact, that when the "logic of rebellion" became apparent, the thirteen colonies—all of which developed along distinct political, social, and cultural lines—united around the radical Whig ideology's guiding principles. These were principles, moreover, that took hold only because *so many Americans owned the land that they worked.* We mustn't forget that they worked it to provide food—food for themselves, their families, their neighbors, other colonies, and, in many cases, a transatlantic market. That necessary and ongoing and identity-shaping activity, and the threat that England eventually posed to it, motivated the American colonies to unite around the essential political imperative that virtue had to be guarded with vigilance. And, as the successful Revolution proved, it not only had to be watched but, when the loss of pristine virtue seemed imminent, had to be defended by any means necessary. When Americans did just that, they were defending their farms *and* their rights, which they came to see as one and the same. In this elliptical but nonetheless powerful way, food remained at the core of America's Revolution.

The Dismantling of an Old Cultural Model

And it wouldn't lose its influence when the war ended. As the dust of the battle settled, J. Hector St. John de Crèvecoeur, an American farmer, asked a famously simple question: "What then is this American, this new man?" Six years earlier, in early 1776, Thomas Paine had published a tract that sold hundreds of thousands of copies and succinctly articulated the colonists' justification for rebellion. *Common Sense* obliterated the misconception that had taught too many colonists to "think better of the European world than it deserves." In so doing, Paine suggested exactly what the new American was not—that is, British.

Foreshadowing Noah Webster's prescient remark that "it is perhaps always true that an old civilized nation cannot, with propriety, be the model for an infant nation, either in manners, fashions, in literature, or in government," Paine was trying not only to spark a fight but also to tell Americans what they would have to do when they won it. The power of the British invasion still captivated many Americans, even as British policies became increasingly invasive. But the enigmatic, consumer-driven mystique of the empire began to wither when Americans started to ask Crèvecoeur's question, ponder Paine's and Webster's answers, and fulfill the inevitable nationalist prerequisite of creating—or at least mythologizing—a new culture. American culture—and, with it, American food—was up for grabs, and everyone knew what it could not look like.

What, then, would it be? And, for our own purposes, what, then, would this new American eat? Perhaps anticlimactically, the new American would eat nothing terribly new, at least not until immigrants from southeastern Europe began to pour through Ellis Island after the Civil

War. This conclusion shouldn't be all that surprising, especially in light of the fact that Americans fought a revolution primarily to continue pursuing the same material interests that bound them to the colonial past. But none of this is to say that American food didn't change. American cuisine would become "American" not through a change in ingredients but, rather, through the way that Americans *thought* about those ingredients. In essence, America's culinary declaration of independence was an *intellectual* declaration of independence more than a revolution in specific culinary style. Americans would continue to do pretty much as they had done before the Revolution; that is, they would continue to artfully blend the local demands of the immediate regional environment with traditions imported from abroad. But they would look at the basic act of acquiring and preparing food in an entirely new light, imbue food with new values, and often taste food with a self-consciously less pretentious mentality, one that arguably lingers to this day.

There were, of course, those who wanted to announce America's presence with authority. Young, brash Americans in particular hoped to burst on the international scene with an explosion of flag-waving, muscle-flexing innovation in every area of life. Benjamin Franklin cautioned against such an impulse, however, noting that "all things have their season, and with young countries as with young men, you must curb their fancy to strengthen their judgment." America's act of cultural creation—for better or worse—eventually followed Franklin's avuncular advice, turning to the past rather than the future to find its inspirational font. Joseph Ellis has described Americans' earliest foray into cultural redefinition as an attempt "to ransack their past for cultural accomplishments in a patriotic effort to provide the new nation with a respectable legacy in the arts and sciences." Before examining the past for the bedrock values that would steadfastly guide American culture into the future, however, Americans couldn't resist the impulse to rhetorically dismantle the culture that, only a couple of decades earlier, they had been building grand pedestals to admire. The process of defining a new American culture—and thus the context for a new American culinary philosophy—began by trashing and thrashing the once revered English culture. It was, in a way, a necessary and therapeutic step in deciding who this new American would be.

The ultimate problem with Europe, as these denunciations repeatedly argued, was that it was old and tired. Its corruption was the result of its age as much as the vile character of its policies. As Webster articulated it, a nation, like a person, "was born, grew up, became old, then died."

In England, "the establishment of an economy based on commerce and manufacturing was a clear sign of the nation's middle age." European culture was, as Webster continued, "highly pernicious" because—in a perversion of Buffon's natural history—it was making "hasty strides to the last stages of corruption" and extinction. James Murray, writing on the eve of the Revolution, agreed. "The decline of virtue and the downfall of nature," he explained, "have *always* kept pace with one another." The reason, once again, had to do with age. He continued, "The basis of government *generally* grows weak as its splendor encreases. Nations are like trees; they make the greatest show when they flourish in *trade, luxury,* and *riches*; but they are then weakest and have *least vital strength.*" John Witherspoon offered his two cents on the matter when he wrote how "a general profligacy and corruption of manners make a people ripe for destruction."

Many commentators, in a slightly more sophisticated version of the growing-old argument, appealed to what was called a conjectural theory of civilization. Adam Smith, who was a staunch supporter of this central idea of the Scottish Enlightenment, explained how "savage and barbarous nations," which America once was, evolved according to "the natural progress of law and government and the arts." But a nation could travel only so far on this arc of civilization before crossing the threshold of decline. When commerce and manufacturing endeavors replaced the more virtuous and vigorous work of agriculture, then a nation was set on the path of ruin. This, in fact, is precisely what went wrong, as Franklin put it, in "many parts of England." It had allowed itself to evolve into a nation with "Landlords, great Noblemen and Gentlemen, extremely opulent, living in the Affluence and Magnificence" and coexisting with a majority who were "tattered, dirty, and abject in Spirit" and living "in the most sordid wretchedness in dirty hovels of Mud and Straw . . . cloathed only in rags." One hundred and twenty years later, the silver-tongued William Jennings Bryan told the Democratic Convention, "Burn down your cities and leave your farms, and your cities will spring up again as if by magic, but destroy our farms and the grass will grow in the streets of every city in the country." Bryan was, of course, speaking about America, but his remark—and the pastoral sentiment supporting it—evoked England and the "wretchedness" into which it had fallen by the late eighteenth century. Americans had no intention of following this example. They would, if they had to, stop themselves cold and put an end to history if grass started to grow in the city. At least this is what they told themselves.

In addition to being old, tired, and caught in the downward spiral of historical decline, Europe, as the young American nation dismantled it, had grown dangerously fond of luxury—luxury on a level that only a handful of Americans, despite decades of equipping themselves with European goods, understood. James Murray, in 1769, wrote by way of historical analogy, "As long as the Romans were virtuous, they enjoyed freedom and liberty; but when *luxury, bribery* and *corruption* were introduced, virtue declined . . . and the foundations of their government were soon overthrown." In case anyone missed the point, he added, "Great Britain now bears a near semblance to what ancient Rome was before the final declension of that mighty empire." An Anglican minister from Philadelphia named William Smith echoed a popular sentiment toward England when he wrote how "Plenty begat Ease, and Ease begat Luxury, and Luxury introduced a fatal corruption of every good and virtuous principle." On the basis of these characterizations of the Old World, Americans finally came to conclude that, indeed, "an old civilization cannot be . . . the model for an infant nation."

The Search for a New Cultural Model

The sun might have been setting on the British Empire, but (with apologies to Ronald Reagan) it was morning in America. Dissecting the perceived evils of the empire was a much easier task than rebuilding a distinctly American culture. Nevertheless, the young nation took solace and found inspiration in Thomas Paine's assertion that it had the "power to begin the world over again" and that it could commence doing so because it had "a blank sheet to write upon." Young Americans might not be too sure what kind of treatise to fill it with, but they did know that they had just marshaled "virtue enough to defend themselves against the most powerful nation in the world." They could take further comfort in the fact that they had the "wisdom to contrive a perfect and free form of government." Americans might have felt as though they had lost their cultural moorings, but the moorings were still there—they just had to be rerooted. A careful examination of the arguments they used to tarnish English culture reveals the hidden facets of a new American culture that came to define who Americans were and, among other things, how they thought about the food they ate. When Americans dismissed the English as lazy, effeminate, luxury-obsessed, old, tired, and hypercommercialized, they simultaneously conceptualized themselves as hardworking, manly, frugal, young, energetic, and—above all else—agricultural. Exploring these themes brings us yet one step closer to understanding how the white Americans who lived in the new republic came to see themselves and their food as rustic, plain, practical, unpretentious, and—perhaps above all else—intimately tied to the land they worked.

It's easy for historians to scoff at the earliest promotional accounts of North America as desperate exaggerations made by settlement organizers hoping to lure families to the New World. Granted, not every free man who worked hard succeeded in achieving the dreams that America's promoters proffered. But what's especially striking by the middle of the eighteenth century is, as Jack P. Greene puts it, "that thousands upon thousands of people did succeed in realizing some significant part of the promise held out by promotional writers." The way they did so, moreover, was lost on nobody, least of all Benjamin Franklin, who exuberantly praised his colonial colleagues for making "a Garden of the Wilderness." Even the British official Thomas Whatley agreed in 1766 that America had "flourished . . . beyond all example in Europe" and that there existed "no Precedence of Example" for the colonies' "improvement." A contributor to the magazine *American Husbandry* pithily encapsulated the agricultural history of colonial America by writing how the colonists "maintained themselves the first year, like the Indians, with their guns and nets, and afterwards by the same means with the assistance of their lands," and, finally, after "a few years," they enjoyed farms that allowed them "to maintain themselves and families comfortably." Another writer noted how after only a few years, typical colonial settlers had "made such Farms as afforded them Necessaries of Life in Plenty" as well as "clean houses, neat, though homely, Furniture, commodious Barns, and a sufficient stock of Horses, Cows, Hogs, Poultry, &c." J. Hector St. John de Crèvecoeur may have best articulated the overall accomplishment of American farming with his assessment that, because of it, "the idle may be employed, the useless become useful, and the poor become rich." "Rich," however, didn't connote the luxuriant and landed wealth that the English elite enjoyed but, rather, nothing more decadent than "cleared lands, cattle, good houses, good clothes, and an increase of people to enjoy them." In short, simple and practical comforts—the timeless benefits of a young America's advertised version of the good life.

Whereas Americans once worked to overcome the hayseed associations of the frontier, they now embraced and bragged about their relative lack of cultivation—a quality reflected in their strong roots in farming. The virtue of the frontier became starkly and especially clear to proponents of the conjectural theory of history. After all, being associated with the frontier meant being far away from the commercialized threshold that England had so recently crossed. Noah Webster grasped the advantages of the wild frontier and its promise of continued agricultural pursuits when he characterized the evolution away from agriculture as "a period that every benevolent man will deprecate and endeavor to retard." America, he continued, should "endeavor to preserve our manners by being our own standards." Otherwise, it would be "hurried down the stream of corruption with other nations." On another occasion, Webster remarked, "In the United States everything that has been done hitherto in the construction of cities is an imitation of the old European . . . mode, and of course is *wrong*."

When the frontier closed, as America learned in the 1890s from Frederick Jackson Turner, commercial and industrial forces garnered power over the nation's economy and life. But until that distant and unwelcome event happened, Americans could and very much did promote the idea that—again, as Franklin phrased it—"*Commerce* . . . is generally *Cheating*," while farming "is the only *honest Way* . . . to acquire wealth." Whereas the frontier, according to Crèvecoeur, represented the nation's "feeble beginnings and barbarous rudiments" as well as "the most hideous parts of our society," it was also the raw material necessary for an "industrious people" to transform into "fine, fertile, well regulated" farms and communities, places where a "general decency of manners" could prevail. A "hundred years ago," Crèvecoeur continued, the colonies were "wild, wooly, and uncultivated." Now they comprised an "immense country" marked by "substantial villages, extensive fields . . . decent houses, good roads, orchards, meadows, and bridges." Thus the colonists went from "barbarous" beginnings to a polished culture through the singular and ongoing act of farming. What, Crèvecoeur wanted to know, was more American than that?

Perhaps no American—and certainly no American with such a high profile—better or more enthusiastically sang the praises of the frontier and the agricultural life it fostered than Thomas Jefferson. His oft-quoted pronouncements on the pastoral ideal have become America's secular scriptures. "Those who labour in the earth," he wrote, "are the chosen people of God, if ever he had a chosen people, whose breasts he has made his peculiar deposit for substantial and genuine virtue." England had succumbed to degenerate behavior as its citizens turned toward manufacturing, but America was—for the time being at least—safe from such a fate because, as Jefferson noted, "corruption of morals in the mass of cultivators is a phenomenon of which no age nor nation has furnished an example." America was truly exceptional in that it could realistically wish "never . . . to see our citizens occupied at a workbench, or twirling a distaff." Indeed, "carpenters, masons, smiths are wanting in husbandry; but, for the general operations of manufacture, let our work-shops remain in Europe." Those work-shops, as England's recent history had shown, bred corruption and made life unnecessarily complicated. And such a turn of events for England was to be expected, Jefferson continued, because dependence on other nations for something as basic as food "suffocates the germ of virtue, and prepares fit tools for the designs of ambition."

Jefferson and men like him considered the specific benefits of husbandry to be endlessly fertile, powerful enough to rally white Americans from all regions and backgrounds behind a radical political ideology, and seductive enough to hold them together—however tenuously—after the American Revolution. The thread running through each and every beneficial aspect of farming, however, was a basic notion that was also intricately tied to the frontier: simplicity. Jefferson implored the young American man to avoid Europe, for once there, "he acquires a fondness for European luxury and dissipation and a contempt for the simplicity of his own country." The simplicity of the farming life enchanted Crèvecoeur, too. After thanking God "that my lot is to be an American farmer," he explained the virtues of his chosen profession. There was the generational connection to his father, who "left me a good farm, and his experience; he left me free from debts, and no kind of difficulties to struggle with." When it came to food, he was set: "Every year I kill from 1500 to 2000 weight of pork, 1200 of beef, half a dozen of good wethers in harvest; of fowls my wife has always a great stock: what can I wish more?" Merely walking onto his farm sent him into rapture: "The instant I enter on my own land, the bright idea of property, of exclusive right, of independence exalt my mind. Precious soil, I say to myself . . . what should we American farmers be without the distinct possession of that soil? It feeds, it clothes us, from it we draw even a great exuberancy, our best meat, our richest drink." Richard Price, a Unitarian minister from Virginia, spoke equally approvingly of "an independent and hardy YEOMANRY, all nearly on a level . . . clothed in homespun—of simple manners—strangers to luxury—drawing plenty from the ground—and that plenty, gathered easily by the hand of industry." He declared, "O distinguished people! . . . may the happiness you enjoy spread over the face of the whole earth."

This single value—simplicity—inspired commentators to look on the American Revolution and the values it confirmed and promoted as nothing less than universally applicable. "In great measure," Paine wrote, "the cause of America is the cause of all mankind." Five years later, in 1781, Abbé Raynal described the American cause as the "cause of the whole human race." The American Revolution, men such as Paine and Raynal thought, was a critical step to lending immediate truth to John Locke's famous claim: "In the beginning . . . all the world was America." With respect to democracy, these optimists may have been onto something. But with respect to food, Americans would enjoin the values of the Revolution with their varied culinary pasts in order to create an "American" food that would find its counterpart nowhere else in the world. American food—growing out of this new American culture of rugged, frontier-inspired simplicity—would indeed become something unique, at least in conception.

Defining an "American" Food

Nobody wrote an early treatise on American food. While America's political Declaration of Independence had its Thomas Jefferson, the nation's culinary declaration was delivered more quietly, with less fanfare, without a single voice, in offhand remarks and casual comments dropped at random. While we cannot point to an outstanding document or defining event to confirm that the American Revolution ushered in an "American" style of food, we can hunt down those scraps of evidence that point to a revolution in the way that Americans came to think about their food and, to an extent, cook it.

The agrarian values that colonists fought the Revolution to protect and preserve became the very values that Americans would use to frame their new foodways. As we've seen, American food was first forged in the wildness of an unfamiliar frontier, leading to a variety of regional cooking and eating styles that remained largely isolated from one another for decades. By the eighteenth century, these regional styles began—through a number of influences—to converge, and, as they did, Americans began to balance regional traditions rooted in the frontier with the increasingly powerful influence of more formalized English foodways. After the Revolution, however, they would shed their association with England and tilt back in the direction of their frontier roots.

This time, however, the embrace of the frontier way of cooking would be much more controlled, driven less by necessity than by the conscious and purposeful embrace of an ideology that favored values such as youth, simplicity, hard work, honesty, virtue, and a lack of pretension. Americans could finally dictate their terms to the frontier rather than the frontier dictating its terms to them. A telling summary of the foodways that emerged with political independence came from the early American dramatist William Dunlap, who promoted his play *The Father* as "a frugal plain repast," contrasting it to the "high seasoned food" dished out by European dramatists. Without in any way intending to, Dunlap points us in the direction of a conclusion to the story of America's culinary origins.

The development of a unique American cuisine began with an angry rejection of English culture and, afterward, a polite refusal of French food. It wouldn't have been unexpected if, after the Revolutionary War, Americans had taken a step toward adopting the relatively fancified cooking tradition of the French. There were plenty of reasons to do so. The Americans and French had been loyal allies during the Revolution; Jefferson had become an inveterate Francophile during the war; and the French were gearing up to fight a revolution of their own based on principles adopted from the Americans. A cultural connection of sorts therefore existed. But evidence that, despite the appeal of French food to America's first four presidents, French gastronomy would go virtually nowhere in early America came in 1793 when the Bostonians served their French residents a meal to honor the French Revolution of 1789. The feast began not with the expected pot-au-feu but with the Bostonians hanging a "Peace Offering to Liberty and Equality" sign around the neck of an ox, leading it to Liberty Square, slaughtering it, and eating it with sixteen hundred loaves of bread, corn mush, turkey, and two hogsheads of punch—an American affair if there ever was one.

The more Americans learned about French food, in fact, the more they came to misunderstand and dislike it, and the more they came to realize what theirs was all about. Patrick Henry, the vocal Revolutionary agitator from Virginia, criticized Jefferson's taste in French food as an effete affectation that made him "abjure his native victuals." Many years later, in 1840, when William Henry Harrison slung mud at his opponent for the presidency, Martin Van Buren, he did so by depicting him as eating pâté de foie gras and *soup à la reine*. Harrison, by contrast, portrayed himself—despite his privileged upbringing—as living in a log cabin and knocking back hard cider on the front porch after a hard day in the fields. The American rejection of French food was, two historians of American food write, "by no means the only demonstration in American history of the curious fact that in America it is politically disadvantageous to be known as a gourmet, as though there were something unmanly in being discriminating about, or even attentive to, what one eats."

But Americans *did* care about what they ate, and much evidence indicates that they wanted their food to be—like their newly articulated political principles—honest, virtuous, simple, free from artifice, and, in a way,

AMERICAN COOKERY,

OR THE ART OF DRESSING

VIANDS, FISH, POULTRY and VEGETABLES,

AND THE BEST MODES OF MAKING

PASTES, PUFFS, PIES, TARTS, PUDDINGS, CUSTARDS AND PRESERVES,

AND ALL KINDS OF

C A K E S,

FROM THE IMPERIAL PLUMB TO PLAIN CAKE.

ADAPTED TO THIS COUNTRY,

AND ALL GRADES OF LIFE.

By Amelia Simmons,

AN AMERICAN ORPHAN.

PUBLISHED ACCORDING TO ACT OF CONGRESS.

HARTFORD

PRINTED BY HUDSON & GOODWIN.

FOR THE AUTHOR.

1796

robust. Newspapers printed recipes for such patriotic dishes as Independence Cake, Federal Cake, Election Cake, and Ratification Cake. And when one tired of patriotic cake, there was always Congressional Bean Soup. For those who followed recipes, however, cookbooks were the norm. The cookbooks that were published in early America, as we've seen, were largely relics of the English system of cookery that, more often than not, are more interesting for their plagiarizing from English sources dating back to the 1730s than for their recording of rough-hewn American innovations. Their use is thus somewhat limited because the recipes were very likely more popular from the 1740s to the 1760s than they were after the American Revolution and into the early nineteenth century.

That said, some sense of America's culinary "return to homespun" comes through in several selected recipes. Choices from American cookbooks after 1796 (when the first one was published) use ingredients native to America in their recipes. In *American Cookery*, Amelia Simmons basically lifted recipes from English cookbooks, but still formally introduced Americans to such foods as "cranberry sauce," "pumpkin pie," Indian pudding, and cornmeal bread. Hannah Glasse's *The Art of Cookery Made Plain and Easy*, published in Virginia in 1805, also reads like an old English cookbook, with the exception of seven wonderful pages, all included under the subtitle "several new receipts adapted to the American mode of cooking." These recipes stand out in stark contrast to those in the rest of the book for their simplicity and homespun nature. A brief sampling conveys a taste of this "American mode" while providing a telling point of comparison to European traditions:

TO MAKE MUSH
Boil a pot of water . . . and then stir in the meal till it becomes quite thick, stirring it all the time to keep out the lumps, season with salt, and eat it with milk or molasses.

TO MAKE A BAKED INDIAN PUDDING
One quart of boiled milk to five spoonfuls of Indian meal, one gill of molasses, and salt to your taste.

Title page of American Cookery, 1796
This cookbook, by Amelia Simmons, is the first to have been published in the United States. Although the recipes were "adapted to this country," they have a heavy British flavor.

TO MAKE PUMPKIN PIE

Take the Pumpkin and peel the rind off, then stew it till it is quite soft, and put thereto one pint of pumpkin, one pint of milk, one glass of Malaga wine, one glass of rose-water, if you like it, seven eggs, half a pound of fresh butter, one small nutmeg, and sugar and salt to your taste.

TO MAKE BLOOD PUDDINGS

Take your Indian meal . . . and scald it with boiled milk or water, then stir in your blood, straining it first, mince the hog's lard and put it in the pudding, then season it with treacle . . . put it in a bag and let it boil six or seven hours.

TO MAKE CRANBERRY TARTS

To one pound of flour three quarters of a pound of butter, then stew your cranberry's to a jelly. Putting good brown sugar in to sweeten them, strain the cranberry's and then put them in your patty pans for baking in a moderate oven for half an hour.

TO MAKE A RAISED PORK PIE

Take six ounces of butter to one pound of flour, boil the butter in a sufficient quantity of water to mix with the flour hot, let the paste be stiff and form it in a round shape with your hands, then put in your pork, season to your taste with pepper and salt, and then bake it for about an hour.

TO MAKE PEACH SWEETMEATS

To one pound of Peaches put half a pound of good brown sugar, with a half a pint of water to dissolve it, first clarifying it with an egg; then boil the peaches and sugar together, skimming the egg off . . . till it is of the thickness of a jelly . . . pears are done the same way.

TO MAKE A POT PIE

Make a crust and put it around the sides of your pot, then cut your meat in small pieces, of whatever kind the pot-pie is to be made of, and season it with pepper and salt, then put it in the pot and fill it with water, close it with paste on the top; it will take three hours doing.

The recipes are unusual in that they were meant to be followed. Unlike the more traditional English recipes published in Glasse's book, they generally use native ingredients, or at least ingredients commonly available throughout America; they are described in a much more basic manner than the English recipes; and they are much easier to carry out than the other recipes she provides. It would have been quite obvious to seasoned readers at the time that most of her recipes were truncated and scaled-down versions of the English standard. The comparison of American pot pie with English mince pie reveals an obvious attempt to reduce the number of steps involved and ingredients used. Glasse's recipe for a traditional English mince pie, for example, is about four times as long and involved. She calls for raisins; currants "picked, washed, rubbed, and dried at the fire"; "half a hundred pippins pared, cored, and chopped small"; sugar "pounded fine"; cloves, nutmegs, and mace "all beat fine"; and layerings with Seville oranges, lemons, and the addition of a parboiled tongue for added flavor. A similar situation can be seen with pork pie. The simplicity of the American recipe for raised pork pie becomes especially obvious when compared with the English recipe for Cheshire pork pie. In this version, Glasse advised the cook to use a *loin* of pork rather than any old cut, to "lay a layer of pork, then a larger layer, of pippins, pared, cored and a little sugar . . . then another layer of pork," and, finally, to add half a pint of white wine.

The pared-down methods characterizing the "American mode" are further evident in a comparison of Glasse's American and English recipes for eel pie. The "American mode" instructed the cook to "skin your eels and parboil them, then season them with pepper and salt, and put them into your paste, with a half dozen raw oysters, one quarter of a pound of butter, and water." Instead of skinning and parboiling eels to clean them, by contrast, the English version demanded that the chef "clean, gut, and wash your eels very well, then cut them into pieces half as long as your finger." It also suggested the addition of "a little beaten mace to your palate." A comparison of how to make sausages reveals an English recipe that insists that the "skin and gristles" be removed and the guts "very nicely cleaned." Neither directive, however, appears in the American version.

The implication couldn't have been any more obvious: the "American mode" had no time and felt no need to remove the guts from eels, cut them into uniform pieces, and pamper the palette with a dusting of hand-milled mace. It saw no need to scrape gristles and skin from a pig before rendering it into sausage. Perhaps it would have back in 1750, when Americans were in awe of the British. But not in 1805, when Americans were in awe of themselves. The nature of a "frugal plain repast," the aspects of the changing attitudes toward American food, discouraged such conveniences.

Glasse's "American mode" section further reflected the reversion to frontier-oriented American food by concentrating heavily on making do with what was available. Her recipes directed brewers to make "spruce beer from shed spruce" and to make treats such as maple sugar, maple beer, and maple molasses. The last of these could "be done in three ways: 1. from thick syrup, obtained by boiling after it is strained for granulation, 2. from the drainings of the sugar after it is granulated, 3. from the runnings of the tree [which will not granulate] reduced by evaporation to the consistence of molasses." Whichever way they made it, settlers could add it to cornmeal for a hearty meal. Another section unique to the "American mode" speaks to the practical nature of American cooking. Titled "Method of destroying the putrid Smell which meat acquires during the weather," it advised the cook to "put [the meat] in a saucepan full of water, scum it when it boils, and then throw into the sauce a burning pit coal, very compact and destitute of smoke, leave it there for two minutes, and it will have contracted all the smell of the meat." The meat could then be used in a soup.

A focus on cooking as a practical rather than a luxuriant or indulgent endeavor—as a task that should be "plain" and "frugal"—was evident beyond Glasse's cookbook. A proliferation of post-Revolutionary beer production especially reflected the more rugged frontier mode of drinking that prevailed in the days before cider and rum replaced beer as daily beverages of choice. Speaking within the context of the Revolutionary embrace of national self-subsistence and simplicity, brewing advocates exhorted women in particular to bring brewing back into the kitchen. "Almost any household can brew," explained Samuel Deane, "without putting himself out too much." Deane echoed the reemerging theme of homespun frugality when he wrote, "Instead of a large copper, which is necessary in a brew house, a large kettle or two may answer the purposes," while "hogshead or barrel tubs, and other vessels, may serve for mashing tubs, backs, coolers, and tins." A new magazine called the *Practical Farmer* instructed readers on how to build a home brewery. If Americans weren't going to make their own beer, they should at least—the commentators exhorted—buy American. Sam Adams drove the message home when he took out an advertisement that remarked, "It is to be hoped, that the Gentlemen of the Town will endeavour to bring our own OCTOBER BEER into fashion again . . . so that we may no longer be beholden to *Foreigners* for a *Credible Liquor*." Brewers crawled out of the woodwork to heed the call. A Virginia brewer introduced his new business with the comment that "the severe treatment we have lately received from our Mother Country would, I should think, be sufficient to recommend my undertaking. . . . [Y]et, the goodness of every commodity is the best recommendation."

Whether American beer was good or not was open to interpretation and taste, but whether it was "American" or not there was little doubt. Local breweries that emerged after the Revolution sparked a revival in beer production and consumption for the very reason that, as we've seen, beer was quintessentially a frontier beverage. And, as it turns out, the frontier was de rigueur. Beer was important because it symbolized the recently revived cultural values of health, simplicity, virtue, frugality, and other aspects of America's agrarian tradition. Beer production was a critical example of how early Americans self-consciously embraced the frontier and its values after the Revolution. It was a clear case of drink reinforcing the nation's new cultural values while shaping its unique foodways.

The results of the beer transition were rapid and lasted well into the 1820s. Philadelphians lowered their rum consumption and increased their beer production and consumption to the extent that, in 1789, the British consul in Philadelphia wrote home to report that not only was homemade porter undercutting British sales in Philadelphia, but, even though "the quality is vastly inferior even to Bath or Bristol porter," it was about to be "sold at ½ less than the London porter . . . to the Southern states." The rapid popularization of domestic beer after the Revolution brought more Americans back to the soil and into their own kitchens and breweries to produce their own alcohol rather than depending on the now foreign West Indies for the ingredients to make rum. While George Hay, James Madison's nephew, complained that "TWELVE MILLION OF DOLLARS have been expended by the United States in purchasing West India spirituous liquors," J. B. Bordley could soon retort with the hopeful remark that, because of local production, "beer is taking place of diluted spirits." Because of beer, "there is more sobriety now observed in the towns than formerly, when West India rum abounded at a third of its present price." Samuel Sewall and other advocates of sobriety would have been proud.

Beer also reinforced the noble business of farming rather than the supposedly deleterious practice of manufacturing and commerce. When Peter Shiras and Robert Smith opened their Virginia brewery, they did so with an advertisement that read, "Farmers who choose to raise Barley, may depend upon having the price of Five Shillings per bushel." It was no coincidence that Jefferson, the nation's leading advocate of frontier agriculture, became a master brewer after the war. He actively forged a powerful cultural association between beer and new American values when he brewed beer from Indian corn, lobbied for a brewing company in Washington, and declared brewing an art done best without formal recipes. When James Barbour inquired about a recipe for ale that he had enjoyed at Monticello, Jefferson replied, "I have no receipt for brewing & I doubt if the operations of malting and brewing could be successfully performed from a receipt." Instead, all one really needed to brew beer were the very same virtues that had served farmers well throughout history and were becoming the buzzwords for a new national character: "great intelligence and diligence."

Although it hardly connoted the kind of health that beer did, whiskey also became a popular beverage after the Revolution, and thus another example of the American effort to consciously promote frontier food and drink as part of a larger process of cultural reconstruction. Despite its frigid place down at –60 degrees on Benjamin Rush's "Moral and Physical Thermometer," whiskey reflected the young nation's renewed attraction to frontier virtues. It joined cider as the nation's preferred strong drink for several reasons. It could be made from Indian corn and rye, by makeshift stills in the backyard, and with the backcountry's ample supply of fuel and fresh water. It had the added benefit of offering hardscrabble farmers in the backcountry an excellent outlet for grain crops that too often otherwise rotted during overland transportation to coastal markets. Whiskey's most powerful ideological benefit, however, was that it joined beer in driving rum out of business. In other words, it was a frontier beverage that replaced a commercial one, and it was thus a drink fully commensurate with the broader cultural transition toward homespun simplicity. "I reckon every horse exported and returned in rum," wrote one anti-rum zealot, "as . . . property lost to the general interest." Chances are that he would have been none too pleased with whiskey as the solution to this problem, but at least a whiskey distiller could—as a young Kentucky man did—mark his bottles with "Born with the Republic" and sell a brand called "Old 1776."

Through their intended and quite concerted turn back toward culinary simplicity after the Revolution, Americans ate familiar foods—both native and imported—under the assumption that eating was more of a practical activity rather than a ceremonial one. Just as American culture had become more pragmatic, so had its food. The British foreign minister who visited Secretary of State James Madison in 1777 spoke volumes about the emerging distinction of American food when he described Dolley's meal as "more like a harvest home supper than the entertainment of the Secretary of State." Dolley, who overheard the remark, retorted how "the profusion of my table arises from the happy circumstances and abundance and prosperity in our country." Enough said.

At the time of this frosty exchange, the American frontier that nurtured a rustic attitude about food was raw but limited—hemmed in as it was by the English and the Spanish. In 1803, however, that limitation lifted when America paid a mere $15 million for the Louisiana Territory. With that acquisition, the frontier became—for all intents and purposes—endless. When Americans began to pour west after 1803, they brought with them their assumptions that food should be simple, rustic, close to home, the fruit of their own labor, honest, and unpretentious. The frontier, suddenly an ever-expanding phenomenon, could—and in many ways did—renew for generations the culinary values that America forged after the Revolution. As the North slowly urbanized and the South evolved into an entrenched plantation society, the West ensured that the foodways of the older regions of America remained true to their Revolutionary roots—rough, simple, honest fare.

The specific ways in which the new frontier around and west of the Mississippi reinvigorated a mode of cuisine not really seen in America since its earliest settlements are evident in the experiences of Meriwether Lewis and William Clark. Their expedition to explore the plant and animal life in America's newest acquisition began in a fifty-five-foot keelboat loaded with 2,000 pounds of cornmeal, 3,400 pounds of flour, 600 pounds of lard, 750 pounds of salt, 3,705 pounds of pork, and 560 pounds of hardtack. When these staples of a rustic American diet ran out, the explorers were reduced to behaving as their forebears had 150 years earlier. They grubbed for roots, relied on Native Americans for food, and consumed wild sweet potatoes, bitterroot, "Indian biscuit root," prairie apples, and *wapatoo*, which, Lewis said, "are never out of season . . . [and are] nearly equal in flavor to the Irish potatoe and afford a very good substitute for bread." As settlers to America did when they first arrived on the east coast, the expedition's venturers marveled at the fish and wild game. Sounding like John Winthrop gushing over the New England cod that were practically jumping into his boat back in 1631, Clark wrote in his journal, "The number of dead salmon floating on the Shores & floating in the river is incredible to say and at this season [the Indians] have only to collect the fish Split them open and dry them on their scaffolds."

Lewis and Clark were soon doing the same. And while it was surely the last thought on their minds as they did so, they were reenacting a culinary habit of adaptation that America had once relied on to turn the earliest east coast settlements into societies. In this way, these men were an apt microcosm of the thousands of American families who would soon pack it up in the East; load a supply of familiar foods onto a wagon drawn by oxen; head west; eat through their provisions; grub, hunt, and barter; build their farms; achieve self-sufficiency; market some surplus goods; acquire a few fineries; improve their standard of living as their own settlement became a society; and, in the process, unwittingly help establish the origins of a national cuisine.

Their kids, once the land was in full use, would then start the process over again. Whether this western expansion breathed new life into American democracy is a thesis that Frederick Jackson Turner proposed and historians have long questioned, but there's no doubt that the movement west acted to preserve the cultural and culinary values that America imbibed as the lessons of the American Revolution matured and sunk in.

Were Americans aware that they were defining a unique culinary tradition? Given that few Americans today conceive of their country as having such a distinction, it seems unlikely. Interestingly, though, their European contemporaries sensed that a change was under way. In 1804, a Frenchman visiting the United States was struck by the almost proud lack of refinement that characterized supposedly sophisticated meals. "They swallow," he wrote of his American hosts, "almost without chewing." The rusticity of the food thoroughly underwhelmed him. The Americans he visited ate "hot bread, half-baked, toast soaked in butter, cheese of the fattest kind, slices of salt or hung beef, ham, etc., all of which is nearly insoluble." Fearing that he might sound inhospitable, the Frenchman could not help but express his opinions that "at dinner they have boiled pastes under the name puddings, and their sauces, even for roast beef, are melted butter; their turnips and potatoes swim in hog's lard, butter, or fat; under the name of pie or pumpkin, their pastry is nothing but a greasy paste, never sufficiently baked." What makes these comments even more revealing about the comparatively rustic nature of American food is the fact that this Frenchman was Constantin-François Chasseboeuf, comte de Volney. With a name like that, we can be assured that he was not having his snobbish taste buds assaulted in backcountry taverns but, rather, dining in style. Albeit American style.

While the tendency might be to dismiss Volney's opinion as exceptionally snooty, he doesn't seem to have been alone. Twenty-five years later, Harriet Martineau, an English visitor to America and the future author of *Society in America* (1837), graciously referred to the United States as a place where "sweet temper diffused like sunshine over the land." Evidently not, however, over its food. At best, she thought it quaint that Americans relied so heavily on simple fare for their sustenance, and she repeatedly noted the popularity of cornbread, buckwheat cakes, eggs and bacon, broiled chicken, hominy, beefsteak, and pickled fish. "A man who has corn," she wrote, "may have everything." In Virginia, however, she found all the food she ate—mainly bread, butter, and coffee—to be stale. The attitudes of her hosts weren't much fresher, in her opinion. "They probably have no idea that there is better food than they set before us," she sneered. A search for mutton turned up nothing, and when Martineau moved from the east coast to Tennessee, her culinary quest actually turned up a gustatory horror. "The dish from which I ate," she recalled after one especially enigmatic meal, "was, according to some, mutton; to others, pork." "My own idea," she concluded, "was that it was dog."

Even in Tennessee, however, they weren't eating dogs. What Martineau failed to understand was that she was visiting a nation that had consciously rejected European culinary habits. Americans had become perfectly at ease with unrefined, unpretentious food. Other foreigners visiting America recognized this defining trait more clearly. Frederick Marryat, an Englishman, observed the offerings at a Broadway market and remarked tellingly on the offerings. "Broadway being three miles long," he explained, "and the booths lining each side of it, in every booth there was a roast pig, large or small, as the center of attraction. Six miles of roast pig!" François-Alexandre-Frédéric, duc de La Rochefoucauld-Liancourt, noted the Americans' seeming contentment with the most simple, monotonous diet. "Indian corn," he wrote, "was the national crop, and Indian corn was eaten three times a day" in addition to salt pork. "In the country," he continued, "fresh meat could not regularly be got, except in the shape of poultry or game; but the hog cost nothing to keep, and very little to kill and preserve. Thus the ordinary American was brought up on salt pork and Indian corn, or rye." Not that Americans disliked salted meat. Thomas Ashe, writing in *Travels in America in 1806*, noted that many Americans preferred it, recalling one timber worker who explained that "your fresh meat, that's too fancy . . . and hain't got strength unto it." Charles Dickens confirmed the pragmatism behind American food when he noted a steady stream of "tea, coffee, bread, butter, salmon, shad, liver, steak, potatoes, pickles, ham, chops, black-puddings, and sausages," explaining that "dinner was breakfast again without the tea and coffee; and supper and breakfast were identical." In *The American Frugal Housewife*, Lydia Maria Child offered advice that might be regarded as the essence of early American food: "Nothing should be thrown away as long as it is possible to make use of it, however trifling that use may be." The men, women, and children moving west of the Mississippi would have, like their fellow citizens back east, thoroughly understood.

The Big Picture

As Americans who came of age during the Revolutionary era knew better than the historians who have studied them, food didn't exist in a vacuum. Food and drink, in fact, were integral to the period's defining events. In representing nothing less than the material success of an early American dream, food and drink in America became a critical manifestation of independence and the virtues that composed it. Americans defended access to their food sources and the right to trade their food with the utmost passion in the 1760s and 1770s. When the British persisted in violating the colonists' most basic constitutional and material rights, the Americans reinvigorated their defense of a hard-earned material way of life by, among other acts, rioting when merchants tried to sell food at unreasonable prices. But food's influence didn't end there. Food and drink and the land on which Americans produced them also predisposed Americans to adopt a radical political ideology that, while unpopular in England, did an effective job of articulating American political concerns from Georgia to Maine—effective enough, anyway, to help a largely fragmented nation fight and win political independence. The American victory in the Revolutionary War inspired a cultural backlash against the mother country—a conscious rejection of the British culture that Americans had been actively embracing only a decade or so earlier. That rejection led Americans to embrace the virtues of the farming life as an explicit cultural and political cause. Thus the virtues of the frontier, as a conscious choice, rather than out of necessity, became an animating force in American life. Food both coincided with and inspired this cultural transition. As Americans idealized a pastoral vision that stressed such attributes as honesty, frugality, simplicity, and lack of pretension, they highlighted that single aspect of geographical and cultural life that Europe lacked: land, land, and more land to replicate the successful creation of a resource-rich society. The costs of its development were legendary in terms of the human suffering it caused, but the ownership of a frontier patch of land was, nonetheless, the single most important factor in making American food what it was.

In choosing "a frugal plain repast" over the "high seasoned food" of Europe, the young nation set a precedent that lasted well into the nineteenth century as a mainstream cultural and culinary standard. By the twentieth century—with the close of the frontier, the rise of great cities, industrialization, regional economic specialization, deep freezes, refrigerators, restaurants, TV dinners, and fast-food outlets—America's tethers to its past became frayed and worn. And now, in the twenty-first century—with agribusiness, a chain restaurant in every strip mall, genetically modified food, big-box stores, commercial stoves in suburban homes, and mad cows— well, those frayed tethers seem to have broken.

But roots can wander, spread underneath the soil in myriad directions, and break through in unexpected places and at unexpected times. American food now seems so mature, and, indeed, it might be fair to say that it has gone the way of commercial decadence, just as English culture did in the late eighteenth century. But those of us who value this nation's culinary past wouldn't be amiss in hoping that some of those dormant roots regenerate and allow us to claim once again, as Thomas Jefferson did in 1785, "How unripe we yet are."

Introduction

1 The opening section, "A Meal," is based on information from Lois Green Carr, Russell R. Menard, and Lorena S. Walsh, *Robert Cole's World: Agriculture and Society in Early Maryland* (Chapel Hill: University of North Carolina Press, 1991), 71, 72, 96, 109, 73, 47–48, 38, 74–75, 103–107.

5 "is one of the means by which a society creates itself" Margaret Visser, *Much Depends on Dinner: The Extraordinary History and Mythology, Allure and Obsessions, Perils and Taboos of an Ordinary Meal* (New York: Collier Books, 1986), 12.

6 "shapes us and expresses us" Ibid., 12.

6 "The large stall-fed ox beef is the best" (and the rest of the quotations in the paragraph) Lucy Emerson, *The New England Cookery* (Montpelier, Vt.: Parks, 1808), 5–8.

7 "Why should not the rich harvest of our hopes" (and the rest of the quotations in the paragraph) Richard Hakluyt, comp., *The Principal Navigations, Voyages, Traffiques and Discoveries of the English Nation* (Glasgow: MacLehose, 1903), 8:299, 303–305.

7 "tooke in less than 2 howers" *The Journal of John Winthrop, 1630–1649*, ed. Richard S. Dunn, James Savage, and Laetitia Yeadle (Cambridge, Mass.: Harvard University Press, 1996), 27

7 "an apt place for the keeping of cattle and swine" Daniel Gookin, *Historical Collections of the Indians in New England* (1792; reprint, Boston: Massachusetts Historical Society, 1848), 185.

8 "a heathan graine" John Gerard, *The Herball, or Generall Historie of Plants* (London: Adam, Issip Joice Norton and Richard Whitakers, 1633), 83.

8 "toyles a man's bodye overmuch" (and the following references to the laziness of Native Americans) Quoted in David D. Smits, "The 'Squaw Drudge': A Prime Index of Savagism," *Ethnohistory* 29, no. 4 (1982): 281–306.

9 "Take eight ounces of mush" Helen Bullock, *The Williamsburg Art of Cookery* (Williamsburg, Va.: Colonial Williamsburg Foundation, 1958), 199.

14 The theme of "Anglicization" is well explored in T. H. Breen, "An Empire of Goods: The Anglicization of Colonial America, 1690–1776," *Journal of British Studies* 25, no. 4 (1986): 467–499.

16 "dependence . . . prepares fit tools for the designs of ambition" Thomas Jefferson, *Notes on the State of Virginia*, ed. William Peden (Chapel Hill: University of North Carolina Press, 1955), 165.

1. Adaptability

19 The story of the rat and the mongoose is from Robert W. Henderson, "Consequences of Predator Introductions and Habitat Destruction on Amphibians and Reptiles in the Post-Columbus West Indies," *Caribbean Journal of Science* 28, nos. 1–2 (1992): 1–10.

21 Information on the Tainos is from Irving Rouse, *The Tainos: Rise and Decline of the People Who Greeted Columbus* (New Haven, Conn.: Yale University Press, 1992), 140–161.

22 "the best people in the world" Samuel Eliot Morison, ed., *Journals and Other Documents on the Life and Voyages of Christopher Columbus* (New York: Heritage Press, 1963), 133.

22 "They are not a people suited to hard work" Quoted in Hugh Thomas, *The Slave Trade: The Story of the Atlantic Slave Trade, 1440–1870* (New York: Simon and Schuster, 1997), 89.

22 For an overview of the smallpox epidemic, see Alfred W. Crosby, *The Columbian Exchange: Biological and Cultural Consequences of 1492* (Westport, Conn.: Greenwood Press, 1972), 35–58.

23 For sugar-mill construction and slavery in sixteenth-century Hispaniola and Santo Domingo, see Thomas, *Slave Trade*, 99–101.

25 Details on sugar production are in Sidney W. Mintz, *Sweetness and Power: The Place of Sugar in Modern History* (New York: Viking), 44–50.

27 The international competition in the slave trade is discussed in Thomas, *Slave Trade*, 182–197.

28 English dominance over the slave trade in the West Indies is covered in Richard S. Dunn, *Sugar and Slaves: The Rise of the Planter Class in the English West Indies, 1624–1713* (New York: Norton, 1972), xiii–xvii.

30 Information on general West African foodways is from P. A. Allison, "Historical Inferences to Be Drawn from the Effect of Human Settlement on the Vegetation of Africa," *Journal of African History* 3, no. 2 (1962): 241–249, and M. A. Havinden, "The History of Crop Cultivation in West Africa: A Bibiliographical Guide," *Economic History Review* 23, no. 3 (1970): 532–555.

33 "Our tillage is exercised in a large plain or common" *The Interesting Narrative of the Life of Olaudah Equiano, Written by Himself*, ed. Robert J. Allison (Boston: Bedford Books, 1995), 39.

34 On Caribbean food, see William F. Keegan and Michael J. DeNiro, "Stable Carbon- and Nitrogen-Isotope Ratios of Bone Collagen Used to Study Coral-Reef and Terrestrial Components of Prehistoric Bahamian Diet," *American Antiquity* 53, no. 2 (1988): 320–336.

36 "The sweet pepper is called *boniatai*" Quoted in Jean Andrews, "The Diffusion of Mesoamerican Food Complex to Southeastern Europe," *Geographical Review* 83, no. 2 (1993): 195.

36 "Thanks to God, that he has given us a sample of all the things of that land" Quoted in Andrews, "Diffusion of Mesoamerican Food Complex," 196.

36 "and brought in them plantans, pinos and potatoes" Quoted in Lennox Honychurch, "Crossroads in the Caribbean: A Site of Encounter and Exchange on Dominica," *World Archaeology* 28, no. 3 (1997): 298.

36 "Many Savage Indians" Philip L. Barbour, Jean Martin, and Bryan Milner, eds., *The Jamestown Voyages Under the First Charter, 1606–1609: Documents Relating to*

the *Foundation of Jamestown and the History of the Jamestown Colony* (Cambridge: Cambridge University Press, 2001), 129.

37 On Caribbean cooking habits, see J. A. Cosculluela, "Prehistoric Cultures of Cuba," *American Antiquity* 12, no. 1 (1946): 10–18.

38 "chiefly owing to the evil practice of mixing sea water with fresh"   Elizabeth Donnan, ed., *Documents Illustrative of the History of the Slave Trade to America* (New York: Octagon Books, 1965), 2:4.

39 "universally considered the greatest benefit"   Sheila Lambert, ed., *House of Commons Sessional Papers of the Eighteenth Century* (London: List and Index Society), 71:144, quoted in Woodville K. Marshall, "Provision Ground and Plantation Labour in Four Windward Islands: Competition for Resources During Slavery," in Ira Berlin and Philip Morgan, eds., *The Slaves' Economy: Independent Production by Slaves in the Americas* (London: Cass, 1991), 48.

39 On malnourishment, see Jerome S. Handler and Robert S. Corruccini, "Plantation Slave Life in Barbados: A Physical Anthropological Analysis," *Journal of Interdisciplinary History* 14, no. 1 (1983): 65–90.

39 "robbing cornfields and slaughtering cattle for food"   Quoted in Richard B. Sheridan, "The Crisis of Slave Subsistence in the British West Indies During and After the American Revolution," *William and Mary Quarterly*, 3rd ser., 33, no. 4 (1976): 619.

39 "their proprietors appropriate only small portions"   *The Papers of Alexander Hamilton*, ed. Harold C. Syrett (New York: Columbia University Press, 1963), 1:61–62.

39 "for want of a sufficiency of Food"   Main Swete Walrond to Clement Tudway, October 9, 1781, Tudway Papers, quoted in Sheridan, "Crisis of Slave Subsistence," 627.

40 "a man who does not know how to fish"   Raymond R. P. Breton, *Dictionnaire Caraïbe–Français* (Leipzig: Platzman, 1892), 59, quoted in Richard Price, "Caribbean Fishing and Fishermen: A Historical Sketch," *American Anthropologist* 68, no. 6 (1966): 1364.

40 "they are marvelously ingenious"   Charles de Rochefort, *Histoire naturelle et morale des îles Antilles de l'Amérique* (Rotterdam: Leers, 1665), 506, quoted in Price, "Caribbean Fishing and Fishermen," 1364.

41 "One goes at night in a canoe" and "The turtle mounts"   R. P. Jean Baptiste Laba, *Nouveau Voyage aux îles de l'Amérique* (Paris: Le Bas, 1742), 312–314, quoted in Price, "Caribbean Fishing and Fishermen,"1365.

41, 42 "They built dams in inlets" and "I have known people for whom a seine"   *Dissertation sur la pêche aux Antilles*, 15–16, quoted in Price, "Caribbean Fishing and Fishermen," 1372.

42 "slaves are obliged to seek out [their food] elsewhere"   Jean Baptiste Thibeau de Chanvalon, *Voyage à la Martinique* (Paris: Bauche, 1763), 108, quoted in Price, "Caribbean Fishing and Fishermen," 1375.

42 "poultry and his [live]stock are his wealth"   Quoted in Bryan Edwards, *History of the British Colonies* (Philadelphia: Humphries, 1805–1806), 4.

43 On yams, see Alan Davidson, *The Oxford Companion to Food* (New York: Oxford University Press, 1999), 856–857.

44 "clean and ameliorated surface to plant"   Woodville K. Marshall, ed., *The Colthurst Journal: Journal of a Special Magistrate in the Islands of Barbados and St. Vincent, July 1835–September 1838* (Millhouse, N.Y.: KTO Press, 1977), 171.

44 "contiguous to the Negro Houses"   Lambert, ed., *House of Commons Sessional Papers of the Eighteenth Century*, 70, 132, quoted in Marshall, "Provision Ground and Plantation Labour in Four Windward Islands," 51.

45 "very husbandlike and beautiful appearance" (and the rest of the quotations in the paragraph)   William Beckford, *Descriptive Account of the Island of Jamaica* (London: Egerton, 1790), 8, 18, 19, 22, 81.

46 "those who are industrious"   George Pinckard, *Notes on the West Indies, Written During the Expedition Under the Command of the Late General Sir Ralph Abercromby* (London: Longman, Hurst, Rees, and Orme, 1806), 2:116.

46 "a pig, a goat, a young kid, some pigeons"   Ibid., 368.

46 "slaves always have time to cultivate their yams"   F. W. N. Bayley, *Four Years' Residence in the West Indies* (London: Kidd, 1830), 92, quoted in Hilary McD. Beckles, "An Economic Life of Their Own: Slaves as Commodity Producers and Distributors in Barbados," in Berlin and Morgan, eds., *Slaves' Economy*, 34.

46 "makes its appearance at the top of a cone" (and the rest of the quotations in the paragraph)   "James Savage Journal," MS. S-43, Massachusetts Historical Society, Boston.

47 For slave meals in the Caribbean, see Diane M. Spivey, *The Peppers, Cracklings, and Knots of Wool Cookbook: The Global Migration of African Cuisine* (New York: State University of New York Press, 1999), 219–221.

48 "several miles to market"   William Dickson, *Letters on Slavery: To Which Are Added Addresses to the Whites, and to the Free Negroes of Barbados* (London: Phillips, 1789), 11, quoted in Beckles, "Economic Life of Their Own," 35.

48 "busy marketeers"   James A. Thome and Joseph Horace Kimball, *Emancipation in the West Indies: A Six Months' Tour in Antigua, Barbados, and Jamaica in the Year 1837* (New York: American Anti-Slavery Society, 1838), 66, quoted in Beckles, "Economic Life of Their Own," 35.

49 "In this Island"   Quoted in Beckles, "Economic Life of Their Own," 34.

49 "tray of vegetables" (and the rest of the quotations in the paragraph)   Bayley, *Four Years' Residence in the West Indies*, 423–424, quoted in Beckles, "Economic Life of Their Own," 38.

49 "depend for a subsistence on robbing the slaves" (and the rest of the quotations in the paragraph)   Dickson, *Letters on Slavery*, 41–42, quoted in Beckles, "Economic Life of Their Own," 39.

50 "of any goods, wares, merchandize"   Samuel Moore, *The Public Acts in Force, Passed by the Legislature of Barbados, from May 11th, 1762 to April 8, 1800* (London, 1801), 154–177.

51 Information on the connection between Barbados and Carolina is from Alan Taylor, *American Colonies* (New York: Viking, 2001), 223–225.

52 "To the owner of every Negro-Man"   Alexander S. Salley, ed., *Narratives of Early Carolina, 1650–1708* (New York: Scribner, 1911), 48.

2. Traditionalism

55 "The English [in New England] make very good Bread"   Quoted in Fulmer Mood, "John Winthrop, Jr., on Indian Corn," *New England Quarterly* 10, no. 1 (1937): 129.

57 "This much I can affirm"   Quoted in Massachusetts Historical Society, *Proceedings of the Massachusetts Historical Society* (Boston: The Society, 1929), 62:318.

57 "The country is yet raw"   Robert Cushman, "Reasons and Considerations Touching the Lawfulness of Moving out of England," in Alexander Young, ed., *Chronicles*

of the Pilgrim Fathers of the Colony of Plymouth (1841; reprint, New York: Da Capo Press, 1971), 265.

57 "heere is foule and fish in great plenty" *Winthrop Papers* (Boston: Massachusetts Historical Society, 1929–1947), 3:166.

57 "the fertility of the soil is to be admired at" Everett Emerson, ed., *Letters from New England: The Massachusetts Bay Colony, 1629–1638* (Amherst: University of Massachusetts Press, 1976), 31.

58 "the colony in a sad and unexpected condition" Ibid., 310.

58 "the people of the country" William Hubbard, *A General History of New England from the Discovery to MDCLXXX* (1704; reprint, New York: Arno Press, 1971), 41.

58 "if theis ship had not come" *Winthrop Papers*, 3:18–19.

58 "This soil is like your woodland in England" Thomas Hutchinson, *History of the Colony and Province of the Massachusetts Bay* (Boston: Fleet, 1764), 1:482–483.

58 "came to no good" William Bradford, *Of Plymouth Plantation, 1620–1647*, ed. Samuel Eliot Morison (New York: Knopf, 1970), 67.

58 "Hay is inferior" Emerson, ed., *Letters from New England*, 310.

59 Information on Native Americans in New England is from M. K. Bennett, "The Food Economy of the New England Indians, 1605–75," *Journal of Political Economy* 63, no. 5 (1955): 369–397.

60 "hand into the water" Chrestien Le Clerque, *New Relation of Gaspesia*, trans. and ed. William F. Ganong (Toronto: Champlain Society, 1910), quoted in William Cronon, *Changes in the Land: Indians, Colonists, and the Ecology of New England* (New York: Hill and Wang, 1983), 39.

60 "From the month of May to the middle of September" Reuben Gold Thwaites, ed., *Jesuit Relations* (Cleveland: Burrows Press, 1897), 3:65–67.

61 "in such multitudes as is almost incredible" William Wood, *New England's Prospect*, ed. Alden T. Vaughan (1635; reprint, Amherst: University of Massachusetts Press, 1977), 56.

61 "For beasts, there are some beares" Francis Higginson, *New England's Plantation* (London: Cotes, 1630), quoted in Massachusetts Historical Society, *Proceedings*, 62:311.

61 "If I should tell you" Wood, *New England's Prospect*, 51.

62 "the paradox of want in a land of plenty" Cronon, *Changes in the Land*, 41.

62 "It is all the same to us" Le Clercq, *New Relation of Gaspesia*, quoted in Cronon, *Changes in the Land*, 40.

62 "They are convinced that fifteen to twenty lumps of meat" Quoted in James Sullivan, "The History of the Penobscott Indians," *Collections of the Massachusetts Historical Society* 1, no. 9 (1804): 228.

63 "the Salvages are accustomed to set fire of the Country" Thomas Morton, *New English Canaan*, ed. Charles Francis Adams (1632; reprint, Boston: Prince Society, 1883), 232.

63 "consumes all the underwood and rubbish" Wood, *New England's Prospect*, 38.

63 "Having burnt up the wood in one place" Roger Williams, *A Key into the Language of America* (London: Dexter, 1643), quoted in Cronon, *Changes in the Land*, 49.

63 On New England's early food supply, see Sarah F. McMahon, "A Comfortable Subsistence: The Changing Composition of Diet in Rural New England, 1620–1840," *William and Mary Quarterly*, 3rd ser., 42, no. 1 (1985): 26–65.

63 "our lands are aptest for Rye and Oats" *Winthrop Papers*, 3:166.

66 "an object of some consequence" Charles Marshall, *An Introduction to the Knowledge and Practice of Gardening* (London: Rider, 1798), 1:25.

67 "it is . . . extremely unlikely" Ann Leighton, *Early American Gardens: For Meate or Medicine* (Amherst: University of Massachusetts Press, 1986), 162.

67 "be southward, a point either to the east or west" Ibid.

67 "A free moderate loam" Ibid., 47.

67 "Let not the ground be glutted with dung" John Abercrombie, *Every Man His Own Gardener: Being a New and Much More Complete Gardener's Kalender than Any Other Hitherto Published* (London: Rivington, 1782), 410; Marshall, *Introduction to the Knowledge and Practice of Gardening*, 1:47.

68 "a free, sweet, and rich soil" (and the rest of the quotations in the paragraph) Marshall, *Introduction to the Knowledge and Practice of Gardening*, 1:46.

68 "one paire of oxen" (and the rest of the quotations in the paragraph) George Francis Dow, ed., *The Probate Records of Essex County, Massachusetts* (Salem, Mass: Essex Institute, 1916), 1:73, 264–266, 153, 161.

68 "Let everything be done now" Marshall, *Introduction to the Knowledge and Practice of Gardening*, 2:102.

68 "in which the loss of a single day is of consequence" Ibid.

69 "short prickly" Abercrombie, *Every Man His Own Gardener*, 1.

69 "a full spade deep" (and the rest of the quotations in the paragraph) Marshall, *Introduction to the Knowledge and Practice of Gardening*, 2:103.

69 "very valuable to the good gardener" Ibid, 106.

69 "turnips on a gentle heat" (and the rest of the quotations in the paragraph) Philip Miller, *Gardener's Kalender: Directing What Works Are Necessary to Be Done Every Month in the Kitchen, Fruit, and Pleasure-gardens, as also in the Conservatory and Nursery* (London, 1732), 51–53.

70 "The products of spring" Marshall, *Introduction to the Knowledge and Practice of Gardening*, 2:112.

70 "It is in this month" (and the rest of the quotations in the paragraph) Ibid, 114–118.

70 "An attention of this sort" (and the rest of the quotations in the paragraph) Abercrombie, *Every Man His Own Gardener*, 452; Marshall, *Introduction to the Knowledge and Practice of Gardening*, 2:123.

71 "no longer decorated with flowers or verdure" Marshall, *Introduction to the Knowledge and Practice of Gardening*, 2:131.

71 "it contains many things of promise" Ibid., 21.

72 "I have seen them as big as a man's arm" (and the rest of Josselyn's quotations in the paragraph) John Josselyn, *New-Englands Rarities Discovered: In Birds, Beasts, Fishes, Serpents, and Plants of That Country* (London: Widdowes, 1672), 34.

72 "our turnips, parsnips, and carrots" Higginson, *New England's Plantation*, 312.

73 "first unto my wife" (and the rest of the quotations in the paragraph) George Francis Dow, ed., *The Records and Files of the Quarterly Courts of Essex County, Massachusetts, 1635–1683* (Salem, Mass.: Essex Institute, 1911–1916), 1:67, 302.

73 On cattle in New England, see Virginia DeJohn Anderson, "King Philip's Herds: Indians, Colonists, and the Problem of Livestock in Early New England," *William and Mary Quarterly*, 3rd ser., 51, no. 4 (1994): 601–605.

73 "three heifers and a bull" Bradford, *Of Plymouth Plantation*, 141.

74 "such wild Fother as was never cut before" Edward Johnson, *Johnson's Wonder-Working Providence, 1628–1651*, ed. J. Franklin Jameson (1654; reprint, New York: Scribner, 1910), 84.

74 "Our beasts grow lousy feeding upon it" Hutchinson, *History of Massachusetts Bay*, 1:84.

74 "as men and cattle increased" *Winthrop Papers*, 2:120.

74 "the abundance of [English] grass" John Smith, *The Generall Historie of Virginia, New England, and the Summer Isles* (1624; reprint, Cleveland: World, 1966), 211.

74 "an apt place for the keeping of cattle and swine" Daniel Gookin, *Historical Collections of the Indians in New England* (1792; reprint, Boston: Massachusetts Historical Society, 1848), 185.

74 "our English-clover grass thrives very well" John Josselyn, *An Account of Two Voyages to New-England* (London: Widdowes, 1675).

75 "eight cowes" (and the rest of the quotations in the paragraph) Dow, ed., *Probate Records of Essex County*, 1:245, 53, 141, 163, 128.

76 "Cows . . . should be treated with constant gentleness" Charles Flint, *Milch Cows and Dairy Farming* (Boston: Williams, 1858), 147.

76 "barn and cow house" (and the rest of the quotations in the paragraph) Dow, ed., *Probate Records of Essex County*, 1:15, 60, 325.

76 "Milk and cream are exceedingly sensitive" Flint, *Milch Cows and Dairy Farming*, 220.

76 "No matter if it is but a single drop" Ibid., 221.

77 Information on butter production is from Gervase Markham, *The English Housewife*, ed. Michael R. Best (Kingston, Ont.: McGill–Queens University Press, 1982), 170–174.

78 "there be many mischiefs and inconvenience" Markham, *English Housewife*, 172.

78 "a churne, 1 firkin" Dow, ed., *Probate Records of Essex County*, 1:192.

78 "If the stomach is preserved from putrefaction" Flint, *Milch Cows and Dairy Farming*, 247–248.

79 Information on meat supplies is from McMahon, "Comfortable Subsistence," 34–38, 60.

79 "deer, bear meat, partridges" Higginson, *New England's Plantation*, 310.

79 "their walke or place of feeding" *Dorchester Town Records* (Boston: Rockwell and Churchill, 1883), 23.

80 "Of all the quadrupeds that we know" John Mills, *A Treatise on Cattle* (London: Whitestone, 1776), quoted in Julian Wiseman, *The Pig: A British History* (London: Duckworth, 2000), xvi.

81 "He asked what meat she had in the house" Dow, ed., *Records and Files of the Quarterly Courts of Essex County*, 4:290.

82 "It is of hard digestion" John Gerard, *The Herball, or Generall Historie of Plants* (London: Adam, Issip Joice Norton and Richard Whitakers, 1633), 83.

82 Information on corn ownership is from McMahon, "Comfortable Subsistence," 30–32.

83 "finished cribbing the corn" *The Diary of Joshua Hempstead of New London, Connecticut* (1758; reprint, New London, Conn.: New London Historical Society, 1970), 14.

83 "wheat bread was reserved" Ibid., 16.

83 On the "Anglicizing" of Indian corn, see Betty Fussell, "Translating Maize into Corn: The Transformation of America's Native Grain," *Social Research* 66, no. 1 (1999): 41–65.

84 "boyle[d] it upon a gentle fire" Josselyn, *New-Englands Rarities Discovered*, 35.

84 "It is light of digestion" Ibid., 36.

3. Negotiation

89 For more on the findings at Monticello, see Diana C. Crader, "The Zooarchaeology of the Storehouse and the Dry Well at Monticello," *American Antiquity* 49, no. 3 (1984): 542–558.

92 "we were entertayned with much Courtesey" (and the rest of the quotations in the paragraph) "Archer's Relation," in Maurice A. Mook, "Virginia Ethnology from an Early Relation," *William and Mary Quarterly*, 2nd ser., 23, no. 2 (1943): 105, 106–107.

93 "he sowes his wheate" Ibid., 108.

93 "caused heere to be prepared for us pegatewk-Apyan" (and the rest of the quotations in the paragraph) Ibid., 110.

93 "fatt lustie manly woman" (and the rest of the quotations in the paragraph) Ibid., 111–113.

95 "In March and Aprill they live much upon their fishing weares" Ibid., 120.

95 "The manner of baking bread is thus" Ibid., 121.

95 Information on the foodways of the Native Americans of the Chesapeake Bay is from Helen C. Rountree, "Powhatan Indian Women: The People Captain John Smith Barely Saw," *Ethnohistory* 45, no. 1 (1998): 1–29.

98 "in one day a Savage will gather enough" *The Complete Works of Captain John Smith*, ed. Phillip L. Barbour (Chapel Hill: University of North Carolina Press, 1986), 1:153.

98 "The men bestowe their times in fishing" Quoted in Mook, "Virginia Ethnology," 121, and David D. Smits, "The 'Squaw Drudge': A Prime Index of Savagism," *Ethnohistory* 29, no. 4 (1982): 285.

99 "one of the Indians shot a bear" Quoted in Smits, "'Squaw Drudge,'" 285.

99 "the natural Production of that Country" Robert Beverly, *The History and Present State of Virginia*, ed. L. B. Wright (1705; reprint, Chapel Hill: University of North Carolina Press, 1974), 156.

100 "Heaven and earth never agreed better to frame a place" John Smith, *A Map of Virginia: With a Description of the Countrey, the Commodities, People, Government, and Religion* (1612), in Lyon Gardiner Tyler, ed., *Narratives of Early Virginia, 1606–1625* (New York: Scribner, 1907), 77.

100 "was not unlike . . . Arabia for spices" Quoted in Alexander Brown, *The Genesis of the United States* (Boston: Houghton Mifflin, 1890), 1:130–131.

100 "if the Lord love us" Peter Force, *Tracts and Other Papers Relating Principally to the Origin, Settlement, and Progress of the Colonies in North America, from the Discovery of the Country to the Year 1776* (Gloucester, Mass.: Smith, 1963), 8–11.

100 "blast the savages off the face of the earth" Susan Myra Kingsbury, ed., *The Records of the Virginia Company of London, 1606–1626* (Washington, D.C.: Government Printing Office, 1906–1935), 3:541.

100 "an idle crue" *A True Declaration of the Estate of the Colonie in Virginia* (London: Barret, 1610), quoted in Edmund S. Morgan, *American Slavery, American Freedom: The Ordeal of Colonial Virginia* (New York: Norton, 1975), 88.

101 "When our people were fed out of the common store" Ralph Hamor, *True Discourse on the Present State of Virginia* (1615; reprint, Richmond: Virginia State Library, 1957), 26, quoted in Morgan, *American Slavery, American Freedom*, 83.

101 "we can plant anywhere" *Travels and Works of Captain John Smith: President of Virginia and Admiral of New England, 1580–1631*, ed. Edward Arber and A. G. Bradley (Edinburgh: Grant, 1910), 1:152, quoted in Morgan, *American Slavery, American Freedom*, 73.

102 "savages have no occupations but leisure ones"   Quoted in Smits, "'Squaw Drudge,'" 282.

102 "were it fully manured and inhabited"   John Smith, *The Generall History of Virginia, New England, and the Summer Isles* (1624; reprint, Cleveland: World, 1966), 22.

102 "they place [these activities] among their sports and leisures"   William Strachey, *The History of Travell into Virginia Britania* (1609; reprint, London: Hakluyt Society, 1953), 83–84.

102 "the little work that is done among the Indians"   Quoted in Smits, "'Squaw Drudge,'" 284.

103 "There is scarce any man amongst us"   Kingsbury, ed., *Records of the Virginia Company*, 3:446.

103 "now must justly be compelled to servitude and drudgery"   *Travels and Works of Captain John Smith*, 2:597.

104 "Nothing is done in anie one of [the plantations]"   Kingsbury, ed., *Records of the Virginia Company*, 4:145, quoted in Morgan, *American Slavery, American Freedom*, 109.

104 Details on the fine art of growing tobacco are in T. H. Breen, *Tobacco Culture: The Mentality of the Great Tidewater Planters on the Eve of the Revolution* (Princeton, N.J.: Princeton University Press, 1985), 45–60.

104 "an experienced planter commonly takes care"   J. F. D. Smyth, *A Tour in the United States of America* (London: Robinson, 1784), 2:129.

104 "about as large as a dollar"   *The Papers of Thomas Jefferson*, ed. Julian P. Boyd (Princeton, N.J.: Princeton University Press, 1953), 7:210, quoted in Breen, *Tobacco Culture*, 47.

105 "When a good shower . . . happens"   G. Melvin Herndon, *William Tatham and the Culture of Tobacco, Including a Facsimile Reprint of "An Historical and Practical Essay on the Culture and Commerce of Tobacco"* (Coral Gables, Fla.: University of Miami Press, 1969), 15.

105 "until the *long season in May*"   Ibid., 14.

105 "spots appearing on the leaf"   Lee Family Papers, MS. L51, fol. 378, Virginia Historical Society, Richmond, quoted in Breen, *Tobacco Culture*, 49–51.

105 "the tobacco, when ripe, changes its colour"   Herndon, *William Tatham and the Culture of Tobacco*, 124–125.

107 "To employ the Fall & Winter well"   Ulrich B. Phillips, ed., *Plantation and Frontier Documents: 1649–1863* (Cleveland: Clark, 1909), 1:112.

108 The transition from servitude to slavery is covered most thoroughly in Morgan, *American Slavery, American Freedom*, 250–315.

108 "to worke in the heat of the day"   Kingsbury, ed., *Records of the Virginia Company*, 3:706.

108 "It would not have been surprising"   Morgan, *American Slavery, American Freedom*, 133.

110 "abuse their servants there with intollerable oppression"   Kingsbury, ed., *Records of the Virginia Company*, 2:442.

110 "she had been sore beaten"   W. L. Sachse, ed., *Minutes of the Norwich Court of Mayoralty* (Norwich, Eng.: Norfolk Record Society, 1942), 15:90, quoted in Morgan, *American Slavery, American Freedom*, 127.

110 "put his yard into her and ravished"   Warren M. Billings, ed., *The Old Dominion in the Seventeenth Century: A Documentary History of Virginia, 1607–1689* (Chapel Hill: University of North Carolina Press, 1975), 161–163. The case is also discussed in

Philip D. Morgan, *Slave Counterpoint: Black Culture in the Eighteenth-Century Chesapeak and Lowcountry* (Chapel Hill: University of North Carolina Press, 1998), 9–10.

112 "But for those with eyes to see"   Morgan, *American Slavery, American Freedom*, 269.

114 "the mess"   David Hackett Fischer, *Albion's Seed: Four British Folkways in America* (New York: Oxford University Press, 1989), 350.

114 "are allowed a peck of Indian corn per week" and "nourishes labourers better"   Quoted in Gregory Stiverson and Patrick Butler, eds., "Virginia in 1732," *Virginia Magazine of History and Biography* 85, no. 2 (1977): 32.

115 "who are not fed with animal food"   Carter Letterbook Ms., 119, Duke University, Durham, N.C., quoted in Philip Morgan, *Slave Counterpoint*, 36.

115 "found themselves so weak"   Mark Catesby, *The Natural History of Carolina, Florida, and Bahama Islands* (London: Jnnys and Manat, 1731), 1:xvii.

115 "the Negroes, while the novelty lasted, seemed to prefer Wheat bread"   Quoted in Philip Morgan, *Slave Counterpoint*, 134.

115 "about 900 lbs. [of pork] . . . for the people"   James A. Bear Jr., ed., *Jefferson at Monticello: Recollections of a Monticello Slave and of a Monticello Overseer* (Charlottesville: University of Virginia Press, 1967), 54.

115 "a grate petition . . . for some meat"   Quoted in Philip Morgan, *Slave Counterpoint*, 136.

115 The anecdote about Landon Carter is recounted in Philip Morgan, *Slave Counterpoint*, 136.

116 Information on Kingsmill Plantation is from William M. Kelso, *Kingsmill Plantations, 1619–1800: Archeology of Country Life in Colonial Virginia* (London: Academic Press, 1984), 176–180.

116 "asked the lent the use of the sein" (and the rest of the quotations in the paragraph)   Philip Morgan, *Slave Counterpoint*, 139.

117 "small houses or huts"   Hugh Jones, *The Present State of Virginia*, ed. Richard L. Morton (1724; reprint, Chapel Hill: University of North Carolina Press, 1956), 75.

117 "to plant little platts for potatoes"   Quoted in Stiverson and Butler, eds., "Virginia in 1732," 32.

117 "great quantities of snaps and collards"   *The Journal of Lieut. William Feltman*, ed. H. C. Baird (Philadelphia: Historical Society of Pennsylvania, 1853), 10, quoted in Philip Morgan, *Slave Counterpoint*, 140.

118 Archaeological evidence is detailed in Diana C. Crader, "Slave Diet at Monticello," *American Antiquity* 55, no. 4 (1990): 690–717.

119 "in the middle of this poverty"   Quoted in Philip Morgan, *Slave Counterpoint*, 115.

121 "I took my gun and endeavored to shoot some partridges"   *The Great American Gentleman: William Byrd of Westover in Virginia, His Secret Diary for the Years 1709–1712*, ed. Louis B. Wright and Marion Tinling (New York: Capricorn Books, 1963), 137.

121 "I resolved to eat no meat today"   Ibid., 133.

121 "fish for dinner and a little asparagus"   Ibid., 14.

121 "nothing but cold roast beef and asparagus"   Ibid., 15.

122 "wonderfully quick of growth"   Robert Beverly, *The History and Present State of Virginia*, ed. David Freeman Hawke (1705; reprint, New York: Bobbs-Merrill, 1971), 168.

122 "my belly out of order"   *Great American Gentleman*, 79.

122 "persuaded him to enter into a milk diet"   Ibid., 206.

123 "I ate some green peas for dinner"   Ibid., 150.

123 "at night we ate some bread and cheese"   Ibid., 131.

123 "I ate fish for dinner" Ibid., 91.

123 "As for fish . . . no country can boast of more Variety" Beverly, *History and Present State of Virginia*, ed. Hawke, 82.

123 "two small fish and some roast mutton" *Great American Gentleman*, 168.

123 "I ate fish for dinner, which they called trout" Ibid., 44.

123 "rode to Kensington" Ibid., 35.

124 "taking the protection of[f] corn" Ibid., 53.

124 "the boatwright was affronted" Ibid., 132.

124 "seaven cowes & heifers" Quoted in Lois Green Carr, Russell R. Menard, and Lorena S. Walsh, *Robert Cole's World: Agriculture and Society in Early Maryland* (Chapel Hill: University of North Carolina Press, 1991), 185.

124 Information on white foodways in the Chesapeake is from Fischer, *Albion's Seed*, 349–354.

125 "fine Pastures as anywhere in the world" Beverly, *History and Present State of Virginia*, ed. Hawke, 318.

125 "hogs swarm like Vermine upon the earth" Ibid., 170.

125 "before they get cold" Helen Bullock, *The Williamsburg Art of Cookery* (Williamsburg, Va.: Colonial Williamsburg Foundation, 1958), 61–62.

125 "When you roast a loin" Hannah Glasse, *The Art of Cookery Made Plain and Easy* (Alexandria, Va.: Cottom and Stewart, 1805), 14–17.

125 "take a sirloin of beef"(and the rest of the quotations in the paragraph) Ibid., 69–70, 51, 277, 255.

126 "The summer heat" Howard C. Rice Jr. and Anne S. K. Brown, eds., *The American Campaigns of Rochambeau's Army* (Princeton, N.J.: Princeton University Press, 1972), 1:66.

126 "Get a thirty gallon cask" Mary Randolph, *The Virginia Housewife: Or, Methodical Cook* (Washington, D.C.: Davis and Force, 1824), 22–24.

126 "After the wet season" Ibid., 24.

126 "The meat is first cut from the bones in thin slices" *The Journal of Nicholas Cresswell, 1774–1777*, ed. A. G. Bradley (New York: Dial Press, 1924) 75–76, 199.

127 "Make fresh pickle often" Elizabeth Raffald, *The Experienced English House-keeper* (Manchester: Harrep, 1769), 293.

127 "Virginians dined; New Englanders merely ate" Fischer, *Albion's Seed*, 352.

128 "I took a whim in my head" *Journal and Letters of Philip Vickers Fithian: A Plantation Tutor of the Old Dominion, 1773–1774*, ed. Hunter Dickenson Farish (Virginia: University of Virginia Press, 1957), 121, quoted in Fischer, *Albion's Seed*, 353.

128 "We rode twenty strong to Colonel Fichous" Durand de Dauphiné, *A Huguenot Exile in Virginia; or, Voyages of a Frenchman Exiled for His Religion, with a Description of Virginia & Maryland*, ed. Gilbert Chinard (1687; reprint, New York: Press of the Pioneers, 1934), 158.

4. Wilderness

131 "cavalances, or red bean, and black-betty" Karen Hess, *The Carolina Rice Kitchen: The African Connection* (Columbia: University of South Carolina Press, 1992), 97. Hess charts the possible origins of various dishes on 98–102.

133 "speedy peopling of the place" Quoted in Peter Wood, *Black Majority: Negroes in Colonial South Carolina from 1670 Through the Stono Rebellion* (New York: Norton, 1974), 21.

133 "wee cannot employ our servants [slaves] as we would" Ibid., 26.

134 "whole business . . . to clear a little ground" Ibid., 26.

134 "wee have but 7 weekes provision left" Quoted in South Carolina Historical Society, *Collections* (Charleston: South Carolina Historical Society, 1857), 5:202.

134 "cattle, company, and good liquor" Alexander S. Salley, ed., *Narratives of Early Carolina, 1650–1708* (New York: Scribner, 1911), 6.

135 "Our design . . . to have planters there and not Graziers" Quoted in South Carolina Historical Society, *Collections*, 5:437–438, and Wood, *Black Majority*, 29.

135 "did formerly transport Severall Negroes out of this Colony" Alexander S. Salley, ed., *Records of the Secretary of the Province and the Register of the Province of South Carolina, 1671–1675* (Columbia: University of South Carolina Press, 1944), 59.

135 "Negro man by name Cato" Quoted in Gary S. Dunbar, "Colonial Carolina Cowpens," *Agricultural History* 35, no. 3 (1961): 125–130.

136 "134 head of cattle" Quoted in Wood, *Black Majority*, 31.

136 "superintenting a number of slaves" *Travels of William Bartram*, ed. Mark Van Doren (1928; reprint, New York: Dover, 1955), 255.

136 "cattell . . . begins to be plentiful" Salley, ed., *Narratives of Early Carolina*, 182.

136 "severall in the country" Ibid.

136 "chief subsistence of the first settlers being by hoggs & cattle" Quoted in Verner W. Crane, *The Southern Frontier, 1732–1870* (Ann Arbor: University of Michigan Press, 1929), 110.

136 "The New Settlers have now great Advantage over the first Planters" Salley, ed., *Narratives of Early Carolina*, 291.

136 "It was [once] reckon'd a great deal to have three or four cows" Thomas Nairne, *A Letter from South Carolina; Giving an Account of the Soil, Air, Product, Trade, Government, Laws, Religion, People, Military Strength, and C. of that Province* (London: Baldwin, 1710), 13.

136 "a Bermudian, being employ'd here with a boy" John Lawson, *A New Voyage to Carolina* (London, 1709), 7.

136 "Barbados and ye rest of ye Caribee Islands" Quoted in Vincent T. Harlow, *A History of Barbados, 1625–1685* (New York: Negro Universities Press, 1969), 283, and Wood, *Black Majority*, 32.

136 "the planter here is but slave" William L. Saunders, ed., *The Colonial Records of North Carolina* (Raleigh: Hale, 1886), 1:746.

137 "the [white] people here are the vilest race of men upon the earth" Quoted in Frank J. Klingberg, "The Indian Frontier in South Carolina as Seen by the S.P.G. Missionary," *Journal of Southern History* 5, no. 4 (1939): 483–484.

137 "no body is obliged to beg or want for food" Nairne, *Letter from South Carolina*, 42.

137 Information on the Piedmont Native Americans is from Richard L. Haan, "The 'Trade Do's Not Flourish as Formerly': The Ecological Origins of the Yamassee War of 1715," *Ethnohistory* 28, no. 4 (1981): 341–358.

137 "nailes of all sizes" Nairne, *Letter from South Carolina*, 43.

137 Information on the trade in skins is from Converse D. Clowse, *Economic Beginnings in Colonial South Carolina, 1670–1730* (Columbia: University of South Carolina Press, 1971), 116–143.

137 "one hunting Indian has yearly kill'd and brought to his plantation" Salley, ed., *Narratives of Early Carolina*, 150.

138 "Guns and Ammunition" Lawson, *New Voyage to Carolina*, 220.

138 "There must be some convenient time given ye Traders"   Quoted in Haan, "'Trade Do's Not Flourish as Formerly,'" 346.

138 "a Judicious man be sent Among the Indjans"   Terry W. Lipscomb, ed., *Journal of the Commons House of Assembly for South Carolina, October 6, 1757 to January 24, 1761* (Columbia: South Carolina Department of Archives and History, 1996), 5.

138 "the first opportunity for an important source of skins"   Clowse, *Economic Beginnings in Colonial South Carolina*, 64.

140 "convenient for procuring game"   *Travels of William Bartram*, 44.

140 "Living in one place year after year"   James H. Merrell, "The Indians' New World: The Catawba Experience," *William and Mary Quarterly*, 3rd ser., 41, no. 4 (1984): 545.

141 "six English-men, three Indian-men" (and the rest of the quotations in the paragraph)   Lawson, *New Voyage to Carolina*, 6–10.

142–144 "We were entertain'd" through "Santee Jack, a good Hunter"   Ibid., 16–26.

144–145 "we were never wanting of a good appetite" through "take a light and go upon them in the Night"   Ibid., 27–45.

145–146 "I concluded, with telling them" through "the herrings in March and April"   Ibid., 52–56.

146 "the civilized Indians . . . making Weares to catch fish"   John Brickell, *The Natural History of North Carolina* (Dublin: Cambon, 1737), 42.

146 "one of our Indian young men, this evening, caught a very large salmon trout"   *Travels of William Bartram*, 61.

146 "For a small consideration"   Brickell, *Natural History of North Carolina*, 42.

147 "By the middle of the eighteenth century"   Harry L. Watson, "'The Common Rights of Mankind': Subsistence, Shad, and Commerce in the Early Republican South," *Journal of American History* 83, no. 1 (1996): 21–22.

147 "many poor familys who Depended on said fishing"   Quoted in Watson, "'Common Rights of Mankind,'" 24.

147 "mullet, witing, black-fish, rock-fish"   James Glen, *A Description of South Carolina* (London: Dodsley, 1761), in Chapman J. Milling, ed., *Colonial South Carolina: Two Contemporary Descriptions* (Columbia: University of South Carolina Press, 1951), 69.

147 "The great devouring trout and catfish are in abundance"   *Travels of William Bartram*, 157.

148 "delights in high loose land"   Glen, *Description of South Carolina*, 16–17.

148 "there are no Wind-Mills in this Province"   Brickell, *Natural History of North Carolina*, 263–264.

148 "the Indian corn, or maize, is of most general use"   George Milligen-Johnston, *Account of the Situation, Air, Weather, and Diseases of South-Carolina* (London: Hinton, 1770), in Milling, ed., *Colonial South Carolina*, 137.

148 "Although most new fields remain for a long time lumbered"   William De Brahm, *Report of the General Survey in the Southern District of North America*, ed. Louis de Vorsey (1799; reprint, Columbia: University of South Carolina Press, 1971), 94.

148 "there are dispersed up and down the Country"   Glen, *Description of South Carolina*, 14.

149 "at Sun-set all the Slaves leave their fields and retire to their Cottages"   De Brahm, *Report of the General Survey*, 93–94.

149 "a place affording many strange Revolutions in the Age of a Man"   Lawson, *Voyage to Carolina*, 12–13.

149 "in the Woods and Fields, are Plenty of wild Turkeys of a large Size" Milligen-Johnston, *Account of the Situation, Air, Weather, and Diseases of South-Carolina*, 139.

149 "great Variety of wild Fowl" Nairne, *Letter from South Carolina*, 13.

149 "the wild Beasts which the Woods of South Carolina afford for Profit" Glen, *Description of South Carolina*, 67.

149 "the master of the house where I was staying" *Luigi Castiglioni's Viaggio: Travels in the United States of North America, 1785–1787*, trans. and ed. Antonio Pace (Syracuse, N.Y.: Syracuse University Press, 1983), 149.

149 "in the company of the overseer of the farm" *Travels of William Bartram*, 38.

150 "From the animal's incapacity to exert speed" William Eddis, *Letters from America*, ed. Aubrey C. Land (1792; reprint, Cambridge, Mass: Belknap Press, 1969), 32, quoted in Timothy Silver, *A New Face on the Countryside: Indians, Colonists, and Slaves in South Atlantic Forests, 1500–1800* (Cambridge: Cambridge University Press, 1990), 96.

150 "came home with horse loads of wild pigeons" *Travels of William Bartram*, 371–372.

150 "South Carolina abounds with black Cattle" Glen, *Description of South Carolina*, 68.

150 "we have likewise Hogs in abundance" Nairne, *Letter from South Carolina*, 13

150 "the cattle feed themselves" Quoted in Wood, *Black Majority*, 29n.47.

151 "plenty of milk, butter, and a very good cheese" *Travels of William Bartram*, 43.

151 "they also have lettuce" (and the rest of the quotations in the paragraph) Johann Martin Bolzius, "Reliable Answer to Some Submitted Questions Concerning the Land Carolina," trans. and ed. Klaus G. Loewald, Beverly Starika, and Paul S. Taylor, *William and Mary Quarterly*, 3rd ser., 14, no. 2 (1957): 239.

151 "one bushel of barley yields about 8 bushels" (and the rest of the quotations in the paragraph) Ibid., 238.

152 "living in a state of Nature" *The Carolina Backcountry on the Eve of the Revolution: The Journal and Other Writings of Charles Woodmason, Anglican Itinerant*, ed. Richard J. Hooker (Chapel Hill: University of North Carolina Press, 1953), 15.

152 "Was there ever such a scene of primitive simplicity!" *Travels of William Bartram*, 38.

152 Information on the Yamasee War is from Haan, "'Trade Do's Not Flourish as Formerly,'" and Clowse, *Economic Beginnings in Colonial South Carolina*, 186–188.

152 "the Creek Indians had a design to Cut off the Traders" William L. McDowell, ed., *Journals of the Commissioners of the Indian Trade* (Columbia: South Carolina Archives Department, 1955), 155.

152 "hear and redress their complaints and grievances" Saunders, ed., *Colonial Records of North Carolina*, 2:177.

153 "one of the most significant events in southern colonial history" Quoted in Haan, "'Trade Do's Not Flourish as Formerly,'" 342.

153 "killing their hoggs[,] fowls" Ibid., 342.

153 "heard [the traders] brag to each other of debauching their [Indian] wives" Public Record Office, *Calendar of State Papers, Colonial Series* 28 (London, 1860–), 247–248.

154 "600 whites . . . and 400 Negros" and "to protect the Settlements" Quoted in Wood, *Black Majority*, 128.

155 The connection between West African slaves and rice is explored in Daniel C. Littlefield, *Rice and Slaves: Ethnicity and the Slave Trade in Colonial South Carolina* (Urbana: University of Illinois Press, 1991), 74–114.

155 "The people being unacquainted with the manner of cultivating rice" Glen, *Description of South Carolina*, 94.

155 "flat low swamps . . . they have a reservoir" Quoted in Littlefield, *Rice and Slaves*, 94–95.

155 "directed the Agents in Africa to send a few, full grown Men" Ibid., 109.

156 "The common idea is, that one Indian, or dextrous negroe" Quoted in Wood, *Black Majority*, 117.

156 "sent his Negro to guide us over the head of a large swamp" Lawson, *Voyage to Carolina*, 14.

156 "as soon as I arrived in the Parish" "Charles Boschi, Oct. 30, 1745," *South Carolina Historical and Genealogical Magazine*, October 1945, 185.

156 "The only Commodity of Consequence produced in *South Carolina* is *Rice*" Glen, *Description of South Carolina*, 95.

156 "rice is raised so as to buy more negroes" Quoted in Philip D. Morgan, *Slave Counterpoint: Black Culture in the Eighteenth-Century Chesapeak and Lowcountry* (Chapel Hill: University of North Carolina Press, 1998), 148.

156 A vivid description of rice cultivation is in Morgan, *Slave Counterpoint*, 147–159.

157 "up to [his] knees and waist in water" John Drayton, *A View of South Carolina, as Respects Her Natural and Civil Concerns* (Charleston: Young, 1802), 119, quoted in Morgan, *Slave Counterpoint*, 152.

157 "the severest work the negroes undergo" Quoted in Morgan, *Slave Counterpoint*, 153.

157 "105 feet long and will save a great deal of time" Bolzius, "Reliable Answer to Some Submitted Questions," 258.

158 "a field in a day or two will be completely drean'd" Quoted in Morgan, *Slave Counterpoint*, 181.

158 "a system of routine" Ulrich B. Phillips, *American Negro Slavery* (Baton Rouge: Louisiana State University Press, 1966), quoted in Morgan, *Slave Counterpoint*, 181.

158 "His master feels no right to call on him" Daniel Turner to his parents [microfilm], Daniel Turner Papers, Manuscripts Division, Library of Congress, Washington, D.C.

158 "several of the negroes did their work in less time than usual" *George Whitefield's Journals* (Carlisle, Pa.: Banner of Truth, 1989), 444.

158 "by one or two in the afternoon" Scotus Americanus [pseud.], *Informations Concerning the Province of North Carolina* (Glasgow: Knox, 1773), in *North Carolina Historical Review* 3 (1926): 616.

158 "are diligent in performing them, and have the rest of the day for themselves" Drayton, *View of South Carolina*, 145.

158 "The daily task does not vary to the arbitrary will and caprice of their owners" Edwin C. Holland, *A Refutation of the Calumnies Circulated Against the Southern and Western States, Respecting the Institution and Existence of Slavery Among Them* (Charleston, S.C.: Miller, 1822), 53, quoted in Morgan, *Slave Counterpoint*, 184.

158 "they are given as much land as they can handle" Bolzius, "Reliable Answer to Some Submitted Questions," 259.

159 "were at liberty to cultivate for themselves as much land as they choose" François-Alexandre-Frédéric de La Rochefoucauld-Liancourt, *Travels Through the United States of North America* (London: Philips, 1799), 1:599.

159 "slaves in their own private fields" Drayton, *View of South Carolina*, 145–147.

159 "there are many planters who, to free themselves from the trouble of feeding and clothing their slaves" Quoted in Frank J. Klingberg, *An Appraisal of the Negro in*

Colonial South Carolina: A Study in Americanization (Washington, D.C.: Associated Publishers, 1941), 7.

159 "The West African and Carolinian climates were similar enough" Wood, *Black Majority*, 120.

159 "Guiney Corne grows very well here" Quoted in South Carolina Historical Society, *Collections*, 5:333.

159 "Guinea Corne, which thrives well here" Lawson, *New Voyage to Carolina*, 83.

159 "propagated, and that chiefly by negroes" Mark Catesby, *The Natural History of Carolina, Florida and the Bahama Islands: Containing the Figures of Birds, Beasts, Fishes, Serpents, Insects, and Plants* (London: Author, 1771), 1:xviii.

160 "an annual herb with mallowlike flower" *Luigi Castiglioni's Viaggio*, 171–172.

160 "on Sundays . . . gather Snake-root" Brickell, *Natural History of North Carolina*, 275.

160 "two or three slaves will gather as many spontaneous Plants in one day" Quoted in Wood, *Black Majority*, 138.

160 "Negroes are the only people that seem to pay any attention" Janet Schaw, *Journal of a Lady of Quality: Being the Narrative of a Journey from Scotland to the West Indies, North Carolina, and Portugal, in the Years 1774 to 1776*, ed. Evangeline Walker Andrews and Charles McLean Andrews (New Haven, Conn.: Yale University Press, 1923), 176.

160 "very expert in hunting" and "an abundance of fish" Quoted in Morgan, *Slave Counterpoint*, 138.

160 "some Negros and others that can swim and dive well" Lawson, *New Voyage to Carolina*, 158.

160 "catch great quantity of fish" Thomas Cooper and David J. McCord, eds., *The Statutes at Large of South Carolina* (Columbia: South Carolina Historical Commission, 1837–1841), 3:270.

161–162 "keeps all Negroes busy" through "corn and beans" Bolzius, "Reliable Answer to Some Submitted Questions," 257–259.

162 "chief sustenance" Milligen-Johnston, *Account of the Situation, Air, Weather, and Diseases of South-Carolina*, 137.

162 "the negroes of Carolina give it a decided preference" David Ramsay, *The History of South-Carolina: From Its First Settlement in 1607, to the Year 1808* (Newberry, S.C.: Duffie, 1858), 123.

162 "one of the principle foods of the Negro" Quoted in Morgan, *Slave Counterpoint*, 135.

162 "their little piece[s] of land" Schaw, *Journal of a Lady of Quality*, 176.

162 "are very industrious and laborious in improving their plantations" Brickell, *Natural History of North Carolina*, 275.

162 "It is tilled by the negroes in April" *Luigi Castiglioni's Viaggio*, 171.

162 "never had any meat except at Christmas" Charles Ball, *Fifty Years in Chains; or, The Life of an American Slave* (1859; reprint, New York: Dover, 1970), quoted in Morgan, *Slave Counterpoint*, 137.

162 "if a master wishes" Bolzius, "Reliable Answer to Some Submitted Questions," 260.

162 "never give [slaves] meat" Reuben Gold Thwaites, ed., *Early Western Travels, 1748–1846* (New York: AMS Press, 1966), 304.

162 "They sell their crops" Bolzius, "Reliable Answer to Some Submitted Questions," 260.

163 "At noon we went on shore" Lawson, *New Voyage to Carolina*, 9.

163 For more on Pinckney's accomplishments, see David L. Coon, "Eliza Lucas Pinckney and the Reintroduction of Indigo Culture in South Carolina," *Journal of Southern History* 42, no. 1 (1976): 61–76.

163 "O! . . . I have planted a large fig orchard" *The Letterbook of Eliza Lucas Pinckney, 1739–1762*, ed. Elise Pinckney and Marvin R. Zahiser (Columbia: University of South Carolina Press, 1997), 34–35.

164 "The country abounds with wild fowl, Venison, and fish" Ibid., 7.

164 "The turkies are extremely fine" Ibid., 39.

164 "a kegg of sweetmeats" Ibid., 44.

164 "some peach trees and our Country potatoes" Ibid., 60.

164 "Negroe pepper" Ibid., 28.

164 "There is no such thing at this time as a wild Turkey to be got alive" Ibid., 119.

164 "I was very early fond of the vegetable world" Ibid., xxv.

165 "all the cooking of these people" (and the rest of the quotations in the paragraph) Woodmason, *Carolina Backcountry on the Eve of the Revolution*, 35.

165 "the ground will bear thistles only while your indolence permits it" Schaw, *Journal of a Lady of Quality*, 162.

165 "the concerns of this Country are so closely connected and interwoven with *Indian Affairs*" Glen, *Description of South Carolina*, 67.

165 "Carolina . . . looks more like a negro country" Quoted in Wood, *Black Majority*, 132.

5. Diversity

169 "Frugality is good, if liberality is joined with it" William Penn, *Some Fruits of Solitude in Reflection and Maxims* (1663; reprint, Bedford, Mass.: Applewood Books, 1996), 24.

169 "live to eat" (and the rest of Penn's aphorisms in the paragraph) Quoted in David Hackett Fischer, *Albion's Seed: Four British Folkways in America* (New York: Oxford University Press, 1989), 539–540.

169 "pampering the lower self" Ibid., 538.

169 "in excess of apparel and diet" James Naylor, *A Collection of Sundry Books, Epistles, and Papers* (London: Sowle, 1716), 46.

171 "provisions are somewhat hard to come by in some places" "Letter of Thomas Paschall," in Albert Cook Myers, ed., *Narratives of Early Pennsylvania, West New Jersey, and Delaware, 1630–1707* (New York: Scribner, 1912), 251.

171 "Houses over their heads and Garden plots" (and the rest of the quotations in the paragraph) "A Further Account of the Province of Pennsylvania, By William Penn, 1685," in Myers, ed., *Narratives of Early Pennsylvania*, 263–265.

171 "the evil Reports that I do understand are given out" (and the rest of the quotations in the paragraph) "Letter of Doctor Nicolas More, 1686," in Myers, ed., *Narratives of Early Pennsylvania*, 284–286.

172 "I have never seen brighter and better corn" "Letter from James Claypole, Merchant," in Myers, ed., *Narratives of Early Pennsylvania*, 292.

172 "Things prosper very well" "Letter from Robert Turner," in Myers, ed., *Narratives of Early Pennsylvania*, 290.

172 "The Peach-Trees are much broken down with the weight of the Fruit" "Letter from the Governor's Steward," in Myers, ed., *Narratives of Early Pennsylvania*, 290.

172 "The cranberries [are] much like cherries for color and bigness" "The Present State of the Colony of West Jersey," in Myers, ed., *Narratives of Early Pennsylvania*, 191.

173 "In the country" John Watson, *Annals of Philadelphia* (Philadelphia: Carey and Hart, 1830), 1:179, quoted in Fischer, *Albion's Seed*, 542.

173 "We eat so moderately" "Edward Shippen to C. J. Edward Shippen," *Pennsylvania Magazine of History and Biography* 30 (1906): 85–90.

173 "Care was usually taken that there should be no waste" *The America of 1750: Peter Kalm's Travels in North America: The English Version of 1770*, ed. Adolph B. Benson (New York: Wilson-Erickson, 1937), 2:629.

174 "as if the fig tree shall not blossom" Frederick Barnes Tolles, Introduction to *The Journal of John Woolman and "A Plea for the Poor,"* comp. Frederick Barnes Tolles (1774; reprint, Secaucus, N.J.: Citadel Press, 1961), 42.

175 The relationship among the Native Americans, English, and French is explored in Richard White, *The Middle Ground: Indians, Empires, and Republics in the Great Lakes Region, 1650–1815* (Lincoln: University of Nebraska Press, 1983).

175 Iroquois foodways are discussed in Dean R. Snow, *The Iroquois* (Oxford: Blackwell, 1994), 66–71.

175 "boile in one kettle" E. B. O'Callaghan and Berthold Fernow, eds., *Documents Relative to the Colonial History of the State of New York*, vol. 4 (Albany: Weed, Parsons, 1853–1887), quoted in Daniel K. Richter, *The Ordeal of the Longhouse: The Peoples of the Iroquois League in the Era of European Colonization* (Chapel Hill: University of North Carolina Press, 1992), 19.

176 "severely straightened for want of provisions" Ibid.

176 "A whole village must be without corn" Gabriel Sagard, *The Long Journey to the Country of the Hurons*, ed. George M. Wrong (1632; reprint, Toronto: Champlain Society, 1939), quoted in Richter, *Ordeal of the Longhouse*, 21.

177 "the native had killed a great number of roe deer" Kalm, *America of 1750*, 2:591.

177 "The Indians do not raise as many pumpkins as they do squashes" (and the rest of the quotations in the paragraph) Ibid., 607.

177 "He treated us to bear meat" *The Notebook of a Colonial Clergyman, Condensed from the Journals of Henry Melchior Muhlenberg*, ed. and trans. Theodore G. Tappert and John W. Doberstein (1742; reprint, Minneapolis: Fortress Press, 1959), 34.

177 "right in the thick of the forest" Ibid.

177 "we were fed on *raccoons*" Ibid., 35.

177 "I have Venison of the Indians very cheap" "Letter of Thomas Paschall," 252.

178 "the Old Inhabitants supplied us with most of the Corn we wanted" Penn, "Further Account of the Province of Pennsylvania," 266.

178 "Game is always to be found" Arthur Butler Hulbert and William Nathanial Schwarze, eds., "David Zeisberger's History of North American Indians," *Ohio Archaeological and Historical Publications* 21 (1910): 22, quoted in James H. Merrell, *Into the American Woods: Negotiations on the Pennsylvania Frontier* (New York: Norton, 1999), 135.

178 "All . . . kinds of wild game are extremely plenty" Quoted in Reuben Gold Thwaites, ed., *Early Western Travels, 1748–1846* (New York: AMS Press, 1966), 130–131.

178 "The gooseberries being now ripened" John Bartram, *Observations on the Inhabitants, Climate, Soil, Rivers, Productions, Animals, and Other Matters Worthy of Notice* (London: Whiston and White, 1751), 64.

178 "If we had but one loaf of bread" *Minutes of the Provincial Council of Pennsylvania, from the Organization to the Termination of the Proprietary Government*, vol. 9 (Har-

risburg: Published by the State, 1851–1852), quoted in Merrell, *Into the American Woods*, 136.

178 "so punctually adhered to"   Bartram, *Observations*, 16.

178 "grown in the woods . . . did not have much taste"   Quoted in Merrell, *Into the American Woods*, 137.

178 "licked by the dogs in lieu of washing"   John Heckewelder, *History, Manners, and Customs of the Indian Nations, Who Once Inhabited Pennsylvania and the Neighboring States* (1876; reprint, New York: Arno Press, 1971), 196.

178 "could eat Indian fare"   William M. Beauchamp, ed., *Moravian Journals Relating to Central New York, 1745–1766* (Syracuse, N.Y.: Syracuse University Press, 1916), 71.

178 "Ind.n Corn Acquash"   Quoted in Merrell, *Into the American Woods*, 138.

179 "constant application of the mind"   Heckewelder, *History, Manners, and Customs of the Indian Nations*, 178, quoted in Merrell, *Into the American Woods*, 151.

179 "I cannot conceive the best white man to be equal to them in the woods"   *The Papers of Henry Bouquet*, ed. S. K. Stevens et al. (Harrisburg: Pennsylvania History Museum Commission, 1972–1994), 206, quoted in Merrell, *Into the American Woods*, 152.

179 "province *in its cultivated state* affords grain of all sorts"   Andrew Burnaby, *Travels Through the Middle Settlements in North America in the Years 1759 and 1760* (London: Payne, 1775), 77.

179 "It is kept by a little old man"   "The Itinerarium of Dr. Alexander Hamilton," in Wendy Martin, ed., *Colonial American Travel Narratives* (New York: Penguin, 1994), 181.

180 For overviews of immigration in the eighteenth century, see T. H. Breen and Timothy Hall, *Colonial America in an Atlantic World: A Story of Creative Interaction* (New York: Longman, 2004), 283–287, and John J. McCusker and Russell R. Menard, *The Economy of British America, 1607–1789* (Chapel Hill: University of North Carolina Press, 1985), 211–236.

180 On ethnicity and the power of economic incentive, see James T. Lemon, *The Best Poor Man's Country: A Geographical Study of Early Southeastern Pennsylvania* (Baltimore: Johns Hopkins University Press, 1972).

181 "There were Scots, English, Dutch"   "Itinerarium of Dr. Alexander Hamilton," 191.

182 "The people are a Collection of divers Nations"   Penn, "Further Account of the Province of Pennsylvania," 260.

182 "of different nations, different languages, and different religions"   Burnaby, *Travels Through the Middle Settlements*, 80.

182 "I dined upon what I never had eat in my life before"   "Itinerarium of Dr. Alexander Hamilton," 205–206.

183 "the Jews never cook any food for themselves on Saturday"   Kalm, *America of 1750*, 2:631.

184 "catch a large number of small eels"   Ibid., 707.

184 "who then came over . . . near bays and rivers"   Ibid., 710.

184 "prepared to-day an unusual salad"   Ibid., 609.

184 "They are careful not to load up the table with food" (and the rest of the quotations in the paragraph)   Ibid., 614–615.

185 "our good hostess treated us to a great rarity"   Muhlenberg, *Notebook of a Colonial Clergyman*, 145–146.

185 "ran away from his English master"   Ibid., 43.

185 "the way of living with respect to food is very poor" Quoted in Linda Grant Depauw, *Founding Mothers: Women in America in the Revolutionary Era* (Boston: Houghton Mifflin, 1975), 84.

185 "venison, moor game, the most delicious red and yellow bellied trout" Quoted in Evan Jones, *American Food: The Gastronomic Story* (New York: Dutton, 1981), 82.

186 "the essence of frugal cuisine" William Woys Weaver, *Pennsylvania Dutch Cooking* (New York: Abbeville Press, 1993), 47.

187 On the mobility of Germans in the eighteenth century, see Lemon, *Best Poor Man's Country*, 84.

187 "Market considerations were more critical than ethnicity" McCusker and Menard, *Economy of British America*, 201.

187 "neighbors may help one another" Quoted in Lemon, *Best Poor Man's Country*, 99.

188 The statistics on grain exports are from McCusker and Menard, *Economy of British America*, 199.

189 "good lands yield" Quoted in Lemon, *Best Poor Man's Country*, 157.

189 "Pleas were voiced to buy improved seed from other areas" Lemon, *Best Poor Man's Country*, 156.

190 For the register of wills, see ibid., 155.

190 "sufficient encouragement has not been given to raise it" Quoted in Lemon, *Best Poor Man's Country*, 156.

190 "a graine [that] produced more increase than any other Graine whatsoever" Kalm, *America of 1750*, 2:615.

190 "Scarce an house but has an apple, peach, and cherry orchard" Quoted in Lemon, *Best Poor Man's Country*, 158.

190 "in great plenty on every farm" *Pennsylvania Gazette*, May 24, 1750, 4.

191 "raises enough cattle to over stock the market" Johann David Shoepf, *Travels in the Confederation*, ed. and trans. Alfred J. Morrison (Philadelphia: Campbell, 1911), 1:213.

191 "not to neglect the timothy seed" Quoted in Lemon, *Best Poor Man's Country*, 160.

191 For an overview of labor choices in Pennsylvania and New York, see Jack P. Greene, *Pursuits of Happiness: The Social Development of Early Modern British Colonies and the Formation of American Culture* (Chapel Hill: University of North Carolina Press, 1987), 127–133.

194 On urbanization, see ibid., 135.

195 "The town is well furnish'd with convenient Mills" Penn, "Further Account of the Province of Pennsylvania," 262.

195 "we have no lack of food here" Muhlenberg, *Notebook of a Colonial Clergyman*, 12–13.

195 "there is no foreign trade carried on from this province" Burnaby, *Travels Through the Middle Settlements*, 72.

195 "The products which came from New Brunswick" Kalm, *America of 1750*, 2:619.

195 "The Swedes who then came over" (and the rest of the quotations in the paragraph) Ibid., 710–711.

196 "The best cider is said to be made in New Jersey and New York" Ibid., 616–617.

196 "few peas are planted in New Sweden" Ibid., 658–659.

196 "In New York several kinds of cheese were made" Ibid., 647.

196 "Farmers sow a considerable amount of buckwheat" Ibid., 634.

196 "some colonists in this vicinity [who] made a pleasant beverage of apples" Ibid., 642–643.

197 "But to give you to understand the full of our Condition" "Letter of Doctor Nicolas More," 285.

198 "When men take their pleasure" Tolles, Introduction to *Journal of John Wool-man*, 43.

198 "I found two strange gentlemen that had come from Jamaica," "Itinerarium of Dr. Alexander Hamilton," 210–211.

198 "A large quantity is gotten this way" Kalm, *America of 1750*, 2:707.

6. Consumption

201 "wooden benches were used" Quoted in Grady McWhiney, *Cracker Culture: Celtic Ways in the Old South* (Tuscaloosa: University of Alabama Press, 1988), 243.

201 "fetherbed & boulster & red rug" (and the rest of the quotations in the paragraph) George Francis Dow, ed., *The Probate Records of Essex County, Massachusetts* (Salem, Mass.: Essex Institute, 1911), 1:285, 287, 336, 138.

203 "sat down on the bed, for chairs and stools there were none" Quoted in Richard L. Bushman, *The Refinement of America: Persons, Houses, Cities* (New York: Vintage Books, 1992), 75.

203 "took up my dinner and laid it on a little table made on the [baby's] cradle head" David D. Hall, ed., *Witch Hunting in Seventeenth-Century New England: A Documentary History, 1638–1692* (Boston: Northeastern University Press, 1991), 40.

204 "I have not seen an oven in a cottage anywhere" *The America of 1750: Peter Kalm's Travels in North America: The English Version of 1770*, ed. Adolph B. Benson (New York: Wilson-Erickson, 1937), quoted in Frances Phipps, *Colonial Kitchens, Their Furnishings, and Their Gardens* (New York: Hawthorn Books, 1972), 23.

204 "a little Room parted from the kitchen" Perry Miller and Thomas Johnson, eds., *The Puritans* (New York: American Book, 1938), quoted in Phipps, *Colonial Kitchens*, 29.

204 "a Loanesome cottage" Kalm, *America of 1750*, 2:70.

205–206 Kitchen inventories are in Phipps, *Colonial Kitchens*, 87–89.

207 For more on home renovations involving kitchens, see J. Frederick Kelly, *Early Domestic Architecture of Connecticut* (New Haven, Conn.: Yale University Press, 1924); Molly Harrison, *The Kitchen in History* (New York: Scribner, 1972); and Phipps, *Colonial Kitchens*.

208 "large open fires . . . used in the days of our fathers" *The Papers of Benjamin Franklin, 1706–1790*, ed. Leonard W. Labaree et al. (New Haven, Conn.: Yale University Press, 1959–1997), 2:424, 425.

209 "commonly built in the English manner" Kalm, *America in 1750*, quoted in Phipps, *Colonial Kitchens*, 95.

209 "pickling my meat" *The Diary of Joshua Hempstead of New London, Connecticut* (1758; reprint, New London, Conn.: New London Historical Society, 1970), quoted in Phipps, *Colonial Kitchens*, 95.

209 "They set out their cabinets and bouffets with much China" "The Itinerarium of Dr. Alexander Hamilton," in Wendy Martin, ed., *Colonial American Travel Narratives* (New York: Penguin, 1994), 229.

209 "kettles, pans, and skillets" Quoted in Phipps, *Colonial Kitchens*, 87.

209 "plantation in Baltimore" (and the rest of the quotations in the paragraph) *Philadelphia Gazette*, February 3, 1746, December 16, 1746, and March 10, 1746; *Maryland Gazette*, November 15, 1742; *New York Journal*, March 18, 1748; *South Carolina Gazette*, August 22, 1735.

212 "do not think themselves aliens, or the less a-kin to those of Great Britain" *State of the British and French Colonies in North America* (London: Millar, 1755), quoted in

Jack P. Greene, *Imperatives, Behaviors, Identities: Essays in Early American Cultural History* (Charlottesville: University of Virginia Press, 1992), 302.

212 "consider themselves to be upon an equal footing"   Ibid.

212 "a single true New England man"   John Barnard, *The Throne Established by Righteousness* (Boston, 1734), quoted in Greene, *Imperatives, Behaviors, Identities*, 301.

212 "Great Britain itself in miniature"   Samuel Keimer, ed., *Caribbeana* (London: Osborn, 1741), ix.

212 "another Great Britain rising in America"   Jonathan Mayhew, *A Sermon Preach'd in the Audience of His Excellency William Shirley, Esq.* (Boston: Draper, 1754), 39.

212 "magnetick Force" through "The result was a strong disposition among the colonists"   Greene, *Imperatives, Behaviors, Identities*, 159.

213 "a licentious idle life"   Ludwig Lewisohn, Introduction to J. Hector St. John de Crèvecoeur, *Letters from an American Farmer*, ed. Ludwig Lewisohn (New York: Boni, 1925), 42–43.

213 "the latest goods imported from England"   T. H. Breen, "An Empire of Goods: The Anglicization of Colonial America, 1690–1776," *Journal of British Studies* 25, no. 4 (1986): 486.

213 "everywhere the pace of business picked up"   Ibid.

213 "pepper, lace, gloves, gunpowder"   Glenn Weaver, *Jonathan Trumball: Connecticut's Merchant Magistrate, 1710–1785* (Hartford: Connecticut Historical Society, 1956), 19.

213 "to build substantial brick store buildings"   Lois Green Carr and Lorena S. Walsh, "Changing Life Styles and Consumer Behavior in the Colonial Chesapeake" (paper presented at "The Conference on Britain and America in the Early Modern Era," Williamsburg, Va., September 5–7, 1985), quoted in Breen, "Empire of Goods," 486.

214 "At the lowest levels of wealth"   Lorena S. Walsh, "Urban Amenities and Rural Self-Sufficiency: Living Standards and Consumer Behavior in the Colonial Chesapeake, 1643–1777," *Journal of Economic History* 43, no. 1 (1983): 111.

214 "it is really possible to obtain all the things one can get in Europe"   Gottlieb Mittelberger, *Journey to Pennsylvania*, ed. and trans. Oscar Handlin and John Clive (Cambridge, Mass.: Harvard University Press, 1960), 37, 88–89, quoted in Breen, "Empire of Goods," 489.

214 "There are 25 stores within 18 miles around me"   Quoted in Carr and Walsh, "Changing Life Styles and Consumer Behavior in the Colonial Chesapeake," quoted in Breen, "Empire of Goods," 31.

215 "We want the British Manufactures"   J. Hall Pleasants, ed., *Archives of Maryland: Proceedings and Acts of the General Assembly of Maryland, 1764–1785* (Baltimore: Maryland State Archives, 1942), 210.

215 "the quick importations of fashion from the mother country is really astonishing"   William Eddis, *Letters from America*, ed. Aubrey C. Land (1792; reprint, Cambridge, Mass.: Belknap Press, 1969), 57–58.

215 "a vast demand is growing for British manufactures"   *Papers of Benjamin Franklin*, 4:259.

215 "could [only] have been used" and "material goods themselves contain implicit meanings and are therefore indicative of attitudes"   T. H. Breen, "'Baubles of Britain': The American and Consumer Revolutions of the Eighteenth Century," *Past and Present* 119 (1988): 75.

215 "submitted willingly to the government of the Crown"   Jack P. Greene, ed., *Colonies to Nation, 1763–1789: A Documentary History of the American Revolution* (New York: McGraw-Hill, 1975), 72.

216 The most thorough studies on material holdings in the Chesapeake Bay include Walsh, "Urban Amenities and Rural Self-Sufficiency," and James Horn, *Adapting to a New World: English Society in the Seventeenth-Century Chesapeake* (Chapel Hill: University of North Carolina Press, 1994), esp. 310–313; for New England, see Gloria L. Main and Jackson T. Main, "Economic Growth and the Standard of Living in Southern New England, 1640–1774," *Journal of Economic History* 48, no. 1 (1988): 24–46; for Kentucky, see Elizabeth A. Perkins, "The Consumer Frontier: Household Consumption in Early Kentucky," *Journal of American History* 78, no. 2 (1991): 486–510.

216 "few countries have ... exhibited so striking an instance of public and private prosperity" David Ramsay, *The History of South-Carolina: From Its First Settlement in 1607, to the Year 1808* (Newburry, S.C.: Duffie, 1858), 10.

217 "much in vogue, it being convenient for many purposes" Trade catalogue (TS573M58d), Downs Collection, Winterthur Library, quoted in Donald L. Fennimore, *Metalwork in Early America: Copper and Its Alloys* (Winterthur, Del.: Winterthur Museum, 1996), 77.

218 "pure and cleane" Thomas Webster, *Encyclopaedia of Domestic Economy* (New York: Harper, 1845), quoted in Fennimore, *Metalwork in Early America*, 90.

218 "to hold coales of fire" Ibid., 100.

218 "the last vessels from London and Liverpool" (and the rest of the quotations in the paragraph) *New York Journal*, June 4, 1767; *South Carolina Gazette*, January 11, 1742; *Maryland Gazette*, October 21, 1746, and August 30, 1747; *Pennsylvania Gazette*, August 11, 1743, and May 15, 1742.

219 "bill of fare for every month of the year" Mrs. Fisher, *The Prudent Housewife: or, Complete English Cook, for Town and Country* (London: Sabine, ca. 1750), 112.

219 "beef soup made of brisket of beef and the beef served up in the dish" (and the rest of the eating calendar) Ibid., 112–118.

220 "a crust of bread" (and the rest of the quotations in the paragraph) Sarah Harrison, *The House-Keeper's Pocket-Book; and Compleat Family Cook* (London: Ware, 1739), 28–29, 44–48, 74–93.

221 "the great secret of health" (and the rest of the quotations in the paragraph) Thomas Hayes, *Concise Observations on the Nature of Our Common Food* (London: Swords, 1790), 8–15.

222 "Soup, broth, or fish" (and the rest of the food presentation) Fisher, *Prudent Housewife*, 122–127.

223 "be assured she can do these [recipes]" Anne Battam, *A Collection of Scarce and Valuable Recipes* (London: Author, 1750), 2.

223 "First then to speak of sallats" (and the rest of the quotations in the paragraph) Gervase Markham, *Country Contentments, or The English Huswife* (London: I. B. for R. Iackson, 1623), 60–64.

223 "to consist of many things" (and the rest of the quotations in the paragraph) Ibid., 63–67.

224 "Take some lamb, rabbit, chicken, pigeon, some forc'd meat balls" Battam, *Collection of Scarce and Valuable Recipes*, 97.

224 "Take two small chickens, two squab pigeons, two sucking rabbits" *Family Magazine: Or Accomplished Housewife and Housekeepers Companion* (London, 1754), 51.

225 "Take twelve artichoke bottoms boil'd tender" Battam, *Collection of Scarce and Valuable Recipes*, 67.

225 "Take the bottoms of six or eight artichokes" *Family Magazine*, 51.

225 "draw it with parsley and roast" Ibid., 38.

225 "Bone a neck and breast of mutton" Battam, *Collection of Scarce and Valuable Recipes*, 48.

225 "blood of an hogge whilest it is still warme" Markham, *Country Contentments*, 70–71.

226 "If you will make pottage of the best and daintiest kind" Ibid., 73.

226 "To make the best ordinarie pottage" Ibid., 72.

227 "principall dish of boild meate which is esteemed in all of Spaine" Ibid., 74.

227 "Jamaican pepper corns" Battam, *Collection of Scarce and Valuable Recipes*, 14–15; see also 37, 151.

227 "to make English hams like those of Westphalia" *Family Magazine*, 41–42.

227 For an overview of cookbooks published first in London and later in the colonies, see Genevieve Yost, "*The Compleat Housewife or Accomplish'd Gentlewoman's Companion*: A Bibliographical Study," *William and Mary Quarterly*, 2nd ser., 18, no. 4 (1938): 419–435.

228 "the house keeping much better than the house" William Byrd, *The History of the Dividing Line Betwixt Virginia and North Carolina*, ed. William K. Boyd (1841; reprint, New York: Dover, 1967), 313.

228 "great many provisions and fruits" Ibid., 315.

228 "the Gentry sometimes rayse a few" through "a bare piece of Housewifery" Quoted in Cynthia A. Kierner, "Hospitality, Sociability, and Gender in the Southern Colonies," *Journal of Southern History* 62, no. 3 (1996): 466–468.

231 "strictly examine the gills" (and the rest of the quotations in the paragraph) Lucy Emerson, *The New England Cookery* (Montpelier, Vt.: Parks, 1808), 5.

231–232 "the large stall-fed ox beef is the best" through "have red legs" Ibid., 5, 7–8.

232 "pale legs" Richard Briggs, *The New Art of Cookery, According to the Present Practice* (Philadelphia: Spotswood, Campbell, and Johnson, 1792), 17.

232 "the most mealy and richest flavor'd" (and the rest of the quotations in the paragraph) Emerson, *New England Cookery*, 10–14.

233 "the large bell pear" (and the rest of the quotations in the paragraph) Ibid., 16–17.

233–235 "be very careful that your pots and covers are well tinned" through "put in a piece of butter as big as a walnut" Ibid., 23–28.

235 "brisk hot fire" (and the rest of the quotations in the paragraph) Ibid., 17–23.

236 "take one pound of veal" (and the rest of the quotations in the paragraph) Ibid., 19–20.

236 "and fry them in butter" (and the rest of the quotations in the paragraph) Ibid., 30–33.

7. Intoxication

241 "found much company" *The Diary of Samuel Sewall, 1674–1729*, ed. M. Halsey Thomas (New York: Farrar, Straus, and Giroux, 1973), 2:742–743. A version of this incident is recounted in David W. Conroy, *In Public Houses: Drink and the Revolution of Authority in Colonial Massachusetts* (Chapel Hill: University of North Carolina Press, 1995), 57.

242 "votaries of strong drink" Cotton Mather, *Sober Considerations* (Boston, 1708), 18.

242 "a pest to society" *Pennsylvania Gazette*, March 15, 1764, 3.

242 "Moral and Physical Thermometer" W. J. Rorabaugh, *The Alcoholic Republic: An American Tradition* (New York: Oxford University Press, 1979), 44.

242 "a general addiction to hard drinking" C. D. Arfwedson, *The United States and Canada* (London: Bentley, 1834), 1:145.

242 "the ruin of half the workmen in this Country" John Adams, *Adams's Works*, ed. Charles Francis Adams and John Quincy Adams (Boston: Little, Brown, 1856), 10:365.

242 "a nation of drunkards" Quoted in Rorabaugh, *Alcoholic Republic*, 5.

243 "the brutish sin of drunkenness" Increase Mather, *Wo to Drunkards: Two Sermons Testifying Against the Sin of Drunkenness* (Cambridge, Mass.: Johnson, 1673).

243 "If I take a settler after my coffee" Quoted in Marie Kimball, "Some Genial Old Drinking Customs," *William and Mary Quarterly*, 2nd ser., 2, no. 4 (1945): 354.

243 The statistics on drinking in the 1790s are from Rorabaugh, *Alcoholic Republic*, 7–9.

244 "good living where there is not good drinking" *Benjamin Franklin: Writings*, ed. J. A. Leo Lemay (New York: Library of America, 1987), 303.

244 "a Creature of God" Quoted in Rorabaugh, *Alcoholic Republic*, 30.

245 The many functions of taverns are elaborated in Conroy, *In Public Houses*, 47–49; Peter Thompson, *Rum Punch and Revolution: Taverngoing and Public Life in Eighteenth-Century Philadelphia* (Philadelphia: University of Pennsylvania Press, 1999), 21–51; and Mark Edward Lender and James Kirby Martin, *Drinking in America: A History* (New York: Free Press, 1982), 1–25.

245 "killed and impoverished Indians in colonial America" Peter C. Mancall, *Deadly Medicine: Indians and Alcohol in Early America* (Ithaca, N.Y.: Cornell University Press, 1995), xi.

246 "there remained neither taverne, beer house, nor place of relief" Quoted in John Smith, *The Travels of Capt. John Smith* (Glasgow: MacLehose, 1907), 91–92.

246 "there are about three hundred men there more or less" Quoted in Stanley Wade Baron, *Brewed in America: A History of Beer and Ale in the United States* (Boston: Little, Brown, 1962), 5.

246 "desiring a small can [container] of beer" William Bradford, *Of Plymouth Plantation, 1620–1647*, ed. Samuel Eliot Morison (New York: Knopf, 1970), 78.

246 "I dare not prefer it before a good beer" William Wood, *New England's Prospect*, ed. Alden T. Vaughan (1635; reprint, Amherst: University of Massachusetts Press, 1977), 16.

246 "good and wholesome beer and bread" *Journal of Richard Mather* (1635; reprint, Boston: Clampp, 1850), 30.

246 "things which were better for you to think of there than to want them here" Francis Higginson, *New England's Plantation* (1630; reprint, New York: Franklin, 1971), 7.

246 "few of the upper planters drinke any water" *Travels of Capt. John Smith*, 176–178.

247 "blood in a proper state" Richard Briggs, *The New Art of Cookery, According to the Present Practice* (Philadelphia: Spotswood, Campbell, and Johnson, 1792), 38.

247 "all the various branches of brewing" Ibid., 539.

250 "intend to keep your ale a great while" Hannah Glasse, *The Art of Cookery Made Plain and Easy* (Alexandria, Va.: Cottom and Stewart, 1805), 195–198.

250 "Wee made of the same in the Countrey some mault" Quoted in Philip Alexander Bruce, *Economic History of Virginia in the Seventeenth Century* (New York: Macmillan, 1896), 2:213.

250 "The fruit, seeds and all, was crushed" Quoted in Kimball, "Some Genial Old Drinking Customs," 349.

250 "If barley be wanting to make into malt" Quoted in Lender and Martin, *Drinking in America*, 20.

251 "Take a large Siffer [sifter] full of bran hops to your taste" Quoted in Baron, *Brewed in America*, 96.

251 "One ounce of senna tree" Ibid.

251 "The stalks, green as they are" *Virginia Gazette*, February 13, 1775, 2.

252 On the ordinary and its expansion, see James E. McWilliams, "Brewing Beer in Massachusetts Bay, 1640–1690," *New England Quarterly* 71, no. 4 (1998): 543–569.

253 For more on cider production, see Thomas Chapman, *The Cyder-maker's Instructor, Sweet-maker's Assistant, and Victualler's and Housekeeper's Director* (London: Steuart, 1762).

254 "two pounds of calcined oyster shells" (and the rest of the quotations in the paragraph) Briggs, *New Art of Cookery*, 11–14.

255 "wild plums and grapes" "Letter of Thomas Paschall," in Albert Cook Myers, ed., *Narratives of Early Pennsylvania, West New Jersey, and Delaware, 1630–1707* (New York: Scribner, 1912), 253.

255 On stills in inventories, see George Francis Dow, ed., *The Probate Records of Essex County, Massachusetts* (Salem, Mass.: Essex Institute, 1916), 1:71, 93, 105.

256 "license to draw liquors for a year" George Francis Dow, ed., *The Records and Files of the Quarterly Courts of Essex County, Massachusetts, 1635–1683* (Salem, Mass.: Essex Institute, 1911–1916), 4:9.

256 "to draw cider and liquors for six months" Ibid., 289.

256 "selling cider by small quantities contrary to law" Ibid., 213.

256 "to keep an ordinary and draw beer and cider" Ibid., 268.

256 "was licensed to sell strong waters out of doors" Ibid.

256 "for scurrilous speeches and tippling" (and the rest of the quotations in the paragraph) Ibid., 1:36.

257 "sell liquors . . . his own boats for a year" Ibid., 4:232.

257 "keep an ordinary . . . to draw liquors" Ibid., 1:424–425.

257 "William Vinsonne had been chosen by the town to keep the ordinary and to sell wine" Ibid.

257 "had his license to sell cider and liquors renewed" Ibid., 4:289.

257 "to punish all the vices which disturb the good order and repose of human society" Cotton Mather, *Optanda: Good Men Described* (Boston: Harris, 1692), 46.

258 "do daily and frequently draw and sell by retail wine" Quoted in Conroy, *In Public Houses*, 59.

258 "There is no place more overrun with wickedness" Quoted in Thompson, *Rum Punch and Revolution*, 23.

258 "as for ordinaries, we are of the opinion that there are too many in this government" Ibid., 23.

258 "all excess is ill: but drunkenness is of the worst Sort" William Penn, *Some Fruits of Solitude in Reflections and Maxims* (1663; reprint, Bedford, Mass.: Applewood Books, 1996), 27.

259 "pens for the sheep, and turkeys" Quoted in Elise Lathrop, *Early American Inns and Taverns* (New York: Tudor, 1926), 80.

259 "one hundred horses could be stabled in the barns" Ibid.

259 "has good Pasture and Provider for horses" *Maryland Gazette*, September 10, 1745.

259 "a large brick kitchen, and a new brick stable" *Pennsylvania Gazette*, October 4, 1745.

259 The reference to the Carolina tavern is from Daniel B. Thorp, "Taverns and Tavern Culture on the Southern Colonial Frontier: Rowan County, North Carolina, 1753–1776," *Journal of Southern History* 62, no. 4 (1996): 671–673.

259 On the licensing of taverns in Philadelphia, see Thompson, *Rum Punch and Revolution*, 26.

260 "permitted Diverse idle and ill disposed persons" Quoted in Thorp, "Taverns and Tavern Culture," 670.

260 "Is it not vile" Benjamin Wadsworth, *Vicious Courses, Procuring Poverty Describ'd and Condemn'd* (Boston: Allen, 1719), 16–17, quoted in Conroy, *In Public Houses*, 75.

261 "at night [there was] Carousing and Drinking" "Journal of a French Traveller in the Colonies, 1765, I," *American Historical Review* 26, no. 4 (1921): 743.

262 "kicking, scratching . . . biting . . . throttling" *The Journal and Letters of Philip Vickers Fithian: A Plantation Tutor of the Old Dominion, 1773–1774*, ed. Hunter Dickinson Farish (Charlottesville: University of Virginia Press, 1957), 183.

262 "aleselling kept poor men from coming upon the parish" Peter Clark, *The English Alehouse: A Social History, 1200–1830* (New York: Longman, 1983), quoted in Conroy, *In Public Houses*, 101.

262 "follow[ing] his other calling" Quoted in Conroy, *In Public Houses*, 103.

262 "an act of charity" Ibid., 106.

262 "It may be a man has met with losses" Benjamin Wadsworth, *An Essay to Do Good* (1716; reprint, Gainesville, Fla.: Scholars' Facsimiles and Reprints, 1967), 21.

263 "4 rooms on a floor" *Pennsylvania Gazette*, April 7, 1746.

263 The reference to sanger is in Thorp, "Taverns and Tavern Culture," 686.

264 The statistics on distilleries are from John J. McCusker and Russell R. Menard, *The Economy of British America, 1607–1789* (Chapel Hill: University of North Carolina Press, 1985), 290–291; see also John J. McCusker, "The Rum Trade and the Balance of Payments of the Thirteen Continental Colonies, 1650–1775" (Ph.D. diss., University of Pittsburgh, 1970), 431–477.

265–266 The trade statistics for rum, molasses, and fish are from McCusker and Menard, *Economy of British America*, 108, 160; those for intraregional trade, from James F. Shepherd and Samuel H. Williamson, "The Coastal Trade of the British North American Colonies, 1768–1772," *Journal of Economic History* 32, no. 4 (1972): 788–809.

265 "William Govane, at his house near Annapolis" *Maryland Gazette*, June 18, 1745.

265 "Barbados, Antigua, and New England rum" *South Carolina Gazette*, September 2, 1743.

267 "the sloop arrived this evening and is now unloading" *The Papers of Henry Laurens*, ed. Philip M. Hamer and George C. Rogers (Columbia: University of South Carolina Press, 1972), 3:150.

267 "Trade among the continental colonies" Arthur Jenson, *The Maritime Commerce of Colonial Philadelphia* (Madison: University of Wisconsin Press, 1963), 3.

267 "the loss of their Crops in New York" (and the rest of the quotations in the paragraph) *Papers of Henry Laurens*, 3:193.

268 "CHOICE Minisink FLOUR" Ibid., 54.

268 "IMPORTED *in the sloop* Dispatch" Ibid., 151.

268 Shipping schedules are based on scores of customs reports printed in almost every issue of the *Pennsylvania Gazette* in the 1740s and 1750s.

269 The statistics on intraregional trade are from Shepherd and Williamson, "Coastal Trade of the British North American Colonies," 788–790. The authors note that "there are some limitations imposed by the data."

270 "The vastness of its extent" Quoted in Jack P. Greene, *The Intellectual Construction of America: Exceptionalism and Identity from 1492 to 1800* (Chapel Hill: University of North Carolina Press, 1993), 134.

271 "continue sober during the Treaty" (and the rest of the quotations in the paragraph) *The Autobiography of Benjamin Franklin*, ed. Leonard W. Labaree et al. (New Haven, Conn.: Yale University Press, 2003), 198–199.

272 "Can it be expected that any law" Quoted in Mancall, *Deadly Medicine*, 27.

272 "It is often bad enough with white people when they are [drunk]" Ibid.

272 "Sometimes you may with Brandy or Strong liquor" *The Discoveries of John Lederer*, ed. William P. Cumming (Charlottesville: University of Virginia Press, 1958), 42.

272 "Sylvester Garland [a trader] had brought to the settlement of Indians of their nation several Anchors of Rum" *Pennsylvania Colonial Records, 1600s–1800s* [CD-ROM] (Novato, Calif.: Learning Company, 2000), 2:33.

272 "is by this opportunity to Deale with them" Quoted in Mancall, *Deadly Medicine*, 51.

273 "Indians drank at least in part" Ibid., 8.

273 "From the 16th to the 26th we co[u]ld do nothing" Ibid., 87.

273 "In a few days this festival exhibited one of the most ludicrous bacchanalian scenes" *Travels of William Bartram*, ed. Mark Van Doren (1928; reprint, New York: Dover, 1955), 214–215.

273 "in full view and to the great horror of all" Nicholas Denys, *The Description and Natural History of the Coasts of North America*, trans. William F. Ganong (1673; reprint, Toronto: Champlain Society, 1910), 448–450.

274 "young men . . . drunk and Mad" Quoted in Mancall, *Deadly Medicine*, 89.

274 "A husband will kill his wife" Ibid., 96.

274 "there are some that do at times hire some of our Squaws to go to Bed with them & give them rum for it" *Journals of Charles Beatty, 1762–1769*, ed. Guy S. Klett (University Park: Pennsylvania State University Press, 1962), 67.

274 "The poor Indians . . . when Drunk are easily cheated" Edmond Atkin, *The Appalachian Indian Frontier: The Edmond Atkin Report and Plan of 1755*, ed. Wilbur R. Jacobs (Lincoln: University of Nebraska Press, 1967), 35–36.

274 "nothing but Rum Drinking and Women Crying" Quoted in Richard White, *The Roots of Dependency: Subsistence, Environment, and Social Change Among the Choctaws, Pawnees, and Navajos* (Lincoln: University of Nebraska Press, 1983), 85–86.

274 "the power of God" and "drunken wretches" Quoted in Mancall, *Deadly Medicine*, 111.

275 "My kindred Indians, pray attend and hear" Ibid, 112.

8. Revolution

279 "That the animals common both to the old and new world" Thomas Jefferson, *Notes on the State of Virginia*, ed. William Peden (Chapel Hill: University of North Carolina Press, 1955), 47.

279 "tremendous struggles of elemental forces" Quoted in Ralph N. Miller, "American Nationalism as a Theory of Nature," *William and Mary Quarterly*, 2nd ser., 12, no. 1 (1955): 76.

279 "replenish the air with heavy and noxious vapors" Adam Ferguson, *An Essay on the History of Civil Society* (1767; Basel: Tourneisen, 1789), 2:177–178, quoted in Miller, "American Nationalism," 79.

280 "*has been . . . and is at present a very barren country*" Abbé Francisco Clavigero, *History of Mexico*, trans. Charles Cullen (London: G. G. J. and Robinson, 1787), 146–147.

280 "every thing carries the vestiges of a malady" Abbé Guillaume-Thomas-François de Raynal, *A Philosophical and Political History of the Settlements and Trade of the Europeans in the East and West Indies* (1779; Edinburgh: Doig, 1792), 5:243.

280 "extensive marshes, great lakes, aged, decayed, and crowded forests" Ferguson, *Essay on the History of Civil Society*, 2:177–178.

280 "coldness and insensibility" William Robertson, *History of America* (1777; London: Strayhan, 1803), 2:233–234.

280 "Vegetables are mediately or immediately the food of every animal" Jefferson, *Notes on the State of Virginia,* 48.

280 "a race of animals . . . has been increased in its dimensions" Ibid.

281 "It may be affirmed with truth" (and the rest of the quotations in the paragraph) Ibid., 56.

281 "best informed of any Naturalist who has ever written" Ibid., 55.

282 "remain in their aboriginal state" Ibid., 54.

282 "But who were these travellers?" and "one sentence of [Buffon's] book" Ibid.

284 "a truly remarkable performance" John J. McCusker and Russell R. Menard, *The Economy of British America, 1607–1789* (Chapel Hill: University of North Carolina Press, 1991), 58.

284–285 For the per capita–income figures, see ibid., 57.

285 "That the colonists were able to produce significant food surpluses" David G. Klingaman, "Food Surpluses and Deficits in the American Colonies, 1768–1772," *Journal of Economic History* 31, no. 3 (1971): 554.

285 "2 hundredweight of flour, 11 bushels of corn" Ibid., 559.

286 On the slight decline in self-sufficiency in New England, see ibid., 563.

286–288 For an overview of the acts passed by Parliament that sparked colonial discontent, see Pauline Maier, *From Resistance to Revolution: Colonial Radicals and the Development of American Opposition to Britain, 1765–1776* (New York: Knopf, 1972).

288 "the ruin of our liberties" (and the rest of the quotations in the paragraph) Quoted in Bernard Bailyn, *The Ideological Origins of the American Revolution* (Cambridge, Mass.: Harvard University Press, 1967), 111–125.

289 "sparked the production of meanings" T. H. Breen, "The Meaning of Things: Interpreting the Consumer Economy in the Eighteenth Century," in John Brewer and Roy Porter, eds., *Consumption and the World of Goods* (New York: Routledge, 1992), 250.

290 "every spot of the Old World was overrun with oppression" Joseph Galloway, *A Candid Examination of the Mutual Claims of Great-Britain and the Colonies: With a Plan of Accommodation, on Constitutional Principles* (New York: Rivington, 1775), 31.

290 "We Look upon [the Tea Act] as unconstitutional *and a Burden*" Quoted in Robert A. Gross, *The Minutemen and Their World* (New York: Hill and Wang, 1976), 46–47.

290 "a fair inheritance, purchased by a waste of blood and treasure" "Proceedings of the Middlesex County Convention," in *The Journals of Each Provincial Congress of Massachusetts in 1774 and 1775, the Committee of Safety* (Boston: Dutton and Wentworth, 1838), 609–614.

290 "burthensome tax" Henry Steele Commager, ed., *Documents of American History* (New York: Appleton-Century-Crofts, 1968), 1:56–57.

290 "violent infringement of our rights" Samuel Eliot Morison, ed., *Sources and Documents Illustrating the American Revolution, 1764–1788* (New York: Oxford University Press, 1929), 95.

290 "unconstitutional *and* entirely destructive" Ibid., 92.

291 "Rioters and their allies claimed" Barbara Clark Smith, "Food Rioters and the American Revolution," *William and Mary Quarterly*, 3rd ser., 51, no. 1 (1994): 6.

291 "uneasiness with those that trade in rum, molasses, and sugar" Quoted in Smith, "Food Rioters," 6.

291 "detrimental to the Liberties of America" Ibid., 7–8.

292 "to make a prey of the friends of the United States" Ibid.

292 All these cases are covered in ibid., 7–30.

292 "The very honey of our bees" J. Hector St. John de Crèvecoeur, *Letters from an American Farmer*, ed. Ludwig Lewisohn (New York: Boni, 1925), 27.

293 "No individual has a Right" (and the rest of the quotations in the paragraph) Quoted in Harry L. Watson, "'The Common Rights of Mankind': Subsistence, Shad, and Commerce in the Early Republican South," *Journal of American History* 83, no. 1 (1996): 13.

293 "the Benefits and Emoluments arising from a Fishery" Ibid.

293 "the keeping open of the River Savannah" Lucius Q. C. Lamar, comp., *Compilation of the Laws of the State of Georgia* (Augusta: Hannon, 1821), 80–81.

293 "an Act to . . . prevent the stoppage of the passage of Fish" Walter Clark and William Laurence Saunders, eds., *Colonial and State Records of North Carolina* (Raleigh: Hale, 1886–1907), 10:87–88.

293 "by fish dams, mill dams, hedges, and other obstructions" Thomas Cooper and David J. McCord, eds., *The Statutes at Large of South Carolina* (Columbia: South Carolina Historical Commission, 1837–1841), quoted in Watson, "'Common Rights of Mankind,'" 24.

294 "many poor familys who depended on said fishing" Clark and Saunders, eds., *Colonial and State Records of North Carolina*, quoted in Watson, "'Common Rights of Mankind,'" 24.

294 "which had been in store since the former war" (and the rest of the quotations in the paragraph) Quoted in Stephen Brumwell, *Redcoats: The British Soldier and War in the Americas, 1755–1763* (Cambridge: Cambridge University Press, 2002), 151–152.

294–295 For the food allowance figures, see ibid., 150–152.

295 "Hence every Government, concerned in the present Enterprise" (and the rest of the quotations in the paragraph) Quoted in Harry M. Ward, *"Unite or Die": Intercolony Relations, 1690–1763* (Port Washington, N.Y.: Kennikat Press, 1971), 77–78.

296 "sheep Fowl & Roots" Quoted in Brumwell, *Redcoats*, 151–152.

296 "very mad" Quoted in Fred Anderson, *A People's Army: Massachusetts Soldiers and Society in the Seven Years' War* (Chapel Hill: University of North Carolina Press, 1984), 87.

296 "the lure of war profiteering was greater than patriotism" Ward, *"Unite or Die,"* 77.

296 For the political and social consequences of the Seven Years' War, see Jack P. Greene, *Understanding the American Revolution: Issues and Actors* (Charlottesville: University of Virginia Press, 1995), 4–5.

297 "a set of *idle drones*" James Wilson, *Considerations on the Nature and the Extent of the Legislative Authority of the British Parliament* (Philadelphia: Bradford, 1774), 6–7, quoted (with the rest of the quotations in the paragraph) in Bailyn, *Ideological Origins of the American Revolution*, 103–104.

298 "Important as all of these clusters of ideas were" Bailyn, *Ideological Origins of the American Revolution*, 33.

299 "Cassandras of the age" Ibid., 47.

299 "public corruptions and abuses have grown upon us" Quoted in Bailyn, *Ideological Origins of the American Revolution*, 33.

300 "any industrious man . . . with his own labor" John Norris, *Profitable Advice for Rich and Poor* (London: Howe, 1712), 109.

300 "scarcely procure a living" Daniel Denton, *A Brief Description of New York: Formerly Called New Netherlands* (London: Hancock and Bradley, 1670), 18.

300 "was devoured by the colonists" Bailyn, *Ideological Origins of the American Revolution*, 43.

301 "What then is this American, this new man?" St. John de Crèvecoeur, *Letters from an American Farmer*, 48.

301 "think better of the European world than it deserves" *The Complete Writings of Thomas Paine*, ed. Philip Foner (New York: Citadel Press, 1945), 1:21.

301 "it is perhaps always true that an old civilized nation" Noah Webster, *An American Selection of Lessons in Reading and Speaking* (Philadelphia: Hogan, 1787), 214–216.

302 "all things have their season" Quoted in Joseph Ellis, *After the Revolution: Profiles of Early American Culture* (New York: Norton, 1979), 11.

302 "to ransack their past for cultural accomplishments" Ellis, *After the Revolution*, 11.

302 "was born, grew up, became old, then died" Noah Webster, *A Collection of Essays and Fugitive Writings* (Boston: Thomas and Andrews, 1790), 2–4.

303 "The decline of virtue and the downfall of nature" James Murray, *Sermons to Asses* (Philadelphia: Dunlap, 1769), 68.

303 "a general profligacy and corruption" *The Works of the Reverend John Witherspoon* (Philadelphia: Woodward, 1802), 3:41.

303 For an overview of the conjectural theory of history, see Jack P. Greene, *The Intellectual Construction of America: Exceptionalism and Identity from 1492 to 1800* (Chapel Hill: University of North Carolina Press, 1993), 117.

303 "savage and barbarous nations" Adam Smith, *The Wealth of Nations*, ed. David S. Landes (New York: Norton, 1998), 565.

303 "Landlords, great Noblemen and Gentlemen" *The Papers of Benjamin Franklin*, ed. Leonard W. Labaree et al. (New Haven, Conn.: Yale University Press, 1959–1997), 19:7.

303 "Burn down your cities and leave your farms" William Jennings Bryan, "Cross of Gold Speech" (available at: www.tntech.edu/history/crosgold.html).

304 "As long as the Romans were virtuous, they enjoyed freedom and liberty" Murray, *Sermons to Asses*, 52.

304 "Plenty begat Ease, and Ease begat Luxury" William Smith, *Discourses on Several Public Occasions During the War in America* (London: Millar, 1759), 76.

304 "power to begin the world over again" *Complete Writings of Thomas Paine*, 1:19.

305 "that thousands upon thousands of people did succeed" Greene, *Intellectual Construction of America*, 89.

305 "a Garden of the Wilderness" *Papers of Benjamin Franklin*, 2:303.

305 "flourished . . . beyond all example in Europe" Thomas Whately, *Considerations on the Trade and Finance of the Kingdom* (London: Millar, 1762), 81.

305 "maintained themselves the first year, like the Indians" Harry J. Carman, ed., *American Husbandry* (New York: Kennikat Press, 1939), 90.

305 "made such Farms as afforded them Necessaries" Roscommon [pseud.], *To the Author of Those Intelligencers Printed at Dublin* (New York: Zenger, 1733), 5, quoted in Greene, *Intellectual Construction of America*, 102.

305 "the idle may be employed" St. John de Crèvecoeur, *Letters from an American Farmer*, 42, 52, 57, quoted in Greene, *Intellectual Construction of America*, 102.

306 "a period that every benevolent man" Webster, *American Selection of Lessons*, 218–219.

306 "In the United States everything that has been done hitherto" Quoted in Ellis, *After the Revolution*, 206.

306 "*Commerce . . .* is generally *Cheating*" *Papers of Benjamin Franklin*, 16:109.

306 "feeble beginnings and barbarous rudiments" (and the rest of the quotations in the paragraph) St. John de Crèvecoeur, *Letters from an American Farmer*, 35, 48–49, 52.

306 "Those who labour in the earth are the chosen people of God" (and the rest of the quotations in the paragraph) Jefferson, *Notes on the State of Virginia*, 164–165.

307 "he acquires a fondness for European luxury" Ibid., 15.

307 "Every year I kill from 1500 to 2000 weight of pork" St. John de Crèvecoeur, *Letters from an American Farmer*, 25.

307 "an independent and hardy YEOMANRY" Richard Price, *Observations on the Importance of the American Revolution* (London: Cassell, 1785), 57–58.

307 "In great measure, the cause of America is the cause of all mankind" *Complete Writings of Thomas Paine*, 1:92.

307 "cause of the whole human race" Abbé Guillaume-Thomas-François de Raynal, *The Revolution in America* (London: Davis, 1781), 172–173.

308 "In the beginning" John Locke, *The Second Treatise of Government*, ed. Thomas Preston Peardon (New York: Liberal Arts Press, 1952), 29.

309 "a frugal plain repast" William Dunlap, *The Father, or American Shandyism* (New York: Hodge, Allen, and Cambell, 1789), 3–4.

309 "abjure his native victuals" Quoted in Waverly Root and Richard de Rochemont, *Eating in America: A History* (New York: Ecco Press, 1976), 112.

309 "by no means the only demonstration in American history" Ibid.

311–314 "several new receipts adapted" through "put [the meat] in a saucepan full of water" Hannah Glasse, *The Art of Cookery Made Plain and Easy* (Alexandria, Va.: Cottom and Stewart, 1805), 137–144.

314 "Almost any household can brew" Samuel Deane, *The New England Farmer* (Worcester, Mass.: Thomas, 1790), 21.

314 "It is to be hoped, that the Gentlemen of the Town will endeavour" Quoted in Stanley Wade Baron, *Brewed in America: A History of Beer and Ale in the United States* (Boston: Little, Brown, 1962), 89.

314 "the severe treatment we have lately received from our Mother Country" *Virginia Gazette*, November 25, 1766.

315 "the quality is vastly inferior" "Letters of Phineas Bond, British Consul at Philadelphia, to the Foreign Office of Great Britain, 1787–1794," in American Historical Association, *Annual Report for the Years 1896–1897* (Washington, D.C.: Government Printing Office), 653.

315 "TWELVE MILLION OF DOLLARS have been expended" Quoted in Baron, *Brewed in America*, 118.

315 "Farmers who choose to raise Barley" Ibid., 85.

316 "I have no receipt for brewing" Ibid.

316 "Born with the Republic" Quoted in Mark Edward Lender and James Kirby Martin, *Drinking in America: A History* (New York: Free Press, 1982), 32–34.

316 "more like a harvest home supper" Quoted in Root and Rochemont, *Eating in America*, 118.

317 "are never out of season" Ibid., 111–112.

318 "They swallow almost without chewing" Constantin-François Chasseboeuf, *View of the Soil and Climate of the United States of America* (London: Johnson, 1804), 55.

319 "A man who has corn may have everything" Quoted in Root and Rochemont, *Eating in America*, 121.

319 "Broadway being three miles long" Frederick Marryat, *A Diary in America* (London: Longmans, 1839), 16.

319 "Indian corn was the national crop" Quoted in Root and Rochemont, *Eating in America*, 122.

319 "your fresh meat, that's too fancy" Thomas Ashe, *Travels in America in 1806* (London: Phillips, 1809), 7.

319 "Nothing should be thrown away" Lydia Maria Child, *The American Frugal Housewife* (New York: Wood, 1838), 3.

Abercrombie, John. *Every Man His Own Gardener: Being a New and Much More Complete Gardener's Kalender than Any Other Hitherto Published*. London: Rivington, 1782.

Adams, John. *Adams's Works*. Edited by Charles Francis Adams and John Quincy Adams. 10 vols. Boston: Little, Brown, 1850–1856.

———. *Diary and Autobiography of John Adams*. Edited by L. H. Butterfield et al. 4 vols. Cambridge, Mass.: Harvard University Press, 1961.

Adams, Samuel. *The Writings of Samuel Adams*. Edited by Harry Alonzo Cushing. 4 vols. New York: Putnam, 1904–1908.

Allen, David Grayson. *In English Ways: The Movement of Societies and the Transferal of English Local Law and Custom to Massachusetts Bay in the Seventeenth Century*. Chapel Hill: University of North Carolina Press, 1981.

———. "The Matrix of Motivation." *England Quarterly* 59, no. 3 (1986): 408–418.

Allison, P. A. "Historical Inferences to Be Drawn from the Effect of Human Settlement on the Vegetation of Africa." *Journal of African History* 3, no. 2 (1962): 241–249.

Anderson, Fred. *A People's Army: Massachusetts Soldiers and Society in the Seven Years' War*. Chapel Hill: University of North Carolina Press, 1984.

Anderson, Robert Charles. "A Note on the Changing Pace of the Great Migration." *New England Quarterly* 59, no. 3 (1986): 406–407.

Anderson, Terry Lee. "Economic Growth in Colonial New England: 'Statistical Renaissance.'" *Journal of Economic History* 39, no. 1 (1979): 243–257.

———. *The Economic Growth of Seventeenth Century New England: A Measurement of Regional Income*. New York: Arno Press, 1975.

Anderson, Virginia DeJohn. "King Philip's Herds: Indians, Colonists, and the Problem of Livestock in Early New England." *William and Mary Quarterly*, 3rd ser., 51, no. 4 (1994): 601–624.

Andrews, Charles M. "Colonial Commerce." *American Historical Review* 20, no. 1 (1914): 43–63.

Andrews, Jean. "The Diffusion of Mesoamerican Food Complex to Southeastern Europe." *Geographical Review* 83, no. 2 (1993): 194–204.

Appleby, Joyce Oldham. "Commercial Farming and the 'Agrarian Myth' in the Early Republic." *Journal of American History* 68, no. 4 (1982): 833–849.

———. *Economic Thought and Ideology in Seventeenth-Century England*. Princeton, N.J.: Princeton University Press, 1978.

Arfwedson, C. D. *The United States and Canada*. Vol. 1. London: Bentley, 1834.

Ashe, Thomas. *Travels in America in 1806*. London: Phillips, 1809.

Atkin, Edmond. *The Appalachian Indian Frontier: The Edmond Atkin Report and Plan of 1755*. Edited by Wilbur R. Jacobs. Lincoln: University of Nebraska Press, 1967.

Austen, Ralph A., and Daniel Headrick. "The Role of Technology in the African Past." *African Studies Review* 26, no. 3 (1983): 163–184.

Bailey, L. H. *The Standard Cyclopedia of Horticulture.* New York: Macmillan, 1950.

Bailyn, Bernard. *The Ideological Origins of the American Revolution.* Cambridge, Mass.: Harvard University Press, 1967.

———. *The Origins of American Politics.* New York: Vintage Books, 1967.

———. *The Peopling of British North America: An Introduction.* New York: Vintage Books, 1986.

Baker, William Avery. *Colonial Vessels: Some Seventeenth-Century Sailing Craft.* Barre, Mass.: Barre Publishing, 1962.

Ball, Charles. *Fifty Years in Chains; or, The Life of an American Slave.* 1859. Reprint, New York: Dover, 1970.

Barbour, Philip L., Jean Martin, and Bryan Milner, eds. *The Jamestown Voyages Under the First Charter, 1601–1609: Documents Relating to the Foundation of Jamestown and the History of the Jamestown Colony.* Cambridge: Cambridge University Press, 2001.

Barickman, B. J. "'A Bit of Land, Which They Call Roca': Slave Provision Grounds in the Bahian Reconcavo, 1780–1860." *Hispanic American Historical Review* 74, no. 4 (1994): 649–687.

Barnard, John. *The Throne Established by Righteousness.* Boston, 1734.

Baron, Stanley Wade. *Brewed in America: A History of Beer and Ale in the United States.* Boston: Little, Brown, 1962.

Bartram, John. *Observations on the Inhabitants, Climate, Soil, Rivers, Productions, Animals, and Other Matters Worthy of Notice.* London: Whiston and White, 1751.

Bartram, William. *Travels of William Bartram.* Edited by Mark Van Doren. 1928. Reprint, New York: Dover, 1955.

Battam, Anne. *A Collection of Scarce and Valuable Recipes.* London: Author, 1750.

Bayley, F. W. N. *Four Years' Residence in the West Indies.* London: Kidd, 1830.

Bear, James A., Jr., ed. *Jefferson at Monticello: Recollections of a Monticello Slave and of a Monticello Overseer.* Charlottesville: University of Virginia Press, 1967.

Beatty, Charles. *Journals of Charles Beatty, 1762–1769.* Edited by Guy S. Klett. University Park: Pennsylvania State University Press, 1962.

Beauchamp, William M., ed. *Moravian Journals Relating to Central New York, 1745–1766.* Syracuse, N.Y.: Syracuse University Press, 1916.

Beaumont, A. B. "Geography of New England Soils." *Economic Geography* 18, no. 2 (1942): 203–208.

Beckford, William. *Descriptive Account of the Island of Jamaica.* London: Egerton, 1790.

Beckles, Hilary McD. *Black Rebellion in Barbados: The Struggle Against Slavery, 1727–1838.* Bridgetown, Barbados: Carib Research, 1984.

Bender, Barbara. "Emergent Tribal Formations in the American Midcontinent." *American Antiquity* 50, no. 1 (1985): 52–62.

Bennett, J. Harry, Jr. "The Problem of Slave Labor Supply at the Codrington Plantations." *Journal of Negro History* 36, no. 4 (1951): 406–441.

Bennett, M. K. "The Food Economy of the New England Indians, 1605–75." *Journal of Political Economy* 63, no. 5 (1955): 369–397.

Berkeley, William. *A Discourse and View of Virginia.* 1663. Reprint, Norwalk, Conn: Smith, 1914.

Berleant-Schiller, Riva. "Free Labor and the Economy in Seventeenth-Century Montserrat." *William and Mary Quarterly,* 3rd ser., 46, no. 3 (1989): 539–564.

Berlin, Ira. "Time, Space, and the Evolution of Afro-American Society on British Mainland North America." *American Historical Review* 85, no. 1 (1980): 44–78.

Berlin, Ira, and Morgan Philip, eds. *The Slaves' Economy: Independent Production by Slaves in the Americas.* London: Cass, 1991.

Beverly, Robert. *The History and Present State of Virginia.* Edited by David Freeman Hawke. New York: Bobbs-Merrill, 1971.

Bidwell, Percy Wells. "The Agricultural Revolution in New England." *American Historical Review* 26, no. 4 (1921): 683–702.

Bidwell, Percy Wells, and John I. Falconer. *History of Agriculture in the Northern United States, 1620–1860.* Washington, D.C.: Carnegie Institution, 1925.

Billings, Warren M., ed. *The Old Dominion in the Seventeenth Century: A Documentary History of Virginia, 1607–1689.* Chapel Hill: University of North Carolina Press, 1975.

Bird, Rebecca L. Bliege, and Douglas W. Bird. "Delayed Reciprocity and Tolerated Theft: The Behavioral Ecology of Food-Sharing Strategies." *Current Anthropology* 38, no. 1 (1997): 49–78.

Bolzius, Johann Martin. "Reliable Answer to Some Submitted Questions Concerning the Land Carolina." Translated and edited by Klaus G. Loewald, Beverly Starika, and Paul S. Taylor. *William and Mary Quarterly*, 3rd ser., 14, no. 2 (1957): 223–261.

Bouquet, Henry. *The Papers of Henry Bouquet.* Edited by S. K. Stevens et al. Harrisburg: Pennsylvania History Museum Commission, 1972–1994.

Bowden, William Hammond. "The Commerce of Marblehead, 1665–1775." Essex Institute, *Historical Collections* 68 (1932): 117–146.

Bradford, William. *Of Plymouth Plantation, 1620–1647.* Edited by Samuel Eliot Morison. New York: Knopf, 1970.

Braund, Kathryn E. Holland. "The Creek Indians, Blacks, and Slavery." *Journal of Southern History* 57, no. 4 (1991): 601–636.

Breen, T. H. "'Baubles of Britain': The American and Consumer Revolutions of the Eighteenth Century." *Past and Present* 119 (1988): 73–104.

———. "An Empire of Goods: The Anglicization of Colonial America, 1690–1776." *Journal of British Studies* 25, no. 4 (1986): 467–499.

———. *Tobacco Culture: The Mentality of the Great Tidewater Planters on the Eve of the Revolution.* Princeton, N.J.: Princeton University Press, 1985.

Breen, T. H., and Stephen Foster. "Moving to the New World: The Character of Early Massachusetts Immigration." *William and Mary Quarterly*, 3rd ser., 30, no. 2 (1973): 189–222.

Brewer, John, and Roy Porter, eds. *Consumption and the World of Goods.* New York: Routledge, 1992.

Brickell, John. *The Natural History of North Carolina.* Dublin: Cambon, 1737.

Briggs, Richard. *The New Art of Cookery, According to the Present Practice.* Philadelphia: Spotswood, Campbell, and Johnson, 1792.

Brown, Alexander. *The Genesis of the United States.* Vol. 1. Boston: Houghton Mifflin, 1890.

Bruce, Philip Alexander. *Economic History of Virginia in the Seventeenth Century.* Vol. 2. New York: Macmillan, 1896.

Bruchey, Stuart Weems. *The Roots of American Economic Growth, 1670–1861: An Essay in Social Causation.* New York: Harper & Row, 1965.

Brumwell, Stephen. *Redcoats: The British Solider and War in the Americas, 1755–1763.* Cambridge: Cambridge University Press, 2002.

Budd, Thomas. *Good Order Established in Pennsylvania and New-Jersey in America*. London: Sowle, 1685.

Bullock, Helen. *The Williamsburg Art of Cookery*. Williamsburg, Va.: Colonial Williamsburg Foundation, 1958.

Burnaby, Andrew. *Travels Through the Middle Settlements in North America in the Years 1759 and 1760*. London: Payne, 1775.

Bushman, Richard, L. *From Puritan to Yankee: Character and the Social Order in Connecticut, 1690–1765*. New York: Norton, 1967.

———. *The Refinement of America: Persons, Houses, Cities*. New York: Vintage Books, 1992.

Byrd, William. *The Great American Gentleman: William Byrd of Westover in Virginia, His Secret Diary for the Years 1709–1712*. Edited by Louis B. Wright and Marion Tinling. New York: Capricorn Books, 1963.

———. *The History of the Dividing Line Betwixt Virginia and North Carolina*. Edited, with an introduction, by William K. Boyd. 1841. Reprint, New York: Dover, 1967.

———. *The Prose Works of William Byrd of Westover*. Edited by Louis B. Wright. Cambridge, Mass.: Harvard University Press, 1966.

Carney, Judith. "Rice Milling, Gender and Slave Labour in Colonial South Carolina." *Past and Present* 153 (1996): 108–134.

Carr, Lois Green, Russell R. Menard, and Lorena S. Walsh. *Robert Cole's World: Agriculture and Society in Early Maryland*. Chapel Hill: University of North Carolina Press, 1991.

———. "The Standard of Living in the Colonial Chesapeake." *William and Mary Quarterly*, 3rd ser., 45, no. 1 (1988): 135–159.

Carson, Jane. *Colonial Virginia Cookery: Procedures, Equipment, and Ingredients in Colonial Cooking*. Williamsburg, Va.: Colonial Williamsburg Foundation, 1985.

Carter, Landon. *The Diary of Colonel Landon Carter of Sabine Hall, 1752–1778*. Edited by Jack P. Greene. Charlottesville: University of Virginia Press, 1965.

Carter, Susannah. *The Frugal Housewife, or, Complete Woman Cook*. New York: Waite, 1803.

Cartwright, Peter. *Autobiography of Peter Cartwright*. Edited by Charles Wallis. 1856. Reprint, New York: Abingdon Press, 1956.

Castiglioni, Luigi. *Luigi Castiglioni's Viaggio: Travels in the United States of North America, 1785–1787*. Translated and edited by Antonio Pace. Syracuse, N.Y.: Syracuse University Press, 1983.

Catesby, Mark. *The Natural History of Carolina, Florida, and Bahama Islands*. Vol. 1. London: Jnnys and Manat, 1731.

———. *The Natural History of Carolina, Florida and the Bahama Islands: Containing the Figures of Birds, Beasts, Fishes, Serpents, Insects, and Plants*. 2 vols. London: Author, 1771.

Chamberlain, Alexander F. "Algonkian Words in American English: A Study in the Contact of White Man and the Indian." *Journal of American Folklore* 15, no. 59 (1902): 240–267.

Chapman, Thomas. *The Cyder-maker's Instructor, Sweet-maker's Assistant, and Victualler's and Housekeeper's Director*. London: Steuart, 1762.

Chasseboeuf, Constantin François de. *View of the Soil and Climate of the United States of America*. London: Johnson, 1804.

Chastellux, François-Jean de. *Travels in North America in the Years 1780, 1781, and 1782*. Translated by Howard C. Rice. 2 vols. New York: Kelley, 1970.

Child, Lydia Maria. *The American Frugal Housewife*. New York: Wood, 1838.

Clark, Christopher. "Household Economy, Market Exchange, and the Rise of Capitalism in the Connecticut Valley, 1800–1860." *Journal of Social History* 13 (1979): 169–189.

Clark, Peter. *The English Alehouse: A Social History, 1200–1830.* New York: Longman, 1983.

Clark, Walter, and William Laurence Saunders, eds. *Colonial and State Records of North Carolina.* Vol. 10. Raleigh: Hale, 1886–1907.

Clayton, John. "John Clayton's 1687 Account of the Medicinal Practices of the Virginia Indians." Explanatory notes by Bernard G. Hoffman. *Ethnohistory* 11, no. 1 (1964): 1–40.

Clowse, Converse D. *Economic Beginnings in Colonial South Carolina, 1670–1730.* Columbia: University of South Carolina Press, 1971.

Coats, Alice M. *Flowers and Their Histories.* New York: Pitman, 1956.

Coclanis, Peter A. "Distant Thunder: The Creation of a World Market in Rice and the Transformation It Wrought." *American Historical Review* 98, no. 4 (1993): 1050–1078.

Coe, Sophie D. *America's First Cuisines.* Austin: University of Texas Press, 1994.

Coelho, Philip R. P., and Robert A. McGuire. "African and European Bound Labor in the British New World: The Biological Consequences of Economic Choices." *Journal of Economic History* 57, no. 1 (1997): 83–115.

Coffey, T. G. "Beer Street: Gin Lane: Some Views of Eighteenth-Century Drinking." *Quarterly Journal of Studies on Alcohol* 27 (1966): 669–692.

Columbus, Christopher. *The Four Voyages of Columbus: A History in Eight Documents.* Edited by Cecil Jane. New York: Dover, 1988.

Combrune, Michael. *The Theory and Practice of Brewing.* London: Haberkorn, 1762.

Commager, Henry Steele, ed. *Documents of American History.* Vol. 1. New York: Appleton-Century-Crofts, 1968.

Conroy, David W. *In Public Houses: Drink and the Revolution of Authority in Colonial Massachusetts.* Chapel Hill: University of North Carolina Press, 1995.

Coon, David L. "Eliza Lucas Pinckney and the Reintroduction of Indigo Culture in South Carolina." *Journal of Southern History* 42, no. 1 (1976): 61–76.

Cooper, Thomas, and David J. McCord, eds. *The Statutes at Large of South Carolina.* Vol. 3. Columbia: South Carolina Historical Commission, 1837–1841.

Cosculluela, J. A. "Prehistoric Cultures of Cuba." *American Antiquity* 12, no. 1 (1946): 10–18.

Cowan, Ruth Schwartz. *More Work for Mother: The Ironies of Household Technology from the Open Hearth to the Microwave.* New York: Basic Books, 1983.

Crader, Diana C. "Slave Diet at Monticello." *American Antiquity* 55, no. 4 (1990): 690–717.

———. "The Zooarchaeology of the Storehouse and the Dry Well at Monticello." *American Antiquity* 49, no. 3 (1984): 542–558.

Crane, Verner. *The Southern Frontier, 1732–1870.* Ann Arbor: University of Michigan Press, 1929.

Craton, Michael. *Searching for the Invisible Man: Slaves and Plantation Life in Jamaica.* Cambridge, Mass.: Harvard University Press, 1978.

Cresswell, Nicholas. *The Journal of Nicholas Cresswell, 1774–1777.* Edited by A. G. Bradley. New York: Dial Press, 1924.

Cressy, David. *Coming Over: Migration and Communication Between England and New England in the Seventeenth Century.* Cambridge: Cambridge University Press, 1987.

Cronon, William. *Changes in the Land: Indians, Colonists, and the Ecology of New England.* New York: Hill and Wang, 1983.

Crosby, Alfred W. *The Columbian Exchange: Biological and Cultural Consequences of 1492.* Westport, Conn.: Greenwood Press, 1972.

Cummings, Abbott Lowell. *Massachusetts and Its First Period Houses: An Essay with Appendices on Architecture in Colonial Massachuetts.* Boston: Colonial Society of Massachusetts, 1979.

————, ed. *Rural Household Inventories: Establishing the Names, Uses, and Furnishings of Rooms in the Colonial New England Home, 1675–1775*. Boston: Society for the Preservation of New England Antiquities, 1964.

Danforth, Samuel. *Piety Encourage*. Boston: Green, 1705.

Daniels, Bruce C. *Puritans at Play: Leisure and Recreation in Colonial New England*. New York: St. Martin's Press, 1995.

Dauphiné, Durand de. *A Hugenot Exile in Virginia; or, Voyages of a Frenchman Exiled for His Religion, with a Description of Virginia and Maryland*. Edited by Gilbert Chinard. 1687. Reprint, New York: Press of the Pioneers, 1934.

Davidson, Alan. *The Oxford Companion to Food*. New York: Oxford University Press, 1999.

Davis, Dave D., and Christopher Goodwin. "Island Carib Origins: Evidence and Nonevidence." *American Antiquity* 55, no. 1 (1990): 37–48.

Davisson, William I., and Dennis J. Dugan. "Commerce in Seventeenth-Century Essex County, Massachusetts." Essex Institute, *Historical Collections* 107 (1971): 113–142.

Deane, Samuel. *The New England Farmer*. Worcester, Mass.: Thomas, 1790.

DeBoer, Warren R. "The Archaeological Evidence for Manioc Cultivation: A Cautionary Note." *American Antiquity* 40, no. 4 (1975): 419–433.

De Booy, Theodoor. "Certain Kitchen-Middens in Jamaica." *American Anthropologist* 15, no. 3 (1913): 425–434.

De Brahm, William. *Report of the General Survey in the Southern District of North America*. Edited by Louis de Vorsey. 1799. Reprint, Columbia: University of South Carolina Press, 1971.

Denevan, William M. "The Pristine Myth: The Landscape of the Americans in 1492." *Annals of the Association of American Geographers* 82, no. 3 (1992): 369–385.

Denton, Daniel. *A Brief Description of New York: Formerly Called New Netherlands*. London: Hancock and Bradley, 1670.

DePauw, Linda Grant. *Founding Mothers: Women in America in the Revolutionary Era*. Boston: Houghton Mifflin, 1975.

DeWolf, Marian. "Excavations in Jamaica." *American Antiquity* 18, no. 3 (1953): 230–238.

Dickson, William. *Letters on Slavery: To Which Are Added Addresses to the Whites, and to the Free Negroes of Barbados*. London: Phillips, 1789.

Donnan, Elizabeth, ed. *Documents Illustrative of the History of the Slave Trade to America*. Vol. 2. New York: Octagon Books, 1965.

Douglas, Mary, ed. *Constructive Drinking: Perspectives on Drink from Anthropology*. Cambridge: Cambridge University Press, 1983.

Dow, George Francis, ed. *The Probate Records of Essex County, Massachusetts*. 3 vols. Salem, Mass.: Essex Institute, 1916–1920.

————, ed. *The Records and Files of the Quarterly Courts of Essex County, Massachusetts, 1635–1683*. 9 vols. Salem, Mass.: Essex Institute, 1911–1916.

Dowd, Gregory Evans. "The Panic of 1751: The Significance of Rumors on the South Carolina–Cherokee Frontier." *William and Mary Quarterly*, 3rd ser., 53, no. 3 (1996): 527–560.

Drayton, John. *A View of South Carolina, as Respects Her Natural and Civil Concerns*. Charleston: Young, 1802.

Dunlap, William. *The Father, or American Shandysim*. New York: Hodge, Allen, and Cambell, 1789.

Dunn, Richard S. *Sugar and Slaves: The Rise of the Planter Class in the English West Indies, 1624–1713*. New York: Norton, 1972.

Earle, Alice Morse. *Home Life in Colonial Days.* 1898. Reprint, New York: Macmillan, 1922.

Eddis, William. *Letters from America.* Edited by Aubrey C. Land. 1792. Reprint, Cambridge Mass.: Belknap Press, 1969.

Edwards, Bryan. *History of the British Colonies.* Philadelphia: Humphries, 1805–1806.

Egnal, Marc. "The Economic Development of the Thirteen Continental Colonies, 1720 to 1775." *William and Mary Quarterly,* 3rd ser., 32, no. 2 (1975): 191–222.

Emerson, Everett, ed. *Letters from New England: The Massachusetts Bay Colony, 1629–1638.* Amherst: University of Massachusetts Press, 1976.

Emerson, Lucy. *The New England Cookery.* Montpelier, Vt.: Parks, 1808.

Equiano, Olaudah. *The Interesting Narrative of the Life of Olaudah Equiano, Written by Himself.* Edited, with an introduction, by Robert J. Allison. Boston: Bedford Books, 1995.

Evelyn, John. *Acetaria: A Discourse of Sallats.* 1699. Reprint, London: Tooke, 1966.

Fairchild, Thomas. "An Account of Some New Experiments, Relating to the Different, and Sometimes Contrary Motion of the Sap in Plants and Trees, Made by Thomas Fairchild, Gardener at Hoxton." *Philosophical Transaction* 33 (1724–1725): 127–129.

Fairfax, Arabella. *The Family's Best Friend; or the Whole Art of Cookery Made Plain and Easy.* London: Henderson, ca. 1755.

"The Family Brewer." *Universal Magazine,* January–April 1748.

Farley, John. *The London Art of Cookery and Housekeeper's Complete Assistant on a New Plan.* London: Barker, 1800.

Feltman, William. *The Journal of Lieut. William Feltman.* Edited by H. C. Baird. Philadelphia: Historical Society of Pennsylvania, 1853

Fennimore, Donald L. *Metalwork in Early America: Copper and Its Alloys.* Wintherthur, Del.: Winterthur Museum, 1996.

Ferguson, Adam. *An Essay on the History of Civil Society.* Vol. 2. Basel: Tourneisen, 1789.

Fewkes, J. Walter. "Relations of Aboriginal Culture and Environment in Lesser Antilles." *Bulletin of the American Geographical Society* 46, no. 9 (1914): 662–678.

Fischer, David Hackett. *Albion's Seed: Four British Folkways in America.* New York: Oxford University Press, 1989.

Fisher, Daniel. "Extracts from the Journal of Daniel Fisher, 1755." *Pennsylvania Magazine and Biography* 44 (1920): 112–115.

Fisher, Mrs. *The Prudent Housewife: or, Complete English Cook, for Town and Country.* London: Sabine, ca. 1750.

Fithian, Philip Vickers. *Journal and Letters of Philip Vickers Fithian: A Plantation Tutor of the Old Dominion, 1773–1774.* Edited by Hunter Dickenson Farish. Charlottesville: University of Virginia Press, 1957.

Flint, Charles. *Milch Cows and Dairy Farming.* Boston: Williams, 1858.

Flint, Clarissa Dillon. "'A Large, an Useful, and a Grateful Field': Eighteenth-Century Kitchen Gardens in Southeastern Pennsylvania, the Uses of the Plants, and Their Place in Women's Work." Ph.D. diss., Bryn Mawr College, 1986.

Force, Peter. *Tracts and Other Papers Relating Principally to the Origin, Settlement, and Progress of the Colonies in North America, from the Discovery of the Country to the Year 1776.* 1836. Reprint, Gloucester, Mass.: Smith, 1963.

Fountain, Daniel L. "Historians and Historical Archaeology: Slave Sites." *Journal of Interdisciplinary History* 26, no. 1 (1995): 67–77.

Franklin, Benjamin. *The Autobiography of Benjamin Franklin.* Edited by Leonard W. Labaree et al. New Haven, Conn.: Yale University Press, 2003.

———. *The Papers of Benjamin Franklin.* Edited by Leonard W. Labaree et al. 32 vols. New Haven, Conn: Yale University Press, 1959–1997.

Fussell, Betty. *The Story of Corn.* New York: Knopf, 1992.

———. "Translating Maize into Corn: The Transformation of America's Native Grain." *Social Research* 66, no. 1 (1999): 41–65.

Gentleman of the Faculty. *Concise Observations on the Nature of Our Common Food, so far as It Tends to Promote or Injure Health.* London: Swords, 1790.

Gerard, John. *The Herball, or General Historie of Plantes.* London: Adam, Issip Joice Norton and Richard Whitakers, 1633.

Gildrie, Richard P. *Salem Massachusetts, 1626–1683: A Covenant Community.* Charlottesville: University of Virginia Press, 1974.

Glacken, Clarence J. "Count Buffon on Cultural Changes of the Physical Environment." *Annals of the Association of American Geographers* 50, no. 1 (1960): 1–21.

Glasse, Hannah. *The Art of Cookery Made Plain and Easy.* Alexandria, Va.: Cottom and Stewart, 1805.

Glen, James, and George Milligan-Johnson. *Colonial South Carolina: Two Contemporary Descriptions.* Edited by Chapman J. Millings. Columbia: University of South Carolina Press, 1951.

Gmelch, George, and Sharon Bohn Gmelch. "Barbados's Amerindian Past." *Anthropology Today* 12, no. 1 (1996): 11–15.

Gookin, Daniel. *Historical Collections of the Indians in New England.* 1792. Reprint, Boston: Massachusetts Historical Society, 1848.

Gottfried, Marion H. "The First Depression in Massachusetts." *New England Quarterly* 9 (1936): 655–678.

Greene, Jack P. "Autonomy and Stability: New England and the British Colonial Experience in Early Modern America." *Journal of Social History* 7 (1974): 171–194.

———. *Imperatives, Behaviors, Identities: Essays in Early American Cultural History.* Charlottesville: University of Virginia Press, 1992.

———. *The Intellectual Construction of America: Exceptionalism and Identity from 1492 to 1800.* Chapel Hill: University of North Carolina Press, 1993.

———. *Understanding the American Revolution: Issues and Actors.* Charlottesville: University of Virginia Press, 1995.

———, ed. *Colonies to Nation, 1763–1789: A Documentary History of the American Revolution.* New York: McGraw-Hill, 1975.

Greene, Jack P., and J. R. Pole, eds. *Colonial British America: Essays in the New History of the Early Modern Era.* Baltimore: Johns Hopkins University Press, 1984.

Grieve, Maud. *A Modern Herbal.* New York: Hafner, 1967.

Gross, Robert A. *The Minutemen and Their World.* New York: Hill and Wang, 1976.

Grubb, Farley. "Redemptioneer Immigration to Pennsylvania: Evidence on Contract Choice and Profitability." *Journal of Economic History* 46, no. 2 (1986): 407–418.

Haan, Richard L. "The 'Trade Do's Not Flourish as Formerly': The Ecological Origins of the Yamassee War of 1715." *Ethnohistory* 28, no. 4 (1981): 341–358.

Hakluyt Society. *The Jamestown Voyages Under the First Charter, 1606–1609.* Cambridge: Cambridge University Press, 1969.

Hall, David D., ed. *Witch Hunting in Seventeenth-Century New England: A Documentary History, 1638–1692.* Boston: Northeastern University Press, 1991.

Hall, Douglas, and Sidney Mintz. *The Origins of the Jamaican Internal Marketing System.* New Haven, Conn.: Yale University Press, 1960.

Hall, Richard. *Acts Passed in the Island of Barbados from 1643–1762.* London: Printed for Richard Hall, 1764.

Hally, David J. "The Identification of Vessel Function: A Case Study from Northwest Georgia." *American Antiquity* 51, no. 2 (1986): 267–295.

Hamer, Marguerite. "The Fate of the Exiled Acadians in South Carolina." *Journal of Southern History* 4, no. 2 (1938): 199–208.

Hamilton, Alexander. *Gentleman's Progress: The Itinerarium of Dr. Alexander Hamilton, 1744.* Edited by Carl Bridenbaugh. Chapel Hill: University of North Carolina Press, 1948.

Hamilton, Alexander. *The Papers of Alexander Hamilton.* Vol. 1. Edited by Harold C. Syrett. New York: Columbia University Press, 1963.

Hamor, Ralph. *True Discourse on the Present State of Virginia.* 1615. Reprint, Richmond: Virginia State Library, 1957.

Handler, Jerome S. *Plantation Slavery in Barbados: An Archeological and Historical Investigation.* Cambridge, Mass.: Harvard University Press, 1978.

———.*The Unappropriated People: Freedom in the Slave Society of Barbados.* Baltimore: Johns Hopkins University Press, 1974.

Handler, Jerome S., and Robert S. Corruccini. "Plantation Slave Life in Barbados: A Physical Anthropological Analysis." *Journal of Interdisciplinary History* 14, no. 1 (1983): 65–90.

Hariot, Thomas. *A Brief and True Report of the Newfoundland of Virginia, Diligentlye Collected and Drawne by John White.* Frankfurt: de Bry, 1590.

Harlow, Vincent T. *A History of Barbados, 1625–1685.* New York: Negro Universities Press, 1969.

Harrison, Molly. *The Kitchen in History.* New York: Scribner, 1972.

Harrison, Sarah. *The House-Keeper's Pocket-Book; and Compleat Family Cook.* London: Ware, 1739.

Hartman, G. (George). *The True Preserver and Restorer of Health.* London: Taylor, 1684.

Havinden, M. A. "The History of Crop Cultivation in West Africa: A Bibliographical Guide." *Economic History Review* 23, no. 3 (1970): 532–555.

Hayes, Thomas. *Concise Observations on the Nature of Our Common Food.* London: Swords, 1790.

Heckewelder, John. *History, Manners, and Customs of the Indian Nations, Who Once Inhabited Pennsylvania and the Neighboring States.* 1876. Reprint, New York: Arno Press, 1971.

Hempstead, Joshua. *The Diary of Joshua Hempstead of New London, Connecticut.* 1758. Reprint, New London, Conn.: New London Historical Society, 1970.

Henretta, James A. "Families and Farms: *Mentalité* in Pre-industrial America." *William and Mary Quarterly*, 3rd ser., 37, no. 4 (1980): 3–32.

Herndon, G. Melvin. *William Tatham and the Culture of Tobacco, Including a Facsimile Reprint of "An Historical and Practical Essay on the Culture and Commerce of Tobacco."* Coral Gables, Fla.: University of Miami Press, 1969.

Hess, Karen. *The Carolina Rice Kitchen: The African Connection.* Columbia: University of South Carolina Press, 1992.

Higman, B.W. "The Slave Family and Household in the British West Indies, 1800–1834." *Journal of Interdisciplinary History* 6, no. 2 (1975): 261–287.

Holland, Edwin C. *A Refutation of the Calumnies Circulated Against the Southern and Western States, Respecting the Institution and Existence of Slavery Among Them.* Charleston, S.C.: Miller, 1822.

Honychurch, Lennox. "Crossroads in the Caribbean: A Site of Encounter and Exchange on Dominica." *World Archaeology* 28, no. 3 (1997): 291–304.

Horn, James. *Adapting to a New World: English Society in the Seventeenth-Century Chesapeake.* Chapel Hill: University of North Carolina Press, 1994.

Hubbard, William. *A General History of New England from the Discovery to MDCLXXX.* 1704. Reprint, New York: Arno Press, 1971.

Hudnut, Ruth Allison, and Haynes Baker-Crothers. "Acadian Transients in South Carolina." *American Historical Review* 43, no. 3 (1938): 500–513.

Hughes, E. *A Treatise on the Brewing of Beer.* London: Lake, 1796.

Hutchinson, Thomas. *History of the Colony and Province of the Massachusetts Bay.* Vol. 1. Boston: Fleet, 1764.

Innes, Stephen. *Labor in a New Land: Economy and Society in Seventeenth-Century Springfield.* Princeton, N.J.: Princeton University Press, 1983.

———. "Land Tenancy and Social Order in Springfield, Massachusetts, 1652 to 1702." *William and Mary Quarterly*, 3rd ser., 35, no. 1 (1978): 33–56.

———, ed. *Work and Labor in Early America.* Chapel Hill: University of North Carolina Press, 1988.

Innis, Harold A. *The Cod Fisheries: The History of an International Economy.* Toronto: University of Toronto Press, 1940.

Jefferson, Thomas. *Notes on the State of Virginia.* Edited by William Peden. Chapel Hill: University of North Carolina Press, 1955.

———. *The Papers of Thomas Jefferson.* Edited by Julian P. Boyd. Vol. 7. Princeton, N.J.: Princeton University Press, 1953.

———. *Thomas Jefferson's Farm Book.* Edited by Edwin Morris Betts. Charlottesville: University of Virginia Press, 1976.

———. *The Writings of Thomas Jefferson.* Edited by Andrew A. Liscomb. Vol. 9. Washington, D.C.: Thomas Jefferson Memorial Association, 1903.

Johnson, Edward. *Johnson's Wonder-Working Providence, 1628–1651.* Edited by J. Franklin Jameson. 1654. Reprint, New York: Scribner, 1910.

Johnson, Joshua. *The Art of Cheese Making.* Albany, N.Y.: Webster, 1801.

Johnson, Richard R. "The Search for a Usable Indian: An Aspect of the Defense of Colonial New England." *Journal of American History* 64, no. 3 (1977): 623–651.

Jones, Alice Hanson. *American Colonial Wealth: Documents and Methods.* New York: Columbia University Press, 1978.

———. "Estimating Wealth of the Living from a Probate Sample." *Journal of Interdisciplinary History* 13, no. 2 (1982): 273–300.

———. "Wealth and Growth of the Thirteen Colonies: Some Implications." *Journal of Economic History* 44, no. 2 (1984): 239–254.

Jones, Alick R. "Dietary Changes and Human Population at Indian Creek, Antigua." *American Antiquity* 50, no. 3 (1985): 518–536.

Jones, Douglas Lamar. *Village and Seaport: Migration and Society in Eighteenth-Century Massachusetts.* Hanover, N.H.: University Press of New England, 1981.

Jones, Evan. *American Food: The Gastronomic Story.* New York: Dutton, 1981.

Jones, Hugh. *The Present State of Virginia.* Edited by Richard L. Morton. 1724. Reprint, Chapel Hill: University of North Carolina Press, 1956.

Josselyn, John. *An Account of Two Voyages to New-England.* London: Widdowes, 1675.

———. *New-Englands Rarities Discovered: In Birds, Beasts, Fishes, Serpents, and Plants of That Country.* London: Widdowes, 1672.

Kalm, Peter. *The America of 1750: Peter Kalm's Travels in North America: The English Version of 1770.* Edited by Adolph B. Benson. Vol. 2. New York: Wilson-Erickson, 1937.

Keegan, William F. "The Ecology of Lucayan Arawak Fishing Practices." *American Antiquity* 51, no. 4 (1986): 816–825.

Keegan, William F., and Michael J. DeNiro. "Stable Carbon- and Nitrogen-Isotope Ratios of Bone Collagen Used to Study Coral-Reef and Terrestrial Components of Prehistoric Bahamian Diet." *American Antiquity* 53, no. 2 (1988): 320–336.

Keimer, Samuel, ed. *Caribbeana*. London: Osborn, 1741.

Kelso, William M. *Kingsmill Plantations, 1619–1800: Archeology of Country Life in Colonial Virginia*. London: Academic Press, 1984.

Kercheval, Samuel. *A History of the Valley of Virginia*. 2nd ed. Woodstock, Va.: Gatewood, 1850.

Kettilby, Mary. *A Collection of Above Three Hundred Receipts in Cookery, Physick and Surgery*. London: For the Executrix of Mary Kettilby, 1746.

Kierner, Cynthia A. "Hospitality, Sociability, and Gender in the Southern Colonies." *Journal of Southern History* 62, no. 3 (1996): 449–480.

Kimball, Marie. "Some Genial Old Drinking Customs." *William and Mary Quarterly*, 2nd ser., 2, no. 4 (1945): 349–358.

Kingsbury, Susan Myra, ed. *The Records of the Virginia Company of London, 1606–1626*. 4 vols. Washington, D.C.: Government Printing Office, 1906–1935.

Kiple, Kenneth F., and Virginia H. Kiple. "Black Tongue and Black Men: Pellagra and Slavery in the Antebellum South." *Journal of Southern History* 43, no. 3 (1977): 411–428.

Klingaman, David C. "The Coastwise Trade of Colonial Massachusetts." Essex Institute, *Historical Collections* 108 (1972): 217–234.

———. "Food Surpluses and Deficits in the American Colonies, 1768–1772." *Journal of Economic History* 31, no. 3 (1971): 553–569.

Klingberg, Frank J. "The Indian Frontier in South Carolina as Seen by the S.P.G. Missionary." *Journal of Southern History* 5, no. 4 (1939): 479–500.

Kulikoff, Allan. "The Economic Growth of the Eighteenth-Century Chesapeake Colonies." *Journal of Economic History* 39, no. 1 (1979): 275–288.

———. "The Origins of Afro-American Society in Tidewater Maryland and Virginia, 1700 to 1790." *William and Mary Quarterly*, 3rd ser., 35, no. 2 (1978): 226–259.

Kupperman, Karen Ordahl. "Fear of Hot Climates in the Anglo-American Colonial Experience." *William and Mary Quarterly*, 3rd ser., 41, no. 2 (1984): 213–240.

Kurtz, Stephen G., and James H. Hutson, eds. *Essays on the American Revolution*. Chapel Hill: University of North Carolina Press, 1973.

Lamar, Lucius Q. C., comp. *Compilation of the Laws of the State of Georgia*. Augusta: Hannon, 1821.

Lamb, Patrick. *Royal Cookery, or, The Compleat Court-cook*. London: For E. and R. Nutt and H. Lintot, 1731.

La Rochefoucauld-Liancourt, François-Alexandre-Frédéric de. *Travels Through the United States of North America*. Vol. 1. London: Philips, 1799.

Late Able Physician. *The Family Magazine: In Two Parts*. London: Osborn, 1741.

Laurens, Henry. *The Papers of Henry Laurens*. Edited by Philip M. Hamer and George C. Rogers. Vol. 3. Columbia: University of South Carolina Press, 1972.

Lawrence, Roderick J. "Domestic Space and Society: A Cross-Cultural Study." *Comparative Studies in Society and History* 24, no. 1 (1982): 104–130.

Lawson, John. *A New Voyage to Carolina*. London, 1709.

Le Clerque, Chrestian. *New Relation of Gaspesia*. Translated and edited by William F. Ganong. Toronto: Champlain Society, 1910.

Lederer, John. *The Discoveries of John Lederer*. Edited by William P. Cumming. Charlottesville: University of Virginia Press, 1958.

Lefler, Hugh T. "Promotional Literature of the Southern Colonies." *Journal of Southern History* 33, no. 1 (1967): 3–25.

Leighton, Ann. *Early American Gardens: For Meate or Medicine.* Amherst: University of Massachusetts Press, 1986.

Lemon, James T. "Agriculture and Society in Early America." *Agricultural History Review* 35 (1987): 76–94.

———. *The Best Poor Man's Country: A Geographical Study of Early Sourtheastern Pennsylvania.* Baltimore: Johns Hopkins University Press, 1972.

———. Comment on "Families and Farms: *Mentalité* in Pre-industrial America," by James A. Henretta [with a reply by Henretta]. *William and Mary Quarterly*, 3rd ser., 37, no. 4 (1980): 115–131.

———. "Urbanization and the Development of Eighteenth-Century Southeastern Pennsylvania and Adjacent Delaware." *William and Mary Quarterly*, 3rd ser., 24, no. 4 (1967): 501–542.

Lender, Mark Edward, and James Kirby Martin. *Drinking in America: A History.* New York: Free Press, 1982.

Leyel, Hilda. *The Truth About Herbs.* London: Dakers, 1943.

Liddle, William D. "'Virtue and Liberty': An Inquiry into the Role of the Agrarian Myth in the Rhetoric of the American Revolution Era." *South Atlantic Quarterly* 77, no. 1 (1978): 15–38.

Lipscomb, Terry W., ed. *Journal of the Commons House of Assembly for South Carolina, October 6, 1757 to January 24, 1761.* Columbia: South Carolina Department of Archives and History, 1996.

Littlefield, Daniel C. *Rice and Slaves: Ethnicity and the Slave Trade in Colonial South Carolina.* Urbana: University of Illinois Press, 1991.

Locke, John. *The Second Treatise of Government.* Edited by Thomas Preston Peardon. New York: Liberal Arts Press, 1952.

Lockridge, Kenneth A. "Land, Population, and the Evolution of New England Society, 1630–1790." *Past and Present* 39 (1968): 62–80.

———. *A New England Town, the First Hundred Years: Dedham, Massachusetts, 1636–1736.* New York: Norton, 1970.

———. "The Population of Dedham, Massachusetts, 1636–1736." *Economic History Review* 19, no. 2 (1966): 318–344.

Loewald, Klaus G., Beverly Starika, and Paul S. Taylor. "Johann Martin Bolzius Answers a Questionnaire on Carolina and Georgia." *William and Mary Quarterly*, 3rd ser., 14, no. 2 (1957): 218–222.

Luffman, John. *A Brief Account of the Island of Antigua.* London: Cadell, 1789.

Maier, Pauline. *From Resistance to Revolution: Colonial Radicals and the Development of American Opposition to Britain, 1765–1776.* New York: Knopf, 1972.

Main, Gloria Lund. "The Correction of Biases in Colonial American Probate Records." *Historical Methods Newsletter* 8 (1974): 10–28.

———. "Probate Records as a Source for Early American History." *William and Mary Quarterly*, 3rd ser., 32, no. 1 (1975): 89–99.

———. "The Standard of Living in Colonial Massachusetts." *Journal of Economic History* 43, no. 1 (1983): 101–108.

———. "The Standard of Living in Southern New England, 1640–1773." *William and Mary Quarterly*, 3rd ser., 45, no. 1 (1988): 124–134.

———. *Tobacco Colony: Life in Early Maryland, 1650–1720.* Princeton, N.J.: Princeton University Press, 1982.

Main, Gloria L., and Jackson T. Main. "Economic Growth and the Standard of Living in Southern New England, 1640–1774." *Journal of Economic History* 48, no. 1 (1988): 24–46.

Main, Jackson Turner. *Society and Economy in Colonial Connecticut.* Princeton, N.J.: Princeton University Press, 1985.

Mancall, Peter C. "'The Art of Getting Drunk' in Colonial Massachusetts." *Reviews in American History* 24, no. 3 (1996): 383–388.

———. *Deadly Medicine: Indians and Alcohol in Early America.* Ithaca, N.Y.: Cornell University Press, 1995.

Manges, Frances May. "Women Shopkeepers, Tavernkeepers and Artisans in Colonial Philadelphia." Ph.D. diss., University of Pennsylvania, 1958.

Markham, Gervase. *Country Contentments, or The English Huswife.* London: I. B. for R. Iackson, 1623.

———. *The English Housewife.* Edited by Michael R. Best. Kingston, Ont.: McGill–Queens University Press, 1982.

Marshall, Charles. *An Introduction to the Knowledge and Practice of Gardening.* 2 vols. London: Rider, 1798.

Martin, John Frederick. "Entrepreneurship and the Founding of New England Towns: The Seventeenth Century." Ph.D. diss., Harvard University, 1985.

Martin, Wendy, ed. *Colonial American Travel Narratives.* New York: Penguin, 1994.

Marx, Leo. *The Machine in the Garden: Technology and the Pastoral Ideal in America.* New York: Oxford University Press, 1964.

Masterson, James R. "Travelers' Tales of Colonial Natural History." *Journal of American Folklore* 59, no. 231 (1946): 51–67.

Mather, Cotton. *Optanda: Good Men Described.* Boston: Harris, 1692.

———. *Sober Considerations.* Boston, 1708.

Mather, Cotton, Benjamin Wadsworth, and Benjamin Colman. *A Testimony Against Evil Customs.* Boston: Kneeland, 1719.

Mather, Cotton, et al. *A Serious Address to Those Who Unnecessarily Frequent the Tavern, and Often Spend the Evening in Publick Houses.* Boston: Gerrish, 1726.

Mather, Increase. *Wo to Drunkards: Two Sermons Testifying Against the Sin of Drunkenness.* Cambridge, Mass.: Johnson, 1673.

Mather, Richard. *Journal of Richard Mather.* 1635. Reprint, Boston: Clampp, 1850.

Matson, Cathy. "'Damned Scoundrels' and 'Libertisme of Trade': Freedom and Regulation in Colonial New York's Fur and Grain Trades." *William and Mary Quarterly,* 3rd ser., 51, no. 3 (1994): 389–418.

Mayhew, Jonathan. *A Sermon Prech'd in the Audience of His Excellency William Shirley, Esq.* Boston: Draper, 1754.

McCusker, John, J. "The Rum Trade and the Balance of Payments of the Thirteen Continental Colonies, 1650–1775." *Journal of Economic History* 30, no. 1 (1970): 244–247.

McCusker, John, J., and Russell R. Menard. *The Economy of British America, 1607–1789.* Chapel Hill: University of North Carolina Press, 1985.

McDonald, Roderick A. *The Economy and Material Culture of Slaves: Goods and Chattels on the Sugar Plantations of Jamaica and Louisiana.* Baton Rouge: Lousiana State University Press, 1993.

McFarland, Raymond. *A History of the New England Fisheries.* Philadelphia: University of Pennsylvania Press, 1911.

McIlwaine, H. R., ed. *Minutes of the Council and General Court of Colonial Virginia.* Richmond: Virginia State Library, 1809–1823.

McMahon, Sarah F. "A Comfortable Subsistence: The Changing Composition of Diet in Rural New England, 1620–1840." *William and Mary Quarterly*, 3rd ser., 42, no. 1 (1985): 26–65.

———. "'A Comfortable Subsistence': A History of Diet in New England, 1630–1850." Ph.D. diss., Brandeis University, 1982.

McWilliams, James E. "Brewing Beer in Massachusetts Bay, 1640–1690." *New England Quarterly* 71, no. 4 (1998): 543–569.

Meager, Leonard. *The English Gardener*. London: Pierrepoint, 1682.

Mendelsohn, Everett. "John Lining and His Contribution to Early American Science." *Isis* 51, no. 3 (1960): 278–292.

Mendez, Helen. *The African Heritage Cookbook*. New York: Macmillan, 1971.

Merrell, James H. "Cultural Continuity Among the Piscataway Indians of Colonial Maryland." *William and Mary Quarterly*, 3rd ser., 36, no. 4 (1979): 548–570.

———. "The Indians' New World: The Catawba Experience." *William and Mary Quarterly*, 3rd ser., 41, no. 4 (1984): 537–565.

———. *Into the American Woods: Negotiations on the Pennsylvania Frontier*. New York: Norton, 1999.

Merrill, Michael. "Cash Is Good to Eat: Self-Sufficiency and Exchange in the Rural Economy of the United States." *Radical History Review* 4 (1977): 42–72.

Middlekauff, Robert. *The Glorious Cause: The American Revolution, 1763–1789*. New York: Oxford University Press, 1982.

Miller, Perry, and Thomas Johnson, eds. *The Puritans*. New York: American Book, 1938.

Miller, Philip. *The Gardeners Kalender: Directing What Works Are Necessary to Be Done Every Month in the Kitchen, Fruit, and Pleasure-gardens, as also in the Conservatory and Nursery*. London, 1732.

Miller, Ralph N. "American Nationalism as a Theory of Nature." *William and Mary Quarterly*, 2nd ser., 12, no. 1 (1955): 74–95.

Miracle, Marvin P. "The Introduction and Spread of Maize in Africa." *Journal of African History* 6, no. 1 (1965): 39–55.

Mittelberger, Gottlieb. *Journey to Pennsylvania*. Edited and translated by Oscar Handlin and John Clive. Cambridge, Mass.: Harvard University Press, 1960.

Mood, Fulmer. "John Winthrop, Jr., on Indian Corn." *New England Quarterly* 10, no. 1 (1937): 121–133.

Mook, Maurice A. "Virginia Ethnology from an Early Relation." *William and Mary Quarterly*, 2nd ser., 23, no. 2 (1943): 101–129.

Morgan, Edmund S. *American Slavery, American Freedom: The Ordeal of Colonial Virginia*. New York: Norton, 1975.

———. *The Challenge of the American Revolution*. New York: Norton, 1976.

———. "The First American Boom: Virginia 1618 to 1630." *William and Mary Quarterly*, 3rd ser., 28, no. 2 (1971): 169–198.

———. *The Puritan Dilemma, the Story of John Winthrop*. Boston: Little, Brown, 1958.

Morgan, Philip D. *Slave Counterpoint: Black Culture in the Eighteenth-Century Chesapeak and Lowcountry*. Chapel Hill: University of North Carolina Press, 1998.

Morgan, W. B. "The Forest and Agriculture in West Africa." *Journal of African History* 3, no. 2 (1962): 235–239.

Morison, Samuel Eliot, ed. *Journals and Other Documents on the Life and Voyages of Christopher Columbus*. New York: Heritage Press, 1963.

————, ed. *Sources and Documents Illustrating the American Revolution, 1764–1788*. New York: Oxford University Press, 1929.

Morton, Julia Francis. *Fruits of Warm Climates*. Winterville, N.C.: Morton, 1987.

Morton, Thomas. *New English Canaan*. Edited by Charles Francis Adams. 1632. Reprint, Boston: Prince Society, 1883.

Muhlenberg, Henry Melchior. *The Journals of Rev. Henry Melchoir Muhlenberg*. Edited by Theodore G. Tappert and John Doberstein. 3 vols. Evansville, Ind.: Lutheran Historical Society, 1982.

————. *The Notebook of a Colonial Clergyman, Condensed from the Journals of Henry Melchior Muhlenberg*. Edited and translated by Theodore G. Tappert and John W. Doberstein. 1742. Reprint, Minneapolis: Fortress Press, 1949.

Murray, James. *Sermons to Asses*. Philadelphia: Dunlap, 1769.

Myers, Albert Cook, ed. *Narratives of Early Pennsylvania, West New Jersey, and Delaware, 1630–1707*. New York: Scribner, 1912.

Nairne, Thomas. *A Letter from South Carolina; Giving an Account of the Soil, Air, Product, Trade, Government, Laws, Religion, People, Military Strength, and C. of that Province*. London: Baldwin, 1710.

Nash, Gary. "The First Decade in Pennsylvania: Letters of William Markham and Thomas Holme to William Penn." *Pennsylvania Magazine of History and Biography* 90, no. 90 (1966): 314.

Nash, R. C. "South Carolina and the Atlantic Economy in the Late Seventeenth and Eighteenth Centuries." *Economic History Review* 45, no. 4 (1992): 677–702.

Naylor, James. *A Collection of Sundry Books, Epistles, and Papers*. London: Sowle, 1716.

Nester, William R. *The First Global War: Britain, France, and the Fate of North America, 1756–1775*. Westport, Conn.: Praeger, 2000.

Nordenskiold, Erland. "The American Indian as an Inventor." *Journal of Royal Anthropological Institute of Great Britain and Ireland* 59 (1929): 273–309.

Norris, John. *Profitable Advice for Rich and Poor*. London: Howe, 1712.

Nyaho, E. Chapman, E. Amarteifio, and J. Asare. *Ghana Recipe Book*. Accra: Ghana Publishing, 1970.

O'Callaghan, E. B., and Berthold Fernow, eds. *Documents Relative to the Colonial History of the State of New York*. Vol. 4. Albany: Weed, Parsons, 1853–1887.

Olwell, Robert. *Masters, Slaves, and Subjects: The Culture of Power in the South Carolina Low Country, 1740–1790*. Ithaca, N.Y.: Cornell University Press, 1998.

Ouellette, Susan M. "Divine Providence and Collective Endeavor: Sheep Production in Early Massachusetts." *New England Quarterly* 69, no. 3 (1996): 355–380.

Paine, Thomas. *The Complete Writings of Thomas Paine*. Edited by Philip Foner. Vol. 1. New York: Citadel Press, 1945.

Parks, Roger N. "The Roads of New England, 1790–1840." Ph.D. diss., Michigan State University, 1966.

Parry, John H. "Plantation and Provision Ground: An Historical Sketch of the Introduction of Food Crops into Jamaica." *Revista de Historia de América* (1955).

Pechey, John. *The English Herbal of Physical Plants*. 1664. Reprint, London: Medical Publications, 1951.

Penn, William. *Some Fruits of Solitude in Reflection and Maxims*. 1663. Reprint, Bedford, Mass.: Applewood Books, 1996.

Perkins, Elizabeth A. "The Consumer Frontier: Household Consumption in Early Kentucky." *Journal of American History* 78, no. 2 (1991): 486–510.

Perry, James R. *The Formation of a Society on Virginia's Eastern Shore, 1615–1655*. Chapel Hill: University of North Carolina Press, 1990.

Pescatello, Ann. *Old Roots in New Lands: Historical and Anthropological Perspectives on Black Experiences in the America*. Westport, Conn.: Greenwood Press, 1977.

Phillips, James Duncan. *Salem in the Seventeenth Century*. Boston: Houghton Mifflin, 1933.

Phillips, Ulrich B., ed. *Plantation and Frontier Documents: 1649–1863*. Vol. 1. Cleveland: Clark, 1909.

Phipps, Frances. *Colonial Kitchens, Their Furnishings, and Their Gardens*. New York: Hawthorne Books, 1972.

Pierson, Hamilton W. *Jefferson at Monticello: The Private Life of Thomas Jefferson, from Entirely New Materials*. 1862. Reprint, Freeport, N.Y.: Books for Libraries Press, 1971.

Pinckard, George. *Notes on the West Indies, Written During the Expedition Under the Command of the Late General Sir Ralph Abercromby*. Vol. 2. London: Longman, Hurst, Rees, and Orme, 1806.

Pinckney, Eliza Lucas. *The Letterbook of Eliza Lucas Pinckney, 1739–1762*. Edited by Elise Pinckney and Marvin R. Zahiser. Columbia: University of South Carolina Press, 1997.

Plantenga, Bart. "*Mysticisme de la bière*: Fermentation, Inebriation and Navigation." *Exquisite Corpse*, no. 8 (available at: http://www.corpse.org/issue_8/index.html).

Pleasants, J. Hall, ed. *Archives of Maryland: Proceedings and Acts of the General Assembly of Maryland, 1764–1785*. Baltimore: Maryland State Archives, 1942.

Powell, Sumner Chilton. *Puritan Village: The Formation of a New England Town*. Middletown, Conn.: Wesleyan University Press, 1963.

Price, Richard. "Caribbean Fishing and Fishermen: A Historical Sketch." *American Anthropologist* 68, no. 6 (1966): 1363–1383.

Price, Richard. *Observations on the Importance of the American Revolution*. London: Cassell, 1785.

Pruitt, Bettye Hobbs. "Self-Sufficiency and the Agricultural Economy of Eighteenth-Century Massachusetts." *William and Mary Quarterly*, 3rd ser., 41, no. 3 (1984): 333–364.

Quitt, Martin H. "Trade and Acculturation at Jamestown, 1607–1609: The Limits of Understanding." *William and Mary Quarterly*, 3rd ser., 52, no. 2 (1995): 227–258.

Rabisha, William. *The Whole Body of Cookery Dissected, Taught, and Fully Manifested, Methodically, Artificially, and According to the Best Tradition of the English, French, Italian, Dutch, &c., or, a Sympathie of All Varieties in Naturall Compounds in That Mysterie*. London: Giles, Calvert, 1661.

Raffald, Mary. *The Experienced English House-keeper*. Manchester: Harrep, 1769.

Rainbolt, John C. "The Absence of Towns in Seventeenth Century Virginia." *Journal of Southern History* 35, no. 3 (1969): 343–360.

Ramsay, David. *The History of South-Carolina: From Its First Settlement in 1607, to the Year 1808*. Newberry, S.C.: Duffie, 1858.

Randolph, Edward. *History of Virginia*. Edited by Arthur H. Shaffer. Charlottesville: University of Virginia Press, 1970.

Randolph, Mary. *The Virginia Housewife: Or, Methodical Cook*. Washington, D.C.: Davis and Force, 1824.

Ratekin, Mervyn. "The Early Sugar Industry in Española." *Hispanic American Historical Review* 34, no. 1 (1954): 1–19.

Raynal, Guillaume-Thomas-François de. *A Philosophical and Political History of the Settlements and Trade of the Europeans in the East and West Indies*. Vol. 5. Edinburgh: Doig, 1792.

———. *The Revolution in America*. London: Davis, 1781.

Rea, John. *Flora, or a Complete Florilege.* London: Marriot, 1676.

Rice, Kym S. *Early American Taverns: For the Entertainment of Friends and Strangers.* Chicago: Regnery Gateway, 1983.

Richter, Daniel K. *The Ordeal of the Longhouse: The Peoples of the Iroquois League in the Era of European Colonization.* Chapel Hill: University of North Carolina Press, 1992.

Robertson, William. *History of America.* Vol. 2. London: Strayhan, 1803.

Root, Waverly, and Richard de Rochemont. *Eating in America: A History.* New York: Ecco Press, 1976.

Rorabaugh, W. J. *The Alcoholic Republic: An American Tradition.* New York: Oxford University Press, 1979.

Rothenberg, Winifred B. "The Emergence of a Capital Market in Rural Massachusetts, 1730–1838." *Journal of Economic History* 45, no. 4 (1985): 781–808.

———. "Farm Account Books: Problems and Possibilities." *Agricultural History* 58 (1984): 106–112.

———. "The Market and Massachusetts Farmers, 1750–1855." *Journal of Economic History* 41, no. 2 (1981): 283–314.

———. "Markets and Massachusetts Farmers. A Paradigm of Economic Growth in Rural New England, 1750–1885." Ph.D. diss., Brandeis University, 1985.

Rountree, Helen C. "Powhatan Indian Women: The People Captain John Smith Barely Saw." *Ethnohistory* 45, no. 1 (1998): 1–29.

Rouse, Irving. *The Tainos: Rise and Decline of the People Who Greeted Columbus.* New Haven, Conn.: Yale University Press, 1992.

Rozbicki, Michal J. "The Curse of Provincialism: Negative Perceptions of Colonial American Plantation Gentry." *Journal of Southern History* 63, no. 4 (1997): 727–752.

Rundell, Maria Eliza Ketelby. *The Experienced American Housekeeper; or, Domestic Cookery, Formed on Principles of Economy for the Use of Private Families.* New York: Johnstone & Van Norden, 1823.

Rush, Benjamin. *Drunkard's Emblem: Or an Inquiry into the Effects of Ardent Spirits upon the Human Body.* 1791. Reprint, Newmarket, Va.: Henkel, 1812.

———. *Letters of Benjamin Rush.* Edited by Lyman H. Butterfield. 2 vols. Princeton, N.J.: Princeton University Press, 1951.

Rutman, Darrett B. "Governor Winthrop's Garden Crop: The Significance of Agriculture in the Early Commerce of Massachusetts Bay." *William and Mary Quarterly,* 3rd ser., 20, no. 3 (1963): 396–415.

———. *Husbandmen of Plymouth: Farms and Villages in the Old Colony, 1620–1692.* Boston: Beacon Press, 1967.

———. *Winthrop's Boston: Portrait of a Puritan Town, 1630–1649.* Chapel Hill: University of North Carolina Press, 1965.

Rutman, Darrett B., Charles Wetherell, and Anita H. Rutman. "Rhythms of Life: Black and White Seasonality in the Early Chesapeake." *Journal of Interdisciplinary History* 11, no. 1 (1980): 29–53.

Sache, W. L., ed. *Minutes of the Norwich Court of Mayoralty.* Vol. 15. Norwich, Eng.: Norfolk Record Society, 1942.

Sagard, Gabriel. *The Long Journey to the Country of the Hurons.* Edited by George M. Wrong. 1632. Reprint, Toronto: Champlain Society, 1939.

Salley, Alexander S., ed. *Narratives of Early Carolina, 1650–1708.* New York: Scribner, 1911.

———, ed. *Records of the Secretary of the Province and the Register of the Province of South Carolina, 1671–1675.* Columbia: University of South Carolina Press, 1944.

Samford, Patricia. "The Archaeology of African-American Slavery and Material Culture." *William and Mary Quarterly*, 3rd ser., 53, no. 1 (1996): 87–114.

Sarbah, J. M. "The Oil-Palm and Its Uses." *Journal of the Royal African Society* 8, no. 31 (1909): 232–250.

Saunders, William Laurence, ed. *The Colonial Records of North Carolina*. Vol. 1. Raleigh: Hale, 1886.

Schaw, Janet. *Journal of a Lady of Quality: Being the Narrative of a Journey from Scotland to the West Indies, North Carolina, and Portugal, in the Years 1774 to 1776*. Edited by Evangeline Walker Andrews and Charles McLean Andrews. New Haven, Conn.: Yale University Press, 1923.

Schwanitz, Franz. *The Origin of Cultivated Plants*. Cambridge, Mass.: Harvard University Press, 1967.

Selig, Robert A. "Emigration, Fraud, Humanitarianism, and the Founding of Londonderry, South Carolina, 1763–1765." *Eighteenth-Century Studies* 23, no. 1 (1989): 1–23.

Sewall, Samuel. *The Diary of Samuel Sewall, 1674–1729*. Edited by M. Halsey Thomas. 2 vols. New York: Farrar, Straus, and Giroux, 1973.

Shepherd, James F., and Samuel H. Williamson. "The Coastal Trade of the British North American Colonies, 1768–1772." *Journal of Economic History* 32, no. 4 (1972): 783–810.

Shepherd, Verene A. "Livestock and Sugar: Aspects of Jamaica's Agricultural Development from the Late Seventeenth to the Early Nineteenth Century." *Historical Journal* 34, no. 3 (1991): 626–643.

Sheridan, Richard B. "The Crisis of Slave Subsistence in the British Wets Indies During and After the American Revolution." *William and Mary Quarterly*, 3rd ser., 33, no. 4 (1976): 615–641.

Shurtleff, Nathaniel B., ed. *Records of the Governor and Company of the Massachusetts Bay in New England, 1628–1686*. 5 vols. Boston: White, 1853–1854.

Silver, Timothy. *A New Face on the Countryside: Indians, Colonists, and Slaves in South Atlantic Forests, 1500–1800*. Cambridge: Cambridge University Press, 1990.

Simmons, Amelia. *American Cookery*. 1796. Facsimile, New York: Oxford University Press, 1958; reprint, New York: Dover, 1984.

Singleton, Theresa A. "The Archaeology of Slavery in North America." *Annual Review of Anthropology* 24 (1995): 119–140.

Smith, Adam. *The Wealth of Nations*. Edited by David S. Landes. New York: Norton, 1998.

Smith, Andrew F., ed. *The Oxford Encyclopedia of Food and Drink in America*. 2 vols. New York: Oxford University Press, 2004.

Smith, Barbara Clark. "Food Rioters and the American Revolution." *William and Mary Quarterly*, 3rd ser., 51, no. 1 (1994): 3–38.

Smith, Daniel Scott. "Population, Family, and Society in Hingham, Massachusetts, 1635–1880." Ph.D. diss., University of California, Berkeley, 1973.

———. "Underregistration and Bias in Probate Records: An Analysis of Data from Eighteenth-Century Hingham, Massachusetts." *William and Mary Quarterly*, 3rd ser., 32, no. 1 (1975): 100–110.

Smith, John. *The Generall Historie of Virginia, New England, and the Summer Isles*. 1624. Reprint, Cleveland: World, 1966.

———. *Travels and Works of Captain John Smith: President of Virginia and Admiral of New England, 1580–1631*. Edited by Edward Arber and A. G. Bradley. Edinburgh: Grant, 1910.

———. *The Travels of Capt. John Smith*. Glasgow: MacLehose, 1907.

Smith, William. *Discourses on Several Public Occasions During the War in America*. London: Millar, 1759.

Smits, David D. "The 'Squaw Drudge': A Prime Index of Savagism." *Ethnohistory* 29, no. 4 (1982): 281–306.

Smyth, J. F. D. *A Tour in the United States of America*. Vol. 2. London: Robinson, 1784.

Snow, Dean R. *The Iroquois*. Oxford: Blackwell, 1994.

Spivey, Diane M. *The Peppers, Cracklings, and Knots of Wool Cookbook: The Global Migration of African Cuisine*. Albany: State University of New York Press, 1999.

St. John de Crèvecoeur, J. Hector. *Letters from an American Farmer*. Edited, with an introduction, by Ludwig Lewisohn. New York: Boni, 1925.

Stephens, James M. "Cassava–*Manihot esculenta Crantz*." University of Florida, Institute of Food and Agricultural Sciences (available at: http://edis.ifas.ufl.edu/MV042).

Stetson, Sarah Pattee. "American Garden Books Transplanted and Native, Before 1807." *William and Mary Quarterly*, 2nd ser., 3, no. 3 (1946): 343–369.

Stith, William. *History of the First Discovery and Settlement of Virginia*. 1747. Reprint, Williamsburg, Va.: Parks, 1969.

Strachey, William. *The History of Travell into Virginia Britania*. 1609. Reprint, London: Hakluyt Society, 1953.

Sullivan, James. "The History of the Penobscott Indians." *Collections of the Massachusetts Historical Society* 1, no. 9 (1804): 207–232.

Taylor, Alan. *American Colonies*. New York: Viking, 2001.

Thacker, John. *The Art of Cookery*. Newcastle: Thompson, 1758.

Thomas, Hugh. *The Slave Trade: The Story of the Atlantic Slave Trade, 1440–1870*. New York: Simon and Schuster, 1997.

Thomas, Peter A. "Contrastive Subsistence Strategies and Land Use as Factors for Understanding Indian–White Relations in New England." *Ethnohistory* 23, no. 1 (1976): 1–18.

Thome, James, and Joseph Horace Kimball. *Emancipation in the West Indies: A Six Months' Tour in Antigua, Barbados, and Jamaica in the Year 1837*. New York: American Anti-Slavery Society, 1838.

Thompson, Peter. *Rum Punch and Revolution: Taverngoing and Public Life in Eighteenth-Century Philadelphia*. Philadelphia: University of Pennsylvania Press, 1999.

Thompson, Vincent. *The Making of the African Diaspora in the Americas 1441–1900*. London: Longman, 1987.

Thorp, Daniel B. "Assimilation in North Carolina's Moravian Community." *Journal of Southern History* 52, no. 1 (1986): 19–42.

———. "Taverns and Tavern Culture on the Southern Colonial Frontier: Rowan County, North Carolina, 1753–1776." *Journal of Southern History* 62, no. 4 (1996): 661–688.

Thwaites, Reuben Gold, ed. *Early Western Travels, 1748–1846*. New York: AMS Press, 1966.

Tully, Alan. *Forming American Politics: Ideals, Interests, and Institutions in Colonial New York and Pennsylvania*. Baltimore: Johns Hopkins University Press, 1994.

Tusser, Thomas. *Five Hundred Points of Good Husbandry* and *A Book of Huswifery*. Edited by William Mayor. London: Lackington, Allen, 1812.

Tyler, Lyon Gardiner, ed. *Narratives of Early Virginia, 1606–1625*. New York: Scribner, 1907.

Ulrich, Laurel Thatcher. *The Age of Homespun: Objects and Stories in the Creation of an American Myth*. New York: Oxford University Press, 2001.

———. *A Midwife's Tale: The Life of Martha Ballard, Based on Her Diary, 1785–1812*. New York: Vintage Books, 1996.

Vaughan, Alden T. "From White Man to Redskin: Changing Anglo-American Perceptions of the American Indian." *American Historical Review* 87, no. 4 (1982): 917–953.

Voigts, Linda E. "Anglo-Saxon Plant Remedies and the Anglo-Saxons." *Isis* 70, no. 2 (1979): 250–268.

W. J. *A Letter from New-England Concerning Their Customs, Manners, and Religion Written upon Occasion of a Report About a Quo Warranto Brought Against That Government.* London: Taylor, 1682.

Wadsworth, Benjamin. *Vicious Courses, Procuring Poverty Describ'd and Condemn'd.* Boston: Allen, 1719.

Walcott, Robert R. "Husbandry in Colonial New England." *New England Quarterly* 9, no. 2 (1936): 218–252.

Walsh, Lorena S. "Urban Amenities and Rural Self-Sufficiency: Living Standards and Consumer Behavior in the Colonial Chesapeake, 1643–1777." *Journal of Economic History* 43, no. 1 (1983): 109–117.

Walton, Gary M., and James F. Shepherd. *The Economic Rise of Early America.* Cambridge: Cambridge University Press, 1979.

Ward, Harry M. *"Unite or Die": Intercolony Relations, 1690–1763.* Port Washington, N.Y.: Kennikat Press, 1971.

Watson, Harry L. "'The Common Rights of Mankind': Subsistence, Shad, and Commerce in the Early Republican South." *Journal of American History* 83, no. 1 (1996): 13–43.

Watson, John. *Annals of Philadelphia.* Vol. 1. Philadelphia: Carey and Hart, 1830.

Weaver, Glenn. *Jonathan Trumball: Connecticut's Merchant Magistrate, 1710–1785.* Hartford: Connecticut Historical Society, 1956.

Webster, Charles. "The Recognition of Plant Sensitivity by English Botanists in the Seventeenth Century." *Isis* 57, no. 1 (1966): 5–23.

Webster, Noah. *A Collection of Essays and Fugitive Writings.* Boston: Thomas and Andrews, 1790.

Webster, Thomas. *Encyclopedia of Domestic Economy.* New York: Harper, 1845.

Weiss, Rona Stephanie. "The Development of the Market Economy in Colonial Massachusetts." Ph.D. diss., University of Massachusetts, 1981.

———. "The Market and Massachusetts Farmers, 1750–1850: Comment." *Journal of Economic History* 43, no. 2 (1983): 475–478.

———. "Primitive Accumulation in the United States: The Interaction Between Capitalist and Noncapitalist Class Relations in Seventeenth-Century Massachusetts." *Journal of Economic History* 42, no. 1 (1982): 103–113.

Welch, Paul D., and C. Margaret Scarry. "Status-Related Variation in Foodways in the Moundville Chiefdom." *American Antiquity* 60, no. 3 (1995): 397–419.

Whately, Thomas. *Considerations on the Trade and Finance of the Kingdom.* London: Millar, 1762.

White, Richard. *The Middle Ground: Indians, Empires, and Republics in the Great Lakes Region, 1650–1815.* Lincoln: University of Nebraska Press, 1983.

———. *The Roots of Dependency: Subsistence, Environment, and Social Change Among the Choctaws, Pawnees, and Navajos.* Lincoln: University of Nebraska Press, 1983.

Williams, Roger. *A Key into the Language of America.* London: Dexter, 1643.

Willoughby, Charles C. "Houses and Gardens of the New England Indians." *American Anthropologist* 8, no. 1 (1906): 115–132.

Wilson, Samuel M. "The Prehistoric Settlement Pattern of Nevis, West Indies." *Journal of Field Archaeology* 16, no. 4 (1989): 427–450.

Witherspoon, John. *The Works of the Reverend John Witherspoon.* Vol. 3. Philadelphia: Woodward, 1802.

Wood, Peter. *Black Majority: Negroes in Colonial South Carolina from 1670 Through the Stono Rebellion.* New York: Norton, 1974.

Wood, William. *New England's Prospect.* Edited by Alden T. Vaughan. 1635. Reprint, Amherst: University of Massachusetts Press, 1977.

Woodmason, Charles. *The Carolina Backcountry on the Eve of the Revolution: The Journal and Other Writings of Charles Woodmason, Anglican Itinerant.* Edited by Richard J. Hooker. Chapel Hill: University of North Carolina Press, 1953.

Woolley, Hannah. *The Gentlewomans Companion; or, a Guide to the Female Sex.* London: Maxwell, 1673.

———. *The Queen-like Closet, or, Rich Cabinet.* 2nd ed. London: For Richard Lowndes, 1672.

———. *The Queen-like Closet, or, Rich Cabinet.* 3rd ed. London: For Richard Lowndes, 1675.

Woolman, John. *The Journal of John Woolman and "A Plea for the Poor."* Compiled, with an introduction, by Frederick Barnes Tolles. 1774. Reprint, Secaucus, N.J.: Citadel Press, 1961.

Wright, Gavin. *The Political Economy of the Cotton South: Households, Markets, and Wealth in the Nineteenth Century.* New York: Norton, 1978.

Yost, Genevieve. *"The Compleat Housewife or Accomplish'd Gentlewoman's Companion:* A Bibliographical Study." *William and Mary Quarterly,* 2nd ser., 18, no. 4 (1938): 419–435.

Young, Alexander, ed. *Chronicles of the Pilgrim Fathers of the Colony of Plymouth.* 1841. Reprint, New York: Da Capo Press, 1971.

Zelinsky, Wilbur. "The New England Connecting Barn." *Geographical Review* 48, no. 4 (1958): 540–553.

Zuckerman, Michael. *Peaceable Kingdoms: New England Towns in the Eighteenth Century.* New York: Knopf, 1970.

215, 218; consumption of alcoholic beverages by, 14–15, 243–244; culture of, after Revolution, 301–308; English opinions of, 212–213; ethnic diversity of, 167–168, 180–186, 192, 195–196, 198; food preparation by, 1–4; as frontiersmen, 5–7; hunting by, 8, 149–150; influence of British culture on, 13–14, 180–183, 197–199; kitchens of, 201–203; natural resources available to, 7; obtaining food by, compared with modern Americans, 4–5; opinions of Native Americans, 8–9, 92–95, 96, 100–103, 141–146, 177–180; political ideology of, related to food, 297–301; population growth of, 180–182, 285; regional foodways of, 10–13; reliance of, on slaves in West Indies, 48–51; wealthy, 99, 102, 115, 119–124, 164, 202–203, 204. *See also* American Revolution; kitchens

Colton, Samuel, 291–292

Columbus, Christopher, 19, 22

Common Sense (Paine), 301

Compleat City and Country Cook, The, 228

Compleat Housewife, or, Accomplished Gentlewoman's Companion, The (Eliza Smith), 229

Concise Observations on the Nature of Our Common Food (Hayes), 221, 228

Constitutional Convention, 293

consumer goods, 210–211, 214–215, 218. *See also* kitchens

cooking, African, 30–34, 91. *See also* slaves

cooking, American: art of, 227–229; boiling in, 233–235; cookware and tableware used in, 3–4, 205–206, 216–218; in eighteenth century, 13–14, 205–206, 216–218; first cookbooks on, 229–230, 237–238, 310–314; influence of British culture on, 13–14, 53, 201–229; influence of Native American foodways on, 8–9; ingredients used in, 230–233; as melting pot of cuisines, 7–10; in Middle Colonies, 12; in New England, 10–11, 230–237; political influences on, 15–16; regional distinctions in, 10–13; after Revolution, 308–320;

roasting in, 235–236; in seventeenth century, 1–4, 5–7, 63–65, 204–205; smoking meat in, 2, 126–127; in South, 12–13; techniques of, 233–237

cooking, English: flexibility of, 222–227; general rules of, 219–222; influence of, on American cooking, 13–14; migration of, to America, 227–229; and pies, 220, 224–225

cooking, West Indian, 34–37

cookware and tableware, colonial, 3–4, 205–206, 216–218

Cope, John, 256

Corbin, Richard, 107

corn, 8–9; grown in Carolina, 148–149; grown in Chesapeake Bay, 114–115; grown in New England, 82–84; use of, in alcoholic beverages, 250; Winthrop on, 55–56

cottagers, in Middle Colonies, 192–193

Craven, Charles, 152

creoles, 212–213

Cresswell, Nicholas, 126–127

Crèvecoeur, J. Hector St. John de, 213, 301, 305, 307

Cross, Michael, 256

Daubenton, Louis-Jean-Marie, 282

De Brahm, William, 148–149

de Castellon, Tomás, 23–24

de Tapia, Cristobal, 23–24

Denton, Daniel, 300

Dickens, Charles, 319

Dickson, William, 50

Diderot, Denis, 218

dining rooms, in Chesapeake Bay, 127–128

Drayton, John, 158, 159

Dudley, Thomas, 58–59

Dunlap, William, 308–309

Economical Manual of Domestic Arts (Löffler), 185–186

Eddis, William, 150, 215

eels, 184, 198–199

Ellis, Joseph, 302

Emerson, Lucy, 230; on cooking ingredients, 230–233; on cooking techniques, 233–237; influence of, on American cooking, 237–238

ARTS AND TRADITIONS OF THE TABLE:
PERSPECTIVES ON CULINARY HISTORY

Albert Sonnenfeld, series editor